INTRODUCTION TO

Social Work
The People's Profession

Ira Colby
University of Houston

Sophia Dziegielewski
University of Central Florida

LYCEUM
BOOKS, INC.

5758 South Blackstone Avenue
Chicago, Illinois 60637

Published by

LYCEUM BOOKS, INC.
5758 S. Blackstone Ave.
Chicago, Illinois 60637
773+643-1903 (Fax)
773+643-1902 (Phone)
lyceum@lyceumbooks.com
http://www.lyceumbooks.com

Library of Congress Cataloging-in-Publication Data

Colby, Ira C. (Ira Christopher)
    Social work : the people's profession / Ira Colby, Sophia Dziegielewski.
        p. cm.
    Includes bibliographical references and index.
    ISBN 0-925065-33-1 (alk. paper)
        1. Social service—United States. 2. Social workers—United States. I. Dziegielewski, Sophia F. II. Title.
HV91.C598 2001
361.3'2'0973—dc21   00-051468

Preface

Your career should be personally rewarding. Feeling a sense of accomplishment when you make a difference in someone else's life provides a natural high that is both uplifting and fulfilling. Social work is a profession that provides ample opportunities to make positive differences in others' lives and to help make our communities better and safer places for all people.

In the pages that follow, you will be introduced to the social work profession, with its obvious strengths as well as its limitations. You will see how social work started, and how the field has grown from humble but deep roots working with poor and underserved populations to the worldwide profession it has become today. Each chapter introduces the beginning professional to what social work involves and the roles social workers perform. Although social work is an old profession rich in tradition, it remains dynamic. With its focus on the "person-in-situation" and the "person-in-environment," the need to address continuous and repeated changes is ongoing. To facilitate this process, the majority of the chapters consider the field of social work and where social workers are typically found; however, suggestions are made for future exploration and expansion of social work practice. These areas provide fertile ground in which social workers can develop new services, allowing the best possible care for the client.

By presenting the many different facets of social work, we attempt to provide a realistic and varied presentation that will help you develop a more authentic understanding and appreciation of the profession. At a minimum you will be exposed to what social workers do and the importance of considering the environmental context that surrounds all decisions. Social workers believe strongly in allowing ethical principles and a respect for cultural diversity to guide all practice decisions. Differences in individuals are acknowledged and concepts such as dignity, worth, and respect, along with a nonjudgmental attitude, provide the cornerstone on which all intervention is built. In part, it is our hope that the success of this book will be measured by whether it can help you make a career decision and answer the following question: Is social work the profession for me? If so, let the book introduce you to the field and what rewards and challenges lie ahead. If not, may you gain an understanding of and respect for the field, an awareness of the needs and struggles that people face, and the knowledge that most of these problems and issues are not self-perpetuated.

Part 1 provides a broad overview of the profession, in which we introduce some of the professional terminology and acronyms. We then discuss the settings where social workers can be found, what social workers actually do, and the salaries they are often paid. After that, albeit briefly, we explore the rich traditions within the field of social work, highlighting how the past clearly relates to the present and making predictions about what the future has in store. This section ends with the definition of a social worker, and what that means when the field is chosen as a professional career.

In Part 2, we introduce the practice of social work at three levels: the micro-, the mezzo-, and the macro-perspectives. In this section we explore the often-misunderstood concept of the "client to be served" and the notion that it can involve more than one person. Although social workers can view clients as individuals, clients are most often addressed in terms of context or systems and can include individuals, families, groups, communities, or policies that either directly or indirectly affect client system well-being. In the chapters in Part 3, several examples of the various practice settings where social workers are employed are presented, along with suggestions for expanding current activities and exploring future development of new areas.

This book is unique in that it will challenge you to synthesize information about successes and events in the field. Activities are included to give the beginning professional a sense of "hands on" learning. These activities will help you develop a more in-depth understanding of the profession. There is also an emphasis on the use of the Internet, a tool that is now part of all our lives. Case examples are used throughout this book to help you see the interface between what is written in the text and how it applies to practice.

This book is an introductory text, so it was not possible for every imaginable topic in the area of social work to be addressed. The "art" and "science" within this field compiled with the restrictions of practicality in publication would never allow it. Therefore, this book provides a broad overview designed to introduce the field and to answer beginning-level questions of those considering this profession as a possible career choice.

On a personal note, we believe that putting a book like this together is never easy—nor should it be. Writing a book takes a lot of hard work: the drafting of chapters from the first proposal to the end product covered a span of well over two years, and the number of rewrites, edits, and so on boggle the mind. Just when we thought it was done, we would discover that more writing was needed. For us this book represents over forty-five years of combined direct practice and teaching experience. We strive to use our passion for the profession to introduce others to this exciting and challenging field. As practitioners, we believe that much is to be learned from the clients we serve. In fact, many of the case examples used in the book have been drawn from our practice experience. Many of the questions our students asked us have been used to guide the chapters and to explore how best to present information. Utilizing our actual experiences in direct practice and as educators helped us present information in a practical and informative way that is sensitive to students' interests and concerns, while taking into account the expectations that social work programs have for a beginning social work course.

This book would not be complete if we did not acknowledge the individuals in our own support systems that have made this effort possible. Ira Colby thanks his wife and best friend, Deborah, who for over thirty years honestly critiqued his teaching, writing, and thinking. Sophia Dziegielewski thanks her family, friends, and colleagues, who respect and support her passion for the field and her "workaholic" ways.

We are grateful for the advice given to our publisher by Steve Anderson, Edward Gumz, Peggy McFarland, Tom Meenaghan, Jane Peller, Dina Rosenfeld, and Gloria Rosenbaum. To all the social workers who graciously allowed us to use their biographical sketches, thank you. Mary Whalen, you are a wonderful photo-grapher with a great appreciation of social workers and the persons with whom they work.

We both recognize the work of Diana Gilloly, whose dedication in editing and re-editing this work cannot be underestimated. Thanks go, lastly, to our publisher, David Follmer, who agreed with us and supported us fully in making this the most accurate depiction of the profession of social work possible.

Now, all that said, we invite you to begin this adventure in learning about one of the oldest helping professions ever developed. May this book and its description of the profession of social work ignite a fire in you, as our careers in social work have in us.

About the Authors

Ira Colby is Dean of the Graduate School of Social Work at the University of Houston; prior to this position he developed and directed the baccalaureate social work program at Ferrum College, taught at the University of Texas at Arlington, and directed a new school of social work at the University of Central Florida. He received his M.S.W. from Virginia Commonwealth University and his Ph.D. from the University of Pennsylvania. He is widely published and has presented papers at state, national and international meetings and forums. His passions are golf and family, not necessarily in that order.

Sophia F. Dziegielewski is Professor in the School of Social Work at the University of Central Florida. Previously she taught in the School of Social Work, The University of Alabama, the Departments of Family and Preventive Medicine and Psychiatry at Meharry Medical College, The School of Social Work at the University of Tennessee, and in the U.S. Army Military College at Fort Benning, GA. She received her M.S.W and her Ph.D. from the Florida State University. Professor Dziegielewski was honored by the National Association of Social Workers as the Tennessee Social Worker of the Year in 1995. She has over 60 publications and lectures widely across the United States.

Table of Contents

List of Boxes and Tables

Part I

The Context of Social Work

Chapter 1

Social Work: The Profession

"CALL ME A SOCIAL WORKER" IS HOW HERMAN MELVILLE, SITTING at his desk in his summer home, in Pittsfield, Massachusetts, might begin a novel detailing his social work experience. As the central character, he describes his work as rewarding and exciting with no two days alike. His cases, he says, run the gamut from simple to complex; while many are successfully resolved, some do not reach a happy ending. Throughout the novel, Herman would clearly set forth the many challenges facing new and rising social workers.

Herman Melville's novel might not make it to the *New York Times* best seller list, but it would be an honest attempt to portray the life and commitment necessary for today's social worker. The profession of social work is an old one whose story begins in the mid-1880s, when professional helping and assistance, often referred to as "social work practice," was first introduced. At this time, social workers were active with all types of people regardless of age, color, or creed, and this helping activity involved individuals, families, groups, and communities, in both public and private social service settings.

These initial efforts at helping have come a long way. As we enter the twenty-first century, the United States has, by government estimates, over half a million professional social workers. More than 160,000 of these workers are members of the **National Association of Social Workers** (NASW), the world's largest professional membership organization for social workers. Its membership comprises professional social workers in all walks of life, from those who work with the elderly to those who work with infants. For the professional training of all these social workers, there are nearly 600 social work education programs, ranging from the baccalaureate to the doctorate level. And that's just in the United States!

Social work professionals are employed in every nation of the world. Schools of social work can be found on every continent. This worldwide activity is represented by the **International Federation of Social Workers**, considered the principal international social work membership association. It held membership meetings in Hong Kong in 1996, Israel in 1998, and Montreal in 2000.

THE PROFESSIONAL SOCIAL WORKER

Considering the enduring popularity of the social work profession, you may ask how and why this interest began and why it continues to grow in scope within the global community. The answer is simple: people across the world and in our

Name: Magaly Ortiz

Place of residence: Miami, Florida

College/university degrees: B.S. in Psychology, Barry University; M.S.W., University of Central Florida

Present position: M.S.W. intern/student and M.S.W. Student Association President

Previous work/volunteer experience:

Case Manager for a sexual trauma recovery center

What do you do in your spare time? I like to exercise, dance, and spend time with family and friends.

Why did you choose social work as a career? One of the things that helped me decide to become a social worker was my parents' divorce, which was a very difficult experience for me. While technically my parents were not taken away from me, I can relate to the fear of losing one's family. In this way, I can empathize and relate on a more personal level with clients who are children of divorced parents.

What is your favorite social work story? I have not been in the field long enough to have many stories, but one that comes to mind occurred when I was an intern working with sexually abused children. I remember the satisfaction of watching a child begin and end her healing journey. It was exciting for me to see the progress and success that children can make with treatment. It was at this time that I knew I was in the right field.

What would be the one thing you would change in our community if you had the power to do so? I would like to change the decision-making power that managed care has on the treatment that our clients receive. Insurance companies make the decisions about how much time a client needs to recover from a mental illness or trauma; however, they do not have the education to determine the medical attention necessary. Therefore, if I had the power to change anything, I would like medical doctors and professionals to be the evaluators in determining the treatment a client should receive.

own neighborhoods face similar problems and need the assistance that social workers provide. When these problems are individual in nature they are referred to as **microsystem** problems. Responsibility for finding solutions to microsystem problems often rests squarely on the shoulders of the individual client or family.

For example, when a single, elderly person falls at home and breaks an arm, he may need to be admitted to a local hospital for treatment. Often after admission, the emergency room physician refers the case to the **hospital social worker**, who is tasked with assessing the client's situation. Suppose that during the **assessment** process, the worker learns that the client has no immediate family and lives alone. Taking into account the needs of the client, the worker must help to develop a plan with the elderly client that ensures provision of the support and services needed. In many cases, this includes arranging home health care so that the client can receive medical services in the home. It can also include ensuring that the client has access to nutritious meals by arranging contact with a **Meals on Wheels** program. To increase socialization and provide mealtime activity, referral to a local neighborhood center's senior citizen's program can be made. Further, individual or group supportive counseling can be provided directly or by referral within the community. The role of the social worker through the microperspective is essential because this role stresses the individual client's personal and social needs in the assessment and **intervention** processes.

Did You Know...The member countries of the United Nations maintain missions in cities throughout the United States. You can learn from them about particular customs and cultural nuances that may affect your work with clients. Also, many international laws that affect practice pertain to individual visitors. If you're not sure about a particular situation, contact the relevant UN mission. Finally, a UN mission can provide you with a great deal of information about its home country's welfare system. (See appendix E for a list of e-mail addresses.)

A second system often addressed in social work is the **mezzosystem**. Through the mezzoperspective social workers highlight the needs of the client by focusing primarily on the environmental systems that can assist the individual. The client is linked directly to support systems that enhance and maximize individual functioning. From a mezzoperspective family and friends are paramount. This perspective also incorporates those social workers who work in administration. These social workers run many of the programs that a client will need and can either initiate or oversee service delivery. When a client's problems are found to be by-products of a larger social system, such as the family or a group, this mezzosystem is usually the primary target of intervention.

Unfortunately, however, many problems have much wider roots in broader community or social institutions. To address these problems a social worker would use what is called a **macrosystem** approach. From the macroperspective, solutions to the problems that clients face must be tied directly to larger systems.

For example, providing decent and safe places to sleep for people who are

uire advocacy with local and state government. The social worker
ate and organize a citywide movement to open a shelter. Indeed,
on for this population is not as simple to accomplish as an inexpe-
rienced obs... r may think. At a minimum, in order to initiate macrochange the
social worker needs to understand housing policy as it affects the homeless. She
must also be knowledgeable about housing options and shelter alternatives used
elsewhere. In addition to this basic knowledge, the social worker must also be
aware of and anticipate resistance from the community that she is trying to serve.
It is important to work with the larger community to get everyone to understand
why a homeless shelter is really needed and to mobilize agreement. When working
within the macrosystem, however, caution should always be exercised; providing a
homeless shelter is much more complicated than simply securing the site and the
funds to construct a building. In implementing this type of change, the social
worker must be sensitive to current community concerns and political issues that
can enhance or impede service assistance and progression.

A list of some of the most serious macrosystem social problems—homelessness, HIV/AIDS, physical and emotional abuse, mental health, substance abuse, and
community development—touches on only some of the areas that make up the
domain of social work practice. As highlighted by Specht and Courtney (1994), the
ultimate goal of the profession is to seek *perfectibility* of the community, whereby
all people are given the opportunity to live their lives to the fullest and to achieve
their own potential. On first sight, the concept of perfectibility of the community
may be alarming, since it appears to represent a utopian goal that is unattainable.
Evaluated more closely, however, the aim of perfectability is not that unusual. Helping clients to improve their life situations and their capacity to achieve their full
potential has been one of the central forces driving the profession since its modest
mid-nineteenth-century beginnings.

�֎ TOWARD A DEFINITION OF SOCIAL WORK

What exactly is social work? Interestingly, although it is a well-established profession, any ten people will probably give you ten different answers. One weekend
morning at a donut shop in Orlando, Florida, we asked ten people to describe what
social workers do. We received the following responses:

- ◆ Social workers give out food stamps and money to freeloaders.
- ◆ I dunno.
- ◆ Don't they work at the welfare office?
- ◆ They help abused kids.
- ◆ My mom had one while she was in the hospital. She really liked that young
  gal!
- ◆ They work in mental hospitals.
- ◆ One helped my wife and I when we adopted our baby. He helped prepare us
  for parenting and has stayed in touch ever since. Now, some four years later,
  he still stays in touch.

- ◆ It is helping poor individuals to get services.
- ◆ Social workers are liberal thinkers that support programs for the poor.
- ◆ Help private and public agencies to help individuals in need.

Activity...Select ten people either at a local mall or at any other shopping area and ask them, "what is social work?" Write down their answers. Also, take notes on their non-verbal reactions to the question.

The variety of responses illustrates two major points. First, the profession is a diverse one, and this diversity means that the roles and tasks that social workers perform are varied and often poorly defined. Second, members of the general public are often confused about the profession. Many people simply do not understand exactly what the mission of this diverse profession really is. This confusion is deepened when social work professionals themselves define what they do on the basis of their scope of practice, using job-specific descriptions such as health care social worker, community organizer, adoptions worker, or mental health counselor. The diversity and broad purview of social work practice makes it difficult to reach a simple, all-inclusive definition of exactly what social work is.

Social work is not the only profession that is difficult to define; however, professions whose tasks are easier to outline are generally received more positively by the community. For example, most people are able to describe accurately what a dentist, a nurse, or a physician does, or they can quickly describe the role of a stockbroker or a lawyer. Defining exactly what a social worker can do, and is expected to do, is a lot more complicated.

Recently, a woman at a holiday party asked her niece what her college major was. The niece proudly announced, "Social work." A disquieting hush spread over the room, and the party seemed to grind to a halt. Some of her relatives looked shocked and glanced around at other family members in astonishment. When her father noted the reaction, he simply shrugged his shoulders and said, "that's nice," secretly hoping this career choice was "just a youthful phase" and that she would change her major before year's end. Today, although she has become a successful university professor of social work, her father and other relatives still refer to her as "a psychologist"! When asked why they keep making this mistake, they reply that they can usually define to others what a psychologist does, but defining social work takes a lot more time and effort. "Besides," her father still asks, "is there really that much of a difference?"

Many social workers, old and new, have at least one or two stories about how their families reacted when they announced that they had selected social work as a career, and many of the stories will be similar to the one above. The confusion surrounding what social workers do, as well as their "image" of working primarily with the poor and disenfranchised in our society, complicates efforts to define what social work is. Or, indeed, what people perceive it to be. Now keeping in mind the difficulties of making a simple definition—just what is social work?

Let us start by considering some of social work's key attributes. First, the pro-

A mother with her children and stepchildren is outside of a Boys & Girls Club. The club offers after-school, weekend, and summer programs and opportunities for children from first grade through high school.

fession involves people helping people. Second, the practice of social work generally involves addressing the needs of **at-risk populations** in a community. Third, in our society there is a belief that people need to be helped and that the community **sanctions** this helping activity. Fourth, most of the activity performed and services provided are agency based. Fifth, social work is a profession and therefore requires some type of professional education and training as well as standards for **ethics** and conduct. Now, let's explore these ideas more fully to develop an understanding of the breadth and depth of the profession.

Thinking about *helping* people focuses our attention on what social workers actually do. Through programs and intervention services, social workers help people—individuals, families, groups, communities, and organizations—in their day-to-day life situations. A hallmark of social work helping is its focus on the interaction between person and social environment. While a psychologist, for example, would consider primarily an individual's psychological state in trying to help, social workers go beyond this to include the interplay between the individual's life situation and social environment.

In the provision of social work services, *at-risk populations* comprise those people who, for any number of reasons, are vulnerable to societal threats. Children and the elderly are often viewed as at-risk populations. Other people considered at risk are those who may be victimized by a person or group through a series of life events that leaves these people susceptible to unwarranted pain and resulting problems.

Sanction refers to the community's "blessing" or recognition of the need for a service or program. Professional sanctioning of services comes in many forms; state licensing and professional certification requirements are two common types. Community funding agents, such as the United Way, can also sanction an activity by supporting it financially. When a funding entity such as the United Way supports a social service agency, it is indicating its belief that the services provided are important to the community good. This type of support is often called having "the good stamp of approval." Having the legitimacy that comes from such support is essential in gaining community approval. Formalized public (or community) sanctioning of the provision of social services can also protect the public by distinguishing between authorized and unauthorized service delivery.

Agency-based practice consists of social work services generally conducted by or delivered under the auspices of social welfare agencies. Agencies can be public, funded by federal, state, or local tax dollars; or agencies can be private, funded by donations or foundations. Most practicing social workers are agency based; however, a small percentage do engage in independent professional social work. Independent practitioners are generally educated at the master's degree level or beyond. A fairly new trend in the field is for professionally trained social workers to become private practitioners in mental health and other health-related settings.

Professional education involves the preparation of individuals in social work practice. It takes place in baccalaureate and graduate-level degree programs at colleges and universities. *Professional training* builds on professional education. Generally, professional training begins in the classroom setting. Later, this educational foundation is expanded and strengthened by experience through the internship process. In their internships, students visit and work in field agencies. At these agencies they can practice the skills they have been taught in school. To further advance their professional training most social workers begin working in the field under the direct supervision of a trained and experienced professional social worker.

The last area among the key components of social work practice has to do with *ethics* and expected conduct. Each profession is established and coordinated under a professional set of standards, often referred to as a "code of conduct," that is designed to govern the moral behavior of those in the field. In social work, NASW through the National Delegate Assembly is tasked with maintaining and updating this document for the profession. It has been said that the social work Code of Ethics is one of the most comprehensive ever written. It is often used as a model for comparison by related professions. A copy of social work's Code of Ethics is included in appendix A of this book, and because it is critical to understanding professional conduct, it will be discussed further in subsequent chapters. In general, when defining social work practice, ethical and moral issues always need to be evaluated. Social workers use the guidelines for professional practice given in the Code of Ethics to understand their moral and legal obligations in assisting their clients.

Social workers entering the field must not only be aware of this document; they must agree to adhere to the standards it sets forth. Any questions about moral and ethical practice should be addressed by using the guidelines it provides.

Did You Know…In August 1996, NASW delegate assembly met in Washington, D.C., and updated social work's previous Code of Ethics. This was the first major revision since 1979. This updated and revised Code of Ethics went into effect January 1, 1997.

SOCIAL WORK DEFINED

A definition of social work is not easy to formulate or apply. Most would agree, however, that the field of social work involves working actively to change the social, cultural, psychological, and larger societal conditions that most individuals, families, groups, and communities face. The helping process emphasizes the use of **advocacy** to create societal conditions that lead to a stronger sense of **person-in-situation** or person-in-environment; this promotes the community good, which benefits all individuals. According to this perspective, social work is directed to two ends: first, to help resolve the micro- and mezzoissues that **clients** face, and, second, to create societal macrochanges that prevent or ameliorate such problems for all individuals, families, groups, or communities.

To initiate the helping process, a social worker may begin by working with an individual or family on an issue. This microlevel work will continue until the issue is resolved; however, the task of the social worker does not end here. This is especially true when the social worker recognizes that the causes of the client's problems are not unique to that client. Many seemingly individual problems have deep roots in the policies and procedures of larger institutions. When these problems have the potential to affect others in the community the social work practitioner must take a macroperspective. If current policies or programs may harm others unless certain changes take place, the social worker is called to action. The worker begins macrointervention and moves to promote changes in the larger system.

For example, Ellen, a social worker employed in a family agency, learned that her client had been evicted from his apartment. After helping the client to find a new apartment, Ellen discovered that the first landlord had not followed eviction procedures as outlined in the city's ordinances. Ellen must decide what to do next. For most social workers the task of helping the client would not be considered complete even though the client now has a safe place to stay. The social worker may feel the need to continue helping this client and future potential clients who may also fall victim to this failed system enforcement. In this case, Ellen could begin working on macroissues by contacting city officials to ensure that local ordinances are enforced and to make them aware of the problems that can occur when ordinances are not enforced. Her advocacy efforts could prevent other people in circumstances similar to her client's from becoming homeless.

In sum, a social worker's immediate focus is usually on a particular client pop-

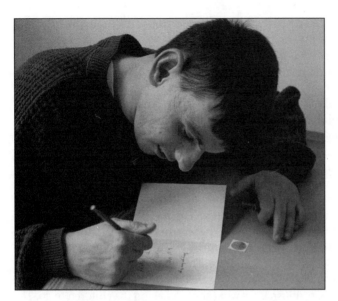

A respite house client writing a note to a social worker who is leaving for a new job. The respite house offers services and weekend-away-from-the-family programs for persons with physical and emotional disabilities. These programs give caregivers and parents a break from their caregiving duties.

ulation, providing service to individuals, couples, or families. These immediate efforts take a micro- or mezzoperspective; however, the macroperspective should never be ignored. Service provision in the field of social work cannot be defined simply, because in order to be successful it often must go beyond the identified client and include the larger system. Social work is both science and art. A skilled social worker must be knowledgeable about all aspects and perspectives of client helping and flexible in their application. The best prepared social workers are those who recognize the importance of helping as a multifaceted process and who can easily move between micro-, mezzo-, and macrosystems with and on behalf of the client populations they serve.

BECOMING A SOCIAL WORKER

People sometimes call themselves social workers even when they do not possess the professional qualification needed to be a social worker. Many times newspaper articles, television news broadcasts, and talk radio hosts refer to "a social worker" whose mishandling of a case led to very negative consequences for an individual or family. The two following case examples are typical.

In the first case, a child abuse report is made to the state child protective services agency, but the child is not removed from the home. A few days later the child dies after a severe beating by the caretaker. The media reports that the social worker responsible for the case did not follow through with a proper investigation and ignored a variety of information and signals. The community is given the impression that if the social worker had just done his job, the child would still be alive. Unfortunately, there is no simple formula for handling such situations or for avoiding them in the first place—even though we want there to be one. The glaring fact is that a child has died and no one was able to help. This is disturbing to everyone, and it is difficult to look beyond the initial fact. However, if the event is not examined more deeply, other children could be placed in harm's way. It is also important to look beyond the media's simplified portrayal of the situation: Due to cutbacks and limited funding, or for other reasons, the person responsible for the investigation may not be a social work professional at all. In fact, this person's college degree and professional training may not be in the area of social work. For example, his education and training might be in the liberal arts, and he may have no formal training in the problem assessment and intervention methods essential to social work practice. Similarly, he may not be familiar with establishing the micro-, mezzo-, and macroperspectives needed to address client situations and problems.

The second case, which involves a young mother reported for child neglect, comes from the authors' firsthand experience. The mother has been sending her children to school without their coats, and the weather is too cold for such attire. A state social service worker visits the house and agrees that the mother seems unfit to handle the needs of her children. The state worker reports that the mother's responses to questions are very basic and brief and that she does not appear to understand the seriousness of what she is allowing the children to do. The worker recommends that all the children be removed from the home before any harm comes to them.

Later the case comes to the attention of one of the authors, who is facilitating the discharge of a client from the hospital. This social worker learns that the client is asking to be released from the hospital against medical advice. When she goes to see the client to discuss the situation, he explains that he recently suffered a small stroke and was immediately taken from his home and admitted to the hospital. He fears that his wife cannot care for their children properly, and he has to go home immediately. His wife is moderately retarded, and he has always handled most of the childcare. After the social worker talks with the client and places several phone calls to help him secure childcare coverage, he agrees to stay in the hospital for the remainder of his treatment. He agrees to stay because the social worker was able to make arrangements with some members of his church who will watch the children until his return home. Later that day, the client becomes very upset when a family friend tells him that his children are about to be removed from home. After receiving permission from the client to release information about the situation the social worker contacts the state worker and tells him about the plan to care for the children. The removal decision is reevaluated, and because support is in place the children are not removed from home or the care of their mother.

In discussing the case, the social service worker obviously is frustrated. His caseload did not give him time to explore disposition options. He was also concerned that a child had died several weeks before in a case very similar to this one. Because of the attention paid to that case, he felt it was best not to take a chance on this one. He also did not realize that the mother was mentally retarded; he thought she might be on drugs or merely resistant to intervention. In trying to understand why he made such a limited assessment, the social service worker reports that he just did not realize the significance of the client's behavior. The worker reports that he has limited on-the-job training and that he often uses opportunities for inservice provision to catch up on his paperwork. Moreover, although this state requires that all social service workers have at least a four-year professional degree, his degree is in physical education.

Cases like these are all too common. For whatever reason—be it a desire to cut costs or a lack of recognition for professional intervention—there is a widespread but false impression that anyone can be a social worker and that anyone can handle the tasks and responsibilities expected of a social worker. Some people even believe they can be their own social workers.

For example, a plumber working for one of the authors asked her what she did for a living. When he heard she was a social worker, he smiled and said, "Oh, never needed one of them before; always do my own social work." When asked what he meant, he said, "Don't need somebody else to solve my problems. I can solve them for my family and myself. I had a lot of training on how to deal with people in school, and that helped." Such comments are very disturbing because they show that many people just don't know what social workers do. When people assume that social work is simply everyday problem solving, they conclude that anyone can do it and that becoming a social worker is open to all.

Confusion also exists among helping and counseling professionals about who can be a qualified social worker. For example, at a 1998 public hearing held by the Florida Board of Mental Health Counselors, Marriage and Family Therapists, and Clinical Social Workers, a board member opposed the licensing of BSW and MSW social workers who do not do clinical social work. A marriage and family therapist added, "Anyone can do social work. There is such a thing as social work with a small 's' and 'w'."

On the surface this statement seems to make sense, and it warrants serious discussion. Certainly, all helping individuals must have "good" hearts and be compassionate as well as willing to help others. But can these qualities alone make someone a *professional* social worker?

Let's make a comparison. Suppose you have a sore throat, feel somewhat congested, and have hot and cold sweats. Your roommate says, "You may be coming down with the flu. Why don't you take brand X over-the-counter cold pills, use some brand Y throat lozenges, and stay home and rest." This could be very good, helpful advice, but does this mean your roommate is a medical doctor, albeit with a small "m" and "d"? Of course not—it seems crazy to even suggest that. Everyone knows that to be a medical doctor you need a formal education and supervised experience in a medical setting. You can't hang out a shingle that says "MD" just because you think you can diagnose some physical ailments.

So what are the requirements for becoming a social worker? Certainly there are personal attributes that a social worker must have. First, a social worker must like working with people. A social worker is involved with people from all walks of life. These people, who come from widely varying backgrounds, can have ideas and expectations very different from the social worker's own. Being aware of and sensitive to the beliefs of others is not always a simple task to accept. In dealing with different people a social worker must really want to understand the troubles that others face. So first of all, a good social worker must genuinely like working with diverse individuals.

Second, a social worker must want to help people. A professional social worker encounters all sorts of client problems, ranging from abuse and neglect, to homelessness, to mental health issues, to community-based substance abuse problems. A good social worker wants to help his clients in their efforts to figure out what is going on and how best to resolve their problems.

Third, a social worker wants the community to be a better place for all people. Through her professional activities, a social worker helps a specific client while at the same time she tries to better the community for all people. For example, ideally social workers want to end poverty and its debilitating effects on people and communities. Social workers envisage communities where all people have access to decent housing and health care. They also strive to end unfair treatment of individuals, the "isms" that face millions of people today—racism, sexism, and ageism. The personal traits that foster the desire to work with and to help individuals, families, and communities are critical ingredients in creating a social worker. To finish the mix, however, these personal traits must be complemented by professional education and training. In the United States, professional social work education takes place in baccalaureate or graduate-level degree programs at specific colleges and universities.

Did You Know...The Council on Social Work Education (CSWE) *is the only national standard-setting and accrediting body for social work education. It was organized in 1952 through the merger of two associations that coordinated baccalaureate and graduate programs, respectively.*

For a U.S. social work program to provide professional education it must meet the **accreditation** standards of the **Council on Social Work Education**. CSWE is the national board that sets and oversees educational standards for social work programs across the United States (see appendix D). Other countries have their own accrediting bodies for social work education. For example, the Canadian Association for Social Work Education is responsible for accrediting programs in Canada, the Joint University Council for Social and Public Administration oversees social work educational programs in the United Kingdom, Finnish programs of social work are associated with the Scandinavian Committee of Schools of Social Work, Brazilian schools of social work are members of the National Association of Schools of Social Work, and Indian social work educational programs are members of the Association of Schools of Social Work. Overall, international accreditation associations can be found in nineteen different nations, in addition to five regional associations (Kendall, 1984).

Regardless of where a professional social work program is located, it must withstand the rigorous scrutiny of an accreditation process, which entails the val-

Name: Carol Ana Naylor

Place of residence: Kalamazoo, Michigan

College/university degrees: B.A., Duquesne University, M.S.W., Western Michigan University

Present position: Full-time social worker on the senior ACT team, Senior Services, Inc., part-time crisis worker at Gryphon Place, a local helpline.

Previous work/volunteer experience: Advocate at ACT of Kalamazoo, lead summer respite worker at Family and Children's Services, direct care worker at Living Ways, volunteer Big Sister at Family Resource Center, volunteer trainer at Gryphon Place.

Why did you choose social work as a career? Quite simply, I feel good when I am helping others. After college, I worked at several jobs as I struggled to find my niche in the world. Working with people was the common denominator in my employment, whether it was waitressing or retail management. Oddly, those jobs seemed to fit naturally into a career in social work. I realized one day that in order to be happy I required something more of myself. Five years ago I made it my mission to become a social worker in the area of mental health. Everyday, I love going to work because I know that what I do matters: it matters to my clients, to my community, and it matters to me.

What is your favorite social work story? When I was an intern at the Battle Creek Veterans Administration Hospital, I spent eight weeks as a substance abuse counselor. This rotation required me to work with down-and-out, chronically alcoholic veterans. I felt helpless counseling many of these men. While I knew they appreciated my insights and active listening skills, I still felt doubtful that I was offering them anything of real value. One vet in particular seemed like a hopeless case. After he left the program, I assumed he would go right back to his previous life of drinking, poverty, and liver problems. Weeks later, I received a note from my supervisor. He included a note from the veteran stating that he felt I had heard him and respected him. He was doing well at a halfway house near his home community. I had no idea until then just how powerful it can be simply to listen and to respect someone. For me, it all relates back to the basic concept of treating people with dignity, which is what social work is all about.

What would be the one thing you would change in our community if you had the power to do so? I feel strongly about the rights of people with chronic mental illness. There has always been a stigma attached to the mentally ill: many people fear, loathe, or discount them. Society often seems not to know what to do with them. I would remove that stigma. I dream of a world where acceptance is abundant—acceptance of all our various colors, sizes, appearance, and harmless eccentricities.

idation of explicit standards of practice (Barker, 1995). Curriculum format and delivery, which is the heart of the educational experience, must be coherent, built on a series of objectives, and offer specific educational content, including a supervised field placement or internship experience; through an internship the social work professional learns to apply in the field environment what has been taught in the classroom. Standards require that the faculty members who teach students possess certain types of degrees and in addition have professional work experience that can facilitate the education process. Accreditation standards also specify that a variety of institutional (e.g., college or university) resources be available. Finally, an accredited program must identify specific behavioral outcomes that all graduates are expected to demonstrate at the end of their course of study.

Activity...Ask to review your social work program's latest "self-study" for accreditation. Compare the self-study to the CSWE's Commission on Accreditation Handbook *and the* CSWE Curriculum Policy Statement *found in appendix D. In order to be accredited your program must conform to these standards. Being part of an accredited program is important for your future development.*

Attending and graduating from an accredited social work program is crucial for the future social work professional. Remember that only a graduate of an accredited social work program is recognized as a professional social worker. Because CSWE accreditation standards apply nationally, the public recognizes that a graduate of a BSW program in California has completed the same minimum educational requirements as a graduate of a BSW program in New Hampshire or Georgia. Uniformity of content through the country means that social workers can be hired in any state and meet specific educational requirements for employment and subsequent licensing in the field. This is particularly important for employers and supervisors of social work professionals because they can then assume that a particular educational background implies familiarity with certain content. Many employers report that this standardization of course content across social work programs makes social workers predictable employees in regard to what they have and have not been trained to do. In fact, an article in *Consumer Reports* in 1995 states that one reason why social workers seemed to fare better than other helping and counseling professions in managed care was that they were more consistent in training and approach (Mental Health, 1995).

Did You Know...The initials BSW stand for Baccalaureate Social Worker and MSW for Master Social Worker. BSSW and MSSW also signify degrees in social work, Bachelor of Science in Social Work and Master of Science in Social Work. The most advanced degrees in social work are the DSW and the Ph.D. In most circles the MSW or the MSSW is considered the highest level needed to practice in the field.

BSW education prepares individuals for entry- or beginning-level social work practice. Baccalaureate studies occur in the junior and senior years of study. **MSW** education prepares individuals for advance practice, also called specialization or concentration practice. (We will explore advanced practice in more detail in chapters 5 and 6.) An MSW program requires two years of full-time study; a person with a BSW degree may be eligible for advanced standing in a graduate program, however, thus bypassing the first year of graduate work through mastery of beginning or foundation knowledge and skills.

A number of schools of social work offer academic programs leading to a doctoral degree, either a **Ph.D** or a **DSW**; such programs are not accredited by the CSWE, however. As a result, doctoral education varies greatly from school to school, with a program's focus set by its faculty's values and beliefs. Individuals pursuing doctoral degrees in social work will for the most part be employed in academic settings, though some will work in agency settings, primarily in administrative, supervisory, or research-related positions.

Social work education is a very large enterprise in the United States. There are close to 600 accredited baccalaureate and graduate programs, and programs are found in all fifty states. In 1997, more than 45,000 social work students were working toward BSWs, 35,000 toward MSWs, and approximately 2,000 toward doctorates. More than 6,500 full-time faculty members were involved in social work education.

MEMBERSHIP ASSOCIATIONS FOR SOCIAL WORKERS

All professionals have the opportunity to belong to membership organizations or associations that represent their interests. An association provides professional self-identity and an opportunity to meet colleagues in order to discuss ideas and share innovations in practice. Some of the most familiar professional associations are the American Medical Association (physicians), the American Bar Association (lawyers), and the National Educational Association (teachers).

Activity…Gather information about your local unit of NASW. Ask one of your instructors or a social worker in the community when your local unit of NASW will be meeting. Try to attend the next meeting. Also, find out when the state board of directors of NASW next meets. These meetings occur several times each year and are held somewhere in the state. Try to attend one of these meetings to see the process firsthand.

The *National Association of Social Workers* is the primary and the largest membership organization for social workers. In 1998, NASW membership totaled more than 160,000 persons. One important point to recognize is that membership is voluntary. Indeed, the federal government estimates that there are more than 500,000 professional social workers in the United States, which means that much less than one-half of all social work professionals are members of NASW.

NASW was first organized in 1955, when five special interest organizations joined together. These five interest groups were the American Association of Group Workers, American Association of Medical Social Workers, American Association of Psychiatric Social Workers, American Association of Social Workers, and National Association of School Social Workers. In addition, two study groups also joined: the Association for the Study of Community Organization and the Social Work Research Group. The ideas of all these groups were merged—to unify the profes-

---

Box 1: Benefits of NASW Membership
✓ Subscription to *Journal of Social Work*
✓ Subscription to *NASW News*
✓ State chapter and local unit memberships
✓ Credit and loan programs
✓ Hospital indemnity option
✓ Toll-free telephone to the NASW Information Center
✓ Representation on Capitol Hill in Washington, D.C., and in state legislatures
✓ Discounts for NASW-sponsored continuing education programs
✓ Subscription discounts for specialty journals (see box 2)
✓ Car rental discounts
✓ Credit card option
✓ Term life insurance options
✓ Malpractice insurance
✓ Job link

---

sion (Alexander, 1995). Today, the national offices of NASW are located in Washington, D.C., only a few blocks from the U.S. Capitol.

NASW regards itself as a bottom-up members' organization. What this means is that governance and direction are established from below and responsibility lies with the units and chapters in each state. Each state has its own chapter of NASW, and each chapter is further subdivided into units. Each local unit covers a geographical area small enough to allow members to attend meetings and programs together.

After joining NASW, each member is assigned to a state chapter and then to a local unit that reflects where the person lives. Most local units conduct quarterly or monthly meetings. These gatherings run the gamut of formality, from the very formal meeting with an invited speaker to the informal after-work get-together. Unit meetings offer social workers from the same geographical area an opportunity to meet on a regular basis and strengthen their professional networks.

The state chapter coordinates activities between the local units and offers ongoing educational opportunities, known as **continuing education,** around the state. It also brings to the attention of its membership issues in the state legislature that could affect the profession or clients being served. Most state chapters provide their members with a monthly newsletter as well as professional and social activities such as an annual or biannual convention. The state chapter is staffed by a paid employee, generally a social worker, and is governed by a board of directors elected by the membership of the state and serving for a prescribed term.

---

*Did You Know...*NASW News, *the monthly newspaper of NASW, is the primary source of news about opportunities for social workers across the United States. Each issue includes a classified section that lists, by state, job vacancies.*

The national office of NASW comprises divisions ranging from membership services to political advocacy to publications. The national office is responsible for carrying out the policy of the national board of directors, which is made up of elected social work members from across the country. The national office also publishes a monthly newspaper that provides an exhaustive overview of social work around the country. Other member benefits include opportunities to purchase life and malpractice insurance and reduced registration fees to national meetings (see box 1).

Box 2: Specialty Journals Published in NASW

Social Work: Premier journal in the social work profession; examines broad topical areas in practice, policy, and theoretical frameworks

Health & Social Work: Covers practice advances, social policy and planning, federal legislation and administrative rule making, innovations in health care, and research

Social Work Abstracts: Provides succinct summaries of articles previously published in a broad range of social work and human service journals

Social Work in Education: Focuses on school social workers and professionals in related disciplines; examines practice and theoretical developments, shifts in federal legislation, and changes at all school levels

Social Work Research: Contains analytic reviews, practice-based research, evaluation studies, theoretical articles, and diverse research studies

---

Through local units, state chapters, and the national office of NASW, individual social workers have numerous opportunities to affect the profession. By holding leadership positions, serving on various committees, and attending local, state, and national meetings, individual social workers mold the profession and give direction to future activities.

In addition to NASW, a number of national special interest social work associations are based on a variety of attributes ranging from race and ethnicity to practice interests (see box 3). Social workers belong to such groups in order to support specific interests. According to Tourse (1995), special interest associations provide professional identity and professional cohesiveness, monitor specialized practice, broaden the sphere of professional influence, and encourage development of specialized theory and practice.

Most special interest groups sponsor an annual meeting, and some publish a journal or newsletter. These organizations' membership rolls are much smaller than NASW's, they often do not have state or local unit groups, and they generally do not have paid staff to run the organization

---

Box 3: Other Social Work Membership Organizations

American Association of Industrial Social Workers: Social workers employed in employee assistance programs

Association for Community Organization and Administration: Community organizers and agency administrators and individuals interested in macroissues

North American Association of Christians in Social Work: Interdenominational association to assist members to develop Christian faith in social work practice

National Association of Black Social Workers: Association to influence practice and policy that impact all black ethnic groups

National Association of Oncology Social Workers: Individuals working with cancer patients

National Association of Puerto Rican/Hispanic Social Workers: Association concerned with advocacy and human services issues that impact the Latino community

National Federation of Societies of Clinical Social Work: State and regional societies that focus on issues relating to clinical social work practice

National Indian Social Workers Association: Association that works to develop understanding of native Americans and Alaska natives in tribal and nontribal organizations

Rural Social Work Caucus: Individuals working in and concerned about rural and small community human services

Society for Social Work Administrators in Health Care: Individuals seeking to promote effective social work health care administration

---

SUMMARY

Social work is a diverse profession. It is not easily defined and, as a result, is often misunderstood by the general public and the greater community. One thing remains prominent: social work is a profession of people helping people. Despite possible confusion about the daily activities of social workers, there is growing recognition that social work plays an important role in today's society. Children, seniors, families, communities, the rich, the poor, and the middle class are all represented among the many clients who benefit directly from social work. Social work clients are found in all quarters of the country. Social work is a global profession.

Today thousands of people studying in colleges and universities are striving to become professional social workers. The role of these new social work professionals is an essential one because it is these individuals who will steer the profession and support the mission of micro-, mezzo-, and macrointervention well into the twenty-first century.

Questions to Think About

1. What do you say to a friend who, after learning that you want to be a social worker, states, "You won't make any money doing that"?

2. What do you think a meeting of professional social workers, such as a local NASW unit meeting, would be like?

3. Do you know any professional social workers? What personal qualities do they have that you think might be useful for a social worker?

4. Do you think there should be one professional membership association, such as NASW, or a number of membership organizations as discussed in this chapter?

5. Why do you think there is a general misunderstanding of social work?

6. What are some ways social workers could help to educate family and friends about what it is they do?

References

Alexander, C. (1995). Distinctive dates in social welfare history. In R. Edwards et al. (Eds.), *Encyclopedia of social work* (19th ed., pp. 2631–2647). Washington, DC: NASW Press.

Barker, R. (1995). *The social work dictionary* (3rd ed.). Washington, DC: NASW Press.

Kendall, K. (1984). *World guide to social work education*. New York: CSWE.

Mental health: Does therapy work? (1995, November). *Consumer Reports*, pp. 734–739.

Specht, H., & Courtney, M. (1994). *Unfaithful angels*. New York: Free Press.

Tourse, R. W. C. (1995). Special-interest professional associations. In R. Edwards et al. (Eds.), *Encyclopedia of social work* (19th ed., pp 2314–2319). Washington, DC: NASW Press.

Chapter 2

Social Welfare: A System's Response to Personal Issues and Public Problems

WHEN YOU HEAR THE WORDS "SOCIAL WELFARE" WHAT COMES TO mind? Many people think of food stamps, child abuse, and low-income housing. Before we begin to explain social welfare, test your knowledge of the subject by taking the following quiz. We expect that as a beginning professional interested in this field, some of your answers will be correct and others will be wrong; just give it your best guess.

Welfare Quiz

1. What is the most costly welfare program?
a) Food stamps   b) Medicaid
c) Low-income housing   d) Social security

2. Who makes up the majority (more than 50 percent) of people receiving public assistance?
a) Mothers and their children   b) Unemployed adults
c) Senior citizens   d) Single females
3. In the United States there are more black individuals than white individuals living in poverty.
a) True   b) False

4. Many individuals who receive welfare benefits have children just to get more money from the government.
a) True   b) False

5. When we talk about the unemployment rate we are referring to those people who are not working at the present time.
a) True   b) False

Name: Leslie Hernandez

Place of residence: Austin, Texas

College/university degrees: B.A. in Psychology, M.S. in Social Work, University of Texas, Austin; Master of Public Affairs, Lyndon B. Johnson School, University of Texas, Austin

Present position: Director of Government Affairs, NASW/Texas

Previous work/volunteer experience: University of Texas Medical Branch, Medical Social Worker; Galveston County Community Action Council, Head Start Director; Health and Human Services Coordinating Council, Indigent Health Care Specialist; Children's Defense Fund, Texas Office, Executive Director; Texas Medical Association, Director of Socioeconomic Research

What do you do in your spare time? My husband is a community activist here in Austin, and I help him by attending meetings, rallies, and demonstrations on issues like preservation of the barrio, the Zapatista uprising in Mexico, and the abolition of the death penalty. I love doing campaign work if I believe in the candidate. I've helped with several campaigns, including Victor Morales's historic bid to unseat Senator Gramm. I also enjoy reading, gardening, cooking (sometimes), and watching my nine (step)grandchildren grow up.

Why did you choose social work as a career? My father is a public servant in the true sense of the word. He was a city manager, director of a state agency, and director of the United Way of Baytown. He and my mother both instilled in me the importance of serving people and communities. For as long as I can remember, I've wanted to do what I could to improve the human condition. One of my colleagues has characterized us as POHOs–People Obsessed with Helping Others.

What is your favorite social work story? Before we began planning for the 1997 Student Legislative Day, I participated in the first Latino March on Washington. It was so deeply moving that I thought "Why not have the students march to the Capitol for a rally before their legislative visits?" We did, and it was very successful. I used a bull horn to lead them in old chants, like "What do we want? Justice! When do we want it? Now!!"

What would be the one thing you would change in our community if you had the power to do so? Not much–just doing away with obstacles that keep people from using their innate power. These include poverty, inferior education, discrimination, lack of access to health care, hunger. . . . There needs to be a balance of power, so that decisions that profoundly affect the lives of the majority are not made by an elite few who don't have a clue.

6. The amount given to the poor in a "welfare" check is the same in all states.
a) True   b) True, but prorated for family size   c) False

7. More than half the people who receive welfare could be working but choose not to.
a) True   b) False

8. Which of the following groups are *not* considered to be welfare recipients by the U.S. government (circle all that apply)?
a) Schoolchildren
b) Seniors receiving social security
c) Armed forces veterans
d) Food stamp recipients
e) College students receiving Pell grants
f) *Medicare* recipients

9. **Aid to Families with Dependent Children** is the name of the *only* federal program that provides cash assistance to poor families.
a) True   b) False

10. In your own words define "social welfare."

Now turn to the back of this chapter to find the correct answers and see how you did. You'll find no answer to question 10. After reading this chapter come back and answer question 10 again. Be sure to compare your two responses to see if your first response is different from your second.

Are you surprised by some of the answers? Think about which questions you got wrong and what you learned from this brief quiz. Clearly, social welfare is a very complicated system that is often misunderstood.

In this chapter we discuss the dimensions of social welfare—in particular, what is meant by the term. We also direct attention to the role of the social work profession as well as that of each individual social worker within our current social welfare system.

TOWARD A DEFINITION OF SOCIAL WELFARE

To begin our discussion of the current social welfare system, we would like you to try this exercise. To prepare, take a piece of paper and a pencil and get ready to write down some of your ideas. First, think of your hometown or where you were raised. Second, imagine that you have the ability to make it into what you consider the "ideal" place to live. What kinds of services are needed to improve this neighborhood or community, bringing it to the perfectability that Specht and Courtney (1994) suggest is the profession's goal?

Use the following list of questions to suggest possible ideas and guide your thinking on this topic.

Housing and Employment

Would everyone have safe and affordable housing?

Would everyone be able to find employment?

Would employment be well paying and include social and health benefits?

Education and Services

Would the education of the young be given top priority?

Would the community help all schools to get the services and supplies they need (e.g., fully equipped classrooms and state-of-the-art technology)—public and private alike?

Would a safe learning environment be provided?

Community Safety and Security

Would senior citizens be protected from abuse and neglect?

Would senior citizens have access to the services they need to complete their activities of daily living?

Would children be protected from exploitation and abuse?

Would domestic violence be tolerated, and what options would be available to those who are victimized?

Would discrimination based on race, color, age, sexual orientation, and the like be tolerated?

Would food services be provided to those who cannot afford to buy their own?

Your own list probably includes many more considerations that you feel are essential to address. Nevertheless, we believe that if you compared your list to someone else's you'd be surprised at how similar the two lists are. Most people agree that in an ideal place, all people are treated with respect and dignity. Further, most people agree that for a community to be responsive, it needs to be a place where members are valued for who they are and what they can offer to their community.

Seems too simple, doesn't it? And, it's true, some issues are much more difficult to address. Most people cannot agree on what services are needed in a community, who deserves these services, and how many services need to be provided. To further complicate things, communities are not static entities. A community needs to shift and change in response to the social, political, and economic conditions that exist at the time. Changing times can create and worsen social problems.

Students in a self-contained public school classroom for persons with emotional disabilities. Biweekly sessions with the social worker help the students to discuss their feelings.

For example, even today poverty plagues more than 13 million people, and of those living in poverty many are women, children, and the elderly. These people are also at particular risk of abuse and neglect, both physical and emotional.

The United States is among the wealthiest countries in the world. It has abundant natural resources and technology; yet many American citizens battle daily with poverty as well as emotional and psychological difficulties that can impede their ability to function at home and in their communities. About one in four children under age 18 live in poverty (Center on Budget and Policy Priorities, 1996). Diverse people, including those of color and alternative sexual orientation, continue to suffer from discrimination and prejudice. Every day millions of children are ill fed, live in unsafe environments, and have no access to high-quality health care services. These are only some of the overwhelming problems that American communities face. Determining who should get service priority is thus a daunting task.

Different people have different impressions about what is needed. With each member of a community asked for input, the list of suggestions will grow. Our purpose in this chapter is not merely to develop a laundry list of society's ills; rather it is to identify how individuals within a community can begin to address them.

When a society strives for community betterment by developing methods and programs to address social needs, this effort is often referred to as **social welfare.** Our perceptions of social welfare vary. The term can bring to mind a myriad of pictures, ranging from the homeless person walking to the shelter to the tornado victim receiving assistance from the Red Cross. From the varied perceptions of social welfare, two common but opposed threads emerge.

On one hand, many people believe social welfare recipients are those who cannot make it on their own and need society's help and intervention. Some people also believe that most recipients are responsible for the misfortunes they are experiencing and, in some cases, have created their own problems. This misperception contributes to the view that welfare recipients are "not worthy" or lack the motivation to help themselves. It is important to note, however, that not everyone feels this way. Many people, on the other hand, believe that some of the problems facing welfare recipients are not of their own making. They think that these problems should be regarded as similar to unexpected crises or traumas. In times of crisis, almost everyone expects victims to seek government assistance; such help is considered a right of citizenship.

The varying opinions that people can hold about government assistance and the wide range of social welfare services that can be provided make an accurate definition of social welfare essential. If the concept is defined too narrowly, people may focus on a few programs that account for only a small portion of welfare spending and decide that welfare policy is too specialized. If social welfare is defined too broadly, people may decide that entitlements are being given too freely and that society's limited resources cannot sustain this policy.

SOCIAL WELFARE DEFINED

Let's approach the concept of social welfare by examining several existing definitions. Later we will formulate a definition of our own.

Social Welfare Is . . .

◆ The assignment of claims from one set of people who are said to produce or earn the national product to another set of people who may merit compassion and charity but not economic rewards for productive service (Titmus, 1965).

◆ "Collective interventions to meet certain needs of the individual and/or to serve the wider interests of society" (Titmus, 1959, p. 42).

◆ A system of social services and institutions, designed to aid individuals and groups to attain satisfying standards of life and health, and personal social relationships which permit them to develop their full capacities and promote their well-being in harmony with the needs of their families and community (Friedlander, 1955, p. 140).

◆ A subset of social policy, which may be defined as the formal and consistent ordering of affairs (Karger & Stoesz, 1994, p. 4).

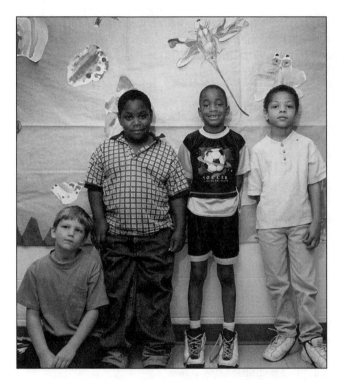

Students with emotional disabilities posing in front of a mural they created during their study of insects.

♦ A nation's system of programs, benefits, and services that help people meet those social, economic, educational, and health needs that are fundamental to the maintenance of society (Barker, 1995, p. 221).

♦ An encompassing and imprecise term but most often it is defined in terms of "organizational activities," "interventions," or some other element that suggests policy and programs to respond to recognized social problems or to improve the well-being of those at risk (Reid, 1995, p. 2206).

♦ A concept that encompasses people's health, economic condition, happiness, and quality of life (Segal & Brzuzy, 1998, p. 8).

♦ Society's organized way to provide for the persistent needs of all people—for health, education, socioeconomic support, personal rights, and political freedom (Bloom, 1990, p. 6).

Close examination of these definitions shows that while the phrasing differs, the content and focus are similar. Let's identify the common themes in these various statements as we develop a comprehensive definition of social welfare. First, social welfare includes a variety of programs and services that yield some type of benefit to their consumers. People participating in any type of welfare-based program benefit because they receive some form of assistance. Many times the assistance, or social provision, is given in cash. At other times social provision is given as **in kind**, for example, as clothes or counseling that the consumer did not have beforehand.

Second, social welfare, as a system of programs and services, is designed to meet the needs of people. The needs to be addressed can be all-encompassing, including economic and social well-being, health, education, and overall quality of life.

Third, the end result of social welfare is to improve the well-being of individuals, groups, and communities. Helping those systems in time of need will later benefit society at large.

RESIDUAL AND INSTITUTIONAL SOCIAL WELFARE

In their classic work, *Industrial Society and Social Welfare*, Harold Wilensky and Charles Lebeaux (1965) attempt to answer a basic question: Is social welfare a matter of giving assistance only in emergencies, or is it a frontline service that society must provide? As part of their discussion, Wilensky and Lebeaux developed two important concepts that continue to frame and influence our understanding and discussions of social welfare: **residual social welfare** and **institutional social welfare**.

Wilensky and Lebeaux (1958) defined the terms as follows:

Residual: Social welfare institutions come into play only when the normal structures of supply, the family and the market, break down.

Institutional: Welfare services are normal, frontline functions of modern industrial society.

Box 1: Examples of Residual and Institutional Program

Residual	Institutional
Food stamps	Social security
Medicaid	Medicare
Head Start	Libraries
Temporary Assistance for Needy Families (TANF)	Health departments
Homeless shelters	Veteran's benefits

Residual Social Welfare

The residual conception of social welfare rests on the "individualistic" notion that people should take care of themselves and rely on government support only in times of crisis or emergency. People are not considered eligible for help until all of their own private resources—which may include assistance from the church, family wealth and inheritance, friends, employers, and so on—have been exhausted. Only then do public welfare efforts at assistance come into play. Therefore, in order to access residual social welfare services, people must first prove their inability to provide for themselves and their families. As a result the help received often carries the stigma of failure.

Qualifying for this type of service is often referred to as **selective eligibility**. When eligibility is selective, social services are delivered only to people who meet certain defined criteria. When a person needs cash assistance as a service, the eligibility determination procedure is commonly called "means testing." To access means-tested programs, people must demonstrate that they do not have the financial ability to meet their specific needs. When a residual type of program provides cash assistance clients must recertify their eligibility every few months. The recertification process is designed primarily to ensure that clients are still unable to meet their needs through private or personal sources.

People who receive residual services are generally viewed as being different from people who receive other kinds of services. They are often regarded as failures because they do not show the rugged individualism that is a cornerstone ideal of our society. Many times beneficiaries of residual programs are labeled as lazy, lacking in morals, and dishonest. They are often accused of making bad decisions and of needing constant monitoring because of their untrustworthiness. In short, people in residual programs carry a **stigma.**

Imagine for a moment that you are standing in the checkout line of your local grocery store. The person in front of you is paying for some items with food stamps. Noting this, you feel compelled to look more closely at what is being purchased. In the grocery cart are potato chips, soda, some candy, and beer, as well as other food items. You have similar items in your own cart. On a piece of paper, write down your first thoughts about this. Be honest, and allow yourself to express any thoughts you might have. One response to this kind of situation is shown in box 2.

Box 2: Food Stamps and the Video Game

Dallas Morning News. Letters to the Editor. January 1, 1983.

Last week I was passing through the checking line at a supermarket. In front of me was a young woman with two children about 5 and 6. She paid for her groceries with food stamps. On their way out they stopped by the store's video game machines. All three played the game, once each. In other words, the woman squandered 75 cents while letting taxpayers pay for the groceries. That money would have bought a dozen eggs for that "poor" family. I wonder if their color TV and stereo are working? I never have objected to my tax dollars being spent to help the truly poor, but I protest vehemently the idea of helping them pay for their entertainment or luxuries.

(Name Withheld)

Dallas, Texas

The response illustrated in box 2 is not unusual. In fact, it is characteristic of the way many people view and react to beneficiaries of residual programs, and it raises some interesting questions. Do people receiving assistance have a right to entertainment? Or when they accept public assistance do they give up their right to the luxuries available to others not dependent on this social welfare service? As we will see in chapter 3 the history of social welfare is marred by a reluctance to help others in need. Residual programs and services are stigmatized, and those who need these types of services are constantly scrutinized. Many people believe that such services, although necessary as temporary forms of assistance or as last-resort charity, reinforce negative behaviors rather than promoting rugged individualism and a strong work ethic.

In summary, residual programs highlight narrow views of helping. Assistance is minimal and temporary and only designed to help people survive immediate problems or crises. These types of programs provide support only when no other support options are available. In other words, a residual program is a program of last resort. In the 1980s, American public welfare programs were categorized as essentially residual in nature. Collectively referred to as "the safety net," these programs could be accessed only after all other avenues of assistance had been exhausted.

There are three important points to keep in mind regarding residual programs. First, these programs are all means tested. To be eligible for benefits people must document their inability to care financially for themselves and their families. In a typical residual program, clients are routinely means tested or recertified for continued eligibility every few months.

Second, residual programs can create barriers for those who seek assistance. Numerous eligibility criteria, which often force clients to produce a variety of supporting documents and evidence, can be disheartening. Continual recertification processes can thus encourage clients to give up, forgoing assistance even when their needs persist.

Third, residual programs carry a stigma, and recipients are not proud to receive services. The **food stamps program** is a typical residual program (see box 1). Food stamp clients must qualify to receive program services, they must be recertified every few months by the state, and they are not viewed positively in the greater community.

Recall the food stamp recipient in our hypothetical grocery checkout line. How often do we look at what the person ahead of us is buying? Do we spend more time scrutinizing the purchases of those who pay with food stamps? If another person had been purchasing exactly the same items and paying with cash would our reactions have been the same? Probably not. Why? Since both individuals would have similar buying habits, why is there a difference in how these two people would be viewed? The sad reality is that the food stamp recipient carries a stigma. Some people believe that beneficiaries of residual programs such as food stamps cannot be trusted, are morally weak, and do not make good decisions. Food stamp clients are often thought to be different from people who do not receive public aid.

Institutional Social Welfare

The second conception of social welfare described by Wilensky and Lebeaux (1965) is institutional social welfare. This definition of social welfare gives it much broader scope and function than the residual definition does. In the institutional conception the community is expected to assist individual members because problems are viewed, not as failures, but as part of life in modern society. This broader community responsibility allows members in need to be provided services that go beyond immediate responses to emergencies. Help is often provided *before* people exhaust all of their own resources, and preventive and rehabilitative services are stressed.

Therefore, an institutional program, as opposed to a residual program, is designed to meet the needs of all people. Eligibility is **universal**. Institutional programs have no stigma attached and are viewed as regular frontline programs in society. In fact, institutional programs are so widely accepted in society that many are not viewed as social welfare programs at all (see examples in box 1). Institutional programs are often called "entitlement programs," meaning that services and benefits are available because of a person's earned status.

In concluding our discussion of residual and institutional provision of social welfare as outlined by Wilensky and Lebeaux we must note the primary weakness of this framework: not all programs and services are easily classified as one or the other; some programs have both institutional and residual attributes. The Head Start program, for example, is institutional in nature but is means tested and restricted to a particular segment of the population. One solution is to expand the traditional dichotomy and classify social programs on a residual–institutional continuum. A program's position on the continuum reflects whether it is more residual or more institutional in design and to what degree. Some questions to help guide the classification process include:

1. Is the program short term or long term?
2. Is the program open to all people or a selected group of people?
3. Do program participants carry a stigma?
4. Does the public embrace the program?
5. Is the program controversial?
6. How would you feel if you were a program participant?

Activity…Ask fifteen to twenty people to define the term "social welfare." Then ask them to list five social welfare programs of which they are aware. Review these responses in light of the work of Wilensky and Lebeaux. Do you notice any patterns in the responses? How many of the responses would you identify as residual, institutional, or a mix of both types? In analyzing these responses do you find that people have a narrow or a broad view of social welfare? How do you feel about the responses you have received? Do you think your respondents' views are accurate?

Although there are ways to classify social programs, the importance of recognizing social stigma, misperception, and its influence on clients can be underestimated. The public does appear openly to support some forms of social welfare, but these feelings and expectations seem to vary based on individual perception and the service that is being received.

IS EVERYONE REALLY ON WELFARE?

Richard Titmus (1965), a famed British social scientist, argued that social welfare was much more than aid to the poor and in fact represented a broad system of support to the middle and upper classes. In his model, social welfare has three branches:

Fiscal welfare: Tax benefits and supports for the middle and upper classes

Corporate welfare: Tax benefits and supports for businesses

Public welfare: Assistance to the poor

Abramowitz (1983) applied the Titmus model to American social welfare. She identified a "shadow welfare state" for the wealthy that parallels the social service system available to the poor. She concluded that poor and nonpoor alike benefit from government programs and tax laws that raise their disposable income. In other words, were it not for direct government support—whether through food stamps or through a childcare tax exemption—people would have fewer dollars to spend and to support themselves and their families.

So, is everyone really on welfare? To address this question, let's focus first on college students. Did you know that college students are probably one of the largest groups of welfare recipients in the United States today? The vast majority of college students first attended public school, which was provided at no cost to them. Why? Because our government subsidizes the public school system. It is important for all children to have nutritious meals, and the daily school lunch is relatively inexpensive to purchase for all school students. In fact, try to buy the same meal in a restaurant and compare costs—the school lunch is much cheaper. Why? Because the government subsidies given to public schools lower the cost of these meals for all students. Okay, that's what happens in public school. Now consider the role of government in a public college. Compare tuition fees at a private college or university with those at a state- or community-supported institution. Why are tuition costs at the public college so much lower? Once again, the answer is simple: because of government subsidies. The government is very involved in subsidizing the educational needs of students at both the elementary and secondary and the college levels. Students are very much in need and dependent on these subsidies in order to complete their educations.

With all the support provided and the need for continuing support, doesn't it sound like welfare? Why then is there no stigma attached to this form of social provision? Some people may say, "I paid for my 'welfare' through taxes on my earnings, which makes me different from those people who did not." There is no easy response to this statement, and such attitudes continue to disturb social work professionals who do not agree with the distinction between the worthy and the unworthy that is often applied to social services. Is there really a difference in the welfare service provided? Could most individuals and families afford to pay the full tuition for college or the costs associated with operating a good-quality public school, including lunch? Government subsidies are important to the maintenance of society and are used by all people.

PUBLIC SOCIAL WELFARE

Social welfare is found in both public and private settings. "Public" refers to programs within the purview of state, federal, or local (city or county) government; "private" refers to services provided for profit and voluntary services.

Federal Welfare

The federal government classifies social welfare into seven areas: social insurance, education, public aid, health and medical programs, veterans' programs, housing, and other social welfare (see box 3). In 1996 the federal government spent more than $1.2 billion in social welfare, approximately 55 percent of all federal expenditures.

Box 3: Federal Social Welfare Programs

Social insurance: Old-age retirement, workers' compensation, disability, unemployment assistance, railroad retirement, public employee retirement

Education: Elementary, secondary, and higher education; vocational education

Public aid: Cash payments under TANF, WIC, general assistance, emergency assistance

Veterans' programs: Assistance to veterans and their families, burial, health and medical programs, education, life insurance

Housing: Public housing

Health and medical programs: Hospital and medical care, maternal and child health programs, medical research, school health, other public health, medical facilities construction.

Other social welfare: Vocational rehabilitation, institutional care, child nutrition, child welfare, OEO and ACTION programs, social welfare not classified elsewhere, food stamps

---

Social insurance has been and continues to be the most costly area of federal welfare, followed by education (see table 1). In fact, these two areas account for more than 72 percent of *total* federal welfare expenses, whereas public aid accounts for only 13.8 percent of the federal welfare budget. It is interesting to note, however, that when "cutting welfare" is discussed, the emphasis is on public aid. But what would happen, for example, if the federal appropriation for food stamps were cut? In 1995 approximately $26 billion was spent on food stamps—certainly a lot of money by anyone's standards. Yet food stamps made up only 1.6 percent of *all* federal expenditures. In other words, cutting food stamps by, say, 50 percent would reduce the federal budget by less than 1 percent.

Table 1: Federal Social Welfare Expenditures, Selected Years (in millions of dollars)

Area	1975	1985	1990
Total	$289,713.7	$732,250.1	$1,050,155.4
Social insurance	123,013.1	369,595.2	513,800.8
Education	80,834.1	127,047.5	258,384.6
Public aid	41,446.6	98,361.8	145,877.7
Health and medical programs	16,742.0	39,053.0	63,790.0
Veteran's programs	17,018.9	27,042.3	30,916.2
Housing	3,171.7	12,598.5	19,468.5
Other social welfare	6,946.6	13,551.8	17,917.6

Source: Social Security Bulletin, 57, no. 1 (spring 1994), 98.
Note: Figures are adjusted for inflation.

State Welfare

State welfare programs differ across the country. Each state is able to develop its own set of social programs to augment the federal government's initiatives. Typically a state establishes rules and provides funds for statewide social agencies. State social welfare agencies include protective services for children and juvenile justice. Funding for state services comes from two sources: **block grants** from the federal government and state tax revenues. A block grant is a lump sum of funds given to a state, which then has the authority to determine how best to spend the dollars. The federal government imposes few rules on block grants, allowing each state to determine how programs will be structured. A state can also supplement block grant funding in order to expand services.

Local Welfare

City and county welfare programs depend on local taxes for funding. Such funds are primarily used for community protection and support, such as police, fire, and other basic local services. Funding and provision of most of these types of local social services are considered mandatory. By contrast, many government officials and community leaders see social welfare provision as a minimal, "fill the gap" measure. Those in power are usually reluctant to develop and sponsor "costly" local services. As with state government programs, the types and levels of local welfare programs vary by municipality. Because of their "gap filling" status, local programs are generally residual in nature. Typical local programs include emergency food relief and housing and clothing vouchers.

PRIVATE SOCIAL WELFARE

Private social welfare consists of for-profit and not-for-profit agencies, also called voluntary agencies or nonprofits. Examples of nonprofits include the United Way, Red Cross, Salvation Army, Boys and Girls Clubs, Girl Scouts, YMCA, YWCA, Jewish Community Centers, Catholic Charities, and Family Services.

> *Activity…Go to your local (county or city) welfare office. Look around and try to get a feel for the setting. What messages does the physical structure send to the clients? Does this environment seem like a typical business setting? Do the setting and staff suggest an interest in serving the clients, and are the clients made to feel important? How does this facility differ from a physician's office? What sorts of informational brochures are available to read? How long do clients wait before a worker sees them?*
>
> *After you've visited a public agency, visit a private social service agency. What differences, if any, do you see between the two agencies? If differences do exist, what are they and why do you think they exist? Should there be any physical differences between public and private agencies?*

According to Karger and Stoesz (1994), private social welfare is not well understood; they characterized it as the "forgotten sector." For the most part, American social welfare has rested within the public domain since the 1930s when the government implemented a series of welfare programs to combat the effects of the Great Depression. As the government took on greater welfare responsibility, the voluntary sector's activities lessened (Karger & Stoesz, 1994). With financial cuts in federal welfare funding in the 1980s and 1990s, however, private welfare has taken on new importance. This forgotten sector is now recognized as a crucial player in the delivery of social services.

The nonprofit sector relies on donations from public foundations and, to a much lesser extent, federal, state, and local governments. In order for nonprofits to provide services, their fundraising efforts must be successful. The success of fundraising depends on three factors: 1) the agency's ability to provide a high-quality program, 2) the agency's ability to communicate its successes, and 3) the community's financial ability to support the program. Karger and Stoesz (1995) noted, "As voluntary agencies become more dependent on the communities in which they are located, their success is tied to the affluence of those communities. Compared with those of wealthier communities, agencies in poor communities are unlikely to fare well" (p. 205). Therefore, in most instances, the level of private social welfare programming available depends directly on the financial well-being of the surrounding community. This dependence on private funding is particularly problematic during periods of economic turmoil, such as recession and rising unemployment. During these periods people have less money and time to donate to private charities, which in turn forces these organizations to make critical choices about which programs to close or cut.

According to the Social Security Administration, the role of the private sector in financing social welfare continues to grow, and this growth is needed to complement public social welfare expenditures and programs. Hoeffer and Colby (1998) referred to the private sector as the "mirror welfare state," a system of services that reflect public programs but are more supportive of the middle and upper classes than the poor.

Private welfare can be categorized into four areas: health, income maintenance (retirement), education, and welfare services. In 1992 private welfare expenditures totaled $824.9 billion, a 75 percent increase over the 1985 level.

As with federal welfare spending it's illuminating to examine where private sector funds are going. In particular, it is not the case that most of the spending, or even most of the increase in spending, is going to millions of poor people to gain the services they need. Of 1992 private welfare expenditures $462.9 billion was spent on private health care; $164.7 billion was spent on income maintenance services, that is, retirement support programs. Thus health and income maintenance together accounted for 78.6 percent of all private welfare expenditures. By contrast, $75.8 billion, 9.2 percent, was spent on private welfare services. So although overall private expenditures have increased, the majority of these funds have gone to assist not the poor but rather the middle and upper classes.

SOCIAL WORK IN THE SOCIAL WELFARE SYSTEM

Social workers make up the primary professional group in the social welfare system. But social work is *not* the sole social welfare profession. Given the broad definition of social welfare used here and in the social work literature, many other professional groups are welfare providers as well. Although it is possible to lump the various professionals together and classify them all as welfare workers, it is more accurate to recognize that some professions are more concerned than others with people's social, health, wellness, and economic welfare needs. A useful way to differentiate among professions is to classify their level of involvement as either primary or secondary.

The primary category consists of professions whose principal efforts are in the provision of social, health, or economic services. The principal activities of professions in the secondary category are not directed toward welfare, but their work does at times involve social, health, or economic service provision (see box 4).

Box 4: Examples of Social Welfare Professionals by Primary or Secondary Classification

Primary	Secondary
Social workers	Police officers
Mental health counselors	Librarians
Schoolteachers	Recreational specialists
Marriage and family therapists	Road crews
Psychologists	Government officials
Psychiatrists	Military personnel
Nurses	
Sanitation workers	

Look at the professionals listed in box 4. What is your opinion of who is included and where they have been placed? Do you think the professionals listed would agree with where we have classified them? For example, how would an elementary schoolteacher react to being described as a welfare worker? We believe that many of the professionals listed above would openly disagree that they are welfare providers. It's possible that the stigma attached to programs and services offered under the rubric of "welfare" might influence their reactions. To explore this possibility, how do you think these professionals would reply to the following question?

> Do you as a professional provide a program, benefit, or service that helps people meet those social, economic, educational, health, and wellness needs that are fundamental to the maintenance of society?

We believe that as this question is framed—without addressing the concept of social welfare provision openly—the vast majority of the professionals listed in box 4, whether classed as primary or as secondary service providers would, answer yes. The simple truth is that although few professionals think of their activities in this way, providing welfare services is an integral part of their jobs.

Our broad definition of social welfare also suggests some rethinking of rigid ideas about social work. The social work profession has its roots in efforts to help the poor and disenfranchised (Hepworth & Larsen, 1993), neither of which is considered a desirable client population according to a narrow definition of social welfare. These efforts historically meant promoting and enhancing individual client well-being albeit in a societal or environmental context.

Over time, however, the traditional role of the social work professional has expanded. According to social work's revised Code of Ethics:

> The primary mission of the social work profession is to enhance human well-being and help meet the basic human needs of all people, with particular attention to the needs and empowerment of people who are vulnerable, oppressed, and living in poverty. A historic and defining feature of social work is the profession's focus on individual well-being in a social context and the well-being of society. Fundamental to social work is the attention to the environmental forces that create, contribute to, and address problems in living.
>
> . . . These activities may be in the form of direct practice, community organizing, supervision, consultation, administration, advocacy, social and political action, policy development and implementation, education, and research and evaluation. (NASW, 1996, p. 1)

For the social work professional, social welfare methods and programs now address diverse populations, which can include those who are homeless, suicidal, homicidal, divorced, unemployed, mentally ill, medically ill, drug abusing, and delinquent, just to mention a few. Moreover, the term "client" is now used inclusively and can mean individuals, groups, families, organizations, and communities. Adopting, in essence, the institutional perspective, the social worker must strive to restore and enhance client wellness and to provide preventive as well as basic, brief services. Strategies to assist clients must address all of these areas because often the factors involved are intertwined and interdependent (Skidmore, Thackeray, & Farley, 1997).

Activity:

OK, You Balance the Federal Budget... *In 1995, the federal budget was $1.68 trillion. Let's say you are a member of the U.S. House of Representatives and are charged with balancing the budget. You will need to cut the federal budget by approximately $200 billion in spending. Find that $200 billion.*

Program	Spending in Billions	Share of Total Spending
Social security	$336.1	20.0%
Interest on national debt	333.7	19.9
Defense	271.6	16.2
Medicare	157.3	9.4
Medicaid	88.4	5.3
Federal pensions and disability	64.7	3.9
Education and training	40.6	2.4
Transportation	39.2	2.3
Veterans' benefits	38.4	2.3
Housing subsidies	26.7	1.6
Food stamps	26.2	1.6
Supplemental Security Income	25.1	1.5
Unemployment	23.8	1.4
Environmental and natural resources	21.9	1.3
International affairs, including foreign aid	18.7	1.1
Law enforcement	17.6	1.1
Families and dependents	17.3	1.0
Science and space	17.0	1.0
Low-income tax credit	16.8	1.0
General government operations	14.5	0.9
Agriculture	14.4	0.9
Nutrition programs	12.3	0.7
Health research and training	11.7	0.7
Community and regional development	7.8	0.5
Disaster relief	4.8	0.3
Energy	4.6	0.3
Other	28.4	1.7
Total	$1.68 trillion	100%

The Fading "Public" versus "Private" Distinction

Changes in the social welfare environment have blurred once clear distinctions in social work—for example, whether an agency that employs a social worker is public or private. For simplicity, "public" agencies are understood to be primarily, if not totally, funded through tax-supported dollars. It is the public agency that is regarded as most representative of social welfare services and programs. Most people believe that these agencies have primary responsibility for residual or means-tested social welfare programs. "Private" agencies, on the other hand, are believed to be voluntarily supported and to rarely have tax-supported dollars as part of their basic budgets. If public and private agencies were distinctly different, these straightforward definitions would suffice. However, in today's social service environment nothing could be further from the truth. There is no longer any clear distinction between public and private agencies because their funding and the services they deliver so often overlap. Many private agencies now actively seek public or tax-supported funds, and many public agencies now contract with private agencies and individual providers to provide services to their clients. Because private agencies can specialize in a way that public agencies, with their broad responsibilities, cannot, such contracts allow public agencies to secure services that they do not have the budget or the skilled personnel to offer on their own.

In addition to this blurring between public and private agencies a dispersion of social workers across both the public and private sectors has placed social work practitioners in new roles. Traditionally, social workers served in the public sector because these agencies and programs assumed primary responsibility for the poor and the underserved. Today, however, social workers practice in many different agencies that have many different goals and allegiances.

Cost Containment versus Quality

For all social workers the current state of social work practice mirrors the turbulence in the general social welfare environment. There is little consistency in the delivery of social welfare services as primary emphasis is placed on cost containment. Social welfare program administrators, forced to justify each dollar billed for services, may reduce the provision of what some see as "expendable services" designed to promote the mental health and well-being of clients. They may be tempted to regard the role of social workers as adjunct to the delivery of care and to cut back on professional staff or replace them with nonprofessionals simply to lower costs. These substitute professionals have neither the depth nor the breadth of training that social work professionals do. The result can be substandard professional services.

The employment of these kinds of paraprofessionals, though cost effective, is not quality driven. When social services are rushed or minimized, issues such as the individual client's sense of well-being, ability to self-care, and family and environmental support may not be considered. The involvement of social work professionals is thus essential to ensuring that personal, social, and environmental issues are addressed and clients are not put at risk of harm.

For social workers, a client who is discharged home to a family that does not want him is at risk of abuse and neglect. A client who has a negative view of herself and a hopeless and hapless view of her condition is more likely to attempt suicide or come to some other harm. Many paraprofessionals and members of other professional disciplines differ from social work professionals in that they do not recognize the paramount importance of culture and environmental factors to efficient and effective practice. Their outlook may enable the delivery of "cheap" service, but the care provided is substandard.

As social service administrators strive to cut costs by eliminating professional social work services the overall philosophy of wellness can be sacrificed. It is important to note, however, that staff reorganizations and reductions in social welfare services are rarely personal attacks on social work professionals. The changes and cutbacks in services and those who provide them are responses to an immediate need—cost reduction. Fluctuating employment and downsizing of social work professionals, as with allied health professionals, simply reflects the fluctuating demands of the current market (Falck, 1990).

SUMMARY

So what is social welfare? The residual view suggests that welfare support should be temporary, only for the poor, and as minimal as possible. If we look at actual public welfare spending, however, it seems that social welfare as practiced is much broader. In fact, everyone in society is a welfare recipient of one type or another.

Similarly, the role of the social work professional is broader than many people expect. Originally, social workers served the poor and disenfranchised; however, over the years the role of the social worker has expanded tremendously. Many social work professionals now provide services outside of the traditional social welfare realm. This diversity of style, task, and approach makes defining exactly what social workers do difficult. Clarity of definition has been further complicated by changes in scope of practice, roles served, and expectations within the client-professional relationship.

In the turbulent social welfare environment social work professionals face a constant battle of "quality of care issues" versus "cost containment measures" for clients (Dziegielewski, 1996). In addition, they must strive to maintain a secure place as professional providers in the delivery of social welfare services.

Quiz Answers

1. d) Social security. According to the federal government nearly 50 percent of all welfare expenditures go to social security retirement payments. Less than 1 percent of the welfare budget is spent on food stamps.

2. a) Mothers and their children. Approximately 60 percent of all welfare recipients, according to the U.S. Bureau of the Census, are mothers and their children.

3. b) False. The majority of people in poverty are white.

4. b) False. Under federal welfare rules a family on welfare that has another baby will not receive any additional benefits.

5. b) False. The unemployment rate identifies only those people not working who actively looked for a job within the past thirty days.

6. c) False. Each state determines the amount a family receives on public assistance. As a result, a person in Florida receives a different amount from someone in Alabama.

7. b) False. According to reports by the U.S. Bureau of Labor Statistics, more than 70 percent of public assistance recipients are women with children, children, and senior citizens.

8. All the groups listed are participants in programs the federal government defines as "social welfare." As a result, all of the groups are welfare recipients.

9. b) False. AFDC was replaced by TANF—Temporary Assistance to Needy Families in 1996.

10. Revise your answer to this question using the information presented in this chapter.

References

Abramowitz, M. (1983). Everyone is on welfare: "The role of redistribution in social policy" revisited. *Social Work, 28*(6), 440–445.

Barker, R. L. (1995). *The social work dictionary* (3rd ed.). Washington, DC: NASW Press.

Bloom, M. (1990). *Introduction to the social work drama*. Itasca, IL: Peacock.

Center on Budget and Policy Priorities. (1996). *Poverty and income trends, 1994*. Washington, DC: Author.

Dziegielewski, S. F. (1996). Managed care principles: The need for social work in the health care environment. *Crisis Intervention and Time Limited Treatment, 3*(2), 97–110.

Falck, H. S. (1990). Maintaining social work standards in for-profit hospitals: Reasons for doubt. *Health & Social Work, 15*, 76–77.

Friedlander, W. (1955). *Introduction to social welfare*. Englewood Cliffs, NJ: Prentice-Hall.

Hepworth, D. H., & Larsen, J. (1993). *Direct social work practice: Theory and skills* (4th ed.). Pacific Grove, CA: Brooks/Cole.

Hoeffer, R., & Colby, I. (1998). Private social welfare expenditures in R. Edwards et al. (Eds.), *Encyclopedia of social work update*. Washington, DC: NASW Press.

Karger, H., & Stoesz, D. (1994). *American social welfare policy: A pluralist approach* (2nd ed.). New York: Longman.

NASW (National Association of Social Workers). (1996, August). *Code of ethics* (adopted by the NASW National Delegate Assembly, August 1996). Washington, DC: NASW.

Reid, P. N. (1995). Social welfare history. In R. Edwards et al. (Eds.), *Encyclopedia of social work* (19th ed.). Washington, DC: NASW Press.

Segal, W., &B Brzuzy, S. (1998). *Social welfare policy, programs, and practice*. Itasca, IL: Peacock.

Skidmore, R. A., M. G. Thackeray, & O. W. Farley. (1997). *Introduction to social work* (7th ed.). Boston: Allyn and Bacon.

Specht, H., & Courtney, M. (1994). *Unfaithful angels*. New York: Free Press.

Titmus, R. (1959). *Essays on the welfare state*. New Haven, CT: Yale University Press.

Titmus, R. (1965). The role of redistribution in social policy. *Social Security Bulletin, 28*(6), 34–55.

Wilensky, H. & Lebeaux, C. (1958). *Industrial society and social welfare*. New York: Russell Sage Foundation.

Wilensky, H. & Lebeaux, C. (1965). *Industrial society and social welfare*. New York, Free Press.

Chapter 3

How Did We Get Here from There?

TIME FOR A BRIEF HISTORY QUIZ:

1. Why is the year 1492 important in American history?
2. The New Deal was the name given to what set of programs?
3. What did the Emancipation Proclamation address?
4. What important event took place in Seneca Falls, New York, in 1848?
5. Where was an immigrant arriving at Ellis Island most likely to be from?
6. What is Salem, Massachusetts, perhaps best known for?
7. The United States acquired California, Nevada, Utah, and parts of Texas, Colorado, New Mexico, and Wyoming as part of what act or event?
8. What document preceded the U.S. Constitution?
9. What does the term "Seward's Folly" refer to?
10. What was at issue in the Dred Scott Case?

So, how did you do? (The answers are at the end of the chapter.) For most people taking this quiz the results are mixed. A few of the questions seem easy while others are complete mysteries. Yet each of these questions addresses a meaningful part of our American history. The importance of being familiar with such events is twofold: 1) it is important to know what has happened simply to be an educated citizen and 2) knowledge of the past can help us to understand both present and future societal developments.

In the field of social work, as in other disciplines, knowing the history of the profession is essential to understanding its past, present, and future. Unfortunately, however, studying history sometimes doesn't seem as exciting as learning about direct social work practice, policy, or social action. When history is discussed in the classroom or in less formal situations, it is almost always received with an air of indifference and reluctance. As one student remarked, "It's over and done with, so why should I be concerned about it? I want to learn how to help people. What happened two hundred years ago won't help me today."

Is this statement really valid? It's true that in social work practice, regardless of the model or technique employed, the emphasis is on the here and now. Nevertheless, most social workers recognize the importance of history in their practice. For

Name: Jorge Munoz Bustamante
Place of residence: Miami, Florida
College/university degrees: M.S.W., Barry University
Present position: Clinical Social Worker
Previous work/volunteer experience:

What do you do in your spare time? What spare time? I am very involved in the lives of my three children and my wife. My daughter is a freshman at Florida International. I have a sixteen-year-old son who is a junior in high school and is very involved in track and field. My thirteen-year-old son is completing middle school. Their activities keep me quite occupied. Additionally, I am involved in the Catholic Physician's Guild, and I offer a presentation called heart-centered-parenting to the community at large. I enjoy sailing and camping whenever I can.

Why did you choose social work as a career? In 1959 my family had to flee Cuba after my father's paint store was confiscated. A West Virginia family that vacationed on the island made possible our entry into the United States by sponsoring us. This family encouraged and supported us even though they had no obligation to do so. From them I learned the deep satisfaction that comes from serving others. In my senior year of college, a friend said to me, "Jorge, have you ever thought about a career in service?" Everything clicked and I signed up for VISTA a few months later. I haven't looked back since.

What is your favorite social work story? After I completed my undergraduate degree in 1973, I helped set up a daycare for migrant children. We would take my old station wagon into the fields and pick up as many preschoolers as we could cram in. We would then take them to the daycare and attend to their needs. As the children began to thrive it was the first time that I fully experienced the power of relieving the misery of others. It was also the first time that I became aware of the tremendous need and lack of resources.

What would be the one thing you would change in our community if you had the power to do so? Meanness and cynicism. In my community I perceive a great deal of fear, hardness, and lack of love and tolerance that act like an acid. People need to be more connected to their healthy and positive selves.

example, when first meeting a client, the social worker asks probing, thoughtful questions about the client's past. This systematic accumulation of information is referred to as gathering a social history or a **psychosocial history**. A social work practitioner would never consider the social history that he completes on each client useless information. In particular, the social history is important to understanding and exploring the client's growth and development process as well as to identifying possible effects of events and relations with others in the client's past.

Activity...Contact the local state NASW office and ask for names of local "Gold Card" members. These are people over age 60 who have been members of NASW for at least twenty-five years. Try to meet them to talk about social work twenty to thirty years ago. What do they see today that is different from when they started out in the profession? How do they think technology is influencing social work and social welfare?

The past offers valuable clues to interpreting the present and anticipating the future. History is essential to helping all of us better understand who we are and how we got here. It also influences our future decisions. Indeed, some people take the extreme position that we are so profoundly influenced by the past that it actually determines the future. This theory is called "determinism."

Whatever degree of importance we place on history, it is obvious that people—sometimes intentionally, sometimes unintentionally—use past experiences as a frame of reference for current and future experiences. For example, a baby only has to burn her hand once not to put it on a hot stove; in adulthood people rarely try this again because they know they can be painfully hurt. Although the causes and effects may not be clearly linked, a similar process can govern the relations we develop throughout our lives. Therefore, the importance of history should not be underestimated. We hope we have sparked your interest in history as a way to understand the roots of social welfare and general aspects of social work practice. In many cases considering the experiences of the past can teach us valuable lessons worth remembering.

Did You Know...Harry Hopkins, a social worker, was one of President Franklin D. Roosevelt's closest friends and was the administrator of a Great Depression program called the Federal Emergency Relief Administration.

This chapter will make a brief foray into social welfare history. Comprehensive examinations of social welfare history have been undertaken by others (Chambers, 1967; Lubove, 1969; Trattner, 1989; Axinn & Levin, 1982; Katz, 1986; Jansson, 1988), and this area is well worth the effort of further investigation. We will briefly examine significant events and trends that influenced the emergence of our current American social welfare system.

THE ELIZABETHAN POOR LAW OF 1601

Most social work historians would agree that the watershed year for social welfare was 1601, when English poor laws were "codified" or brought together under one law. This codification is commonly called *the Elizabethan Poor Law of 1601*. Colonial America adopted the central tenets of this law, and many of its principles continue to underpin the design and implementation of our current social services.

An important note of caution: Let's not fall into a simple trap and believe that welfare began with the Elizabethan Poor Law of 1601. Karger and Stoesz (1994) tracked the development of the English poor laws back through a series of events to the mid-fourteenth century. Gilbert and Specht (1981, p. 17) noted that modern-day social welfare has roots in the Reformation period and the Middle Ages. And Trattner (1989), in his classic work *From Poor Law to Welfare State*, traced the roots of American welfare efforts to the ancient Greeks and Romans! In advanced social policy courses, you'll learn more about the rise of social welfare as a system, but for our purposes, we will begin with the Elizabethan poor laws.

Before 1601 in Europe welfare attempts to assist people in need were generally viewed as the province of the church. With the advent of the industrial era, great changes occurred in society. Many new and better paying jobs were created, and men and women of all ages were encouraged to apply. Rural communities began to decrease in population as people left the limited and shrinking opportunities of farm life for what the industrialized cities offered. Unfortunately, the promise of more jobs and a better way of life was not fulfilled for everyone, and many became unemployed and homeless. The newly destitute turned to the churches, the traditional providers of assistance to the poor. With the ranks of the poor growing to unprecedented levels, however, these urban churches did not have the resources or the expertise to cope with the swelling numbers of rural migrants and their assorted needs.

Faced with a growing population of urban poor, the English government implemented a series of sweeping reforms in an attempt to gain control of this problem. The result, the 1601 poor laws, radically changed the form, function, and scope of welfare assistance. First, the poor laws redefined welfare as no longer a private affair but a public responsibility. Second, the 1601 laws identified local government as the public entity responsible for the poor. Last, the poor laws denied relief if family resources were available (Katz, 1986, pp. 13–14).

In addition to setting the parameters for public aid, the 1601 poor laws divided potential recipients into two groups, the **worthy poor** and the **unworthy poor.** The worthy poor included the ill, the disabled, orphans, and elders. These people were viewed as having no control over their life circumstances. A second group of the worthy poor consisted of people who were involuntarily unemployed. Although they were seen as bearing some responsibility for their own situations due consideration was given to the fact that their misfortunes were beyond their control. The unworthy poor, on the other hand, included the vagrant or able-bodied who, while able to work, did not seek employment (Cole, 1973, p. 5).

Overall, when services were provided, assistance was first given to the worthy poor who were considered helpless to control their situations. Some assistance was provided to those who were involuntarily unemployed. No assistance was given to the unworthy poor, who were treated with public disdain.

COLONIAL AMERICA

The provision of public assistance in colonial America was tenuous at best. Influenced by strong Puritan and Calvinist views, most citizens regarded both the worthy and the unworthy poor as morally flawed. They believed that the poverty-stricken had somehow caused their own distress. This belief released society from any obligation to lend assistance and implied that it was the impoverished individual who was responsible for finding and providing a remedy. Aid or **charity assistance**, in any form, was thought to lead to an "erosion of independence and self-respect; the spread of idleness and the loss of the will to work; the promotion of immorality in all its ugly forms; and the increase in public costs through the growth of poorhouses and jails" (Katz, 1986, p. 40). Benjamin Franklin, for example, strongly opposed public aid: "[The] 'natural state' of working persons was one of sloth, wastefulness, and dissipation. The Common people do not work for pleasure, but for necessity" (Williams, 1944, p. 83). Relief, Franklin felt, simply provided an opportunity for people to return to their natural state of laziness at the expense of others.

Did You Know…In 1931, Jane Addams, social worker and founder of Hull House, was the first American woman to win the Nobel Peace Prize.

Based on a weak commitment to a public welfare system, American colonists developed a dual system of relief that was modeled on the English poor laws of 1601. The resulting programs provided aid to the worthy poor, who in this case comprised the ill, seniors, orphans, widows, and veteran soldiers. The unworthy or able-bodied poor, which included the involuntarily unemployed, were provided little if any assistance.

Assistance to the worthy poor was grudgingly given, primarily in the form of **outdoor relief**, which provided minimal assistance to individuals and families in their homes. The unworthy poor were not provided aid in their homes and often were encouraged to move on to another county. If assistance was required, the unworthy poor were required to return to their counties of origin to receive it. The unworthy poor were eligible, however, for **indoor relief**—the poorhouse.

Funds to support the worthy and unworthy poor were collected by local taxes assessed by the local **overseer of the poor**. In many ways this overseer was a colonial version of a social worker. The overseer was responsible for identifying who constituted the poor, what their needs were, and what the community should do to address their needs.

Selected Dates in American Social Welfare History

1601	Elizabethan Poor Law enacted by the English parliament.
1642	Plymouth Colony enacts first poor law in the colonies.
1657	Scots Charitable Society, first nonprofit organization focused on the provision of welfare, founded in Boston.
1773	First public mental asylum opens in Williamsburg, Virginia.
1790	First public orphanage opens in Charleston, South Carolina.
1798	U.S. Public Health Department established.
1817	Gallaudet School, a school for the deaf, founded in Hartford, Connecticut.
1822	Kentucky opens first public asylum for deaf people.
1829	First asylum for the blind opens in Massachusetts.
1841	Dorthea Dix begins investigations into mental institutions in the United States.
1853	The Reverend Charles Loring Brace organizes Children's Aid Society.
1854	President Pierce vetoes federal legislation designed to use federal land for state asylums.
1865	Freedmen's Bureau is organized.

Check the *Encyclopedia of Social Work* under Distinctive Dates in Social Welfare History (Alexander, 1997) for other dates and events. What events in social welfare history impress or surprise you? What do you think is the most important social welfare event on the list? Why?

In general, the availability and accessibility of colonial public services reflected Franklin's negative view of relief. These programs were often designed with a punitive intent, in an effort to shame people out of their poverty. Typical of this approach was the auctioning of the poor into apprenticeships and indentured service to the lowest bidder—that is, the person who would charge the community least for taking a pauper off its hands. Another example of this reluctant attitude toward helping the poor is the treatment of a widow in Hadley, Massachusetts. In 1687, this woman, who had no resources of her own, was forced to live for two-week periods with those families who were "able to receive her" (Trattner, 1989, p. 18). Further, in Pennsylvania those receiving aid were required to wear a scarlet letter "P" sewn on their right sleeves "with the first letter of the county, city, or place of his or her residence underneath" (Heffner, 1913, p. 11). Even more extreme was a 1754 North Carolina law that allowed vagrants to be whipped in the public square simply because of their impoverished state (Rothman, 1971, p. 25).

Did You Know…Jeannette Rankin, a social worker, was the first woman elected to the U.S. Congress, representing Montana, in 1916.

Not all potential recipients of social welfare services were viewed negatively in colonial America. For example, veteran soldiers who had fought for the colonies were given a more honored status because, when poor, they were generally con-

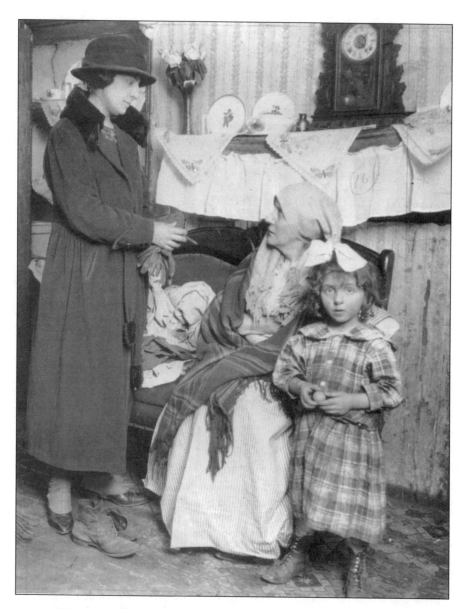

A United Charities of Chicago caseworker or visiting housekeeper calling on a family about 1909. Formed when the Relief and Aid Society merged with the Bureau of Charities, United Charities of Chicago was the city's oldest private welfare organization. It was the best known of the family service agencies and worked on prevention, easing desperate social situations, and creating better living environments.

sidered to be among the worthy poor (Axinn & Levin, 1982, p. 31). As early as 1624, veterans could expect to receive social welfare benefits as a right earned by the service they had provided. It was believed that since veteran soldiers had shown their willingness to risk life and limb in defense of their nation they deserved public aid if they needed it. Providing relief to veterans was not considered the responsibility of the town; rather it was the obligation of the colony. In addition, veterans did not have to satisfy residency requirements in order to receive aid (Axinn & Levin, 1982, p. 31). In summary, two of the primary components of colonial poor relief legislation—local responsibility and residency—did not apply to veterans because they enjoyed the status of the worthy poor.

NINETEENTH-CENTURY REFORM EFFORTS

Throughout American history, immorality and pauperism have been tightly linked by the idea that poverty is a direct result of an individual's flawed character. Nineteenth-century programs intended to help the poor sought to do so by changing their behavior and making them overcome their personal failings. At the same time public opinion turned hostile toward all those living in poverty. As Benjamin Disraeli lamented following passage of the punitive 1834 British poor law reform, it was "a crime to be poor" (Trattner, 1989, p. 49).

Despite the strong resistance to helping the poor, poverty was widespread enough that some form of relief was necessary. Welfare organizations became more formalized and commonplace, particularly in large urban areas. The most prominent agencies for the delivery of social welfare services and programs for the poor were almshouses and asylums, charity organization societies, and settlement houses.

Almshouses and Asylums

The roots of service provision for the poor and disabled can be traced back as far as the 1700s to the first **almshouses**. Almshouses, also called "poorhouses," were intended to be places of refuge for the poor, medically ill, and mentally ill of all ages. In colonial times, however, caring for the family and its members was considered a private matter, and people who had any kind of family support were kept at home. Therefore, the almshouse was an "option of last resort," providing shelter and relief for society's outcasts—those who were poor, incapacitated, or suffered from contagious disease. Severely underfunded, almshouses were dirty and disease filled, and the workers who staffed them, who can be regarded among the earliest practical social workers and health care providers (Dziegielewski, 1998), often became ill.

Did You Know...In 1713 William Penn founded the first almshouse, in Philadelphia. In 1736 a second almshouse was founded at Bellevue Hospital in New York. The almshouse in Bellevue usually housed the mentally ill and later became one of the most famous mental health hospitals in the country.

At one point, almshouses housed all of the poor. However, eventually children were removed from almshouses by the efforts of the Children's Aid Society and later placed in orphanages. In 1851 the mentally ill were also removed and sent to improved facilities and asylums primarily through the crusading efforts of Dorthea Lynde Dix. Basically, the almshouse as "holding tank" was replaced with more segregated forms of institutionalized care such as orphanages and other residential facilities, referred to as "asylums."

Asylums, the most common human service organizations in the 1800s, became the homes for the blind, deaf and dumb, and insane and developed regimented programs formed by a guiding trinity of work, religion, and education. Tightly regulating an inmate's life with scheduled activities throughout each day, according to Rothman (1971, p. 145), reflected belief in the "therapeutic value of a rigid schedule." For example, in the Pennsylvania Hospital, patients were awakened at 5:00 A.M., "received their medicines at six, and breakfast at 6:30; at eight o'clock, they went for a physical examination, and then to work or to some other form of exercise. At 12:30 they ate their main meal and then resumed work or other activities until six, when everyone joined for tea" (Rothman, 1971, p. 145).

As can been seen from this cumbersome schedule, labor was a central component of asylum life. Inmates, as they were being taught jobs, learned the "value" and "importance" or work. This training, coupled with the regimented schedule, in theory imparted "habits. . . necessary for patients' recovery" (Rothman, 1971, p. 146). A poem allegedly written by a young woman in the Texas Asylum for the Blind reveals the negative side of work as the cornerstone of welfare programming:

> *Work, work, work*
> *till the brain begins to swim;*
> *work, work, work*
> *till the eyes are heavy and dim;*
> *seam, gusset, and bond,*
> *bond, gusset, and seam*
> *till over the buttons I fall asleep*
> *and sew them on in dream.*

Did You Know...The first American charity organization society was established in Buffalo, New York, in 1877.

Charity Organization Societies

A second innovative approach to combating poverty was the **Charity Organization Society** (COS), founded in London, England, in the mid-1800s. Besides its significance as a social welfare development, the COS is important to the history of social work because some social work historians view its founding as the profession's birth event. The first American COS, modeled after the British program, was founded in Buffalo, New York, in 1877 by the Reverend Humphrey Gurteen.

In the mid-1800s, charitable efforts proliferated in American cities, resulting in many duplicated and uncoordinated programs. COSs sought to organize the various charities within a city in order to reduce program duplication. A second objective was for COSs to certify the needs and claims of clients in a systematic, investigative fashion. Thus only those in need could receive services from the various charities. Finally, COSs sought to change the lives of the poor through home visits by volunteers.

COSs subscribed to the philosophy that poverty was a consequence of moral decay and the eradication of the slum depended on the poor's recognizing and correcting their personal deficiencies (Boyer, 1978, p. 144). The **friendly visitor**, a key volunteer in the COS movement, was to establish a personal relation with each client through "home visits" and by serving as a role model, to help the poor change their behavior. The 1889 Buffalo Charity Organization Society Handbook declared that the friendly visitor soon would be

> a power in the home. In a very short time the houses would be clean and
> kept clean for her reception. Her advice would be sought. . . . In a word, all
> avoidable pauperism would soon be a thing of the past when the poor
> would regard the rich as their natural friends. (Gurteen, 1882, p. 117)

Women volunteers, particularly those from middle and upper class families, were preferred for the role of friendly visitor. These women would be able to demonstrate and foster the values of the successful family to less fortunate individuals and families. In essence, by psychological and social osmosis, poverty and its companion evils would be uprooted through the kind works of middle class ladies. Specifically, Gurteen wrote,

> [All that is] needed to make our work a grand success. . . is hundreds of
> women from the educated and well-to-do classes, especially women of our
> city, who as mothers and daughters, coming from bright and happy
> homes—homes adorned by virtue and radiant with love, can impart to the
> cheerless tenement or the wretched hovel, a little of their own happiness.
> (1882, p. 116)

The COS movement also relied on female volunteers to staff the various organizations. As COSs became more accepted and formalized, the role of women changed. For example, COS women, by the end of the nineteenth century, were paid for their work, and COSs became a primary employment arena for women. It is interesting to note, however, that the first COS administrators were men and the first female administrator, Mary Richmond, was not appointed until late 1891.

Did You Know...Frances Perkins, a social worker, was the first woman appointed to the U.S. cabinet when in 1933 she was named secretary of labor.

In summary, the COSs were an important development in the history of social work because they provided the basis for the modern social service agencies of today. The workers they employed were some of the first to deliver social services

The Infant Welfare Society was founded in 1911 when the Milk Commission and the Children's Hospital Society joined forces. It trained nurses to staff milk distribution stations where they weighed babies, promoted proper nutrition, and provided mental and emotional guidance for women, children, and families.

in the home setting to poor and disenfranchised people. COSs provided an opportunity for systematic investigation of those in poverty and need. Home visitation, which today remains a highly valued social work intervention technique, allowed volunteers to learn more about individuals and their environments.

Did You Know... The first social work educational program started in 1898 as a summer training course at the New York Charity Organization Society. It later became Columbia University School of Social Work.

Settlement House Movement

Another major British innovation also crossed the Atlantic during the mid-1800s and made a significant impact in the American social service arena. Known as the Settlement House Movement, its philosophy was remarkably different from that of the COSs. The Settlement House Movement sought the causes of poverty in macro- rather than microsystems. For example, poor education, lack of health care, and inadequate housing were considered the primary reasons for poverty. The settlement house was an actual house in a neighborhood where the workers lived year-round coordinating and providing programs, activities, and services directed to the needs of their neighbors.

The most famous nineteenth-century settlement house was Hull House, founded by Jane Addams and Ellen Gates Starr in 1889. Located in a poor west side Chicago neighborhood, Hull House forged a strong bond between neighborhood immigrants and social workers with its efforts to bridge the gulf between rich and poor. By the beginning of the twentieth century there were more than one hundred settlement houses located in the United States.

The Settlement House Movement initiated the macromodel for social work practice, more commonly referred to as "community organization" and "group work practice." Problems were seen as resting not with the individual but at the larger organizational or community level. Poverty was the result not of an individual's lack of morality but of a system that kept wages low, did not enforce housing or health codes, and maintained a marginalized working class. Through client empowerment, problems could be confronted and social resources redistributed.

Did You Know...The Scots Charitable Society, organized in Boston in 1657, was the first voluntary society in the colonies to focus on welfare needs.

THE TWENTIETH CENTURY

At the dawn of the twentieth century, the United States was poised to become a world economic leader. By the 1920s, economic prosperity seemed to come within reach of a growing number of Americans. Yet for blacks and immigrants economic gains were elusive. Blacks continued to suffer racism and discrimination under nineteenth-century Jim Crow laws. As immigration increased, laws inspired by xenophobia (fear of foreigners) framed social policy initiatives.

The prosperity of the first quarter-century quickly unraveled in the worldwide depression of the 1930s. By 1929, 1.6 million people were unemployed, and by the mid-1930s, nearly one in four Americans were unemployed.

Everyone knew someone—a brother, sister, father, mother, aunt, uncle, grandparent, or friend—who was out of work. Poverty was no longer a distant concept reserved for blacks, immigrants, and other minorities. Very quickly, the philosophy that the poor were morally depraved and had no work ethic became unacceptable because now more people had become poor who were never poor before. The new poor were everyone's friends and family and didn't fit the image of the lazy, immoral poor.

With the presidential election of Franklin Roosevelt, relief measures were immediately put in place, followed by the ambitious **New Deal** programs. These programs were funded and coordinated at the federal level and dramatically changed government's ambivalent role in social welfare.

The most important New Deal initiative was the Economic Security Act of

1935, which established the social security system to provide cash assistance to retired workers. This act—which also established the precursors of AFDC and unemployment insurance—became the organizing framework for the federal social service system. By the end of the twentieth century, it has been amended on numerous occasions to include cash assistance, health benefits, and services for the disabled, the blind, families, children, and seniors.

The New Deal included initiatives directed toward a variety of people. The Federal Emergency Relief Act, the Civilian Conservation Corps, and the Works Progress Administration formed the backbone of the New Deal. All of these programs were unprecedented in that they were developed and coordinated by the federal government, but like local relief efforts of the nineteenth century they made work a condition of relief.

Activity…Go to a library and read, generally on microfilm, newspapers from the 1930s. Try to get a feel for life during the depression. Then visit a local nursing home or senior center to meet people who lived during the depression. Ask them how the depression affected their families and neighbors and how did it influence the rest of their lives.

The New Deal essentially affirmed the federal government's role in social welfare. The national effort was unparalled in American history, until the massive social movement of the 1960s.

Social Reform in the 1960s

By 1960, slightly more than one in five Americans lived in poverty. In 1962, Michael Harrington's classic work *The Other America: Poverty in the United States* helped the nation to rediscover this poverty in its backyard. The short book had a profound impact within the halls of Congress and reawakened nationwide debate on the role of government in combating poverty.

In the early part of his administration, President Lyndon Johnson declared a "war on poverty" that would make full use of the nation's resources. The resulting initiative—later referred to as the "Great Society" programs—brought a new federal presence into local communities far different from previous welfare program efforts. Guided by the phrase "maximum feasible participation" of the poor, welfare programs involved the poor in local decision making in their neighborhoods and communities.

The coordinating agency for the Great Society was the Office of Economic Opportunity (OEO). Typical new welfare strategies include assistance to newborn babies and their mothers (Women, Infants, and Children—WIC), preschool education (Head Start), health care for seniors (**Medicare**) and the poor (**Medicaid**), employment programs for young adults (Job Corps), community action programs that encouraged neighbors to marshal resources, legal services for the poor, food stamps, and model city projects that were designed to provide assistance to the poorest neighborhoods.

The Great Society was spurred by a newfound belief that the nation could fight and win any battle it chose, and the War on Poverty had no borders. The Peace Corps, developed in 1965, sent volunteers to nations around the world to work in poor communities. Volunteers in Service to America (VISTA) was a domestic version of the Peace Corps with volunteers working in low-income American neighborhoods.

By the end of the 1960s, the Great Society was under growing attack for being too costly with too few benefits to the larger society. During the presidential administration of Richard Nixon, the influence of the OEO was minimized, and numerous programs were scraped. In their place Nixon proposed an innovative guaranteed annual income for the poor—a "negative income tax." Known as the Family Assistance Program (FAP), Nixon's plan would have subsidized a poor family by $2,400 a year. FAP required work or job training with the states eventually having full responsibility for program operation. This controversial proposal was ultimately rejected by Congress, but it was nevertheless a dramatic attempt to establish a minimum income based on work requirements.

The 1980s and Beyond: A Return to the Work Ethic

With the election of Ronald Reagan to the presidency and a more conservative Congress, public service relief programs became targets of a massive attack. Numerous federal public assistance programs were eliminated while others had their funding cut and their eligibility requirements tightened to weed out the unworthy poor. The results of this realignment were dramatic. Palmer and Sawhill (184, pp. 363–379) found that 500,000 families were removed from AFDC and an additional 300,000 families received reduced benefits. One million people were eliminated from food stamp rolls. In 1985, the National Anti-Hunger Coalition charged that the federal government was not spending allocated funds for the WIC nutrition program, depriving thousands of pregnant women and newborn infants of health and nutrition services.

Children, women, seniors, and minorities were the primary victims of the Reagan welfare reforms. The message of the 1980s was clear: First, public assistance was contributing to the national debt. Second, only the truly needy, the poorest of the poor, would be helped with a "safety net" to ensure survival. Third, welfare was a state and a local, not a federal, concern.

The safety net approach places responsibility for helping the poor and disadvantaged at the doorstep of local government and private sources; the federal government becomes a resource of last resort. To achieve this purpose the Reagan administration adopted three overriding goals with regard to income security programs: 1) reduce short-term spending by implementing changes in entitlement programs; 2) turn over welfare responsibility to the states; and 3) promote reliance on individual resources rather than create and maintain dependence on governmental benefits (Storey, 1982). The result was

a patchwork of programs at the federal, state, and local level that results in gross inadequacies in education. . . . We have developed too few resources to prevention and maintenance, and too many to picking up pieces after the damage is done. On the other hand, the United States has established a broad welfare system for the non-poor while the middle and upper classes and corporate America are able to take advantage of many benefits and, to a large extent, have become dependent on government support. (American Assembly, 1989, p. 34)

Welfare reform continued in the 1990s with the 1992 presidential election of Bill Clinton, who promised to "end welfare as we know it." His ambition came within reach with later developments in Congress. The midterm congressional election in 1994 brought a Republican sweep and in their "Contract with America" conservative congressional Republicans made welfare reform a top priority.

In 1996 Congress essentially ended federal relief programs with the passage of the Personal Responsibility and Work Opportunity Reconciliation Act. The new law abolished specific categorical programs and provided federal block grants to the states. Today, the federal government is no longer responsible for operating public welfare programs. No longer does the country have a national welfare program. Rather each state operates its own set of public welfare services, each with its own set of eligibility criteria, program rules, and benefits. Another way of looking at public welfare is to recognize that the nation has fifty different welfare programs, each operating under a different set of rules. Commonalities come from conditions placed on federal block grants: a lifetime limit of five years of relief, a work requirement, and participation in job-training programs.

According to the Federal Welfare Reform Act of 1996, all adult welfare recipients are required to work, be registered for work, or be participating in a job-training or educational programs. The food stamp program—now run by the states—has similar eligibility criteria; failure to follow these work guidelines results in program disqualification. This welfare reform act also ended the AFDC program, in place since the New Deal. It was replaced by Temporary Assistance for Needy Families (TANF), a short-term program that incorporates lifetime limitations and work requirements.

The 1996 welfare reform is an example where knowledge of history can help us to understand what is happening today. The philosophy that undergrids today's welfare provision reflects some of Franklin's admonitions. The reluctance to acknowledge government responsibility continues. And with a lifetime limit on years of eligibility for welfare, so do deep concerns about dependence. Recipients are to be forced into a totally independent and self-reliant mode of existence.

SUMMARY

American social welfare history is marked by a deep mistrust of the poor. Persistent beliefs that the poor are immoral and lacking either the ability or the desire to work have inspired repeated attempts to condition relief on work and improved behavior—and, above all, to make relief as difficult to obtain as possible. Social welfare is much bigger than simply programs to support the poor and disadvantaged such as Section 8 housing and food stamps. The federal government provides support to a variety of groups: banks requiring bailouts, farmers needing subsidies, and cities requiring federal loans to make payrolls are just some of the many acceptable forms of welfare. In these circumstances, however, bankers, farmers, and mayors do not consider themselves "welfare recipients"; rather, federal supports are viewed as necessary subsidies that benefit the community.

Workfare, training programs, and stringent program eligibility requirements, coupled with ongoing recertification in order to continue receiving even minimal assistance, are the punitive features of today's federal and state welfare systems. When it comes to poverty Americans are inclined to blame the victim as much as ever. Rather than maintaining a dignified helping system accessible to the poor, American welfare policy is designed to exclude people and to discourage clients by constantly setting hurdles to eligibility.

Throughout its history, finding the appropriate balance between public and private responsibility has plagued American social welfare. There is a clear record of national ambivalence and resistance toward welfare services and the poor. The current debate on welfare is an extension of a discussion threaded through the nation's fabric since colonial times. The lack of national consensus on who is to receive what type of social provisions for what period of time and on how these services will be funded means that the debate will continue well into the twenty-first century.

Movies to See

Movies on social welfare history rarely win Academy Award consideration or excite producers. The following videos, while not specifically detailing social welfare history, help us to better understand people and their conditions in the past.

Across the Sea of Time: 1920s New York City through the eyes of Russian immigrants.

All Mine to Give: Orphaned children in turn-of-the-century Wisconsin are put in different homes in order to survive.

America, America: In the 1890s, a Greek youth immigrates to New York City; emotional presentation of an immigrant's challenges.

April Morning: A solid portrayal of a teenager's life in the American colonies immediately before the American Revolution.

Attacks on Culture: A brief, forty-nine minute, examination of the U.S. government's legislative attacks on Native Americans.

Autobiography of Miss Jane Pittman: An examination of life from the Civil War through the 1950s as remembered by a 110-year-old former slave.

Avalon: A Russian Jewish immigrant family moves to New York City.

Black West: An examination of African American cowboys, the unsung heroes of the West.

Grapes of Wrath: Classic John Steinbeck story of family's search for a better life than in 1930s depression Oklahoma.

The Molly Maguires: Interesting film set in the 1870s Pennsylvania coal country, as the Irish try to organize a union.

Roll of Thunder Hear My Cry: Black teen copes with depression, poverty, and racism in 1930s Mississippi.

Separate but Equal: An examination of Thurgood Marshall as the NAACP attorney whose U.S. Supreme Court case led to the end of segregation.

Sounder: A sharecropper is forced to steal to feed his family; family deals with poverty and racism in the 1930s.

Wild Women of the Old West: The stereotype of the quiet housewife is broken with this analysis of women in the 1800s.

A Woman Called Moses: An examination of the life of Harriet Ross Tubman, a fugitive slave, founder of the underground railroad, and leader in the abolitionist movement.

Quiz Answers

1. In October 1492 Christopher Columbus reached the Bahamas, marking Europe's first documented contact with the Americas.

2. The New Deal was the name given to a set of social and economic programs established under the leadership of President Franklin D. Roosevelt in the 1930s to combat the depression.

3. The Emancipation Proclamation freed slaves in areas (rebellion states) no longer loyal to the union.

4. In Seneca Falls, New York, in 1848 women rights advocate Elizabeth Cady Stanton organized a convention that generated a declaration of women's rights.

5. Earlier immigrants arrived from northern and western Europe. By 1900, there was a significant rise in people from eastern and southern Europe.

6. In the late seventeenth century nineteen people were executed for witchcraft in Salem, Massachusetts.

7. In 1845 the United States annexed most of what is now Texas. Mexico ceded the remaining land in 1848 following the Mexican-American War.

8. The Articles of Confederation, adopted in 1777, united the colonies; it created a one-house congress.

9. In 1867, William Seward negotiated the purchase of land, now Alaska, from Russia for $7.2 million. It was called "Seward's Folly" because, until the discovery of gold, people saw little value in the far away purchase.

10. Dred Scott, a Missouri slave, sued for his freedom in 1847. The 1857 Supreme Court decision held that slaves were property and had no claim to the rights of citizenship.

References

Alexander, C. A. (1997). Distinctive dates in social welfare history. In R. Edwards et al. (Eds.), *Encyclopedia of social work, 1997 supplement* (19th ed.). Washington, DC: NASW Press.

American Assembly. (1989, November). *The future of social welfare in America*. New York: Columbia University, Barnard College.

Axinn, J., & Levin, H. (1982). *Social welfare: A history of the American response to need* (2nd ed.). New York: Harper and Row.

Boyer, P. (1978). *Urban classes and moral order in America, 1820–1990*. Cambridge, MA: Harvard University Press.

Chambers, C. A. (1967). *Seedtime of reform: American social service and social action, 1918–1933*. Ann Arbor: University of Michigan Press.

Cole, B. (1973). *Perspectives in public welfare: A history* (3rd printing). Washington, DC: Government Printing Office.

Dziegielewski, S. F. (1998). *The changing face of health care: Practice in the era of managed care*. New York: Springer.

Gilbert, N. & Specht, H. (1981). *The emergence of social welfare and social work* (2nd ed.). Itasca, IL: Peacock.

Gurteen, H. (1882). *A handbook of charity organization*. Buffalo, NY: Charity Organization Society.

Harrington, M. (1962). *The other America: Poverty in the United States*. New York: Macmillan.

Heffner, W. (1913). *History of poor relief legislation in Pennsylvania, 1682–1913*. Cleona, PA: Holzapfel.

Jansson, B. (1988). *The reluctant welfare state: A history of American social welfare policies*. Belmont, CA: Wadsworth.

Karger, H. & Stoesz, D. (1994). *American social welfare policy: A pluralist approach* (2nd ed.). White Plains, NY: Longman.

Katz, M. B. (1986). *In the shadow of the poorhouse: A social history of welfare in America*. New York: Basic Books.

Lubove, R. (1969). *The professional altruist: The emergence of social work as a career, 1880–1930*. New York: Atheneum.

Palmer, J., & Sawhill, I. (1984). *The Reagan record*. Cambridge, MA: Ballinger.

Report of the Trustees and Superintendent of the Texas Institute for the Blind. (1886). Austin, TX: Tripplet and Hastings.

Rothman, D. (1971). *The discovery of the asylum social order and disorder in the new republic*. Boston: Little, Brown.

Storey, J. R. (1982). Income security. In J. Palmer & I. Sawhill (Eds.), *The Reagan experiment* (Vol. 5, pp. 361–392). Washington, DC: Urban Institute Press.

Trattner, W. (1989). *From poor law to welfare state: A history of social welfare in America* (4th ed.). New York: Free Press.

Williams, H. (1944). Benjamin Franklin and the poor laws. *Social Service Review, 18*, 77–79.

Chapter 4

So You Want to Be a Social Worker!

THERE ARE NUMEROUS JOBS FOR SOCIAL WORKERS THROUGHOUT the country in cities, suburbs, and rural communities. According to the U.S. Department of Labor, between 1998 and 2008 employment opportunities for social workers will grow by 36.1 percent and unemployment will be "low" within the social work ranks (www.dol.gov). The growth in positions will be in both public and private agencies, large and small alike. On any given day social work job opportunities across the country are listed in *NASW News*.

Social Workers: Our 450-bed long-term care facility needs caring candidates to work with our social services team. LTC experience and BSW preferred. We pay 100% of employee's HMO & life insurance PLUS other excellent benefits. EOE. (Florida, 1998)

Escape the Rat Race and Come to the Beautiful Coast of Maine: Xxxx is a small, nonprofit agency that provides a variety of mental health and family support services throughout a four-county area. Employment opportunities exist in the following programs: INTENSIVE HOME-BASED/OUTPATIENT THERAPIST. Minimum of BSW required. SCHOOL-BASED/OUTPATIENT THERAPIST. MSW required; LCSW preferred delivering individual and group therapy in schools and individual, group, and family therapy. MEDICAL SOCIAL WORKER in exciting collaborative effort with a local home health agency. BSW required; MSW preferred. All applicants must possess flexibility, creativity, strong personal ethics, and a good sense of humor. (Maine, 1998)

Outpatient Clinician: Upper Valley Mental Health Center located in NH is seeking outpatient clinician to work with dynamic, consumer-focused team of professionals, serving adults, children, and their families. Applicants must have excellent communication and teamwork skills. We offer varied recreational opportunities and a family-oriented environment. Prefer licenses/certified MSW applicants. (New Hampshire, 1998)

Long Term Care Social Worker: Xxxx has an opportunity for a social worker to join our dedicated team of professionals. Ideal candidate will have experience with MDs and discharge planning as well as knowledge of commu-

Name: Barbara W. White
Place of residence: Austin, Texas
College/university degrees: Florida A &M, B.S., Florida State University, B.S., M.S.W., Ph.D.
Present position: Centennial Professorship in Leadership and Dean, School of Social Work, University of Texas at Austin
Previous work/volunteer experience: Associate Dean at the School of Social Work at The Florida State University, President of the National Association of Social Workers (NASW), a member of the Board of Directors of the International Association of Schools of Social Work, President of the Council on Social Work Education, (CSWE) Fulbright scholar on Women's Issues in India, member African American Women's Hall of Fame, 1999 recipient of the International Rhoda G. Sarnat Award for significant international or national contributions to advance the public image of professional social work

What do you do in your spare time? Read, travel, and attend theater.

Why did you choose social work as a career? I chose social work as a way to help fight social injustice and man's inhumanity to man.

What is your favorite social work story? During the Christmas holiday season, members of my faculty and staff visit a local nursing home with our own Santa. We bring musicals and become carolers and gift bearers. The responses from the residents provide a reminder of how much there is to do in our society to help improve life;'s quality for so many of our citizens.

What would be the one thing you would change in our community if you had the power to do so? I would address the issues that face one of our most vulnerable populations, our youth. I would eliminate homelessness and hopelessness among our youth.

nity resources. Strong organizational skills, desire and ability to function independently a must. (New Jersey, 1998).

Chief Executive Officer: Founded in 1984, a community mental health center is seeking an individual to fill the position of chief executive officer. In the spectacular Matanuska-Susitna Valley, approximately 40 miles northeast of Anchorage, Alaska, our location offers the conveniences, amenities, and cultural events found in nearby Anchorage, while recreational opportunities abound just outside your door in a rural, family-oriented community. With a broad continuum of programs, including residential services, case management, crisis respite, and a freestanding psychological assessment center, the agency addresses the behavioral health needs of adults, children, and youth within the Mat-Su Borough and surrounding communities. Qualifications for the position include an advanced behavioral degree; proven strengths in planning and leadership; 3 years of work experience as a chief executive, or 5 years as a senior-level manager, preferably within the mental health field. Knowledge of state mental health regulations, managed care concepts, and strategic planning is also required. Reporting to the board of directors, the CEO is responsible for facilitating organizational effectiveness and achieving business objectives while ensuring the successful provision of services to our consumers. The position offers a salary range of $75–95,000 DOE. Relocation assistance may be available.

Community Advocate: Passionate individual willing to work long hours for a small salary. Neighborhood-based substance abuse prevention organization requires person to assist in community planning, grants development, and training. BSW required; must like people and want to help a community confront the challenges and threats of lost funding/program services. Salary: $20,000. EOE.

Do these prospective jobs sound interesting to you? You can read advertisements of this type in every issue of *NASW News*, the monthly newspaper of NASW. There is an array of employment opportunities for BSW, MSW, and DSW or Ph.D. practitioners in every state. What is probably most exciting to the job seeker is that social work positions offer a variety of challenges working with individuals, groups, families, organizations, and communities.

This chapter explores the nature of employment opportunities in the field of social work. We first discuss the educational requirements to become a social worker and the role that accreditation standards play. Then we take an overview of prospects for social workers today, presenting salary and employment projections into the twenty-first century. We conclude with tips on finding that first social work job.

THE EDUCATION OF A SOCIAL WORKER

What makes a person a social worker? The answer is simple: a baccalaureate or master's degree—that is, a BSW, BSSW, or BA or BS in social work or an MSW, MSSW, or MA or MS in social work— from a program accredited by the Council of

Social Work Education. When students graduate from either of these kinds of degree programs in social work, they are considered to have practice degrees. A degree in sociology, psychology, anthropology, or any other "ology" does not make a person a social worker. The major difference between a degree in social work and these degrees is that sociology, psychology, and anthropology are science-based. People who major in these fields may specialize in practice or complete practice-based courses, but they are not *based* in practice as social work graduates are. It is also important to note that working in a social agency for ten years, even under the tutelage of a degreed social worker, does not alone make a person a qualified social worker. Further, a doctoral degree in social work, a Ph.D. or a DSW is not recognized as a *practice* degree. These programs are not regulated by CSWE, and their graduates are considered researchers, administrators, educators, or scientific practitioners. As a result, entry into the social work profession is limited, and those interested in becoming social workers must pass through at least one of the two doors.

Having said this, maybe it's not quite that simple. Not to muddy the waters, but in some states, it is possible to be licensed to practice social work without having a degree in social work. For example, some states may choose to "grandfather in"—or make exceptions for—certain individuals to practice or sit for a qualifying exam. Generally, each state sets its own criteria and deadlines for this type of exception so it is best to contact the state licensing board directly to find out if and how these exemptions are made. For example, in Alabama certain client protection workers for the state have been grandfathered in and are therefore eligible to be licensed as baccalaureate-level social workers; these individuals do not have BSWs, a standard requirement in most states. West Virginia uses a similar practice. Caution should be exercised, however, because people who use this nontraditional door into the field of social work may be disappointed if they move from the granting state. Other states may not honor their designated status, and no appeal based on reciprocity is possible. Remember, the best way to ensure entry into the field of social work is the traditional way: earning a baccalaureate or master's degree in social work from a program accredited by CSWE. Since grandfathered exceptions are so rare and policies vary from state to state, based on state need and requirements, we'll operate on the premise that a bachelor's or master's degree is the only way to enter the profession.

The difference between someone who simply wants to help and someone who is trained in the professional skills to give help is pronounced. Nevertheless, some professionals from other disciplines feel the strong requirements that must be satisfied to qualify as a social worker are unfair. That most states require a professional social worker to have either a bachelor's or a graduate college degree in social work strikes them as elitist. In fact, they might say, a lot of good people carry out important activities on behalf of individuals in need, and these helping workers should also be considered social workers. Most professional social workers would disagree because they believe that social work is indeed a profession and, as such, must have clear rules and requirements for entry.

To support this position, let's look at some professions and see what they require for entry:

Law: Completion of a baccalaureate degree in any discipline; graduation from a law program, accredited by the American Bar Association; passage of a state bar examination. At one time, a person was able to "sit" for the bar exam without graduating from a law program. In such cases, the individual was required to have worked in a law office, under the mentorship of a board-certified lawyer, that is, one who had passed the bar exam, for a number of years. This practice is no longer allowed.

Medicine: Completion of a baccalaureate degree, preferably in the hard sciences; graduation from a medical school, accredited by the American Medical Association; passage of a state medical examination. As with law school, medical school was in the past not a requirement for practice, but that too is no longer the case.

Nursing: Education in the scientific basis of nursing under defined standards of education and concern with the diagnosis and treatment of human responses to actual or potential health problems (PDR: Medical Dictionary, 1995). Most nurses have completed their education in accredited programs and can practice at the level appropriate to their educational qualifications. For example, a licensed practical nurse has graduated from an accredited school of practical (vocational) nursing (one year of training), passed the state exam for licensure, and is licensed to practice by the state authority. Similar requirements with varying education exist for the other levels of nursing at the associate, bachelor's, and graduate levels. An individual without a degree in nursing may assist a nurse in daily routines; often this individual is called a "nurse's aide." Regardless of education nurse's aides are not nurses and cannot perform the traditional duties of nurses licensed at different levels of skill acquisition.

Physical Therapist: Completion of a baccalaureate degree, with emphasis on biology, chemistry, physics, and social sciences, or graduation from a graduate physical therapy program, accredited by the Commission on Accreditation in Physical Therapy Education; in 1998, a doctorate in physical therapy was offered by eight programs. Baccalaureate, master's, and doctoral level practitioners must pass a state exam before they are considered qualified to practice in the area of physical therapy.

Lawyers, physicians, nurses, and physical therapists are only a few of the professions that require professional education regulated by a professional accrediting body and, usually, passage of a state examination to practice. Examples of specific requirements for entry into particular professions abound.

Up to the nineteenth century, people were not required to complete any formal education in order to enter particular professions. Rather, someone hoping to enter a profession studied and worked as an apprentice under a practicing member of that profession who was recognized as experienced. This mentoring model was acceptable for three main reasons. First, at that time the relatively small number of colleges and universities were geographically inaccessible to many. Second, since there were fewer schools the number who could participate in higher education was limited by the availability of educators and seats. Third, few families could afford the costs of a college education. Higher education was reserved for the elite and, for the most part, white males. With these limits on access to former education most aspiring professionals found it productive to learn under the watchful eye and guidance of a successful practitioner.

With the spread of the public state college system and the democratization of all higher education the historical barriers were slowly chipped away. As formal education became more accessible many professionals moved their courses of study from the practical to the academic setting. Social work was no exception.

> *Did You Know…In 1997–98, Texas had more accredited BSW programs (28) than any other state. Counting programs in candidacy as well, New York leads the nation with twenty-seven accredited programs and six in candidacy, for a total of thirty-three BSW programs. California led the nation in accredited MSW programs, with twelve for the same time period (Lennon, 1998).*

The first documented educational training program in social work was a six-week-long summer institute offered in 1898. Sponsored by the New York Charity Organization Society, this program is credited with helping to found the Columbia University School of Social Work. Before this summer institute was held almost all social work training took place within agencies and was provided by agency staff. In the years that followed social work education became a fixture of higher education. By 1998 there were 651 BSW, MSW, and DSW/Ph.D. social work programs in American colleges and universities (table 1). There were also hundreds of social work education programs in other countries around the world.

Table 1: Number of Accredited BSW, MSW, and Ph.D. Programs

Year	BSW	MSW	Ph.D.	BSW and MSW in Candidacy	Total
1998	410	126	62	53	651
1996	388	117	56	52	613
1994	382	112	55	45	594
1992	374	106	53	41	574

Source: Lennon (1998).

The twentieth century was critical for the developing field of social work. During this time social work was transformed from a volunteer activity into an established profession requiring a clearly designed education. When apprenticeship occurs now it is intertwined with or follows a competency-based education provided within the rigorous setting of baccalaureate or graduate study.

ACCREDITATION AND WHY IT MATTERS

As an aspiring social work professional you should be aware of the accreditation standards your social work program must meet. By meeting these standards your program assures you, and others, that when you complete its requirements you will be well prepared for your future career. Because of the importance of this information we present an overview of accreditation and explain how it relates directly to your development as a professional in the field of social work.

Council on Social Work Education

The Council of Social Work Education is the primary national organization that oversees and provides guidelines for social work education in the United States. The council was organized in 1952 with the merger of the National Association of Schools of Social Administration (NASSA), which had coordinated baccalaureate education, and the American Association of Schools of Social Work (AASSW), the membership body for graduate programs (Beless, 1995). In 1998, the number of CSWE member schools included 410 baccalaureate and 126 master's accredited programs (see table 1). In addition, 53 programs were in **candidacy**, or preaccreditation status. While not regulated by CSWE, there were 62 social work doctoral programs.

Activity...Visit the CSWE web page at www.cswe.org and look for the listing of schools, colleges, departments, and programs of social work. Compare and contrast programs from around the country; compare urban and rural programs, large and small colleges/universities. What difference, if any, do you find? What kinds of electives do programs offer? How do BSW and MSW programs differ? What patterns of interesting educational activities do you find?

Although the council was formed by the merger of two organizations that concentrated on baccalaureate and graduate education respectively, undergraduate education appeared to take a back seat to graduate studies (Leighninger, 1987). It wasn't until 1974 that CSWE implemented accreditation standards for baccalaureate programs. As Gardellia (1997) noted, BSW and MSW educational programs were never fully integrated—that is, they have never viewed each other as equal partners—which has created tension between the groups. Moreover, the CSWE board of directors initially included ten seats for BSW educators and twenty seats for MSW educators (Gardellia, 1997, p. 39). Today, BSW and MSW educators hold equal numbers of seats on the board of directors, but tension remains between graduate and undergraduate educators, albeit at a lower level than in the early 1970s.

For social work students knowing how CSWE business is conducted can be helpful in understanding why their educational program is organized in a particular manner. CSWE is governed by twelve commissions: Accreditation, Education Policy, Field Education, Gay Men/Lesbian Women, Minority Group Concerns,

Middle school students meeting with a social worker to discuss various school and family issues.

National Legislation and Administrative Policy, Women, Social Work Practice, Program Research, and Publications and Media (Beless, 1995, p. 634).

Commission on Accreditation: The primary function of CSWE is the accreditation of baccalaureate and master's degree programs. Accreditation is coordinated by the **Commission on Accreditation**, a twenty-five-member committee that includes social work educators representing both BSW and MSW faculties, BSW and MSW students, and social work practitioners. These commissioners are volunteers who are appointed by the president of CSWE for three-year terms; a commissioner may serve no more than two consecutive terms, or a total of six years. A professionally paid staff supports the commission. The commission influences the direction of social work education through such activities as maintaining and updating accreditation standards; conducting commissioner **site visits** to programs in candidacy; voting on candidacy status, initial accreditation, and **reaffirmation**; and assuring the quality of social work education and of the commission's functions.

Curriculum Policy Statement: The **Curriculum Policy Statement** (CPS), written by the Commission on Educational Policy, is a critical document to social work educators and program developers. The CPS descries in broad terms the essence of social work education at the undergraduate and graduate levels. The document is so important to education that accreditation standards require social work students to be familiar with it. As a social work student you need to be aware of this policy statement, and if your program is being reaccredited, you might be asked to tell the site visit team what you believe it says.

The CPS pronounces on a number of different subjects, including "the purpose of social work education and the essential knowledge, skills, and values expected of graduates" (Beless, 1995, p. 633). According to the CPS, the BSW is the entry-level degree, and a BSW practitioner's interventions are developed within a **generalist practice** framework. The MSW is the advanced practice degree, and an MSW practitioner's interventions are developed within a **specialist practice** framework.

Generalist and specialist social workers can be characterized as follows:

Generalist: A social work practitioner whose knowledge and skills encompass a broad spectrum and who assesses problems and their solutions comprehensively. The generalist often coordinates the efforts of specialists by facilitating communication between them, thereby fostering continuity of care.

Specialist: A social work practitioner whose orientation and knowledge are focused on a specific problem or goal or whose technical expertise and skill in specific activities are highly developed and refined. (Barker, 1991)

Accreditation Standards for Social Work Programs

Educational Content for Baccalaureate and Master's Programs: The CPS requires that all social work educational programs include a liberal arts perspective and professional foundation content. The liberal arts perspective, according to accreditation standards,

> enriches understanding of the person-environment context of professional social work practice and is integrally related to the mastery of social work content. . . . It provides an understanding of one's cultural heritage in the context of other cultures; the methods and limitations of systems of inquiry; and the knowledge, attitudes, ways of thinking, and means of communication that are characteristic of a broadly educated person. (CSWE, 1994, pp. 99–100, 138)

That is why before you were allowed to enroll in your social work classes you were required to complete several courses in certain liberal arts. The completion of these courses satisfies part of the social work program's liberal arts educational requirement. Content areas completed most often are English, additional electives in the arts and humanities, science, history, political science, sociology, anthropology, and psychology. A point to remember: accreditation standards do not specify liberal arts courses that must be completed; rather it is your program faculty who have identified courses they feel will prepare you for the social work program's course of study.

According to the CPS, the specific content of the professional foundation is determined by "new advances in practice knowledge, as well as the accumulated knowledge of social work education and the social work profession" (CSWE, 1994, p. 139). The professional foundation *is* the same for all accredited educational programs (see box 1). A BSW student in New York studies the same foundation content as a BSW student in Austin, Texas. As a result, the professional foundation is common ground for all social workers whatever their individual agency settings, client populations, practice functions, or practice methods. This common educational content is a real asset. In particular, the professional foundation helps supervisors and coworkers to know what new social workers have been taught and what has been stressed in their formal education. No such uniformity in educational content exists for some related disciplines such as the various counseling specialties.

Box 1: Professional Foundation of Social Work Ethics

Social work values and ethics: Specific social work values and ethics and their implications for social work practice.

Diversity: Value and richness of human diversity and the impact on the social work process.

Promotion of social and economic justice: Dynamics and results of economic and social injustice, including all forms of social oppression and discrimination.

Populations at risk: People of color, women, and gay and lesbian persons; other at-risk populations related to the program's mission.

Human behavior and the social environment: Theories and knowledge focusing on the human bio-psycho-social development; those systems in which individuals live; and those systems that impact the system development.

Social welfare policy and services: History, mission, and purpose of the social work profession; methods of policy analysis and the development of social policy, including political and organizational systems.

Social work practice: Generalist social work practice with individuals, families, groups, communities, and organizations.

Research: Scientific approach to the evaluation of social work practice.

Field practicum: Work in a social services agency during which time the student engages in supervised social work practice to apply classroom learning.

Baccalaureate in Social Work (Educational Model): The typical baccalaureate social work program begins in the sophomore year of college and requires four to five semesters of study. Accreditation standards demand some form of admission process. Limited access programs require a formal application and review process for admission. Admission may depend on such criteria as cumulative grade point average (GPA), successful completion of the liberal arts requirements, reference letters, and a narrative statement. In programs that are not limited access, admission depends on successful completion of the liberal arts requirements. Whether access to a program is limited or not depends on school policy.

Activity...Meet with a social work advisor to discuss your program's admission process. Is the program a limited access program? What is the application process? Are all applicants accepted into the program? What are some of the reasons people are denied admission to the program? Explore with the advisor the program's liberal arts requirements. Why are these specific courses required? Are you surprised by some of the required courses?

Accreditation standards require that students receive at least 400 hours of field education, though a particular program may demand more than this minimum. Programs currently use a number of models to address the **field placement** requirement. One option is "block placement," in which the student is assigned to an agency full time, forty hours a week, for an entire semester. A second approach, "concurrent placement," assigns the student to an agency one to three days a week while the student takes courses, usually for two semesters. A third approach combines concurrent and block placements: concurrent placement is made in the student's junior year of study and block placement in the senior year. This approach allows the student to be assigned to different agencies. What's more important to remember is that whatever field model your program uses you must complete at least 400 hours in the field practicum. Because this requirement is set forth in the accreditation standards your program is very unlikely to allow modifications or exceptions.

Master of Social Work (Educational Model): Professional education at the master's level requires the equivalent of two academic years of full-time study and combines two components, foundation and specialization, in the program of study.

The professional foundation content is the same as for baccalaureate programs and is most often studied in the first year. Specialization takes place during the equivalent of the second year of full-time study and builds on the foundation education. According to the social work educational model, specialization must be firmly rooted in the foundation content. A specialization can be designed around different areas of social work practice (see box 2); second-year courses and field

Table 2: Number of BSW, MSW, and Ph.D./DSW Students and Graduates of Accredited Programs

Year	1998	1997	1996	1995	1994
BSW students	42,443	48,050	56,038	42,974	45,604
BSW degrees awarded	11,435	12,356	10,305	10,511	10,288
MSW students	31,759	35,559	35,468	32,283	33,212
MSW degrees awarded	13,660	15,058	14,484	12,976	12,856
MSW applications made, first year	34,533	40,075	44,968	43,024	46,247
Ph.D./DSW programs	62	58	56	56	55
Ph.D./DSW students	2,102	2,436	2,087	1,949	2,097
Ph.D/DSW degrees awarded	266	286	258	279	294

Source: Lennon (1998).

education should reflect this specialization area. Accreditation standards demand that MSW students complete at least 900 field hours. Students complete two placements, one in the foundation year and another in the specialization year, and these must total to a minimum of 900 hours.

A common complaint among newly enrolled first-year graduate students is that their field placements are not in their intended areas of specialization. Students need to remember, however, that first-year field placements are intended to be generalist in nature and to allow students to apply foundation knowledge, theories, and skills studied in the classroom. Specialization knowledge, theories, and skills are developed in the equivalent of the second year of study; it is at this point that specialization placements occur.

Box 2: Specialization Models

Methodology: Specialization by intervention, such as critical social work, community organization, or group work

Setting: Specialization by agency setting or type, such as child welfare, mental health, criminal justice, rural practice, or gerontology

Population group: Specialization by a specific client population, such as children, families, women, and seniors

Problem area: Specialization by a focused problem, such as alcohol, tobacco, and other substances, mental illness, family violence, and poverty

Combination: Combination of specialization, such as methodology and population growth, for example, clinical social work with children.

Students choosing a graduate program should know that not all programs offer a choice of specialization; some provide only one track of advanced study. A colleague has remarked that when reviewing admission folders for her graduate program, she feels that students know little about the program they are applying to. One student, for example, wanted to study administration, but the school only offers a clinical specialization. The student had a GPA of 3.8 and a Graduate Record Exam (GRE) score of 1,175. The admission committee, nevertheless, rejected the student's application because the student's career interests did not match the school's mission and curriculum. The applicant was very angry and complained about his rejection. Even when the committee's rationale was explained to him, he did not accept the decision, saying "What I want to do professionally has nothing to do with the type of program I want to apply to." The moral of this story: Make sure that your career goals match the school's mission and educational program.

Advanced Standing (Educational Program): Some graduate programs offer "advanced standing." Advanced standing, which is limited to graduates of CSWE baccalaureate programs, allows these students to have certain courses waived because they learned the content in their baccalaureate studies. Advanced stand-

Name: Sam Hickman

Place of residence: Charleston, West Virginia

College/university degrees: B.A., Marshall University
M.S.W. West Virginia University

Present position: Executive Director, NASW/West Virginia

Previous work/volunteer experience: Hospital social work
director; Federal Mental Health Disaster Program Grant
Director; Soil Conservation Service volunteer

What do you do in your spare time? I play and sing Appalachian folk music, coach youth
soccer, cook, garden, and bike.

Why did you choose social work as a career? My mother held social work/human services
jobs while I was growing up. I often got to sit on the lap of the mental health department
director or juvenile court judge. When entering a part-time M.S.W. program came up, it
was a natural fit.

What is your favorite social work story? I have two that I would like to share. First, after
discussing nursing home care with a somewhat confused elderly woman, she looked up at
me from her hospital bed and said, "You damn Republican!" Second, last April at a conference we organize, we passed the hat on the spur of the moment and raised over $600 for
storm victims in the southeast. We gave it to the Red Cross.

*What would be the one thing you would change in our community if you had the power to
do so?* I would pay respectable salaries to women who choose to stay home to care for
young children. I believe this is where healthy families begin.

ing reflects the CPS stipulation that a graduate program not require course work to be repeated once it has been mastered.

Social work is the only profession that offers an advanced standing option in its educational model. Even within social work advanced standing is very controversial in both theory and practice. The profession's ambivalence toward advanced standing is seen in its inconsistent application. Some programs waive the entire foundation year of study while others limit the exemption to one or two courses, some require successful completion of content-specific examinations, and some programs do not offer an advanced standing option at all. Some programs require BSW practitioners to enroll in the graduate program within a specific time period, ranging from four to seven years, following their baccalaureate graduation; otherwise, they are not eligible for advanced standing and are required to complete the regular two-year curriculum.

Ph.D./DSW (Educational Program): CSWE does not regulate doctoral study. As a result, doctoral programs differ in required courses, program structure, and specialization. Generally, a doctorate is required for people who teach in BSW or MSW programs. While not required for agency practice, there is a small, but growing trend in agencies to hire upper level administrators who hold doctoral degrees.

Two types of doctoral degrees are associated with social work, the Ph.D. and the DSW. The Ph.D. is the familiar Doctorate of Philosophy; DSW designates a Doctorate in Social Work. Basically, the two degree are more similar than different. When doctoral programs first originated in the field of social work, the DSW was awarded. As time passed and social workers were hired as educators, schools changed the doctorate to a Ph.D., and today that is the more common designation in academia. Both degrees require approximately the equivalent of two years of full-time study, passage of a comprehensive qualifying examination, and successful completion of a written dissertation. It is important to remember, however, that because doctoral-level programs, unlike master's and bachelor's programs, are not accredited by CSWE, careful exploration to find the right match between student and program is essential.

SOCIAL WORKERS TODAY

According to U.S. Department of Labor (1998, p. 4) employment projections through the year 2006, social work is tenth among professions that have the fastest growth, highest pay, and lowest unemployment. A 1998 *U.S. News and World Report* special issue on careers identified social work as one of the "20 hot job trends" with growing opportunities.

The Department of Labor identified 585,000 social work jobs in 1996; 40 percent of these jobs are in state, county, or local government, but as the government contracts for more and more services from the private sector, many jobs will shift to private agencies (1998, p. 157). According to Gibelman and Schervish (1997, p. 5), the number of people employed in social work and holding social work degrees will range from 645,000 to a high of 693,000.

No single information source provides a detailed overview of social work employment. One starting point is Gibelman and Schervish's (1997) analysis of the NASW membership. Their study, though based on a self-reporting survey of NASW members and thus not representative of all degreed social workers, nevertheless gives useful insight into the profession.

What Are Social Workers Paid?

Probably of most interest to people considering social work as a career is salary: how much can I make? Well, you won't be poor, and you'll be able to live a comfortable life. Table 3 reports NASW's recommended minimum salary scale for employers, which is meant to be modified to reflect regional differences. These NASW data are somewhat old, reflecting 1990 salaries, but they give a starting point. In 2000 as part of Social Work Month, the annual celebration of the profession held every March, NASW noted that for 1997, median salaries (50% above and 50% below) were $35,000 for an MSW and $25,000 for a BSW (www.nasdc.org/NASW/SWMonth2000/salaries.htm). Median social work salaries by setting were hospitals ($35,000), federal government ($46,900), child welfare ($32,000), and colleges and universities ($50,000).

Table 3: NASW Salary Scale

	1990	1996[a]
BSW	$20,000	$23,320
MSW	25,000	29,150
ACSW[b]	30,000	34,980
Advanced[c]	45,000	52,471

[a]Adjusted for cost of living using the consumer price index.
[b]Academy of Certified Social Workers: MSW plus two years of post-MSW experience required
[c]Ph.D. of DSW degree required.

Source: Gibelman and Schervish (1997).

The median salary for social workers in 1995 was $34,215. Average salary by practice area ranged from a high of $40,472 (occupational social work) to a low of $33,158 (aging). Other practice areas included mental health ($39,626), school social work ($38,871), criminal justice ($36,963), medical health ($36,340), and children/families ($34,865).

Helpful Tips for Applying to Graduate School

There are more applicants to graduate programs than there are seats available. As a result, people are rejected. So, how do you strengthen your chances for admission?

1. Determine what you wish to do as a professional. You need to have a good idea of the type of work you wish to pursue—the more specific you are, the easier your application choices will be. Do you want to work with children or seniors, or doesn't it matter? Do you want to develop knowledge in clinical social work or community practice? Are you interested in developing expertise in mental health, criminal justice, or some other setting?

2. Identify the graduate programs that match your career interests. Begin with the CSWE web site, www.CSWE.org, and look at the various graduate programs. Contact those programs that interest you and ask for an "MSW application packet" and "graduate bulletin."

3. Be sure to follow the application process as outlined. Don't deviate from the school's application procedure, deadlines, or requirements; if you do, you are virtually guaranteeing your rejection.

4. Keep copies of all application materials. On average, each graduate program receives 385 applications. A university's graduate office probably processes thousands of applications. In short, it is easy for papers to be lost given the large number of applicants.

5. Don't pester the school by calling to ask what is happening with your application. What did the application packet and graduate bulletin say about letting you know? Call *only* after an excessive amount of time has passed from the stated notification date.

6. Your GPA is one of the most important pieces of information schools use in the admission process. While a high GPA doesn't guarantee admission, a low GPA doesn't help.

7. Recognize that reference letters are important, but most applicants generally receive strong letters. Admission committee members generally look at what letters do not say rather than what they say.

8. Most programs require the applicant to submit a written statement or responses to certain questions. Without a doubt this is one of the most critical items in the application packet. The written statement gives the admission committee the only direct vehicle to your soul. Be sure to answer all questions, and most important, make sure your statement is grammatically correct. Yes, spelling counts! A sloppy, poorly written paper tells the committee a great deal about how you approach your work. Treat the statement as the most important document you have ever written. Spend time with it. Have friends read it with a critical eye; take their comments seriously.

9. No matter how high your GPA and GRE score might be, you are not entitled to be accepted into any graduate program. No one is guaranteed acceptance into a limited access program. Assume that you will be rejected and that you need to work to minimize your liabilities and maximize your strengths.

As might be expected salary increased with education. Forty-six percent of BSWs earned between $20,000 and $30,000 while 67 percent of Ph.D./DSW holders earned more than $40,000. The largest proportion of MSWs, 38 percent, earned between $30,000 and $40,000.

Agency administrators' average salary was $44,147, followed by educators ($40,780), researchers ($40,347), policymakers ($38,445), trainers ($48,076), clinical practitioners ($35,355), and community organizers ($34,620).

As with any profession, gender discrimination exists. In 1995 men earned on average $37,503 compared to $34,135 for women. Gibelman and Schervish (1997, p. 135) found that the women's salary was below the median salary. Salary discrimination based on ethnicity was minimal, according to Gibelman and Schervish (1997, p. 136), and not statistically significant.

Activity...Check out the New Social Worker Online *web page (www.socialworker.com). You'll find a number of discussion boards and chat rooms dealing with a variety of topics, including careers, ethics, student forums, general items, announcements, and resource recommendations. Questions about jobs and salaries are hot topics on this web site.*

Where Do Social Workers Work?

To better understand *where* job opportunities might be, let's look at social work practice from four interrelated perspectives: job function, auspices, setting, and practice area:

Function: What Do I Do?
Direct service
Management/administration
Consultant
Planning

Supervision
Policy development/analysis
Research
Education/training

Auspices: Where Do I Work?
Public, local
Public, state
Public, federal
Public, military

Private nonprofit, sectarian
Private nonprofit, nonsectarian
Private for profit, proprietary

Setting: What Type of Agency Do I Work In?
Social service agency
Private practice, self-employed
Private practice, partnership
Membership organization
Hospital
Outpatient facility

Nursing home
Criminal justice system
College/university
Elementary/secondary schools
Non–social service organization
Group home

Practice Area: What Is My Practice Area?

Children and youth

Community organization/planning

Family services

Criminal justice

Group services

Mental health

School social work

Services to the aged

Alcohol and other substance abuse

Developmental disabilities

Occupational

Public assistance

Any set of choices, one from each list, defines a social work position. For example, you can be a supervisor (function) in a private nonprofit, sectarian (auspices) nursing home (setting), providing services to the aged (practice area). Or you might provide direct service (function) in a public, local (auspices) outpatient facility (setting) as an alcohol and substance abuse counselor (practice area). The thousands of potential combinations demonstrate the versatility of social work employment opportunities.

Another way to discover the breadth of the social work profession is to examine CSWE studies of social work education programs. Each year the council collects these data in order to track the state of the profession and to detect possible trends in education. In its 1996 study the council identified fourteen different practice area concentrations in most social work schools (see table 4). The data in table 4 reinforces the impression of diversity in social work, although mental health, child welfare, and family services stand out as the three most popular concentrations among students.

Table 4: Fields of Practice among 34,358 Graduate Students in Social Work Education

Field	Percentage of Students
Aging	2.7%
Alcohol or substance abuse	1.5
Child welfare	7.8
Community planning	1.0
Corrections	1.0
Family services	7.4
Group services	.4
Health	5.1
Mental health	11.0
Mental retardation	.3
Occupational social work	.8
Public welfare	.2
Rehabilitation	.2
School social work	3.5
Other	3.7
Combinations	2.6
Not determined	21.6
None (methods only)	29.2

Source: Lennon (1998).

GETTING A SOCIAL WORK JOB AFTER GRADUATION

There's no secret to finding a job, whether in social work, law, nursing, or any other profession: it takes a great deal of hard work and a lot of patience on the part of the job seeker. While jobs in general are available, it takes time to find the one that is right for you. A rule of thumb is that it takes three to four months to find a job from the time you begin your search in earnest. So if you want to have a job by June, you'll need to have your resume prepared and your search strategy developed and implemented no later than the preceding February.

A note of caution: Be prepared not to get the *one* job you've always wanted. Even for the most experienced social worker a job rejection letter hurts. Great jobs are waiting for competent social workers—they key is finding a position in which you can make full use of your knowledge, skills, and potential.

Did You Know…By the late 1990s, of all social workers
   87.9% were women

   88% were white, 5.7% African-American, 1.8% Asian-Americans, and 2.8% Latino

   86% held MSWs, 5% doctorates, and 10% BSWs

   41–45 years was the median age range

   23% lived in the Mid-Atlantic region, while the East South Central had the fewest social workers, 3.6%

   10% had more than twenty-five years of experience, while the average range was six to ten years

   77% were employed full time

   38% were employed in mental health, followed by 25% in family services

   39% were employed in private, nonprofit settings, followed by 27% in private for-profit settings

   69% were in direct service, while 15% held management positions (www.naswdc.org)

Prepare Your Resume Carefully

Be sure your resume is up to date. You can get an easy-to-use resume software program at the college bookstore or computer store. There are also any number of books on resume writing that you can review. Ask your academic advisor or some other social worker for tips and ideas about what to highlight. Consider taking advantage of your school's job placement office by attending a resume-writing workshop. But recognize that most helpers in the resume-writing process are not well versed in social work; their work is geared to a general audience and does not reflect the nuances of social work. The key is to ask social workers in the field what they did and what they listed on their resumes.

Be sure your resume is clean and as error free as possible—no spelling errors, no photocopies with wrinkled edges, and so on. Your resume is your introduction to a potential employer, and you want to make the best impression possible. Consider writing an initial goal or objective for the type of work you want to do in the field. Be sure to link the contents of this statement with the job you are applying for. You may not have much paid clinical or administrative experience, so be sure to highlight volunteer experiences and start with your most recent field placement. For other tips and suggestions present a draft of your resume to a favorite social work instructor or a social worker in the field. Listen to their suggestions carefully because they have been through the employment process; hearing their "words of wisdom" *first* might save you a great deal of time and effort later.

Attend Local NASW Meetings

To facilitate your job search, attend local NASW meetings as often as you can. You can begin to network by attending meetings and becoming active with this group as soon as you declare your major. Dues for a student are a real bargain! Simply contact your state NASW office for information about your local unit and for the name of a contact person. You should be able to get an NASW membership application from your school's social work office or through the state NASW office.

While attending local NASW unit meetings you'll make new friends, begin to develop a professional network, and keep abreast of issues within your new social work community. Moreover, the monthly or bimonthly meetings often include time for members to announce job opportunities. Most people would be surprised at how much information about job openings and availability is spread by word of mouth and through these types of informal networks. For example, you may even get firsthand information on a position that has just become available from the contact person within the agency.

> *Activity...Attend a local NASW meeting. Talk to members about finding jobs and see what hints they can give you.*
>
> *Get on the World Wide Web and see what kind of jobs you can find in at least five different states. Try looking in large cities as well as small towns.*
>
> *Read a number of job announcements and look for qualifications that are* minimum requirements *versus those that are* preferences.
>
> *Visit your school's job placement office. See what the staff recommend about putting together a* job search packet. *Remember, it's never too early to begin collecting material for your resume.*
>
> *Put together a draft resume and pass it around asking for suggestions on how to make it better.*

Use Your Field Placement Experience

Each student must complete a field placement. Don't be surprised if your field agency offers you a position following graduation. The field site has the luxury of assessing your work; if you do an excellent job the agency may ask you to consider moving into a regular position. An agency benefits from hiring a field placement student who has already worked in the agency, because this "new" employee can be moved into a regular position more quickly and with less orientation time. Furthermore, there is little need for an initial skill and knowledge assessment period because the agency, through the internship experience, is well aware of the student's practice abilities and thus the level of supervision needed. Employment in a field placement agency also has advantages for the student accepting the job. The student already knows the agency and how she will fit into the overall organization. Based on direct experience the student knows that it is the setting in which she wants to start a social work career.

Read Local and National Newspaper Advertisements

Local newspapers, *NASW News*, and your state NASW chapter newsletter publish countless employment announcements. Familiarize yourself with the range of jobs that are available as well as the jobs that interest you the most. Read each advertisement carefully, and when you apply for a job be sure to follow the instructions; if it asks for a resume and the names of three references, provide just that— no more and no less.

Look closely at the words used in the announcement. Words such as "must have" or "minimum" or "required" signal baseline qualifications that the successful candidate must possess. For example, if the announcement requires an MSW degree and five years of post-MSW experience, don't apply if you are a newly graduated BSW or an MSW with three years of experience. On the other hand, words such as "should have" or "preferred" signal not minimum criteria but preferences. These words introduce the agency's wish list for the desired candidate, and employers understand that they often don't get everything on their wish lists. Let's say you find an interesting job for which you meet the minimum requirements but not the preferences, go ahead and apply.

Use the Internet

If you'd like a job outside of your local area, the World Wide Web and the Internet can be your best friends. Through the Web you can locate newspapers, state NASW offices, and employment services across the country. Use the Web's search engines to identify employment opportunities.

Get to Know Your Social Work Faculty Advisors and Instructors

One of your best sources of employment information and strategies is your program faculty. They are very interested in your success, they have years of experience, and they know people in the field in the surrounding community who can help you. Your social work teachers have probably had contact with most local agencies, and a good word, phone call, or reference letter from a faculty member can be one of your greatest aids in getting your first job.

Don't forget that many programs use adjunct or part-time faculty to supplement their full-time faculty. Adjunct faculty members who are employed full time in the community can help you in your job search because they are tied into the local informal social work network.

Did You Know...All states have some form of licensing or regulation of social work practice, but in many states such regulation is limited to MSW or advanced practice and does not apply to BSW practice. Be sure to check with your academic advisor to learn more about your state's particular licensing requirements.

NASW also regulates MSW and advanced social work practice through the Academy of Certified Social Workers (ACSW). A practitioner with an ACSW certification meets the following criteria: 1) NASW membership; 2) MSW degree; 3) two years or 3,000 hours of post-MSW experience; and 4) passage of a multiple choice examination, given after the experience requirement is satisfied. A social worker does not need to have the ACSW, but state law may require a practitioner to be licensed.

Explore Your Social Work Student Association or Club

Your program's social work student association or club can help in your job search. The association can invite area agency directors to provide workshops or panels on finding a job. The club can also sponsor a job fair on campus at which area agencies set up booths, distribute agency information, and recruit potential employees. The fair can be coordinated with the program's field office and the local NASW unit. Probably the best time to hold a job fair is in the spring, when most potential graduates are looking for jobs.

A job fair is a win-win-win situation. Students win because they have immediate access to potential employers. Agencies win because the fair is a cost-effective recruiting mechanism that reaches a large pool of potential job applicants. The social work program and university win because the job fair is a positive public relations tool that strengthens ties between the university and the community.

Last Thoughts about Your Job Search

We often get caught up in salary and look for the best paying jobs. Yes, salary is important, but consider other aspects of the job as well. Who works at the agency? What kind of colleagues will you have, and can you learn from them? Your first job will be a major source of knowledge and experience. Will the job be exciting and offer you a variety of learning opportunities? What kinds of benefits are in place? These can range from health care and vacation time to pets—one organization allows staff members to bring their pets to work each Friday. (Now what does that say about the organization?)

A few years ago, a student came into the office very excited about a job offer she had received in New York City as a childcare worker. She said, "I'm getting a great salary. They're going to pay me $35,000!"

But what does $35,000 mean to a new, twenty-one-year-old social worker? Sounds like a great deal, but not really. Use the Web to find salaries for comparison purposes; the easiest way is to search for "salary converters." For example, as you can see in table 5, $30,000 in one city means something quite different somewhere else.

Table 5: A Salary of $30,000 in Houston, Texas, Is the Same As . . .

City	Salary
Hartford, CT	$32,054
New York City (Manhattan)	89,842
Orlando, FL	30,017
Chicago, IL	56,053
Los Angeles, CA	44,371
Santa Fe, NM	36,858
Portland, OR	37,612
London, England	60,214
Dublin, Ireland	51,784
Rome, Italy	55,799
Jerusalem, Israel	47,369

Source: www.homefair/com/calc/sale.html, March 2000.

Remember that you need to be happy with what you find. Make sure the setting offers you an opportunity for continued professional growth and self-fulfillment.

SUMMARY

Students entering social work will find the field rich in opportunities. The profession's future is bright.

In embarking on a professional career in social work the selection of an educational program is important. A social work career should begin with either a baccalaureate or a master's degree, and this degree must come from a CSWE-accredited program. Request admission information directly from the programs you are interested in attending. Programs are located in every state in the United States and throughout the world. (See appendix D for U.S. programs.) Be sure to gather information early so you have plenty of time to prepare what is required. Some baccalaureate programs have open admission, while others use a formal admission process. Admission to graduate program, on the other hand, is usually competitive, and about 40 percent of applicants are turned down.

Employment possibilities for social workers can be found in both public and private settings. They involve a wide range of activities and tasks and a variety of practice areas. Simply stated, practice opportunities for social work professionals are open and diverse.

The key to a successful work experience in social work is planning your education carefully—whether BSW or MSW—and making the most of it. Take advantage of your educational opportunities to develop new knowledge, theories, and skills that will make you more competent. Remember, before you can help the individuals, groups, families, and communities that you will serve, you must first help yourself to be the best equipped professional, with the best foundation of education and training possible.

References

Barker, R. L. (1991). *The social work dictionary* (2nd ed.). Washington, DC: NASW Press.

Beless, D. W. (1995). Council on social work education. In R. Edwards et al. (Eds.), *Encyclopedia of social work* (19th ed., pp. 632–636). Washington, DC: NASW Press.

U.S. Department of Labor, Bureau of Labor of Statistics. (1998). *Occupational handbook, 1998–1999 edition*. Washington, DC: U.S. Government Printing Office.

CSWE Council on Social Work Education. (1994). *Handbook of accreditation standards and procedures*. Alexandria, VA: Author.

Gardellia, L. G. (1997). Baccalaureate social work. In R. Edwards et al. (Eds.), *Encyclopedia of social work, 1997 supplement* (19th ed., pp. 37–46). Washington, DC: NASW Press.

Gibelman, M., and Schervish, P. H. (1997). *Who we are, a second look*. Washington, DC: NASW Press.

Leighninger, L. (1987). *Social work: Search for identity*. Westport, CT: Greenwood.

Lennon, T. (1998). *Statistics in social work education in the United States, 1998*. Alexandria, VA: CSWE.

PDR: Medical Dictionary. (1995). *PDR medical dictionary (1st ed.)*. Montvale, NJ: Medical Economics.

U.S. News and World Reports: 1998 Career guide. (1997, October 27).

Part **II**

The Practice of Social Work

Chapter 5

Social Work Practice

STEVE, AN UNDERGRADUATE SOCIAL WORK STUDENT, STOPPED BY to see one of the authors in his office. Steve was enjoying his introduction to social work class, he had not missed a session, and he believed his final grade would be high. Steve often had questions to ask and really enjoyed taking part in class discussion, so it was no surprise when he asked a question: "So, how do you do it?" Not quite sure what he meant by "it" the instructor asked Steve to clarify what "it" was. Very seriously he said, "You know, social work. How do you 'do' social work?"

Today, some fifteen years after this visit, Steve, who now has an MSW along with his BSW degree and is employed in a public mental health facility, laughs about that question. "I guess I was looking for that magical pill you give a client, the one thing we do to help a person in pain. I just believed that social workers had a bag of tricks that 'poof' solved the person's problems. How wrong I was."

Pondering how exactly to "do" social work is where most professionals start, and even for seasoned practitioners, the quest never ends. Steve, like so many beginning social workers, was unsure of what to do in social work practice and was hoping for a simple answer. Wouldn't it be wonderful if the unique and ambiguous challenges of human life could be easily addressed by giving a pat answer, taking a simple pill, or using a standard procedure. It's tempting, but wholly unrealistic. If social work practice required nothing more than simple prescriptions, then there would be limited need for formal education beyond the basics, for supervision, or for continuing education.

In fact, the practice of social work stems directly from the mission of the profession, which is not simple or standardized. If you look at the definition of social work set forth in chapter 1, you'll be looking in the right direction for practice guidance. Social workers seek to enhance social function, promote social justice, and help people to obtain resources.

Did You Know...The number of social work jobs doubled in the 1930s, from 40,000 to 80,000, as public sector income maintenance, health, and welfare programs were created in response to the depression (NASW, 1993).

Changes in the detailed definition of social work have occurred over time, yet the basis for social work practice has not changed:

Name: Nicole Todd-Thomas
Place of residence: Kalamazoo, Michigan
College/university degrees: Western Michigan University,
B.S.W., University of Chicago, School of Social Service
Administaration, A.M.
Present position: Director of operations of the Boys and
Girls Clubs of Greater Kalamazoo
Previous work/volunteer experience: Community organizer,
mental health advocate, Big Sister, human rights activist,
childcare worker

Why did you choose social work as a career? I have always been drawn to working with people, particularly youth. I chose social work because it is one of the few disciplines that focus on empowering groups and individuals within the context of their environment

What is your favorite social work story? One of the benefits to working in this field is the opportunity to work in a variety of settings with various individuals. While living in Chicago, I had the opportunity to work at a Boys & Girls Club in the Robert Taylor Homes. Since this housing project is notorious for gangs, drugs, and violence, many of the youth with whom I worked were frequently stereotyped as gang-bangers. Working with these kids and their families, I had the chance to see first-hand the inaccuracy of this stereotype. The most of the kids I encountered were just like the young people I worked with in other settings: they had families who loved them and cared for them, they strove to be successful, they desired love and affection, and they liked to laugh and have fun. People need to realize that most individuals living in poor areas are not violent; rather, they are hard working, loving family members attempting to survive in a society that often criminalizes poverty.

What would be the one thing you would change in our community if you had the power to do so? Of course, my first answer is to eliminate poverty. But, more realistically, within the context of our society, if I had the power, I would change the way in which our community approaches social problems. I think it is crucial that all people within our community take responsibility and recognize that all of our lives are affected when social injustices exist. If it is a community-wide problem, then it is a community responsibility.

Today's definition: Social work is the professional activity of helping individuals, groups, or communities to enhance or to restore their capacity for social functioning and to create societal conditions favorable to their goals (NASW, 1993).

Traditional definition: "Social work seeks to enhance the social functioning of individuals, singly and in groups, by activities focused on their social relationships which constitute the interaction between man [individuals] and his [or her] environment. These activities can be grouped into three functions: restoration of impaired capacity, provision of individual and social resources, and prevention of social dysfunction" (CSWE, 1959, p. 54).

The tasks that social workers undertake, the agencies in which they work, and the social policies they support are aimed toward three overarching goals: to enhance client social functioning, to remedy client dysfunction, and to promote social justice (Hepworth & Larsen, 1986, p. 13–15). BSW and MSW educational programs, through course work and field practicum experiences, develop the necessary value-driven knowledge and skills to support social work practice.

It is important to recognize, however, that you will only be introduced to practice in general terms in parts 2 and 3 of this book. You will not be qualified to do social work after reading these chapters. Remember, your career in social work is just beginning and numerous courses and field experiences are in front of you. It is these that when put together will provide you with the foundation for social work practice. This chapter will review the basic concepts related to the delivery of social work services and examine the helping process and its application to the practice of social work.

Before we begin to explore the "doing" of social work, however, we need to remind ourselves that the practice of social work is intended to achieve the profession's purpose of helping clients. A question that must be explored is: Why have you decided that this is the profession for you? Be honest with yourself as you explore the areas of social work practice and decide which holds your interest the most. The initial motivation for many helping professionals comes from wanting to learn more about themselves and their families. This is not unusual, nor is it particularly problematic. However, when this is part of your motivation for choosing the field you must be ultra-aware that the helping services you provide are not designed to help you—they are for the client. Other typical reasons for choosing a helping profession include the need to be needed, the desire to give something back to society and humankind, the need to care for others, and the desire for prestige and professional status. As you embark on a helping career it is essential first to examine what motivated you and why. Later, ask for feedback from other professionals who know you, particularly your social work teachers and professionals experienced in the field. Remember, choosing a career path is not simple or quick. Nor is staying in the field automatic. For many of us, the pressures created by the kind of work we do require constant self-examination throughout our educational and professional careers. Some students may decide relatively early that this is not the work for them. After all, a helping career is not the best choice for everyone, and it is a good idea to establish this before putting a great deal of time, effort, and expense into pursuing it.

Activity... Is Social Work Practice Really For Me? *On a piece of paper write the following questions and answer them individually. For this exercise you may at first feel more comfortable answering them by yourself. Later you may choose to discuss your answers with your instructor or academic advisor. Feel free to add questions to this list. You might also want to save your answers and revisit them later in your professional career.*

What first attracted you to the profession of social work?

What needs of your own are likely to be met by serving as a social worker?

Who in your life has been instrumental in helping you choose this career?

Have you ever received help from a social worker? What did you like most about this person? What did you like least?

What do you believe you can contribute to the field of social work?

In what ways do you believe this profession can help to make you feel like a better person?

CONCEPTS ESSENTIAL TO SOCIAL WORK PRACTICE

We have described social work practice as both art and science. The art of social work involves the sensitive coordination of complex activities to help clients. The science entails selecting, merging, and understanding potentially voluminous amounts of information and applying the conclusions to a specific case situation. While many are successful in learning the science of the profession, the art is difficult to acquire. The interplay of art and science means that effective social work practice grows from the relation between knowledge, skills, and values and ethics (see box 1). Social work practice requires unique skills, either specialized or generalist in nature, that are derived from specific knowledge areas and guided by a clear, fundamental set of values and ethics.

Skills

That we speak of "doing" social work implies that a social worker has a set of specific skills that she uses in practice. These skills, which are inseparable from the helping process, include the ability to perform critical tasks in working with clients: basic communication, exploration, assessment and planning, implementation, goal attainment, termination, and evaluation of the services rendered (Hepworth & Larsen, 1986).

Skill building and acquisition are the bridge between values and knowledge and all subsequent social service activities (Vass, 1996). Unless knowledge and val-

Box 1: Dynamic Interplay of Knowledge, Values and Ethics, and Skills

ues underlie skills the practice of social work is undefined and vague. Social workers must have basic competencies in the following skill areas:

- ◆ Cognitive skills, including analytic skills and the capacity to evaluate and understand research
- ◆ Administrative skills, including record keeping and report writing
- ◆ Interpersonal skills, including verbal and nonverbal skills, understanding, self-awareness, use of authority, working with diversity, working in partnership, and the ability to make and sustain positive working relationships
- ◆ Decision-making skills, including authority and responsibility
- ◆ Use and management of resources (Vass, 1996, p. 63)

A social worker must be able to balance many critical aspects of the practice relationship with each client. For example, the worker must first establish and then maintain a worker-client environment of trust. In this environment the client can feel safe when revealing emotions and thoughts that might disturb an untrained practitioner, because for the skilled worker the ethical values of client worth, dignity, and self-determination are paramount. The worker also must know how and when to approach those of the client's problems that need further explanation and exploration. The skilled social worker is well versed in empathetic communication and helps the client to clarify and confront what may be difficult issues to address. In short, the skilled professional social worker is an expert at establishing a positive worker-client relationship in which problem identification, helping, addressing, and subsequent healing can take place.

Did You Know...Often you will hear social workers discuss "an empathetic relation-ship" or read in the social work literature about the importance of "empathy" in the social work process. What is the difference between empathy and sympathy? It was once described as follows:

Sympathy is what you feel when you begin actually to feel the pain of the client. In a sympathetic relationship the helping professional cannot be objective or render the nonjudgmental intervention required. Say, for example, you wear a size 8 shoe and your client wears a size 7. If you actually put the client's shoes on your own feet, your feet will be so squeezed that you cannot concentrate on the issues the client is facing.

Empathy, on the other hand, is what you feel when you remain in your own shoes while imagining what it is like for the client in his or her situation. The client's situa-tion is assessed based on direct observation and information provided by the client or people from the client's environment. In an empathetic relationship the helping pro-fessional uses objective and subjective information and professional helping skills to truly understand the client's situation and the pain that the client is experiencing.

Knowledge Base

The practice of social work is based on a specific body of scientifically tested knowledge. Practice evolves from the knowledge base as social work skills first developed in the academic curriculum later mature through field experiences and continuing education. Without the appropriate knowledge base and awareness of the theoretical constructs that undergird professional practice, skills would be nothing more than a series of unrelated actions that cannot address total person-in-situation who is at the heart of professional social work practice. Conversely, knowledge evolves from current practice through practice-based research and evaluation of social work interventions. Without such research and evaluation, social work knowledge would quickly become static, outdated, and unfounded.

In many ways, knowledge drives all of a professional's daily actions with and on behalf of clients. Knowledge supports practice in its efforts to be client centered and directed to the unique situation of each client. The knowledge base of profes-sional practice premises, skills, and techniques allows social workers to choose the specific set of skills clearly embedded in a theoretical framework that best apply to a particular client situation. In other words, to achieve client-centered practice, the professional knowledge base must come first.

To create a consistent and comprehensive knowledge base of professional practice all social work educational programs require mastery of foundation con-tent in nine areas: social work practice, human behavior and the social environ-ment, social welfare policy and services, social policy, field practicum, research, diversity, social work values and ethics, populations at risk, and promotion of social and economic justice (see box 1 in chapter 4).

Knowledge needs to be directed toward three areas for the development of integrated, competency-based social work practice:

◆ *Knowledge that informs the social worker about the client*: Psychology, sociology, social problems, social policy, and antidiscrimination

◆ *Knowledge that helps the worker plan appropriate intervention*: Social work practice theory and models of intervention, methods of social work intervention, and processes involved in social work intervention.

◆ *Knowledge that clarifies the worker's understanding of the legal, policy, procedural, and organizational context in which his practice occurs*: Federal, state, and local public legislation; social welfare policy and procedures; and organizational contexts (Vass, 1996).

Values and Ethics

Values and ethics are the third critical component of social work practice. At the start of your social work education, perhaps during the application procedure itself, you were probably introduced to our professional Code of Ethics. This document can be called an "ought to" guide: it specifies how social workers ought to conduct themselves and their helping activities in the professional setting. We cannot emphasize too much of the importance of becoming familiar with this code from the very start of your career and learning how it will apply to your practice activities.

Activity...As a class or by yourself look at the NASW Code of Ethics, in appendix A, and think about how it will shape your practice experiences. Which parts of the code do you find comforting and compatible with your beliefs? Which parts are more difficult for you to understand or support?

All professionals embrace specific values. Although social work values are spelled out in a number of documents, the primary reference for the profession's value base is the NASW Code of Ethics (reproduced in appendix A). The code establishes a set of clear beliefs that define ethical social work practice and thus act as a unifying force among all social workers. The way we work with and on behalf of others, how we view social issues, and the remedies we consider for individual, group, or community ills are all firmly rooted in our value base. Reamer (1995, p. 894) identified the following core values for the social work profession:

◆ Individual worth and dignity of people
◆ Respect for people
◆ People's capacity for change
◆ Client's right to self-determination
◆ Client's right to confidentiality and privacy
◆ People's right to opportunities to realize their own potential
◆ Social change
◆ People's right to adequate resources and services to meet basic needs
◆ Client empowerment
◆ Equal opportunity
◆ Antidiscrimination
◆ Diversity
◆ Willingness to transmit professional knowledge and skills to others

As you read the code and consider Reamer's points, several common themes begin to emerge, but let's look at three in particular.

First, all people, no matter who they are or what their circumstances, should be treated with respect and civility. Respect and civility are cornerstones of a just society. We show respect in any number of ways: being on time for appointments, and apologizing to clients when we're late; calling people Mr. or Ms. until they ask us to do otherwise; listening to others without interruption, and without looking at our watches during interviews.

Second, when given the opportunity, people have the ability to participate in solving their own problems. We understand that not all people can participate fully in such processes, but we also recognize that everyone should be encouraged to participate as much as possible. We support client participation when we help them to figure out ways to identify and deal with their problems; we do not say, "If I were you, I would. . ." Clients have strengths, and we must help them to discover and use these strengths as energy sources for change.

Third, although it's not stated explicitly in the code or among Reamer's points, we can infer the basic principle that we do no harm to people. Our work is to help not harm. We cannot hold back any effort if we believe it will help our clients.

As you become more familiar with the Code of Ethics, compare it with other value statements, such as that of the International Federation of Social Workers (appendix B). What similarities do you find? The words and phrases may be different, but the respect for the human condition and the goal of social change are the same.

As professionals, social workers must pursue the art of helping within a context shaped by values and ethics. Practice that is not guided by values or ethics has no meaning because such practice will fail to recognize the unique circumstances of our clients, their individual needs, and appropriate change strategies. Unless we operate within an ethical framework our clients might as well be telling their problems to a computer!

DIFFERENTIATING BETWEEN GENERALIST AND SPECIALIST SOCIAL WORK PRACTICE

Social work practice is organized around two principal conceptual models, the generalist and the specialist. Generalist social work is more broadly defined and targeted toward a wider variety of clients and problem areas. Specialist social work is more narrowly defined with a sharper focus on specific issues or a particular client population.

Generalist Practice

Landon (1995) has asserted that regardless of how hard the profession has tried, there still is no completely agreed upon definition of generalist practice—although, he did believe consensus existed on key elements of the definition. First, most professional social workers agree that generalist social work practice is primarily reserved for BSW social workers, although a few graduate programs now offer a specialization reflective of additional course work in the area of advanced generalist practice. Second, generalist social workers are prepared for entry-level social work practice. Last, in generalist practice social workers most often apply some type of "systems approach" to professional practice and subsequent intervention. According to the *Social Work Dictionary* a social work generalist is a practitioner "whose knowledge and skill encompasses a broad spectrum and who assesses problems and their solutions comprehensively" (Barker, 1991, p. 91).

The broad-based generalist approach to social work practice integrates the client's needs with those of the environment. In accepting the importance of the person-in-situation social workers are leaders in understanding and interpreting the interaction between behavioral, psychological, and social factors in the client's condition with environmental factors that the client faces daily.

Generalist social work follows a multilevel integrated process for addressing the interplay between personal and collective issues applying it to a variety of human systems, such as societies, communities, neighborhoods, complex organizations, and formal groups, as well as individuals and families (Miley, O'Melia, & Dubois, 1998). According to Miley, O'Melia, and Dubois (1998) generalist practice depends on four major principles. First, generalist practice recognizes the importance of human behavior and the connection between this behavior and the social and physical environments that surround each human being. Second, generalist practice understands that changes in the client's environment must include changes in systems interactions to better the environment for all affected. Third, generalist practice works at every level of a system to assist in bringing about needed changes. Last, generalist practice assists in macropractice while also conducting research on the efficacy and effectiveness of the approaches that are used.

Specialist Practice

The specialist social worker provides a more focused, higher level of intervention. A specialist always possesses an MSW degree and is prepared for advanced social work practice. According to the *Social Work Dictionary* a specialization is "a profession's focus of knowledge and skill on a specific type of problem, target population, or objective" (Barker, 1991, p. 225). Social work specializations have developed in a number of ways over the years. One comprehensive scheme categorizes the various social work specializations into eight different types:

Models
◆ *Methods*: casework, group work, community organization
◆ *Fields of practice*: school, health care, occupational social work
◆ *Population groups*: children, adolescents, and elderly people
◆ *Problem areas*: mental health, alcohol and drug abuse, corrections, mental retardation

Specific Factors

- *Geographic areas*: urban, rural, neighborhoods
- *Sizes of target*: individual (micro), family group (mezzo), and community (macro)
- *Specific treatment modalities*: behavior modification, ego psychology, Gestalt therapy, cognitive therapy
- *Advanced generalist* (Hopps & Collins, 1995, p. 273)

After an extended period of MSW practice, the specialist worker is eligible for independent practice. Through state licensing laws for practice (see chapter 15 for a fuller discussion of licensing and regulation of social work practice) and professional practice certifications the MSW practitioner can move into private practice or practice independently within the agency context.

Social work is one of the most diverse fields of practice imaginable. Specialist social workers are found in numerous settings: public and private agencies, public and private hospitals, clinics, schools, extended care facilities, private practice, private business, police departments, courts, and countless other workplaces, too numerous to name. But the multiplicity of practice specializations has created a major weakness, a professional Achilles' heel if you may. Meyer (1976) said it best when she wrote, "[Whereas] other professional specialists become expert by narrowing their parameters, social workers have had to increase theirs." This diversity in practice and settings makes it difficult for the broader community to understand what social workers do. And given the wide range of our specializations, any attempt to reduce or narrow our efforts will, as Hopps and Collins (1995) suggested, create tension, conflict, and fragmentation within the profession.

In summary, generalist and specialist social workers have different focuses. Specialization of social work practice usually occurs at the master's level. Specialist social workers are all first trained in the generalist approach to practice and later embark on more specialized career tracks by choosing more concentrated areas in which to apply their skills. It is also in specialization that many professional educators believe "real" training as counseling professionals and therapists occurs. MSW social workers with supervised experience (and certification or licensure) are usually free to engage in full non–clinically supervised counseling activities. In the field of social work, the master's degree is generally considered the terminal practice degree. For those studying at the doctorate (DSW or Ph.D.) level the focus is on research or science rather than clinical practice.

THE EMERGENCE OF EMPIRICALLY BASED SOCIAL WORK PRACTICE

It is safe to say that the public expects high-quality service and "state of the art" care (Shortell & Kaluzny, 1994). Whether we pay for services directly through out-of-pocket costs or indirectly with our tax dollars, we want to receive the best services possible. These expectations extend to social workers, and indeed, the profes-

Name: Janina Henson-Dinio
Place of residence: Kitsap County, Washington
College/university degrees: B.A. in Journalism, St.
Theresa's College; M.S.W., University of Washington
Present position: Therapist, Case Manager,
Consultant/Minority Mental Health Specialist
Previous work/volunteer experience: Public Relations,
Advertising and Training Manager, International Corporate Bank; teacher of Spanish and journalism; writer
for local newspaper

Why did you choose social work as a career? I had always been sensitive to the need
to help and provide human services. As an activist in my country of origin—the
Philippines—I was part of a group that sought to address social inequity. When I
emigrated to the United States, I saw that the need to serve minority communities is just as great here. Even today, many services available to mainstream
communities are not accessed by minority communities owing to lack of information and to language and cultural barriers. I see my role in the community as
being a conduit of information from minority communities to professional and
volunteer service providers and vice versa.

What is your favorite social work story? On many occasions, I have thought of going
back to journalism due to the pressures of changing state and federal contract
requirements and the unrelenting pace of change. At these times, I hesitated
from taking that crucial step when people stopped me on the street and thanked
me for the support and assistance I had provided them in a time of need. This
"psychic income" compensates for a lot of the aggravation associated with clinical social work in the community mental health setting.

*What would be the one thing you would change in our community if you had the power to
do so?* I have been in the helping profession for less than a decade. For social
workers to survive stress and burnout, I would implement true outcome-based
practice and decrease regulations. If bureaucrats are truly to manage by outcomes, social workers must be given the leeway to develop the objectives and
programs necessary to achieve desired outcomes, guided by quality and service
norms rather than regulations.

sion itself expects all services and activities performed on behalf of clients to be of the highest quality. Yet how do we demonstrate to the public that our activities are effective?

Social workers have historically been accused of avoiding the use of empirical techniques to establish practice efficiency and effectiveness. As we move into an era of professional accountability and client rights, however, all this has changed. Challenges made to the profession to prove service effectiveness and ensure that interventions are germane to client issues are being embraced.

The challenge to tie empirical research and evaluation to practice is not new. For example, in 1976 Fischer wrote the following:

> It seems to be difficult to avoid the conclusion that unless major changes are made in the practice methods—and hence, the effectiveness—of casework, our field, if not the entire profession of social work, cannot long survive. Indeed, unless such changes are made, it is not clear that as a field, we deserve to survive. On one hand, we have the option of choosing—and building—a new revitalized future for social casework, one rooted in the superordinate principle that our primary if not our sole allegiance is to serve our clients with demonstrable effectiveness. On the other hand, we can continue our outmoded practices, denigrate and resist new approaches to practice, and bury our collective heads in the sand when confronted with the vaguest hint of a threat that we may not be doing all in our power to provide effective services. (p. 310)

The new revitalized casework that Fischer envisaged is today called **empirically based social work practice**. All social workers, generalist and specialist alike, are expected to apply its principles to their activities. The *Social Work Dictionary* defines empirically based social work practice as "a type of intervention in which the professional social worker uses research as a practice and problem-solving tool; collects data systematically to monitor the intervention; specifies problems, techniques, and outcomes in measurable terms; and systematically evaluates the effectiveness of the intervention used" (Barker, 1991, p. 119).

For the beginning social work professional, it is important to understand that in empirically based social work practice, the application of clear-cut research and evaluation models is guided by four broad ideas. First, research findings must be relevant to practice by assessing the change in a client's level of effectiveness after a specific intervention directed at a specific problem. Second, applications, practice and evaluation models, and findings are to be drawn from research reports. Third, research findings are to be disseminated so that the results are known in the practice community. Finally, other social work professionals should be able to interpret, understand, and apply what they read to what they do. Empirically based practice mandates that in developing a practice intervention with a client, the practitioner must include systematic research activities that will provide feedback on the intervention's effectiveness and may give additional information on how the client's ability to resolve the problem can be strengthened.

Box 2: Social Work Process

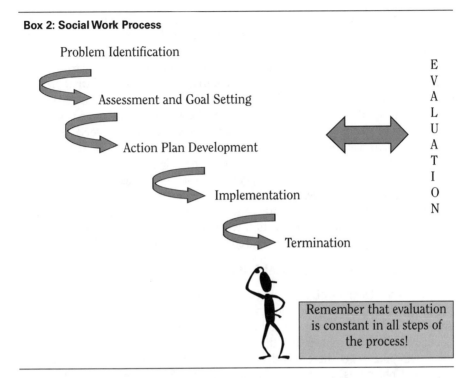

Problem Identification

Assessment and Goal Setting

Action Plan Development

Implementation

Termination

E
V
A
L
U
A
T
I
O
N

Remember that evaluation is constant in all steps of the process!

THE STEPS IN PROFESSIONAL HELPING

Work with clients in social work practice has five steps. These are illustrated in box 2. Note that evaluation is not a distinct step but rather takes place throughout all steps of the social work process.

Step 1: Problem Identification

The first step involves problem identification. The social worker helps the client to identify and concretely define the problem(s) to be addressed by the intervention process. The client's problems are discussed thoroughly, and the client is made aware that the social worker is serious and dedicated in his efforts to help. It is in this initial step of the helping process that the social worker establishes the rapport that will characterize the remainder of the practice experience. A working alliance is developed that allows the client to begin to feel comfortable yet eager to embark on changes. The practitioner avoids simply giving advice to the client.

The social worker is a professional who at all times remains objective in educating, advocating, facilitating, and intervening on behalf of the client. Moreover, as ironic as it may sound, the social worker always begins to plan for termination of the practice encounter early. In fact, as will be explained in chapter 6, termination should be discussed and decided in the first session. The client is thus well aware of what is coming and what needs to be accomplished by the end of the therapeutic term.

At the end of each session or meeting the technique of "summarization" is used. The client is asked to state what was covered in the session and what progress was made in regard to the identified goals and objectives. Never summarize the session content for the client: it should always be done in the client's own words. Letting the client state what he or she got from the session helps the social worker to determine what really was accomplished and whether both client and social worker are aiming toward the same intervention outcomes.

It is also during this initial step that the social worker decides how accountability or practice effectiveness will be evaluated after the intervention is completed. Exactly what will be measured, and how, varies from case to case. No "magic pill" ensures empirically based practice. We hope, however, that knowing its importance piques your interest in the research course you have yet to take.

Step 2: Assessment and Goal Setting

The second step involves helping the client to set goals and objectives that can be accomplished. Worker and client assess the client's need for assistance and how specifically the problem can be addressed. The "goal" is the overall end that the client wants to accomplish and the "objectives" are the concrete steps that the client will take to get there and that allow measurement of the outcome. Setting goals and objectives, when done adequately, has the following valuable consequences:

- ◆ Ensures that worker and client agree on intervention focus and purpose
- ◆ Provides to the client on how to address the problem, while providing a basis for continuity of session content across the intervention process
- ◆ Provides a basis for selecting appropriate treatment strategies
- ◆ Assists the social worker to structure session content and monitor progress of the intervention
- ◆ Gives outcome criteria (the objectives) for measurement of intervention effectiveness

When setting goals and objectives the following always apply. First, the goal and objectives must relate to what the client wants to achieve at the end of the intervention. Second, the goals and objectives must be defined in explicit terms so that the client knows what is expected of him or her. Third, the objectives must be feasible. Clients must believe they can succeed in the process, otherwise they may become disheartened and drop out of the intervention process. Fourth, the goals and objectives must be consistent with the skills and abilities of the helping professional. Social workers should never try to address medical problems that they know little about. For example, if the social worker does become unsure of her abilities, supervision, consultation, and continuing education options should be explored before the social worker goes any further in the intervention process.

Ensuring quality of services in this way is important for the client and the social worker.

Fifth, whenever possible, goals and objectives should be stated in positive rather than negative terms. Sixth, all goals should be mutually negotiated with the client; however, if you have reservations about a goal or objective you must say so. Clients need your input in their decision making. Be sure, though, that your hesitation reflects concern for the client's good and not your own personal bias.

Step 3: Action Plan Development

Once goals and objectives have been clearly identified, the social worker helps the client to develop a plan of action. The role of the social worker is paramount in identifying strategies for action and change. The worker may be able to provide the direct supervision or consultation necessary to implement the plan. Often, however, the social worker does not have the required expertise—he may be a generalist when a specialist is needed—and will contract with another provider or use work strategies to assist the client in meeting the objectives.

The action plan may include one task or a series of tasks. Each task is specific and clear and supported by a time frame to be monitored by both worker and client. Each task builds on previous efforts, and together they lead to the goals and objectives identified. As with goal setting, each task must be understood by both client and worker and, most important, must be within the client's ability to achieve.

Every action plan must have clearly established contingency plans. These plans specify what the rewards will be for completion of the practice strategy agreement and what the consequences will be for noncompliance. Clients must participate in this part of the change process because they will be the ones who must accept the consequences of their action or inaction.

Step 4: Implementation

Implementation takes place when the client is ready to put the plan into action. During implementation, the worker and client together monitor the client's progress; this activity is part of the evaluation that is the empirical side of our practice.

Through monitoring, worker and client are able to assess progress toward the goal, judge the effectiveness of the intervention and/or tasks, examine the client's reactions to the progress or lack thereof, and enhance motivation (Hepworth & Larsen, 1986). Ongoing monitoring also allows worker and client to identify barriers as well as strengths in the process. New strategies can be built to overcome or cope with the barriers. And most important, monitoring provides the client with feedback on positive experiences that in turn reinforce the change efforts.

Implementing an action plan can be intimidating for a beginning social worker. Social work practice knowledge is essential because the social worker will be expected to use multiple practice strategies to assist the client. These can involve the application of planned skills such as modeling, behavioral rehearsal, role playing or simply the use of paper-and-pencil exercises in which the client writes down feelings experienced as well as steps to be completed in the action plan. Referrals for additional help and assistance should also be considered and discussed at this time—for example, additional individual therapy, group therapy, couples therapy, or family therapy.

Step 5: Termination

The last step in the social work process involves termination. Client and social worker end their working relationship and describe how any change strategy that has been developed will be continued. Many clients realize at termination that they want additional help. If this happens, the social worker informs the client of options for continued intervention and emotional growth by giving appropriate referrals. Referrals for group therapy, individual growth-directed therapy, couples therapy, and family therapy can be considered.

Evaluation and Follow-Up

Successful practice intervention achieves significant changes in a client's levels of functioning and coping. Measures that can substantiate these changes are essential to empirically based practice. Measuring intervention effectiveness can be as simple as making a follow-up phone call to discuss how things are going, or as structured as scoring the client's behavior on a standardized scale at the beginning of treatment and at the end and then comparing the two. Scales that measure depression, trauma, and so forth, are readily available. If more advanced methods of measuring practice effectiveness are expected, more advanced training and planning are warranted.

Planned practice evaluation and follow-up at the termination of intervention is essential, but these are steps that have historically been forgotten. As a matter of fact, when you consider the five steps in the social work process, research and evaluation seem to be missing. And if these are missing, how does the process we've outlined lead to empirically based social work practice? In fact, they're not missing—it's simply that they're not a *separate* step: research and evaluation should be included at each step of the helping process.

PRACTICE APPLICATION: THE ROLE OF THE MEDICAL SOCIAL WORKER

Ms. Martha Edda had been living with her family for approximately a year. Before then she had lived independently in her own apartment. Ms. Edda had to leave her apartment after a neighbor found her unconscious. The apartment was unsafe, with rotted food, urine, and feces throughout. Upon discovery, Ms. Edda was immediately admitted to the hospital. Originally, she was believed to have had a stroke; later she was formally diagnosed with a neurological condition called "vascular dementia." Doctors believed that she was in the moderate to advanced stage of this condition because Ms. Edda, at age 62, had pronounced movement and memory difficulties.

An elderly man leaves a rural West Virginia home after a visit from a home healthcare worker. In many such rural areas there is a shortage of physicians and medical facilities.

After discussion with the hospital social worker, it became obvious that Ms. Edda needed a supervised living arrangement. Joan, Ms. Edda's daughter, admitted how guilty she felt about what had happened to her mother, but she did not feel she could handle her mother at home. The social worker reminded Joan that the family would be able to benefit from Ms. Edda's receiving services from a home health care agency and that a community daycare program could be explored. After convincing her family to give it a try, Joan took her mother home.

Once in Joan's home, Ms. Edda did receive home health care services. However, much to her daughter's surprise all services stopped after just two months because Ms. Edda's physical therapy was discontinued. Joan relied heavily on these services, particularly the nurse's aide who helped to give Ms. Edda a bath. Ms. Edda weighed 170 pounds and could not help in getting herself into or out of the tub. Joan recruited the help of her husband, who reluctantly agreed. Unfortunately, Ms. Edda could not get into the adult daycare center in the area because no spaces were available. She was placed on a waiting list. Ms. Edda required help with all of her activities of daily living, and her daughter was afraid to leave her at home alone during the day. So Joan quit her job to help care for her.

On the morning of January 12, Joan found her mother lying face down in her bed. She had become incontinent of bowel and bladder, she was unable to speak, and the features appeared distorted on the left side of her face. When Joan could not rouse her mother she panicked and called an ambulance. Ms. Edda was immediately transported to the emergency room.

In the emergency room, the staff began to run numerous tests to see if Ms. Edda had had another stroke. Plans were made to admit her to the hospital, but no beds were available. Because Ms. Edda needed supervised monitoring and a hospital bed might become available in the morning, an agreement was made to keep her in the emergency room overnight. In the morning she was admitted to the inpatient hospital. While in the hospital Ms. Edda remained incontinent and refused to eat. She was so confused that the nurses feared she would get out of bed and hurt herself, so she was placed in restraints for periods throughout the day.

After two days most of the medical tests had been run and were determined to be negative, and Ms. Edda's vital signs remained stable. The physician felt that her admission to the hospital could no longer be justified, and the social worker was notified of the pending discharge. On placing the call to prepare Ms. Edda's family for her return home the social worker was told that the family would not accept her and that they wanted her placed in a nursing home. The social worker was concerned about this decision because she knew that Ms. Edda did not have private insurance to cover a nursing home stay and she was too young to be eligible for Medicare. This meant that an application for Medicaid would have to be made. This state-funded program had a lower reimbursement rate, and most privately run nursing homes drastically limited the number of Medicaid clients they would accept. After calling around the social worker was told that no beds were available.

When the social worker explained her discharge problem to the physician, he simply stated, "I am under pressure to get her out, and there is no medical reason for her to be here. Discharge her home today." Since it was after 4:00 P.M. and the administrative offices had closed for the day, the social worker planned to try to secure an out-of-area placement the following day.

When the physician returned at 6:00 P.M., he wanted to know why the client has not been discharged. The nurse on duty explained that a nursing home bed could not be found. The physician became angry and wrote an order for immediate discharge. The nurse called Ms. Edda's family at 6:30 P.M. and told them about the discharge. Ms. Edda's family was angry and asked why she was not being placed in a nursing home. The nurse explained to the family that discharge orders had been written and she was only trying to do her job. Ms. Edda's daughter insisted on speaking to the discharge physician prior to picking up her mother. A message was left for him, and at 8:00 P.M. her call was returned. The physician sounded frustrated when he told Joan that all medical emergencies had been addressed and Ms. Edda had to leave the hospital immediately. Ms. Edda's daughter became furious and yelled, "If she is still incontinent and in restraints, how do you expect me to handle her?" Hearing how upset Joan was, the physician softened his voice and said, "I will put the nurse on the phone to update you on her condition. In addition, the social worker will call you in the morning to arrange home health care services."

When Ms. Edda's daughter arrived at the hospital, her mother was hooked to an IV, wearing a diaper, and still in restraints. Pleased to see a member of Ms. Edda's family the nurse sent for a wheelchair, unhooked the intravenous tubing, removed the restraints, and helped place Ms. Edda in the wheelchair for transport to the family's car.

Discussion: Unfortunately, situations like this one continue to exist. This case example is a true depiction of events. The social worker was responsible for discharge planning, but many other issues needed to be addressed to best serve the client and her family. With perseverance, and the help of the hospital social worker

Joan was eventually (several months later) able to place her mother in a nursing home. However, the strain on Joan was so great that she ended up asking to be placed on medication to combat depression. Joan also began to fight with her husband and children over numerous issues related to the time required for her mother's care and the loss of the second source of family income. As in most American families, her earnings were used not only to supplement basic needs (rent, food, etc.) but also to pay for family luxuries (movies, eating out, etc.). It is clear that in such situations the price of the "cost effective" managed care strategy far exceeded the dollar value placed on it: the client and her family became silent victims. The role of the social worker—officially labeled a "discharge planner"—is involved considerably more than just finding a place for the client to go. Referrals, counseling, and openness to service flexibility make the social work professional an invaluable member of any interdisciplinary team. (Case scenario is adopted from Dziegielewski, 1998)

DIVERSITY TOPIC: SOCIAL WORK PRACTICE WITH SEXUAL MINORITIES

Several issues are common to practice with gay men and lesbians. Before discussing these issues, however, we emphasize that most problems confronting these groups are no different from those experienced by heterosexuals. Furthermore, a person with a nonheterosexual orientation is not necessarily seeking help with difficulties related to sexual orientation. Nonjudgmental assessments can assist in identifying the exact nature of the client's concerns. Some clients may prefer to be helped by competent gay or lesbian professionals, and such requests should be respected whenever possible.

Personal and Social Acceptance

One practice issue that may be unique to gay male and lesbian clients is the personal and social acceptance involved in admitting to themselves and others that they are attracted to people of the same sex. This can be a very confusing and upsetting time. Although this identity confusion often begins in adolescence or early adulthood, it can occur at any age (Berger, 1986). Moreover, acknowledging such feelings can be problematic because they are often viewed as violating accepted beliefs. The client is thus more susceptible to alienation from family and friends. Indeed, antihomosexual messages often come from parents, peers, and the community. Such messages can affect an individual's self-concept and self-esteem, and the choice to accept this stigmatized role can be difficult.

Just as homophobia may be manifested in people who surround the nonheterosexual, the individual can also internalize it. Internalized homophobia can cause gay men or lesbians to hate or resent themselves, to feeling inferior to their heterosexual friends. They may become frightened of what they feel and wonder how they can fit into society. These feelings can be confusing and may result in their denying, hiding, or justifying their nonheterosexual preferences (Nichols, 1989). Berger (1986) suggested that for intervention to be effective a task-centered approach should be employed. In this approach, clients must accomplish certain tasks, such as learning how to manage information about themselves and deriving support from peers. Performing such tasks can help clients to gain self-acceptance. Berger (1986) warned, however, that in discovering and accepting themselves, many people pass through a militant phase characterized by a need to assert their homosexuality. This phase is a normal part of the adjustment process and should not be viewed as a pathological state. When acceptance by significant others is an issue, practitioners should consider the following questions: 1) How much information about self-identity and sexual preference should be released? 2) How should this information be conveyed to the client's parents, family, friends, heterosexual peers, and employers?

Family Structure and Patterns

A second practice issue concerns family structure and patterns. Although many gay men and lesbians establish and maintain satisfying long-term relationships (McWhirter & Mattison, 1984; Hyde, 1990), the factors that keep heterosexual couples together do not always apply to nonheterosexual couples. For example, nonheterosexual couples generally differ from heterosexual couples in that their relationships tend to be nonmonogamous (Nichols, 1989; Kelly, 1990). Nonheterosexual couples may also change partners more often than their heterosexual counterparts; in the homosexual culture, this behavior is usually viewed as acceptable. A second difference is financial. Partners in nonheterosexual couples tend to be financially independent. The incentive to stay together for purely financial reasons rarely exists. A third difference is that nonheterosexual couples less often have children living in the home. Therefore, relationships are not maintained for the sake of the children. Often, it is easier to let go of a relationship than to address the family and social prejudices that such an unconventional relationship attracts. Therefore, nonheterosexual couples may benefit greatly from couples counseling or group couples counseling focused on increasing communication skills, a critical issue.

Socialization

A third practice issue concerns socialization for nonheterosexual couples, in particular, the fact that many nonheterosexual couples (especially gay men) use gay bars as a social outlet (Nichols, 1989; Kelly, 1990; DiNitto & McNeece, 1990). These bars serve a variety of needs that might be met for heterosexual couples through church affiliation, community centers, and country clubs. Although many gays have formed their own churches and community groups (Hyde, 1990), the gay bar is still the primary venue of socialization (DiNitto & McNeece, 1990). Therefore, leisure time in the lifestyles of many gays is spent in a drinking milieu. This environment is not a healthy one for developing long or satisfying relationships (DiNitto & McNeece, 1990). Research has been limited on substance abuse by gay men and lesbians, and this is an area that needs attention and research.

The role of social workers is twofold: 1) to initiate and support further research in the area of alcohol consumption and its relation to the substance treatment offered to this population and 2) to become aware of and suggest alternative means of homosexual socialization. Some alternatives to bars include Alcoholics Anonymous (AA) groups (some of which are specifically offered to gay individuals) and groups and organizations (social and religious) dedicated to supporting the gay movement. Many of these activities and services available to the gay community are advertised in publications designed for gay men and lesbians and in local newspapers.

AIDS

Acquired immune deficiency syndrome (AIDS) remains a tremendous issue in the gay community. When society first acknowledged the disease it was termed gay-related immune deficiency (GRID), because it was believed that only homosexuals could contract it (Stulberg & Smith, 1988). Sexually active gay men and bisexual men are still the largest group of individuals at risk for AIDS. Society's attempt to make AIDS a problem belonging solely to homosexuals has helped to increase both the level of homophobia in general and the anxiety, fear, and doubt experienced by gay men themselves. The internalization of homophobic feelings in regard to the disease has become more prominent (Kreiger, 1988). Just as society has blamed the homosexual, the homosexual may blame himself or herself. In the past, frequent impersonal sexual contacts allowed gay men to avoid exploring their feelings. With fewer, more consistent relationships, intimacy between partners becomes very important, and this new role can produce anxiety. The role of the therapist is crucial in supportive counseling and education of gay men about the disease, its transmission, and safe sex practices.

The treatment effectiveness of a counseling-education approach to preventing AIDS transmission was measured by a team of AIDS researchers in Sydney, Australia (Muhall, 1990). This team took one hundred asymptomatic homosexual men and tracked them from 1983 through 1990. Muhall (1990) stated that he and his research associates believed that their intervention might have stopped the spread of AIDS into the research group. According to the researchers, a highly significant decrease in the number of sexual partners among group members was reported. A decline in the frequency of unsafe sex practices, with increased use of condoms, was also evidenced. The researchers concluded that the counseling and education of homosexual men had reduced their use of sexual practices that were thought to be unsafe.

Both Puckett and Bye (1987) and the AIDS researchers in Australia have argued that education is a powerful tool in changing sex-related behavior. In support of this contention, Flowers, Miller, Smith, and Booraem (1994) reported positive responses by 771 gay and bisexual men to single-session STOP AIDS discussion groups. This study found a significant increase in reported belief in personal efficacy in controlling the spread of the HIV virus and intended safer sex practices after just one single-session intervention.

Haney (1988) believed that psychological support at the time of diagnosis was extremely important in "preventing reactions of fear and anger from being transformed into self-destruction" (p. 251). The bleak prognosis for disease sufferers can complicate their adjustment, and they may have the following reactions: suicidal ideation or intent, denial of the disease, anger, hostility, frustration, and depression. Each of these feelings and emotions must be treated as a normal part of the acceptance process, and dysfunctional degrees of such feelings must be treated on an individual basis.

Haney (1988) suggested that we change the mindset of the professional community in dealing with the patient—from preparing him for death, to preparing him for life. This can be accomplished in part by decreasing negative talk. For example, instead of saying "There is nothing we can do" and "You have so many months to live," focus on the possibilities of living. Concrete problem-solving skills are essential; focus on what can and cannot be done. Kreiger (1988) suggested the following stepwise approach used to helping people to understand and cope with the sexual transmission of AIDS: 1) dispense accurate information about the condition and transmission of AIDS, 2) assess the client's fear of prior exposure, 3) help the client to learn to protect self and others, 4) assess support systems and encourage the building of support network, and 5) address related issues and fears as they apply.

In summary, it is important to stress that those afflicted with AIDS had lives before diagnosis, and they continue to live after it. The goal of the social worker is to work with clients to improve the quality of their lives in the here and now. Social workers who work with gay men and lesbians need to be aware of the psychosocial effects that AIDS can have on the gay community. Social workers also need to promote and support groups, policies, and programs that combat AIDS-related discrimination against the gay community (Stulberg & Smith, 1988).

Overall, social workers must be knowledgeable about and nonjudgmental toward gay men and lesbians (Kelly, 1990; Hyde, 1990; Falco, 1991). As products of society, most of us have been socialized into stereotypical and prejudicial behaviors that we must now identify and work to eliminate. Identifying how our traditional beliefs and values (what we believe to be right and wrong) affect us is not an easy task. Homophobic behavior needs to be viewed in the same context as any other prejudice against a particular minority group—women, blacks, and so forth. The social worker must first educate himself or herself on the subject, for example, by reading the professional literature and attending workshops, inservices, and seminars that cover nonheterosexual behavior in general and homophobic reactions in particular. Such education should review myths and realities, lifestyle issues, sexual practices, parenting, religious concerns, health issues, and specific counseling about communicable diseases. In treating AIDS victims in particular, Grossman and Silverstein (1993) have suggested a support group format for the professional health care worker. Here workers can be helped to relieve their stress and burnout when dealing with their own emotional reactions or frustrations.

Social workers should also be involved in educating others, including other mental health professionals. Martin and Lyon (1984) have documented that some male therapists subscribe to the myth that all a lesbian really needs is a good heterosexual experience with a man. Others may use homosexual-based jokes and stories for entertainment. Such behavior must be discouraged; humor at the expense of others is neither funny nor professionally responsible.

Some gay, lesbian, and bisexual individuals may be reluctant to disclose their lifestyle preference to the helping professional. For example, research has shown that lesbians are less likely than primarily heterosexual women to disclose their sexual orientation (Cochran & Mays, 1988). Such reservations make it essential that the client feel comfortable with the social worker. As noted earlier, some homosexual individuals may prefer a homosexual therapist to a heterosexual one because they do not have to explain as much of what they are experiencing or feeling to someone with a similar orientation. When clients express such preferences it is important to refer them, if possible, to the treatment they are requesting.

Social workers must also become familiar with resources in the gay and lesbian communities. For example, a client once came into the office and stated that he was ready to come out; however, he could no longer attend his regular church and he did not want his only social contacts to be provided by the local gay bar. The social worker knew what churches would accept gay men and the phone number and contact person for a local gay men's support group, to the client's great relief. Social workers must know what resources are available in order to perform the roles of educator, counselor, advocate, and broker that are all part of our social work domain.

Social workers in practice with gay men and lesbians must not adhere to the sickness or mental illness theory that has been maintained for years. According to Gonsiorek (1982), researchers in the 1960s and 1970s gathered overwhelming evidence that homosexuality is not related to psychopathology or psychological maladjustment. This does not mean, however, that gay men and lesbians have no problems, only that their problems many times are similar to those experienced by heterosexuals. Like everyone, gay men and lesbians also have unique problems that make knowledge of their lifestyles of paramount importance for social workers. Sexual identity problems can include fears and repercussions of coming out (Gramick, 1983), denial and suppression of homosexual erotic fantasies (Storms, 1980), and changing roles in midstream from a heterosexual family system to a homosexual one. Proctor and Groze (1994) have further reminded practitioners that many gay, lesbian, and bisexual adolescents and young adults have suicidal feelings that they attribute to issues of sexual identity. These are only a few examples of the unique problems that can originate in this group.

Do not pity or try to change sexual orientation. Sexual orientation belongs to the person as his or her own right and responsibility. Your role is not merely to help clients adjust to their problems. Your role as social worker is to help clients identify their problems, establish plans of action to address them, and provide support and guidance as they work through the process. At all times, social work practitioners must adhere to the highest ethical and moral standards. These include the client's right of self-determination and respect and support for whatever sexual preference a client chooses (Wyers, 1987). Being a gay man, a lesbian, or a bisexual in a homophobic society is a heavy burden for even the strongest person. What better goal for social workers than to support this unnecessarily stigmatized group?

SUMMARY

Social work practice evolved from mid-eighteenth- and nineteenth-century efforts to assist the poor. In those early years activities were carried out by volunteers, with few organizational supports and limited training if any. Today the profession has a well-established knowledge base, a clearly articulated value orientation, and diverse practice methodologies and interventions, all of which are transmitted to the new practitioner through formal educational processes.

The practice of social work is generally conducted in one of two major frameworks: the generalist and the specialist. That the profession has both members who can work with a wide range of clients and members who can focus more sharply on particular groups of clients is our greatest strength. This is the reason we find social workers in so many different types of social agencies and organizational settings.

Social work practice has never been static. It has evolved dramatically since its beginnings, and it will continue to change in the future. To grow and adapt, practice must be conducted within a systematic, well-thought-out process that allows both the use and the production of scientifically tested knowledge and skills and that is founded on a clear, coherent set of professional values.

References

Barker, R. L. (1991). *The social work dictionary* (2nd ed.). Washington, DC: NASW Press.

Berger, R. (1986). Gay men. In H. Gochros, J. Gochros, & J. Fischer (Eds.), *Helping the sexually oppressed* (pp. 162–180). Englewood Cliffs, NJ: Prentice-Hall.

Boehm W. (Ed.) in Council on Social Work Education. (1959). *Social Work Curriculum Study,* (Vol. 1). Washington, D.C.: author.

Cochran, S. D., and Mays, V. M. (1988). Disclosure of sexual preference to physicians by black lesbian and bisexual women. *Western Journal of Medicine, 149* (5), 616–619.

DiNitto, D. M., & McNeece, C. A. (1990). *Social work: Issues and opportunities in a challenging profession.* Englewood Cliffs, NJ: Prentice-Hall.

Dziegielewski, S. F. (1998). *The changing face of health care practice: Professional practice in the era of managed care.* New York: Springer.

Falco, K. L. (1991). *Psychotherapy with lesbian clients.* New York: Brunner/Mazel.

Fischer, J. (1976). *Effective casework practice: An eclectic approach.* New York: McGraw-Hill.

Flowers, J. V., Miller, T. E., Smith, N., & Booraem, D. C. (1994, April). The repeatability of a single-session group to promote safe sex behavior in a male at-risk population. *Research on Social Work Practice, 4* (2), 240–247.

Gonsiorek, J. C. (1982). Results of psychological testing on homosexual populations. In W. Paul, J. D. Weinrich, J. C. Gonsiorek, & M. E. Hotvedt (Eds.), *Homosexuality: Social, psychological and biological issues.* Beverly Hills, CA: Sage.

Gramick, J. (1983). Homophobia: A new challenge. *Social Work, 28*, 137–141.

Grossman, A. H., & Silverstein, C. (1993, March). Facilitating support group for professionals working with people with AIDS. *Social Work, 38* (2), 144–151.

Haney, P. (1988). Providing empowerment to the person with AIDS. *Social Work, 33* (3), 251–253.

Hepworth, D., & Larsen, J. A. (1986). *Direct social work practice: Theory and skills* (2nd ed.). Chicago: Dorsey.

Hopps, J. G., & Collins, P. M. (1995). Social work profession overview. In R. Edwards et al. (Eds.), *Encyclopedia of social work* (19th ed., pp. 2266–2282). Washington, DC: NASW Press.

Hyde, J. (1990). *Understanding human sexuality*. New York: McGraw-Hill.

Kelly, G. (1990). *Sexuality today: The human perspective*. New York: Duskin.

Kreiger, I. (1988). An approach to coping with anxiety about AIDS. *Social Work, 33*, 263–264.

Landon, P. S. (1995). Generalist and advanced social work practice. In R. Edwards et al. (Eds.), *Encyclopedia of social work* (19th ed., pp. 1101–1108). Washington, DC: NASW Press.

Martin, D., & Lyon P. (1984). Lesbian women and mental health policy. In L. E. Walker (Ed.), *Women and mental health policy*. Beverly Hills, CA: Sage.

McWhirter, D. P., & Mattison, A. M. (1984). *The male couple: How relationships develop*. Englewoods Cliffs, NJ: Prentice-Hall.

Meyer, C. (1976). Social work practice (2nd ed.). New York: Free Press.

Miley, K. K., O'Melia, M. & Dubois, B. L. (1998). *Generalist social work practice: An empowering approach*. Boston: Allyn and Bacon.

Muhall, L. (1990). Australian counseling program may have halted the spread of AIDS in a select group. *AIDS Conference Bulletin, 1*, 21–24.

NASW (National Association of Social Workers). (1993). *Choices: Careers in social work*. Washington, DC: Author.

Nichols, M. (1989). Sex therapy with lesbians, gay men, and bisexuals. In S. Leiblum & R. Rosen (Eds.), *Principles and practices of sex therapy* (pp. 269–296). New York: Guilford.

Proctor, C. D., & Groze, V. K. (1994, September). Risk factors for suicide among gay, lesbian and bisexual youths. *Social Work, 39* (5), 504–513.

Puckett, S. B., & Bye, L. L. (1987). *The stop AIDS project: An interpersonal AIDS prevention program*. San Francisco: Stop AIDS Project.

Reamer, F. (1995). Ethics and values. In R. Edwards et al. (Eds.), *Encyclopedia of social work* (19th ed., pp. 893–902). Washington, DC: NASW Press.

Shortell, S. M., & Kaluzny, A. D. (1994) Foreword. In S. M. Shortell & A. D. Kaluzny (Eds.), *Health care management: Organizational behavior and design* (3rd ed., p. xi). Albany, NY: Delmar.

Stulberg, I, & Smith, M. (1988). Psychosocial impact of the AIDS epidemic on the lives of gay men. *Social Work, 3* (3), 277–281.

Storms, M. D. (1980). Theories of sexual orientation. *Journal of Personality and Social Psychology, 38*, 783–791.

Vass, A. (1996). *New directions in social work competencies, core knowledge, values, and skills*. Thousand Oaks, CA: Sage.

Wyers, N. (1987). Homosexuality in the family. *Social Work, 32* (2), 143–148.

Chapter 6

Frameworks and Theoretical Foundations

IN HIS FIRST FIELD PLACEMENT JUAN, A SOCIAL WORKER WORKING with older people, often found himself struggling. He joked that he was waiting for the single-problem client to come in so that he could carefully choose the very best method of helping. Although he sincerely wanted to help his clients to address their problems and he remembered what he had been taught in school, the thought of applying this knowledge was frightening. In school Juan had learned numerous intervention methods that supported his generalist approach to practice, but he was concerned that he would not interpret the client's problems correctly or would make the wrong decisions when he began helping activities. Ideas such as the "individual worth" and "dignity" of each client were strong in his memory. He knew that he should never compromise his professional values or show lack of respect for the client's culture, values, and beliefs. For Juan, as for many beginning social work professionals, discovering the best thing to do never seemed easy.

Furthermore, Juan was never sure exactly who his client was. Was it the person suffering from the problem? Was it that person's family? Was it the group or community in which the person lived? Or was the "client" even more extensive—was it the policy or legislation that led to the client's problem that required change? Or was it all of the above?

Juan's experience is quite normal for a beginning social worker. As we've commented, social work is not purely a science. Many aspects of helping have much more about them that is art. The skills required to practice this art take time and experience to develop and, in fact, also depend on continual updating of the science of social work.

Deciding how best to handle a client's situation is never easy, nor should it be. The best practice interventions require constant assessment, reassessment, and collaboration with other professionals. Furthermore, on any professional team, options will vary on how to interpret, best select, and apply strategies of helping. Remember, applying helping skills to problem situations is an art; situations vary and options are diverse. This diversity if one of the strengths of social work, and an important part of the helping process is identifying and supporting alternative and

Name: Diane DesPlantes

Place of residence: Plainfield, New Jersey

College/university degrees: B.A., Fordham University; M.S.W., Hunter Graduate School of Social Work

Present position: Clinical Therapist

Previous work/volunteer experience: Counselor for sexually abused children, Director of E.D.F., Bilingual Counselor, Parenting Education Educator for N.J. Hispanics for Higher Education, and Plainfield Teen Parenting Program

What do you do in your spare time? I enjoy reading, body building, and gardening.

Why did you choose social work as a career? I was heavily influenced by my personal experiences with poverty, being a woman of color. I am aware of the struggle to have a voice within my culture and of the obstacles outside of my culture. It created a desire within me to help others in all communities who are lost and without a voice.

What is your favorite social work story? When I first arrived at the Juvenile Correctional Facility, the administration, guards, and other personnel treated me in an offhand way, as though as a social worker I was nothing more than an ineffective bleeding heart. After a few months of hard work I was glad to see this impression change. The administration and staff marveled at the positive effect my sessions had on the clients. Clients' written assessments displayed the positive changes that had occurred through therapeutic interventions. Now, the climate has changed and I am greeted with respect and approval.

What would be the one thing you would change in our community if you had the power to do so? Many professionals are focused on their own achievements and lose sight of the fact that college teaches theory and not the practical life experiences needed for patient-centered treatment. We need to come out of our comfortable worlds and be more empathetic with those cultures, beliefs, and economic situations that are different from our own.

innovative strategies. The goal is not chaotic improvisation, however. The general practice consensus is that all interventions with a client should take place within a practice framework and have clear theoretical foundations.

In this chapter we introduce generalist social work practice. From this orientation all clients—individuals, families, and groups—are viewed through a culturally sensitive "lens"; this means that client strengths are recognized and supported at each step of the helping process. We also discuss the three most common approaches to social work practice: micropractice, mezzopractice, and macropractice. Social workers must be well versed in all three, though their efforts to assist clients may be concentrated at only one or two of the levels.

THE GENERALIST SOCIAL WORKER

Generalist social workers are employed in a variety of agencies, both public and private, and must develop helping relationships with all kinds of clients. Generalist work therefore, as articulated in the CSWE Curriculum Policy Statement, requires a broad range of knowledge and skills that allow problems and their solutions to be assessed comprehensively (Barker, 1999). Moreover, generalist social workers often coordinate and help to expand on the work of other professionals. In such cases the generalist is an invaluable member of the helping team, not only facilitating communication but fostering continuity of care (Barker, 1999).

> *Did You Know...In 1998 the field of social work in the United States celebrated a century of professional social work education and recognized more than 100 years of contributions to the well-being of individuals, groups, families, communities, and the natural environment. This was such an important event that Volume 43, Number 6, of the NASW journal* Social Work *was dedicated to accomplishments in social work practice.*

Taking an Empowering Approach to Practice

In today's social work practice environment, the idea of "empowerment" should not be underestimated. It is the uniqueness of the individual, group, or community that we much accentuate in each step of the helping process, whatever method of practice we select. Almost all clients respond favorably when they are acknowledged for their strengths and challenged to achieve their full potential.

Empowerment, as a central theme of social work practice, reflects the profession's emphasis on strengths and suggests that the client has the ability to make decisions and pursue change. So often in looking at a problem we focus on the "pathology" rather than on the strengths that the client brings to the situation. For example, when addressing the needs of a disabled client, we can focus on his inability to participate fully at the workplace. This narrow view ignores valuable information, however. The client may be having trouble functioning and may have been unsuccessful in some ways, but what about the ways in which success has been achieved? The disabled often overcome barriers that the nonhandicapped may not even notice. Social workers must ask what strengths the client has and how the client has overcome obstacles in his life. The emphasis is placed on the client's strengths, resiliency, and coping style, with a clear focus on the client's ability to succeed. What makes more sense if you want to motivate and support someone: focusing on strengths and successes or on problems and failures?

Empowerment also requires that we work to provide access to the resources and knowledge necessary for a client to succeed. We can't expect clients to succeed if they don't have the resources; at the same time, resources without knowledge yield limited positive results.

Trust, respect, and treating the client with civility are all part and parcel of empowerment. Without these core ingredients, we cannot foster the client's sense of self-worth and ability to look realistically at and resolve a problem.

Did You Know... The Hollis-Taylor report, a study conducted in 1951, showed that the social work profession was becoming increasingly specialized and fragmented in the delivery of services. Many social workers were treating client problems on a case-by-case basis. The report emphasized a more generic orientation to social work practice, with greater concern for social issues and social action. Many objectives set in this report were accepted by the profession and now form the basis of what is taught in many schools of social work today (Barker, 1999).

People often say, "Social workers empower their clients"—as if social workers have a bag of magic dust that we sprinkle on clients. Poof, we empower the client! In reality, empowerment comes from within. Social workers help clients to find and sharpen the skills and tools they possess and to look for the resources they may need. Social workers facilitate the empowerment process, but it is clients themselves who make it happen.

The Systems Perspective

Social work's mission is to engage in helping activity that enhances opportunities for all people in an increasingly complex environment. Social work professionals deal with a variety of human systems—individuals, couples, families, groups, organizations, and communities. In its simplest form a "system" consists of parts that interact so that a change in one part can affect all the others and the relations among them.

In future social work classes and texts, you'll come across the term "client system." The addition of the word "system" to "client" indicates that an individual, her family, her group, and her community are all related; all are part of the individual's "galaxy" of relations, where each relation influences the others. In considering the client system we focus on the individual within her relations with other parts of her system and seek to understand the extent to which other parts of the system influence the client.

Although a client may initially seek help alone, the social worker may determine after assessment that the client system needs to expand and include a spouse or a significant other to increase the chances of positive change. Consider the case

Activity...Look at yourself as a system. Identify the components of your "galaxy"—family, friends, associations, workplace, and other aspects of your life. Imagine arranging these items with "me" in the middle and drawing a circle around each one to indicate the portion of your environment that it makes up. Do any of the circles overlap? For example, do you work with any members of your family? Is one circle more influential than the others? Why? Do any of the circles influence the others?

described in box 1: the social worker was given a referral to see one client, Don; but after meeting and talking with him, the social worker realized the importance of including Don's wife and his dietician. A basic assessment, intervention plan, and referral process initiated by the social worker helped to harness the strengths of the client system, thereby helping Don to promote his own physical health.

In addition to addressing Don's particular needs the social worker believed that advocacy might be needed in order to help other clients like Don. The social worker talked with other professionals in the hospital to see whether anything similar had occurred before. It soon became apparent that what had happened to Don wasn't unusual. The discussions that the social worker initiated led to the issue being brought before the hospital's quality care management team. Later, the hospital developed a new protocol that required all diabetic clients to be interviewed and information about their living situations to be assessed. This advocacy did not benefit Don directly, but it did benefit others who could now be prevented from falling into a situation similar to what Don experienced.

For the generalist social worker who uses a system's perspective, helping activity assumes four roles: education, advocacy, facilitation, and intervention. While performing these helping activities social workers often go beyond working with the originally identified client.

First, education of the client is essential. Education is intended to make clients aware of the services they need as well as to empower them to address problems that previously seemed insurmountable. The social worker's practice activities often involve helping clients to secure the information they need and fostering connections that link clients to services and resource systems that can contribute to resolving their problems.

Social workers can educate clients in many different areas. For example, in Don's case the social worker helped to provide education by meeting with Don, his wife, and the dietician to discuss the medical need for Don to maintain the proposed diet and the consequences if he does not. The worker facilitated the dialogue between the dietician and the family and helped to support both in asking questions and clarifying discussion. After the meeting, Don's wife understood what was needed from her, and Don's diet compliance improved dramatically. This case demonstrates how a social worker can assist by educating the entire client system—the client, his family, and other members of the delivery team.

Education is important in all practice settings. Child abuse, domestic violence and incest dynamics, parent-child relations, caregiving, homemaker services, and

Box 1: The Case of Don: The Systems Perspective

Don, a 54-year-old man who was not following his diabetic diet, was referred to a social worker for discharge planning. Don's medical condition was worsening and his physician had become very frustrated with Don's noncompliance with his assigned treatment. According to the physician, Don was well aware that he was causing himself harm and might actually lose his eyesight if he did not change his behavior. In the interview with the social worker, Don appeared resistant. He stated that he was trying but that he found it hard to stick to his diet. He was too busy and tired when he got home from work to worry about the food he ate.

During the interview the social worker explored Don's situation by asking questions about his lifestyle, his job, and whether he lived alone. Don stated that he had been married for thirty years and had no children. Don's wife was a homemaker who prepared most of the meals, which included packing him a sack lunch to take to work every day. In an attempt to find out more about Don's support system the social worker asked Don if his wife had participated in the dietetic counseling he was provided. Don seemed surprised and said no, she had not. When asked why his wife had not participated in any of the educational sessions about his condition, Don replied that she had not been invited.

With Don's permission, the social worker called his wife to talk about their both coming in. The social worker also asked Don if he would come back and bring his wife so that they could discuss his diabetic condition with the dietician and his physician. At Don's request the social worker agreed to join them in these meetings, helping Don and his wife to explore what they needed to do to safeguard his health. The meetings were arranged, and the couple was counseled prior to discharge. After this intervention and at a six-week follow-up Don continued to follow his diet regime. He even joked that his wife was enjoying the cooking classes that she had attended and now he never knew what he was going to eat for lunch or supper.

health care, just to name a few, are areas where education commonly takes place. Social workers understand the importance of going beyond the traditional bounds of counseling. They can assist in educating clients to better maintain the safety, security, and wellness not only of themselves but of their families.

Activity...Go to the library and find the journal Social Work, *Volume 43, Number 6. Think about what the articles in this special issue tell you about the following questions:*

1. What types of contributions did social workers make in micro-, mezzo-, and macropractice?

2. How do social workers feel about the Code of Ethics, and what does it mean to each area of social work practice discussed in this chapter?

3. What issues in the history of social work do you believe helped to make the profession what it is today?

4. What issues in the field of social work need the attention of today's workers?

Indeed, social workers are uniquely placed to participate in education, particularly in the areas of prevention and continued health and wellness: "As a go-between of services, the social worker is the linkage between the person and a system of support that maintains health, or that may be the means of detecting illness early, or of preventing deterioration of the problem" (Skidmore, Thackeray, & Farley, 1997).

Second, advocacy helps clients to identify their own strengths and use individual and community resources to support their efforts to change. Advocacy does not always mean doing something *for* the client; it often means helping or teaching the client how to do things for herself. Issues of individual worth and dignity must always be considered. Therefore, every social worker must know how to maintain cultural integrity while fostering change, allowing diversity to flourish.

Third, facilitation consists of making connections among different resource systems that enhance their responsiveness and usefulness. The social worker may contact agencies that can support the client as well as mobilize the client and others in the client system. It is here that we find direct intervention, whereby the social worker actually makes the connections that are needed to help the client—for example, transportation to a medical appointment, or registration with such programs as Meals on Wheels. Direct intervention occurs when the client is unable to intervene on his own behalf or simply needs assistance to do so successfully.

PERSON-IN-SITUATION: GUIDING THE PRACTICE FRAMEWORK

Generalist practice is more than simply combining methods of practice such as casework, group work, and community organizing. It requires a theoretical practice framework involving structured ideas and beliefs that provide a foundation for helping. To this framework we apply knowledge and theory that is consistent with social work values and ethics from a person-in-situation context, which differentiates social work from other helping professions. Most professional social workers feel strongly that practice must be guided by theory. Practice that recognizes no theory is deficient and deprives the client system of the professional helping activity that the social worker should provide.

The systems perspective is part of the conceptual framework that social workers use to understand and assess human relations in context. It reflects the person-in-situation or person-in-environment stance that has always underpinned social work practice, focusing attention on an individual, a collective, a policy, a program, a practice, or any concrete or abstract unit in dynamic interaction with an environment.

A practice framework must also always address issues of human diversity. As we have stated throughout this book social workers always recognize and respect human diversity when forming and maintaining professional relations. Furthermore, social workers are committed to promoting social justice and professional ethical conduct. Social work has historically been concerned with oppressed and disadvantaged populations. The profession's focus on human diversity and social justice reinforces its ethically driven commitment to serving people who do not receive an equitable share of social resources. This commitment and adherence to a professional code of conduct is essential for any type of professional practice, be it generalist or specialist.

> *Did You Know...Lee Frankel (1867–1931) was an early social work educator and developer of family casework theories and practice. He established the Training School for Jewish Social Work in New York and became a national leader in early health and welfare organizations (Barker, 1999).*

For beginning social work professionals deciding where to begin and how best to engage the client can be difficult because this choice must be linked to the theoretical principles that underlie certain types of helping activity. To accomplish this goal, the social worker reviews the client's situation and based on the client's needs decides what theoretical perspective to use. In other words, the client, not the worker's comfort with or allegiance to a particular practice theory, drives the choice of perspective. The theoretical practice approach and helping strategy employed are firmly based in the reality of the client's environment.

At times making this linkage may seem too difficult or time-consuming, but acknowledging the relation between environment and practice method is critical. For example, one of the authors worked with an elderly male client with a history of alcohol abuse who received treatment only to be discharged back into an environment that encouraged him to resume drinking. The return to his previous environment negated much of the influence of the intervention and started a pattern of repeated rehabilitation attempts with numerous admissions to treatment centers. He always seemed to respond well while in the program but on discharge quickly relapsed into alcohol abuse. After numerous interventions had failed with this client he was referred to a social worker. The social worker assessed his situation thoroughly and examined the type of home environment to which he was returning. The social worker discovered that because of his instability and troubles with alcohol the client was unable to maintain a bank account. Therefore, when it came time for him to cash his social security check he used the local bar as his bank: His check would arrive each month, he would pick it up, and there was only one place to cash it—that local bar. To complicate matters, the bar would only cash checks if a purchase was made. It's clear what the consequences were. Assessing the client's discharge environment was a critical component in applying the helping strategy. To assist the client the social worker initiated a supervised living arrangement and helped the client to get a bank account of his own, where his social security check was directly deposited.

In formulating a helping strategy the method chosen must be congruent with the needs and desires of the client system being served as well as reflective of the values and ethics of the social work profession. Beginning social workers often feel trapped within a system driven by social, political, cultural, and economic factors so powerful that they influence the practice techniques and skills that are utilized. In addressing the needs of the poor, the disadvantaged, and those who are culturally different from the majority culture, it is the diversity of problems and of people who experience them that makes social work practice an art. How can social workers constantly evaluate what is happening to the client and whether societal factors—race, sexual orientation, and so forth—affect the way a problem is viewed? How can the beginning professional take into account all system variables that affect the helping relationship? How does a social worker maintain the dignity and worth of each client served and ensure that her own feelings and prejudices never enter the helping relationship?

Did You Know...The term "homophyly" acknowledges that people derive comfort and support from people who are like themselves. Culturally sensitive social work practice recognizes this phenomenon. It is one reason why social workers are always encouraged to use a client's own naturally occurring support network whenever possible. Clients are more likely to achieve needed changes when they can work within a system that is familiar to them.

There are no easy answers to these questions. To address each of these questions and give it the attention it deserves would take several books just to begin. Yet it is critical that each client system be treated individually, no matter how similar a case may be to one the social worker has already encountered.

SELECTING A PRACTICE METHOD

A multitude of factors must be considered in selecting the most appropriate practice method. Who makes up the client system? What is the target of change? What resources are available to the client system? What is the probability of success given the many elements that can affect the situation? This already sounds complicated, and in fact, it is only a small part of what needs to be considered when choosing a practice method. You'll learn more about these factors, and others, in future social work practice classes.

Although it is beyond the scope of this book to explain the many theoretical and practice frameworks available to social workers and how to use them, we explain the most common practice methods: micro-, mezzo-, and macropractice:

Microlevel practice: More commonly called direct or clinical practice with target populations including individuals, families, and groups; primarily uses face-to-face interaction with client

Mezzolevel practice: Involves agency administration with minimal client contact; examines agency effectiveness and policy implementation

Macrolevel practice: Defines client more extensively to include the community or organizations; often deals with broader social problems that impact the community (Hepworth & Larsen, 1990)

In the broadest of terms, micropractice is undertaken with individuals, families, and groups; mezzopractice directs our attention to organizational administration; and macropractice involves change within larger systems, such as communities and organizations. You might be thinking that we're playing semantic games, that micro, mezzo, and macro are just new names for casework, group work, and community practice. This is not really true because all three perspectives—micro, mezzo, and macro—apply a systems perspective to analyzing the presenting problem. For example, there are not foci in micropractice; the individual's system is the focus—note the use of singular versus plural. Micropractice involves an individual client with a presenting problem, and our work includes assessment of the system's role in creating, sustaining, or solving the problem—in fact, the system may play all three roles.

As we discussed in a number of places in this book, social work has two significant professional goals. The first is to help people to achieve their potential and to adjust more effectively to the demands of their environment. The second is to make social resources more responsive to people's needs, particularly for poor and disadvantaged people, who often are avoided or neglected. Incorporating these goals into the helping process reinforces social work's dual focus on personal and social problems and emphasizes the importance of linking micro-, mezzo-, and macrochange efforts.

Micropractice

In box 2 we present the case of Maria, who became a client but not through her own choice. Following her rape, she became almost immobilized, unwilling to leave her apartment or see others. A victim's advocate social worker proved instrumental. She was a constant presence for Maria during the critical time following the rape. The advocate explored issues from Maria's childhood and identified unresolved feelings that had resurfaced with the rape. Rather than trying to provide in-depth clinical help to Maria, the advocate referred her to a more advanced, MSW social worker, who had expertise in violence against women. The skilled worker was able to help Maria by using a mezzointervention model that employed a variety of process, education, and therapeutic techniques. Group sessions helped to validate Maria's experiences and those of the other group members as well as to consistently examine the broader system's impact on each of their lives.

In micropractice, as in all social work methods, social worker and client work together to establish goals and objectives and to develop the steps that must be taken to reach these goals. A typical microapproach has social workers dealing with clients, family members and significant others, and at times other groups of people. Maria, for example, was first seen as an individual and later referred to the group setting to continue the intervention process. Had Maria's family lived in the same geographic area they too may have become directly involved in the healing process.

Mezzopractice

Mezzopractice involves minimal face-to-face client contact, focusing rather on administrative intervention within the agency organization. Typical administrative titles include supervisor, unit director, director, executive director, chief executive office, and president.

Box 2: The Case of Maria: Micropractice

Maria, at age 22, was a victim of rape at her workplace. At the outset of the criminal investigation she met a victim's advocate, who was a BSW social worker employed by the police department. The advocate brought Maria to the hospital and became a major support person for her in the following days. During one of their conversations, the advocate learned that Maria had been a victim of sexual abuse during her childhood. The rape, compounded with her childhood experiences, now had put Maria in a very vulnerable emotional and psychological state: she was unable to go to work or meet family or friends, saying that she would rather just stay at home. Maria was blaming herself for the rape, stating, "I deserved it. Look at my whole life. I deserve it all." The BSW advocate quickly recognized that Maria needed more in-depth help. She referred Maria to a family service agency, where Maria first took part in individual sessions with an MSW social worker.

After a month, the social worker asked Maria how she felt about joining a group of women who had been raped. At first Maria refused, but with gentle, persistent encouragement from the social worker she reluctantly joined the weekly group. Maria's group included seven other women aged 18 to 52. All of the participants reached out to Maria and welcomed her. The social worker, who facilitated the group, told Maria that she did not need to talk unless she wanted too. Discussion at Maria's first group meeting focused on a particular topic, "The Court Hearing." Women shared their fears about the hearings, and some who had been through the courts shared their experiences. Subsequent sessions looked at anger control, relationship building, and becoming a survivor. Maria became an active member of the group and after one year joined the police department as a volunteer victim's advocate.

But don't leave this chapter with the impression that microworkers do not engage in mezzoactivities. In fact, any competent social worker will be knowledgeable and possess basic abilities in mezzotasks. Organizing your workload, preparing monthly reports, conducting policy analysis, supervising staff, and making public presentations to service groups are all mezzotasks that microworkers will find themselves undertaking.

Did You Know...Hull House is the most famous of all settlement houses, founded in Chicago in 1889 by Jane Addams. Settlement houses were community centers where poor and disadvantaged residents of the area could go for help. These centers were major innovators in social reform.

Individuals in mezzoroles develop expertise in a number of areas but particularly the following:

◆ Policy formulation and implementation
◆ Program development
◆ Funding, budgeting, and resource allocation
◆ Management of internal structures

- Staff and professional supervision
- Organizational and professional representation with internal and external groups
- Community presentations
- Ongoing evaluation of agency effectiveness (Hepworth & Larsen, 1990)

Generally, you will find MSW workers assigned to mezzopositions in agencies, while BSW workers are limited to direct service lines. This may not be the case in rural and small communities, however, where with fewer MSW professionals available, the BSW worker is more likely to find an administrative assignment. Although their knowledge and skills may not be as broad and as deep of those of MSW practitioners, baccalaureate practitioners do possess beginning knowledge and skills in mezzowork.

Macropractice

Macropractice directs the worker's attention to change in the larger community, organizational, and policy arenas. Typically called "community organization," macrowork involves helping individuals, groups, and communities who have common interests to deal with "social problems and to enhance well-being through planned collective action" (Barker, 1999, p. 90). Typically, micro- or mezzopractice identifies problems, needs, concerns, or issues that need to be addressed through larger change strategies (Netting, Kettner, & McMurtry, 1993). Just as micropractitioners and mezzoworkers have specialized knowledge and skills, so too does the macroworker. The macroworker has expertise in the following areas:

- Communities, their composition and type—for example, geographic or professional
- Power structures within communities and influence within communities
- Policy-making procedures
- Human service organizations, their purposes, functions, and constituencies
- Dynamics and nuances of social problems
- Macro-specific tasks such as collaboration and capacity building, negotiation, task group dynamics, marketing, research and analysis, and teaching

Macropractice builds on private issues that become public matters. Substance abuse, for example, involves individuals. Yet the abuse quickly becomes a public matter when it leads to increased crime related to the selling of drugs, lack of workforce participation or missed work due to drug abuse, poor school grades and eventual dropout, and family dysfunction. In the example described in box 3, the macroapproach involved a not-so-subtle nonviolent confrontation with a local storeowner. The owner wasn't sure which would be worse: the wrath of the drug dealers or the lack of neighbors who would purchase items from his store. He decided the latter, and with help from the local police department, drug sales disappeared from the area. An interesting note: when the group's organizer was told that the dealers were only going to another neighborhood, he responded, "Then that's their problem and they will have to organize them out of the community like we did."

In this application of macropractice the social worker helped the group to develop a plan of action and supported the group as it organized itself. The worker facilitated the process, helped to mobilize significant agencies and local leaders, and provided background research—essentially providing the neighborhood group with the tools it needed to become successful. What began as an individual problem ended up as a community macroissue whose resolution brought about significant changes in the daily lives of individuals, families, and organizations in the neighborhood.

Box 3: The Case of a Drug-free Community: Macropractice

A drug-related shooting took place in the middle of the day in a poor area of town. A few people gathered that evening in a local church and decided that they had had enough, but they didn't know what to do. One of the participants was a social worker from the local neighborhood center. She suggested that the group in fact knew what it wanted—a drug-free community—but now needed to figure out where to begin in order to make this happen. The group expanded and created a neighborhood drug-free task force to act as a "conduit" for the community. Neighbors were invited to share their frustrations at meetings held in churches, school halls, and the neighborhood center. Local social service agencies and elected and appointed officials were asked to come and listen to the neighbor's concerns.

Out of these meetings came a plan for a march through the neighborhood, with the police leading the parade and marching with citizens. The group decided to include a social action activity by marching to the primary spot where drugs were sold, a mom and pop convenience store, one block from the public elementary school. Once at the store, the marchers, about two hundred people, formed a long single-file line, and each walked in without saying a word and left one dollar on the counter. The police stood in front of the store and within minutes there was a noticeable disappearance of the drug pushers! Over the following weeks, the storeowner worked with the local task force and police; the drug pushers stopped selling in the neighborhood and moved out of the community. The storeowner joined the task force when it took on other substance abuse issues in the community.

Did You Know...Mother Jones was Mary Harris Jones (1830–1930), a community organizer and labor union advocate who led many strikes against inhumane treatment of children and adults. She advocated better child labor laws and less dangerous working conditions in the mining and steel industries (Baker, 1999).

In Brief: Short-Term Intervention Approaches

Having looked at micro-, mezzo-, and macropractice, we would not be helpful if we didn't touch on one major issue facing social workers who practice at the microlevel.

Scenes in a migrant farm worker camp in Michigan. Workers come to Michigan in June to pick strawberries and leave in late fall after the apple harvest. The workers travel in vans and trucks as they move from one region of the country to another, following the harvest cycles.

Whether we like it or not, current social work practice is now dominated by brief, or short-term, practice models. There are many reasons for this trend, but the major influence is money: getting the "biggest bang for the buck." Insurance companies, as third-party payers (those who pay a provider for services for another person, thus "third party"), and health care organizations limit the time during which a client system may receive a service. Simply stated, third-party payers will not underwrite long-term intervention if a short-term model will help, even if the end is less desirable than what a longer term approach may yield. Social workers therefore employ time-limited approaches as a major practice model.

In other cases clients simply don't have the time, desire, or money for long-term social work microservices. People today are working more hours, sometimes two jobs, and have less time to devote to the "self." With less time available, they are unwilling to commit extra time and energy to go beyond simply addressing the cause of the problem. Practitioners can become frustrated when the presenting problem and the underlying issues clearly require a long-term model but the client system, for any number of reasons, is only willing to look at the surface issue.

So often, new social workers aren't all interested in social welfare policy. Students taking policy courses often complain, "Why do I need this course? It has nothing to do with social work!" The ongoing national debate about health insurance and resulting services shows one reason why we need to understand policy and how to influence its scope and design. Our practice grows out of policy: Change policy and you can change practice. Change the ways that third-party payers reimburse for service and you can change your practice. These days insurance rarely covers long-term encounters, and short-term, time-limited practice is the norm.

So what do we mean by short-term, or brief, practice? Short-term practice generally ranges from six to eight meetings (Wells & Phelps, 1990); however, as many as twenty have been noted (Fanger, 1995). For many social workers only seeing a client system once is becoming commonplace.

We must realize social work practice encounters are going to be brief. Planning for this short duration in implementing a helping strategy is critical; lack of planning can result in numerous unexpected endings for the client (Wells, 1994) and can also contribute to feelings of failure and decreased job satisfaction for the social work professional (Resnick & Dziegielewski, 1996).

WE ALL MAKE MISTAKES!

A number of years ago a t-shirt often worn at social work gatherings had a Superman logo on the front; but rather than a big "S" the yellow and red lettering spelled out "Super Social Worker." The apparent exaggeration was ironic because at times the efforts of social workers really did seem Herculean. No one can dispute, however, that social workers are human beings and therefore unlike Superman are vulnerable and capable of making mistakes. However hard we try, everyone of us is subject to err. Social workers are only human!

Therefore, all social workers must try to minimize the number of mistakes they make and, of course, mitigate any potential harm to the clients served. Moreover, a mistake should be viewed as a "learning moment." A natural reaction may be to act defensively and try to blame someone else; however, professionals must take responsibility for what they do. When in supervision with a trained professional, the beginning social worker has the opportunity to explore a mistake and replay what happened, as if watching it on videotape. It is important to evaluate what actually happened and what might have happened had some other strategy been implemented. Social workers use professional supervision as a forum for these detailed discussions so that the same or similar mistakes can be avoided in the future. The most powerful resource that a social worker has is the ability to seek supervisory help or peer consultation about a problem.

TOPIC: CULTURALLY SENSITIVE PRACTICE

Social workers must help clients to maintain cultural integrity and must respect diversity. The term "ethnic identity" is generally defined as common heritage, customs, and values unique to a group of people (Casas, 1984; Queralt, 1996; Worden, 1999). Social science researchers often gather information on race and ethnicity, yet the difference between the two concepts is pronounced. Race is partially based on physical characteristics of genetic origin (Helms, 1990). Ethnicity embraces a much broader range of commonalities, such a religion, customs, geography, and history. These commonalities between individuals and within a community define and bond members, thereby giving an ethnic backdrop to everyday life. Ethnicity can thus influence thinking and feeling and can pattern behavior in both obvious and subtle ways. Generally, however, it is easy to overlook the deeper influence of ethnicity because it often appears to be natural and to consist simply of daily behavior—for example, what individuals eat or how they react.

Activity...Ethical, culturally sensitive social work practice emphasizes the concepts of "respect," "self-determination," and "remaining nonjudgmental." Together with a fellow student, and without using any references, outline briefly what you understand each of these ideas to mean. Then consult a social work resource such as the Social Work Dictionary *or the* Encyclopedia of Social Work *and define them again. Compare your first set of definitions with the second. Were there any differences? If so, what were they?*

The development of ethnic identity occurs on a continuum determined by acceptance of one's ethnicity (Helms, 1990). Clients may either embrace or reject their ethnicity, depending on how it relates to personal identity or to identity ascribed by a particular reference group that dictates behavior and decision-making practices (Helms, 1990). Personal identity is how an individual sees himself whereas ascribed identity is how society values or perceives him. Crucial to understanding the concept of ethnicity is realizing that although it is a potent factor in the professional helping relationship, it is not easy to identify and the degree to which it influences life decisions and behavior is not the same for every client.

When providing culturally sensitive practice social workers must avoid applying a narrow cultural "lens" that can interpret client system traditions and problem-solving processes as abnormal or dysfunctional. In mental health, for example, social workers must thoroughly understand, appreciate, and assess cultural differences in order to enable providers to develop culturally compatible services for the clients that they serve. For example, the social worker who works with an Asian client needs to be aware of Asian customs and expectations. In Asian cultures, there may be resistance to outside intervention as family matters are viewed as private. It is important for the social worker to be aware of and to respect this cultural tradition and to know how it can affect the helping relationship. Culturally sensitive services must extend beyond the general task of making services more accessible and include specifically relevant therapeutic interpretations to guide the framework being used (Leon & Dziegielewski, 1999).

One last issue in providing culturally sensitive practice from a systems perspective is that for the time being, the beliefs and values of social workers and other helping professionals generally reflect those of the greater society. These workers may view different client systems through their own cultural lens and consequently overlook the need to help the client and his system to maintain cultural and ethnic heritage as well as feelings of integrity throughout the intervention process. Professional helpers must be aware of their probable tendency to assess clients based on their own values, beliefs, biases, and stereotypes (Boyd-Franklin, 1989; Dupper, 1992). Lack of awareness of ethnicity and culture may distort perceptions of clients and of their family dynamics. The potential danger here is that the client's right to self-determination may be violated (Hepworth & Larsen, 1993). Providing ethnically sensitive practice requires social workers to very clearly assess clients and client systems in regard to the effects that culture, environment, and family can have on behaviors and responses. Being aware of ethnicity and culture and accepting diversity are essential in culturally sensitive practice.

Did You Know…Examinations such as those used to measure intelligence can be "culturally biased" and thereby inaccurately depict an individual's intelligence or aptitude. For example, a test may ask questions about American history that place immigrants at a disadvantage. Social workers need to be aware of this potential problem and must work with each individual client to ensure that he or she is represented fairly and accurately.

In closing, culturally sensitive practice requires that the social worker:

◆ Identify and discuss the impact of psychological problems than can result from adaptation to a new situation or environment
◆ Encourage the development of positive and supportive peer relations
◆ Encourage relations outside of the client system that can help to reduce feelings of isolation and facilitate transition
◆ Help the client to develop new coping skills with which to negotiate the new environment

SUMMARY

To understand the practice of social work you must appreciate the broad range of activities and areas that practice involves. Choosing from among the varied roles and tasks that social workers perform, as well as identifying what constitutes the client system, is not easy within the dynamic social work practice environment. So it is not uncommon for beginning professionals to struggle with basic practice principles and how best to help the client they serve. Our advice is simple: Don't worry! This can happen even with the most experienced MSW practitioner. Deciding what helping approach to use and when to apply it requires a delicate balancing act among the needs of the client, the demands of the environment, the skills and helping knowledge available to the social worker, and the sanction of the social welfare agency.

Today's society suffers from a multitude of complicated problems that need to be addressed, and social workers, like other helping professionals, are being pressured to assess and address them as quickly and as effectively as possible. Varied social work roles and fluctuating environmental influences reinforce the ongoing need for educational preparation and training in practice. Even after receiving a degree, every social worker needs to enhance his knowledge and skill bases while developing new areas for more effective practice. We must all continue learning and growing in order to anticipate the needs of our clients.

Social workers believe that competent ethical practice is more than simply helping clients by using what is known. It also involves knowing the client, respecting cultural diversity and the uniqueness of the individual, assessing the environmental situation, and recognizing the strengths and limitations of the intervention strategy employed as well as the resources available to the client. The social worker must decide what method of change to use and at what level—micro, mezzo, or macro—the client will best be served.

Microapproaches to social work practice help clients, whether individuals, families, or groups, to feel better about themselves and to address previous relationship experiences that are affecting new or current relationships. Mezzopractice strengthens an agency's ability to respond more congruently with worker practice needs and client issues. And macropractice confronts larger issues that affect individuals, families, groups, or communities.

In this chapter and in chapter 5 you have been exposed, albeit briefly, to social work practice. You've read a few case scenarios and seen how different social workers have tried to help their clients. These cases offer you a glimpse of the exciting, challenging, and often frustrating world of the practicing social work professional.

Social workers are needed in the practice arena to address the wide array of social problems. And yes, while social workers face numerous external pressures from funding groups, we cannot allow these to limit our practice strategies. Clients need and continue to want supportive services, and as the number of people suffering from anxiety and depressive disorders, self-destructive behavior, and life-threatening illnesses continues to grow, so does the need for social workers who engage in professional practice.

References

Barker, R. L. (1999). *The social work dictionary* (4th ed.). Washington, DC: NASW Press.

Boyd, N. (1989). *Black families in therapy*. New York: Guilford.

Casas, J. M. (1984). Policy, training, and research in counseling psychology: The racial/ethnic minority perspective. In S. D. Brown & R. W. Lent (Eds.), *Handbook of counseling psychology* (pp. 785–831). New York: Wiley.

Dupper, D. (1992). Separate schools for black males. *Social Work in Education, 14*(12), 75–76.

Fanger, M. T. (1995). Brief therapies. In R. Edwards et al. (Eds.), *Encyclopedia of social work* (19th ed., pp. 323–334). Washington, DC: NASW Press.

Helms, J. E. (Ed) (1990). *Black and white racial identity: Theory, research, and practice*. Westport, CT: Praeger.

Hepworth, D. H., & Larsen, J. A. (1990). *Direct social work practice* (3rd ed.). Belmont, CA: Wadsworth.

Hepworth, D. H., & Larsen, J. A. (1993). *Direct social work practice: Theory and skills* (4th ed.). Pacific Grove, CA: Brooks/Cole.

Leon, A. M., & Dziegielewski, S. F. (1999). The psychological impact of migration: Practice considerations in working with Hispanic women. *Journal of Social Work Practice, 13*(1), 69–82.

Netting, F. E., Kettner, P., & McMurtry, S. (1993). Social work macro practice. New York: Longman.

Queralt, M. (1996). *The social environment and human behavior: A diversity perspective*. Boston: Allyn and Bacon.

Resnick, C., & Dziegielewski, S. F. (1996). The relationship between therapeutic termination and job satisfaction among medical social workers. *Social Work in Health Care, 23*(3), 17–35.

Skidmore, R. A., Thackeray, M. G., & Farley, O. W. (1997). *Introduction to social work* (7th ed.). Boston: Allyn and Bacon.

Wells, R. A. (1994). *Planned short-term treatment* (2nd ed.). New York: Free Press.

Wells, R. A., & Phelps, P. A. (1990). The brief psychotherapies: A selective overview. In R. A. Wells & V. J. Giannetti (Eds.), *Handbook of the brief psychotherapies* (pp. 3–26). New York: Plenum.

Worden, M. (1999). *Family therapy basics* (2nd ed.). Pacific Grove, CA: Brooks/Cole.

Part **III**

Settings for Social Work Practice

Chapter 7

Poverty and Income Maintenance

THROUGHOUT ITS HISTORY THE CORE FUNCTION OF THE SOCIAL work profession has been service on behalf of those who are economically, socially, or politically disadvantaged. From the earliest efforts of the COSs and settlement houses of the nineteenth century, social workers have always tried to help people to achieve their potential and participate in the development of their communities.

As we enter the new millennium, the United States has experienced unparalleled economic growth. There are more millionaires and billionaires than at any time in U.S. history. The stock market has boomed to new and unexpected heights. Unemployment and inflation have reached their lowest levels in decades, and new job opportunities abound. All of these developments are signs of a growing, prospering economy. Yet as Chelf has noted, even with all these gains the United States remains a society of sharp economic contrasts (1992, p. 21). While many Americans live in affluence, a large part of the population is unable to benefit from the nation's economic triumph.

Poverty is determined primarily by income because it is income that allows the purchase of necessary material resources (Coulton & Chow, 1995, p. 1874). Closely tied to poverty and income is the ability, or inability, to purchase or access high-quality health care, decent and safe housing, and an adequately nutritious diet. As Darby wrote, "Being poor hurts. By itself, poverty diminishes the quality of life" (1996, p. 3). Certainly, many heroic examples exist of people and families who have risen above the limitations of poverty by taking full advantage of public welfare programs and services. But such cases are rare. Living in poverty far more often is associated with negative life experiences that can leave deep scars. Crime, low educational attainment, inadequate health care, substandard housing, and minimum wage employment with little opportunity for promotion are among the many debilitating experiences faced by the poor. For the economically disadvantaged— that is, people who cannot financially support themselves and their families—life is not easy.

Imagine what it would be like not to have enough money to feed, clothe, or house yourself and your family. Now imagine what it would be like if, in addition to these troubles, you were viewed negatively and treated differently simply because your income is low.

Poor people are often regarded as contributing less than their share to society. Indeed, with our society's emphasis on rugged individualism, it's difficult not to view the poor in a negative light. Well-educated people who we believe should

Name: Denise L. Young

Place of residence: Orlando, Florida

College/university degrees: B.A. at Oakland U in Rochester, MI. M.S.W. at Florida State U in Tallahassee, FL. Ph.D. at University of Michigan in Ann Abor, MI

Present position: Associate Vice President for Academic Affairs

Previous work/volunteer experience: Director of International Studies; Director of Program Review in Academic Affairs for the SUS with responsibilities including social work; teacher in and director of gerontology program; worked in adult foster care and mental health.

What do you do in your spare time? I am an avid world traveler. Not just to the comfortable places, but to places that help you comprehend the human condition. When not traveling abroad, I take advantage of the natural beauties of this country-camping, hiking, collecting rocks and bugs, and learning about the environment. I try to pass on the family tradition of helping others by having our family deliver meals on holidays, donate items, and read about children's lives in other communities and lands. I have young children, so there isn't a lot of spare time.

Why did you choose social work as a career? Helping others has been a family tradition for generations. My great-great-grandmother had 8 biological children and adopted 7 more. My great-grandmother was the community midwife, my father was in the medical corps, and my mother and sister are social workers. I like the action orientation of social work, which teaches us how to attempt to change what we find wrong in the world, no matter how complicated or difficult that may be.

What is your favorite social work story? I have no one favorite story, but am spellbound by any story where someone took a chance, made a difference, and perhaps even turned someone else's life around.

What would be the one thing you would change in our community if you had the power to do so? I would have a community where each person, no matter their challenges and differences, would have an appropriate place to live and access to all the services and support they needed in order to reach their own potential. A place without holes in the safety net or cracks in the system, where people are not blamed for conditions beyond their control.

know better sometimes make statements like "Poor people are disadvantaged because they don't work or try hard enough to better themselves." Many people also believe that recipients of social welfare services are immoral because they often have live-in partners while maintaining single-parent families. These misconceptions about the poor are more than just a matter of perceptions; these false assumptions often determine how poor people are treated and what services they are given.

Think about it. Can you remember any discussions you've had with friends or family about people who are impoverished? How were these people characterized? How often have discussions of this type become emotionally charged? Did your friends or family members feel strongly about what they'd seen or believed to be the case? Now think about pronouncements you've heard politicians make in the heat of political campaigns. How did the politicians present the issue of poverty, and what kinds of plans were proposed to address it? Why do you think people who want to hold office seem constantly to attack poverty-related social programs? We believe the reason is that most of the time politicians wish to please their constituents, so they pander to widespread beliefs and attack these programs as costly and wasteful.

Regardless of your opinion about people who live in poverty, it is clear that the poor and disadvantaged inspire strong emotions. Views and expectations about those living in poverty are founded on myths and stereotypes that unfortunately are assumed to be fact. We actually know quite a lot about poverty, however, particularly that the state of poverty is persistent. Poverty affects all races and ages. Poverty affects both men and women. Poverty is found in urban, suburban, and rural communities. Those who live in poverty are often disadvantaged or disenfranchised by the greater society. Finally, poverty cannot be isolated within a particular segment of society. Through its effects on educational performance and crime, poverty affects everyone in society and the quality of life for all people.

Did You Know...In 1995, in the United States 36.4 million people, 13.8 percent of the population, were living in poverty.

In this chapter, we first try to cut through many of the myths that surround the poor and impart critical information to make you a more informed helper. We then look at several important social programs and assess their effectiveness within a framework of facts rather than mythology.

POVERTY DEFINED

According to the *Social Work Dictionary* **poverty** is *"the state of being poor or deficient in money or means of subsistence"* (Barker, 1995, p. 177). Other definitions similarly stress the link between resources and livelihood: Poverty is a *"condition of being without basic resources"* (Segal & Brzuzy, 1998, p. 78). *"Poverty is a simple and complex phenomenon . . . [that can be] defined as deprivation"* (Karger & Stoesz, 1994, p. 130). *"Poverty is generally thought of as material deprivation"* (Coulton & Chow, 1995, p. 1867).

The children in this photo are siblings. They live with their parents in this trailer and another the same size. The trailers are in a parking lot at the edge of a large city in Ireland.

Two ideas further refine the concept of poverty: **absolute poverty** and **relative poverty**. Absolute poverty is determined by comparison with a fixed numerical standard that is applied in all situations and usually reflects bare subsistence. Relative poverty is determined by comparison with some normative standard that may reflect a living standard far higher than subsistence. Absolute measures are usually income based. For example, if a person's annual income is below a certain figure, then the individual is regarded as poor. On the other hand, a relative measure—though still income based—would compare the individual with someone else. A single person with a $35,000 annual income is not absolutely poor but *is* poor relative to Bill Gates, the richest man in the world. A second kind of relative measure is based on the ability, or inability, to meet a standard set and approved by the community. For example, if immunizations are expected but a family cannot afford them for its children, then that family is considered poor by this measure. Absolute measures make it easy to count people and minimize subjective variables. The key is identifying a threshold below which people are counted as poor. Relative measures are much more difficult to formulate or to reach consensus about. They are also difficult to use. For example, people sometimes say that poor people in the United States have it easy compared to poor people elsewhere. But this is like trying to compare apples with oranges. Different countries have different beliefs, values, and economic and social systems—all of which affect the standards by which people are judged to be poor.

Measuring Poverty

The U.S. government measures poverty using a standard called the **poverty threshold**. Mollie Orshansky, director of the Social Security Administration in 1963, conceptualized the poverty threshold as an absolute measure so that statistical processes could be used to simply count the number of poor. Orshansky's formula is based on the amount of money that a family must spend on food and on the portion of overall income that this expense constitutes. Orshansky assumed that a family spends one-third of its total income on food. After calculating the cost of a minimum, or economy, food plan as determined by the Department of Agriculture, she multiplied that amount by three to establish the poverty threshold. This value, which is essential in determining benefits, is updated annually and adjusted for inflation (Coulton & Chow, 1995, p. 1867). It is also adjusted for family size and age (see table 1) and to reflect the increased cost of living in Hawaii and Alaska. Its application is simple: a person or family whose gross income falls below the poverty threshold is counted as being in poverty.

Did You Know...According to the National Center for Children in Poverty in 1998, 23.2 percent of the children under age 6 live in poverty in the United States.

Having explained the poverty threshold calculation, let's complicate matters a bit. The poverty threshold was the government's original attempt to establish a poverty measure, under the oversight of the Social Security Administration, and its

---

Table 1: Social Security Administration Poverty Threshold, Selected Years

			Number of People in Family					
Year	Single Person under Age 65	Single person over Age 65	Two	Three	Four	Five	Six	Seven
1996	$8,163	$7,525	$10,233	$12,516	$16,036	$18,952	$21,389	$24,268
1995	7,763	7,309	9,933	12,158	15,569	18,408	20,804	23,552
1994	7,710	7,108	9,661	11,821	15,141	17,900	20,235	22,923
1993	7,518	6,930	9,414	11,522	14,763	17,449	19,718	22,823
1992	7,299	6,729	9,137	11,186	14,335	16,952	19,137	21,594
1991	7,086	6,532	8,865	10,860	13,924	16,456	18,587	21,058
1990	6,800	6,286	8,509	10,419	13,359	15,792	17,839	20,241
1985	5,593	5,156	6,998	8,573	10,989	13,007	14,696	16,656
1980	4,290	3,949	5,363	6,565	8,414	9,966	11,269	12,761

Source: "Poverty in the United States: 1996." Series P60–194. E. Baugher and L. Lamisow-White (1997).

purpose is to establish a basis for counting retrospectively the number of people who live in poverty. Each year, however, another branch of the federal government, the Department of Health and Human Services (HHS), is responsible for issuing poverty guidelines. These prospective guidelines, which closely approximate the poverty threshold, are used in determining financial eligibility for certain federal programs (see table 2). The poverty guidelines are needed because the poverty threshold data for a given year are not generated until summer of the following year (Institute for Research on Poverty, www.ssc). Thus, poverty thresholds for 1998 were not published until 1999, and agencies using these data to determine program eligibility at the beginning of the year 2000 would then be using two-year-old information.

Table 2: Department of Health and Human Services Poverty Guidelines, 1998

Number of People in Family	48 Contiguous States	Alaska	Hawaii
1	$ 8,050	$10,070	$ 9,260
2	10,850	13,570	12,480
3	13,650	17,070	15,700
4	16,450	20,570	18,920
5	19,250	24,070	22,140
6	22,050	27,570	25,360
7	24,850	31,070	28,580
8	27,650	34,570	31,800
For each additional person add	2,800	3,500	3,220

Source: Federal Registrer, 63, (no. 36). (February 24, 1998), pp. 9235–9238.

An important point to remember: the HHS poverty guidelines are used for determining eligibility for many federal programs but not for all of them. Examples of federal programs that use the HHS guidelines are Head Start, Low-Income Energy Assistance Program, food stamps, National School Lunch and School Breakfast programs, Legal Services for the Poor, Job Training Partnership Act, WIC, and Job Corps. Some of these programs use a percentage multiple of the guidelines, such as 125, 150, or 180 percent (Institute for Research on Poverty, 1998). For example, a program may use 125 percent of the HHS guidelines to determine eligibility. In 1998 this eligibility standard for a three-person family was a $13,650*125%, or $17,062.50; in other words, a family of three was eligible for the program if its income was below $17,062.50. The percentages of the HHS guidelines used by different programs are established by congressional committees and, predictably, can create a great deal of confusion between programs. Moreover, several well-known programs are not tied to the HHS guidelines: Supplemental Security Income, Social Services Block Grant, Section 8 housing, the Earned Income Credit, and Temporary Assistance for Needy Families.

Activity...Using the 1998 poverty guideline for a family of four, $16,450, imagine what life is like. You'll have $1,370.83 each month for expenses. Using Orshansky formula's assumption, one-third of your income, $456.94, goes for food, leaving you $913.89 for other expenses including housing, transportation, health care, clothing, recreation, and so on. Put together a monthly food menu—what type of meals, and so forth—with the $456.94. Find a place to live and set up other expenses with the remaining $919. The two children are ages 5 and 13, and the two adults are the biological parents.

Now, how realistic do poverty guidelines seem to be? What does this exercise tell you about the level at which poverty guidelines are set? If this were your family of four and these were the resources you had available, could you make ends meet?

Did You Know...A single parent with two children making the minimum wage and working forty hours a week will not make enough money to raise this family above the poverty threshold. This parent, in 1995, would need to make $6.02 per hour to be above the poverty threshold or $6.56 to be above the HHS guideline.

Other Considerations in Measuring Poverty

Setting poverty thresholds and thus establishing exactly who will be counted as poor is very controversial. Orshansky's definition, when examined closely, has all sorts of limitations. First, it doesn't consider geographical differences in cost of living, other than for Alaska and Hawaii—and this is an important consideration in the United States. Go back to table 5 in Chapter 4 to see how far the same amount of money goes in different cities. Second, the threshold is based on food costs but does not adjust for the different nutritional needs among children, women, women of child-bearing age, and men. Last, assuming that one-third of a family's income is spent on food purchases is itself problematic. Over the years this has not proved to be a well-founded assumption.

Did You Know...In statistics the mean, median, and mode are indicators of how a set of numbers tends to focus around central values. Applied to income, the mean income *is the average income of a population; 50 percent of the population has income above* median income *and 50 percent below; and the* mode income *is the most frequently occurring income.*

Beyond problems with the formula used to determine poverty is the question of what should or should not be counted as income. For example, should federal cash subsidies such as social security retirement payments be counted as income? Should income be established as the pretax or the posttax amount? Should the cash value of in-kind benefits from federal subsidy programs such as food stamps and Section 8 housing be counted as part of a family's income?

As exhibited in table 3, how income is defined affects actual poverty estimates. Moving down the table, income is adjusted in steps so that we can observe the effects on the poverty rate: first, government cash benefits are removed; then private nonwage income is added, federal tax payments are removed, the primary antipoverty tax credit is added, state tax payments are removed; and finally government benefits are added successively. By the time we reach definition 14, which includes *all* government benefits in income, the poverty rate is much lower than under the current model—3.5 percentage points, which is a 25 percent decline in the rate.

Table 3: Impact of Taxes and Transfers on Poverty Estimates, 1995

Selected Income Definitions	Number with Income Below Poverty Threshold (in thousands)	Poverty Rate
1: Current model	36,425	13.8%
2: Definition 1 less government cash	57,643	21.9
4: Definition 2 plus capital gains and employee health benefits	55,558	21.1
6: Definition 4 less social security and federal income taxes	58,388	22.1
7: Definition 6 plus Earned Income Tax Credit	55,061	20.9
8: Definition 7 less state income tax	55,505	21.0
9: Definition 8 plus non-means-tested government cash transfers	37,176	14.1
11: Definition 9 plus value of Medicare and regular school lunch	36,177	13.7
14: Definition 12 plus the value of Medicaid and other means-tested government noncash transfers	27,190	10.3

Source: Baugher and Lamison-White (1996).

The data presented show that federal programs do improve income levels and thus remove individuals from poverty. The data also show, however, that people who rely on federal benefits for large parts of their income are extremely vulnerable to the slightest modifications in program eligibility conditions and benefit levels.

So, are we really doing a disservice to all poor people when we count such uncertain income? What rate do you believe most accurately reflects existing poverty—the 13.8 percent determined by definition 1 or the 10.3 percent determined by definition 14, or one of the other rates? Does it really matter which definition is used? If the official poverty rate declined slightly because governmental subsidies were added to income calculations don't you think this information would be used to justify reductions in welfare programs? And, if welfare programs actually were reduced, wouldn't the poverty rate rise again?

Nevertheless, agency administrators and welfare advocates often argue that data produced by a standardized process applied consistently from year to year, even if the process is rife with potential measurement flaws, are essential. Such numerical measures allow a community to follow *trends* in poverty and to assess the effects of different attempts to reduce poverty among its citizens. In other words, even though the poverty rate itself may have little intrinsic meaning it is nonetheless important because its fluctuations over time serve as a *barometer* of economic well-being.

Number in Poverty versus Poverty Rate

Note that our discussion of measuring poverty started with counting the *number* of people in poverty but is now framed in terms of the poverty *rate*. The poverty rate is a more illuminating way to quantify poverty because it provides context by expressing the number of people in poverty as a percentage of the total population. This context is important for two reasons. First, the scale of poverty is difficult to judge if we know only the number of poor people: One thousand people in poverty is a far more serious problem if the total population is 2,000 than if it is 100,000. The poverty rates, 50 percent and 1 percent, show how different the two situations are. Second, trends in poverty cannot be judged by changes in the number of poor people alone. Suppose over a decade the number of people in poverty rises from 1,000 to 2,000. If the total population remains stable at 100,000, the poverty rate has doubled from 1 to 2 percent; if, however, the population grows from 100,000 to 200,000, the poverty rate is unchanged at 1 percent—the rate distinguishes between worsening poverty and population growth.

Did You Know...In 1995, the number of people living below the poverty threshold totaled 36,500,000, or 13.8 percent of the U.S. population. To think about how large this number actually is, consider that the total population of the Northeast—Maine, New Hampshire, Vermont, Massachusetts, Connecticut, Rhode Island, and New York—is slightly smaller. Or consider that the total population of the following states approximates the number of people in poverty: Idaho, Montana, North Dakota, South Dakota, Wyoming, Colorado, Utah, Nevada, Arizona, New Mexico, Nebraska, Oklahoma, Iowa, Louisiana, and Arkansas. That the United States is one of world's most technologically advanced societies and has one of the highest standards of living makes it difficult to comprehend the number of Americans who live in poverty.

Examine table 4, and remember that the U.S. population has grown every year since the nation's founding. You can now "read" different eras in the recent history of poverty. In the 1960s the number of people in poverty actually declined, a dramatic development, as evidenced by the sharp drop in the poverty rate from 22 to 12.1 percent. This decrease was achieved primarily through the federal government's activist War on Poverty. Over the following years the poverty rate fluctuated, peaking at 15.2 percent in 1983 and 15.1 percent in 1993, while the number in poverty trended steadily upward with the growing population. Indeed,

Table 4: Poverty Status, 1959–95

Year	Number in Poverty (in thousands)	Poverty Rate	Year	Number in Poverty (in thousands)	Poverty Rate
1995	36,425	13.8%	1976	24,975	11.8%
1994	38,059	14.5	1975	25,877	12.3
1993	39,265	15.1	1974	23,370	11.2
1992	38,014	14.8	1973	22,973	11.1
1991	35,708	14.2	1972	24,460	12.5
1990	33,585	13.5	1971	25,559	12.5
			1970	25,420	12.6
1989	31,528	12.8			
1987	31,745	13.0	1969	24,147	12.1
1986	32,221	13.4	1968	25,389	12.8
1985	32,370	13.6	1967	27,769	14.2
1984	33,700	14.4	1966	28,510	14.7
1983	35,303	15.2	1965	33,185	17.3
1982	34,398	15.0	1964	36,055	19.0
1981	31,822	14.0	1963	36,436	19.5
1980	29,272	13.0	1962	38,625	21.0
			1961	39,628	21.9
1979	26,072	11.7	1960	39,851	22.2
1978	24,497	11.4			
1977	24,720	11.6	1959	39,490	22.4

Source: Baugher and Lamison-White (1996).

although poverty rates in the mid-1990s were far below the 1959 level, the numbers in poverty were not far different.

WHO ACTUALLY CONSTITUTE THE POOR?

Poverty cuts across all races, ethnic groups, and ages and darkens the lives of both men and women. In this country there has always been a myth that the poor are almost all nonwhite. Yet this is far from true (see table 5). Numerically there are more whites in poverty than any other single race. However, poverty rates for blacks and those of Hispanic origin are much higher than that for whites.

The data in table 5 also undermine the idea that most poor people should be supporting themselves. Children—those under age 18—account for about 40 percent of all poor, and seniors—those age 65 and over—account for almost 10 percent.

Poverty and Location

For the most part, the poor live in metropolitan areas (77.8 percent), with 45.7 percent living in central cities. These statistics mirror what most people believe,

Table 5: Profile of Persons in Poverty, 1995

Subpopulation	Number in Poverty (in thousands)	Poverty Rate in Subpopulation
Total	36,425	13.8%
White	24,423	11.2
Black	16,267	29.3
Asian and Pacific Islander	1,411	14.6
Hispanic origin	8,574	30.3
Male	4,512	6.1
Female	4,972	7.6
In families	27,501	12.3
Under 18 years	14,665	20.8
18 to 24 years	4,553	18.3
25 to 34 years	5,196	12.7
35 to 44 years	4,064	9.4
45 to 54 years	2,470	7.8
55 to 59 years	1,163	10.3
60 to 64 years	996	10.2
65 years and over	3,318	10.5
Lives in metropolitan areas	28,342	13.4
Lives in central city	16,269	20.6
Lives outside metropolitan areas	8,083	15.6
Northeast	6,445	12.5
Midwest	6,785	11.0
South	14,458	15.7
West	8,736	14.9

Source: Baugher and Lamison-White (1996).

namely, that poor people primarily live in urban areas and the inner city. Few Americans think of the poor as living in rural areas or small communities, which seem tranquil places not generally associated with poverty. Yet 22.2 percent of the poor live in such communities. And indeed poor people living in rural areas and small communities present a unique challenge to service providers because the services and resources they need are often too few or too difficult to access.

Did You Know…The term "Hispanic" is unique to the United States? No other nation uses this word. "Pertaining to the culture of Spanish- and Portuguese-speaking people…this term is often applied to people of Latin American ethnic background…Some people prefer the term 'Latino'" (Barker, 1995, p. 216). According to the U.S. Bureau of the Census, which first used the word in 1980, a person of Hispanic origin can be of any race. This means that people who describe themselves as Hispanic can have diverse backgrounds and very different mores and cultural expectations.

Poverty and Race

As table 6 clearly shows poverty rates for blacks and Hispanics have been about three times that for whites for years. Averages by decade show that over time the differences have lessened, but they remain extreme.

Minority groups are affected to very different extents by poverty. Poverty rates can vary greatly from one racial or ethnic group to another.

Poverty and Gender

Landrine and Klonoff (1997, p. 3) began their exploration of discrimination against women by observing that numerous studies have documented continuing discrimination against women in a wide variety of arenas including employment,

Table 6: Poverty Rates by Race and Hispanic Origin; 1959–95

Year	All Persons	White	Black	Hispanic
1995	13.8	11.2	29.3	30.3
1994	14.5	11.7	30.6	30.7
1993	15.1	12.2	33.1	30.6
1992	14.8	11.9	33.4	29.6
1991	14.2	11.3	32.7	28.7
1990	13.5	10.7	31.9	28.1
1989	12.8	10.0	30.7	26.2
1988	13.0	10.1	31.3	26.7
1987	13.4	10.4	32.4	28.0
1986	13.6	11.0	31.1	27.3
1985	14.0	11.4	31.3	29.0
1984	14.4	11.5	33.8	28.4
1983	15.2	12.1	35.7	28.0
1982	15.0	12.0	35.6	29.9
1981	14.0	11.1	34.2	26.5
1980	13.0	10.2	32.5	25.7
1975	12.3	9.7	31.3	26.9
1970	12.6	9.9	33.5	22.8[a]
1965	17.3	13.3	41.8[b]	
1959	22.4	18.1	55.1	NA
1990–95	14.3	11.5	31.8	29.7
1980–89	13.8	11.0	32.9	27.6
1970–79	11.8	9.0	31.6	23.1[c]
1960–69	17.5	13.7	37[d]	NA

Source: Baugher and Lamison-White (1996).

[a]Data for 1972.
[b]Data for 1966.
[c]Data for 1972–79.
[d]Data for 1966–69.

housing, health care, and social services. In particular, they stated, "thousands of studies" have shown that women are systematically paid less than men (Landrine & Klonoff, 1997, p. 5). Even social workers, members of a profession that proudly advocates for social and economic justice, work in organizations and agencies that discriminate against women. Gibelman and Schervish (1997, p. 135) found that in 1995 the median income for female social workers was $34,135, compared to $37,503 for their male counterparts! Schervish's findings are supported by a CSWE study that reported that female social work faculty members receive lower salaries at all academic ranks than their male colleagues (Lennon 1997, p. 24).

During the twentieth century, American family structure underwent significant changes. Two-parent families declined while single-parent families increased; birthrates declined for the general population but rose dramatically among teenagers; and women entered the workforce in great numbers. The United States now has many single-parent families that depend on the wages of a female head of household for their income.

Female-headed families are three times more likely to be in poverty than all families (table 7). Even more disturbing are the data for black and Hispanic female-

Table 7: Poverty Rates for Families by Race and Hispanic Origin; 1959–95

| Year | All Families | Families with Female Householder, No Husband Present | | | |
		Total	White	Black	Hispanic
1995	12.3%	36.5%	29.7%	48.2%	52.8%
1994	13.1	38.6	31.8	50.2	54.8
1993	13.6	38.7	31.0	53.0	53.2
1992	13.3	39.0	30.8	54.0	51.5
1991	12.8	39.7	31.5	54.8	52.7
1990	12.0	37.2	29.8	50.6	53.0
1989	11.5	35.9	28.1	49.4	50.6
1988	11.6	37.2	29.2	51.9	55.0
1987	12.0	38.1	29.6	54.1	55.6
1986	12.0	38.3	30.6	53.8	52.9
1985	12.6	37.6	29.8	53.2	55.7
1984	13.1	38.4	29.7	54.6	56.2
1983	13.9	40.2	31.2	57.0	55.1
1982	13.6	40.6	30.9	58.8	60.1
1981	12.5	38.7	29.8	56.7	55.9
1980	11.5	36.7	28.0	53.4	54.5
1975	10.9	37.5	29.4	54.3	57.2
1972	10.3	38.2	27.4	58.1	53.5
1965	15.8	48.9	35.4	65.3[a]	NA
1959	20.8	49.4	40.2	70.6	NA

Source: Baugher and Lamison-White (1996).

[a]Data from 1966.

headed households. In 1995, 48.2 percent of black female-headed families and 52.8 percent of Hispanic female-headed families were in poverty—nearly one in two families!

This hierarchy of poverty faithfully reflects income inequalities. Median income for all families in 1990 was $31,551. For two-parent families it was $39,076, for families headed by divorced women $15,762, and for families headed by a never-married woman $8,337 (Besharov, 1996, p. 35). Again race and ethnicity make a difference. Ethnic and gender discrimination together generate extremely low salaries for minority women and "impair women's ability to support themselves and their children" (Landrine & Klonoff, 1997, p. 8).

> if a job paid White men $20,000, then White women received $15,000, Black women $12,200, and Latinas $11,000 for the same work.
>
> If a job paid White men $35,000, then White women received $26,250, Black women $21,350, and Latinas $19,250 for the same work.
>
> If a job paid White men $50,000, then White women received $37,500, Black women $30,500, and Latinas $27,500 for the same work. (p. 8)

The group with perhaps the greatest risk of poverty consists of teenage parents and their children. The Children's Defense Fund (1998, pp. 81–82), a national nonprofit children's advocacy organization, has reported a reversal and slow decline in teenage pregnancy in the 1990s, but only 25 percent of teens giving birth were married. According to the Congressional Budget Office, within one year of giving birth to their first child, 50 percent of unwed teenage mothers go on welfare, and within five years, 77 percent are receiving welfare benefits (Basharov, 1996, p. 35).

Poverty and Age

The younger the person, the more likely he or she is to live in poverty. In 1995, 20.8 percent of children were in poverty and the age cohort with the next largest poverty rate was young adults, ages 18 to 24 (table 8). In the primary work years,

Table 8: Poverty Rates by Age Group, 1995

Age	Percentage below Poverty Threshold
Under 18 years	20.8%
18 to 24 years	18.3
25 to 34 years	12.7
35 to 44 years	9.4
45 to 54 years	7.8
55 to 59 years	10.3
60 to 64 years	10.2
65 years and over	10.5

Source: Baugher and Lamison-White (1996).

ages 25 to 54, poverty rates decrease. Finally, for people in retirement and relying on fixed incomes, poverty rates increase.

Despite a rise in poverty rates with retirement the percentage of seniors in poverty is lower than the rate for the whole population—13.8 percent. This was not always the case. In 1959, 35.2 percent of seniors lived in poverty compared with 22.4 percent of all people; and between 1967 and 1970, the senior poverty rate ranged from 29.5 to 21.6 percent, compared with a range of 14.2 to 12.6 percent for the whole population. The sharp decline in the poverty rate for seniors was a result of specific federal legislation (Jansson, 1993, p. 306). The Older Americans Act of 1965, the Supplemental Security Act, and the indexing of social security retirement checks in the early 1970s all helped to raise seniors' fixed incomes above the poverty threshold. It's important to recognize that the reductions in senior poverty are primarily due to federal support that pushes income levels slightly above the poverty threshold. Karger and Stoesz (1994, p. 135) reported that in addition to seniors in poverty, another 7 percent are "near poor," with incomes just above the poverty threshold.

Did You Know…Children have been getting poorer as our nation grows richer. American children are twice as likely as adults to be poor. Children in the United States are 1.6 times more likely to be poor than those in Canada, 2 times more likely than those in Britain, and 3 times more likely than those in France or Germany. What is most astonishing is that the United States is the wealthiest of these nations and has the lowest unemployment levels (Children's Defense Fund, 1998).

Of all the figures we have discussed so far those that probably disturb people the most are the ones that involve our nation's children. One in five children, 14,665,000 in 1995, are in poverty. Even worse, almost one in four children under age 6 live in poverty (table 9). While trends since 1970 are gloomy, child poverty rates declined two years in a row from 1993 to 1995. Yet given the nation's economic strength and growth of the 1990s, we would expect lower poverty rates for all people. "If America's periods of economic recovery do not start pulling children out of poverty sooner, faster, or for more years than they have been, America's child poverty problem never will show lasting improvement" (Children's Defense Fund, 1998, p. 17).

We know that poverty has negative consequences for those who live in it, but what specific effects does it have on children? What exactly does it mean to be a child raised in an impoverished home? Some facts can help to answer these questions:

1. Poor children are twice as likely as nonpoor children to have stunted growth, iron deficiency, and severe asthma.

2. Low-income children are three times more likely to die during childhood.

3. Poor children are more likely to die before their first birthdays than children whose mothers smoked during pregnancy.

Table 9: Poverty Rates for Children, 1959–95

Year	Under Age 18	Under Age 6
1995	20.2%	23.7%
1994	21.2	24.5
1993	22.0	25.6
1992	21.9	25.0
1991	21.8	24.0
1990	20.6	23.0
1989	19.6	22.5
1988	19.5	22.6
1987	20.3	22.4
1986	20.5	21.6
1985	20.7	22.6
1984	21.5	23.4
1983	22.3	24.6
1982	21.9	23.3
1981	20.0	22.0
1980	18.3	20.5
1975	17.1	18.2
1970	15.1	16.6
1965	21.0	NA
1959	27.3	NA

Source: Children's Defense Fund (1998).

4. Every year spent in poverty increases the chances that a child will fall behind grade level by age 18.

5. Every year at the current child poverty rate costs the nation $36 billion in lost future productivity because poor children are less educated and less effective workers (Children's Defense Fund, 1998, pp. 17–18).

We've seen that race and ethnicity affect poverty rates for women and for the general population, so we shouldn't be surprised to learn that race and ethnicity also affect age-specific poverty rates. In 1995 poverty rates were 41.5 percent for black youths and 39.3 percent for Hispanic youths, compared with 16.2 percent for white youths. Poverty rates were 25.4 percent for black seniors and 23.5 percent for Hispanic seniors, compared with an overall senior poverty rate of about 10 percent (Baugher & Lamison-White, 1996, pp. C-5–C-7). These numbers represent long-standing inequalities.

WHY IS THERE POVERTY IN A WEALTHY NATION?

Entire university courses are devoted to studying how poverty can exist in the midst of great wealth. Countless books and articles also attempt to answer this

Subsidized housing in a small midwestern city. These units were built for low-income working-class families and are located on the edge of the city.

question. The breadth of this topic allows us only to review some theories put forth to explain why poverty continues to exist.

Karger and Stoesz (1994, pp. 146–152) identified four theories of poverty: the culture of poverty, the underclass, eugenics and poverty, and the radical school of poverty. Each differs markedly from the others, and depending on your philosophical and political views you may have strong reactions, positive or negative, to some or all of the theories:

> *Culture of poverty*: Poverty and its traits are transmitted from one generation to the next. Behavior is learned and repeated. There is a sense of hopelessness, indifference, and dependence and a focus on the present rather than the future. Impulse control is lacking, and resignation and disintegration of the family if pervasive.

> *Underclass*: A population is clustered around similar behaviors and beliefs and is outside the dominant or majority section of society. Its neighborhoods deteriorate, employment opportunities diminish, and marriage rates decline. The underclass is on the outside looking in and is not able to access society's opportunity structure.

> *Eugenics*: Poverty is tied to genetics. Accumulation of wealth depends on ability, which is directly related to intelligence, which is inherited. The "most capable" citizen should receive the greatest benefits, which in turn will stimulate this group to take greater leadership in society.

Radical school: Poverty is exploitation of one group of people by another. The purpose of poverty is to provide a source of cheap labor—the cheaper the labor, the greater the profits. A second purpose of poverty is to provide the middle class with a group to whom it can feel superior, which moderates tension between the middle and upper classes.

Each of these theories is much more elaborate than the brief summaries we give here. At the end of the chapter we list further reading on these four theories.

Setting forth another perspective Darby (1996, p. 20) listed five factors that have produced poverty:

Decline in low-wage jobs: Fewer jobs are available for the labor pool.

Immigration: New immigrants take low-paying jobs away from unemployed residents.

Decline in labor force participation and work effort: Work effort among men is down over the long term.

Breakdown of traditional family structures: The number of single-parent families has increased, particularly among blacks.

Drugs: Alcohol, tobacco, and other drugs (ATOD) continue to plague the most disadvantaged populations. ATOD use among inner city youth is increasing.

According to Darby, these five factors are intertwined. Therefore, efforts to address poverty that are limited, in that they are only aimed at one of these five areas, can be futile. Rather, efforts must be coordinated to target all of these areas.

Johnson and Schwartz (1988) divided the causes of poverty into three broad areas: economic, social, and political. Economic causes relate to unequal distribution of income across society, inadequate income supports in public assistance programs—TANF and food stamps, for example—and unemployment and underemployment rates. Social causes of poverty refer to negative views the public holds of the poor, the strong belief in self-reliance, and discrimination against people based on race, ethnicity, and gender. Political causes include lack of participation in the political process by the poor and unjust social policies. Poverty and welfare programs are not popular in political circles and seem to be more vulnerable to public scrutiny and cutbacks than other public programs.

PROGRAMS TO AID THE POOR

It is time to examine current programmatic responses to poverty in the United States and to consider how these programs are viewed and how their recipients are treated. This section presents a brief overview of major public assistance programs.

In chapter 3 we learned that the modern welfare system has its roots firmly planted in the Great Depression of the 1930s and the passage of the Economic Security Act of 1935. A second major federal welfare initiative occurred in the 1960s with the advent of President Johnson's War on Poverty. Finally, a third, dramatic shift in federal social welfare programs for the poor took shape with the passage and implementation of the Personal Responsibility and Work Opportunity Reconciliation Act of 1996.

This act was a sweeping reform of the role of the federal government in welfare provision. This 1996 act dramatically restructured programs to aid the poor and ended the nation's six-decade-old guarantee of cash assistance to poor families.

Temporary Assistance for Needy Families

The 1996 act created a new federal program, Temporary Assistance for Needy Families (TANF), which replaced AFDC. TANF differs from AFDC in several ways:

1. States no longer have to help all families judged by the federal government to be in poverty but can use their own definitions of poverty and eligibility.

2. Parents must work within two years of receiving their cash benefits, and the option to shorten this two-year period is given to each state.

3. States must impose a sixty-month (five year) lifetime limit on TANF aid, and although states can shorten this length of time, they are not allowed to expand it. Therefore, five years is the lifetime limit.

4. Funds are given to states in block grants, which allow each state significant discretion in how to use the funds (Children's Defense Fund, 1998, p. 1).

Implementation of state discretion and time limits: No longer is cash assistance to the poor an entitlement, it is now short term and variable (Ginsberg, 1998, pp. 188–189). Taking advantage of the flexibility allowed by the federal legislation some states modified TANF services by setting stricter time limits on how long someone in poverty could receive cash assistance. For example, Florida and Georgia set their limits at 48 months, Indiana and Montana at 24 months, and Utah at 36 months (Children's Defense Fund, 1998, p. 4). Furthermore, some states limit the number of consecutive months a family can receive assistance: Arizona, Florida, Louisiana, Massachusetts, Oregon, South Carolina, Tennessee, and Virginia. South Dakota allows no more than 6 months of aid in a 12-month period (Children's Defense Fund, 1998, p. 4). Time spent on TANF as a child does not count toward an individual's 60-month lifetime limit.

All this variation takes place within an iron constraint, however. The lifetime limit of 60 months is a national limit. If a person receives TANF aid for 50 months in one state and then moves to a state with a lower time limit, such as Florida, then the second state's limit has already been exceeded and the person receives no further TANF aid there. Even if the person had moved to a state that had not lowered its time limit, only a further 10 months of TANF assistance would be available.

Work requirements: TANF requires adults to work, a significant departure from the AFDC program and the philosophy behind the War on Poverty of the 1960s. The law mandates that by 2002, a person must work a minimum of thirty hours each week, a rise from the twenty weekly hours required in 1997. A child's TANF benefits can be reduced or eliminated if the parent is not participating fully in the program.

Few forms of preparatory education and job training meet the work requirement. For example, adults over age 20 attempting to earn GEDs and most people working toward college degrees are not eligible for TANF. Community service may be used in place of work, but this option is left to the discretion of individual states.

As with most TANF implementation issues, states can establish their own guidelines on how soon a person must be working to avoid elimination from TANF rolls. Virginia requires a person to be employed within ninety days; other states demand employment within twenty-four months.

Child care: An important component of TANF is the requirement that communities provide childcare to TANF participants. As adults, in unprecedented numbers, are now required to work, there will be large increases in demand for childcare program slots; children cannot be left at home, unattended and unprotected. Funding is required for childcare services to support low-paid employees passing through the TANF system. Unfortunately, according to the Children's Defense Fund (1998, p. 6), not enough funds have been appropriated to support childcare for all of the poor. Social work professionals will be needed to assist these parents in finding low-cost childcare so that they can maintain their jobs.

Did You Know...To qualify for TANF aid a minor parent must live at home with parent(s) or in a home supervised by an adult. Also a teen mother must attend school or a training program once her baby is twelve weeks old.

Food Programs

Food stamps: The Federal food stamp program was designed to fight hunger and malnutrition. Prior to the Great Depression, no national coordinated effort addressed these fundamental issues. The problem was largely left to the states and local communities to deal with. For the most part, antihunger programs distributed actual food items. This practice moved to the national level when, in 1933, the Federal Surplus Relief Corporation was created to distribute surplus food.

The first food stamp program project, which ran from 1939 to 1943, used two types of stamps, blue and orange. Blue stamps could be used only for surplus commodities, while orange stamps allowed the purchase of any type of food.

In 1961, a demonstration food stamp program was started. It led in 1964 to the passage of the Food Stamp Act. Under the auspices of the Department of Agriculture, clients received stamps that allowed them to purchase certain American-grown or -produced food at certain supermarkets.

Did You Know...In 1997 the average amount of food stamps per person per meal was less than $.80.

The 1996 welfare reform efforts included a $27 billion cutback in the food stamp program over six years, to be achieved primarily by reducing, denying, or ending assistance to needy families.

In 1997, 21.4 million people living in 8.9 million households received food stamps. The maximum food stamp benefit for a family of three was $321 per month. Income eligibility for such a family was $17,340, or $1,445 per month. The family is also limited to at most $2,000 disposable assets, such as savings and checking accounts, and one car with a value no more than $4,650. Slightly more than 50 percent of food stamp participants are children who live in single-parent households. Ninety-one percent of food stamp households live below the poverty threshold, and nearly 23 percent of the households have earned income—that is, income earned from a job. The program cost to the federal government was $24.3 billion, of which $22.4 billion, or 92 percent went directly to benefits.

School lunch and breakfast and other food programs: Other federal food programs we need to consider in addition to food stamps include the National School Lunch and Breakfast Program, WIC, and Meals on Wheels. Targeted toward the poor, these programs were developed as supplements for specific vulnerable population groups.

In 1995 the school lunch and breakfast programs provided meals at reduced prices or free to 25.7 million poor students. Nationwide, 57 percent of all students in slightly more than 92,000 schools participated in the school lunch program; 6.3 million students in 60,000 schools participated in the breakfast program (U.S. House, 1991). Income eligibility for a family of three was $16,400.

The Special Supplemental Nutrition Program for Women, Infants, and Children (WIC) was enacted in 1972 to provide nutritional counseling and basic food supplements to prenatal and postpartum low-income women and their children. According to the Children's Defense Fund (1998, p. 43), every $1 spent on WIC saves $3.50 in future federal supports including health, education, and cash assistance. Women generally receive food vouchers that entitle them to certain items including milk, eggs, cheese, infant formula, cereals, and fruits and vegetables. The type and amount of food is specified, limiting the adult's selection. In 1995, the maximum income for a family of four was $29,693. WIC served 6.9 million individuals on a monthly basis (U.S. House, 1991), but with the 1996 welfare reform package, reduction in funding reduced the caseload by 200,000 each month. Nearly 45 percent of all babies born in the United States and 98 percent of eligible infants are involved in WIC. Even so, WIC only serves about 60 percent of eligible women, infants, and children.

Targeted to supplement and improve the nutritional needs of seniors in poverty, the Meals on Wheels program began in 1972. In some instances, meals are provided in the senior's home, while in other cases, meals are provided at a central location such as a senior center. An important and unintended benefit of the program is that seniors, many of whom are isolated, are provided daily contact with others. Volunteers who deliver meals to seniors are able to check on the elderly and ensure that all is fine with them.

Supplemental Security Income

Supplemental Security Income (SSI) was enacted in 1972 by combining three categorical programs that had been part of the Economic Security Act: Old Age Assistance, Aid to the Blind, and Aid to the Totally and Permanently Disabled. Prior to 1972, these three programs had been run by the states. With the creation of SSI, operations were transferred to the federal government.

SSI is a means-tested public assistance program. Age is not an eligibility requirement. Potential clients include the mentally retarded, those over age 65 who have little or no income, those who are legally blind, those disabled because of physical or mental impairment, some people who are visually impaired but do not meet the requirements for blindness, addicts and alcoholics in treatment, and children under age 18 who have an impairment comparable to those that determine eligibility for adults.

In 1995 slightly more than 6.5 million people participated in SSI (U.S. House, 1991). In addition to the income limitation, applicant resources must be minimal. Assets were limited to $2,000 for an individual and $3,000 for a couple, excluding a home; the value of a car was limited to $4,500. Average monthly SSI benefits were $219 ($2,628 per year) for an individual and $534 ($6,408 per year) for a couple. States, while not able to modify eligibility criteria, may increase monthly benefits.

Legal Immigrants

One of the most radical changes introduced by the 1996 welfare reform act was the sweeping elimination of legal immigrants from all public programs. Legal immigrants become eligible for public assistance only when they become citizens or have worked for forty calendar quarters (ten years). A public outcry led to the amendment of the law to allow legal immigrants receiving SSI on or before August 26, 1996, to continue to receive payments. Yet, this wasn't the case for all programs. As a result of the legislation approximately 300,000 legal immigrant children were removed from food stamp rolls (Children's Defense Fund, 1998, p. 7).

Ginsberg (1998, p. 192) identified the rationale behind this decisive move against immigrants: Legal immigrants should seek and obtain citizenship. Until then new immigrants are expected to support themselves or find assistance from private sources, including family or sponsors.

Earned Income Credit

The Earned Income Credit (EIC), also called the Earned Income Tax Credit, is a tax credit for working families with low incomes. One of the Clinton Administration's major welfare initiatives, it was developed to stimulate work among the poor. Eligible working families, either with or without children, pay less federal income tax or receive a larger tax refund.

In 1997, a family with one child and an annual income less than $25,760 was eligible for the EIC; the maximum credit was $2,210. For a family with two children and an annual income less than $29,290, the maximum EIC was $3,656. In most cases, the EIC benefit does not affect other program benefits such as housing supplements, TANF, food stamps, Medicaid, and SSI.

SUMMARY

Poverty cuts across all races and ethnic groups, both genders, and all age groups—indeed, more whites are poor than any other group. Nevertheless, poverty *rates* reveal that some groups are especially vulnerable. Women, minorities, and children suffer disproportionately from poverty. One in five of all children are in poverty and one in four of children under age 6.

No consensus exists about causes of poverty, and theories to explain it are diverse and controversial. The ideas proposed range from an individual's genetic makeup to deep, complicated structures of society.

All social work professionals need to be aware that 1996 was a pivotal year in redirecting sixty-one years of entitlement programs and that as a result governmental antipoverty strategies have changed dramatically. Public programs are now time limited with greater state discretion in imposing limits. In most cases, once a family exhausts its TANF lifetime limit it is left to its own devices. TANF represents a new direction in welfare programming that stresses employment and penalizes clients who do not work or are unable to meet program requirements on a consistent basis.

As social work professionals, what does this mean for us? The social worker's role in public assistance programs is not as clear as it once was. A visit to your local food stamp or TANF office reveals that few, if any, of the workers are professional social workers. The public may believe that social workers run these programs, but the reality is that we do not. The need to assist the poor remains, however, and many people still believe that this is where social workers as professionals need to be.

Poverty and its ravages can't be washed away by finding people jobs and wishing them well. Clients need to be linked with appropriate resources; they need workers who understand the emotional and psychological toll that poverty takes and who can suggest how best to respond to this person turmoil. Someone with a personal problem expects the best possible professional service from the social worker at the local mental health center. A patient in the hospital expects high-quality care from the hospital's social worker. Why should a poor person expect and receive a lower level of care?

A probably more important question concerns the sixty-month limit on welfare. What happens at the end of five years? Do we really believe that people forced without proper education into low-paying jobs will be self-sufficient within sixty months? And remember, a number of states have shorter time limits, some as short as twenty-four months. Where will these people go? Will they simply disappear? Of course not. They will remain in our communities—some more visible than others.

Some people will say that they were given a chance and we shouldn't do anything else. But what will happen when the first child dies on the streets because a parent's TANF time expired? What will happen when our country experiences an economic recession and jobs are just not available?

The poor will always be part of our society, and we must have public policies in place that protect them rather than cause them harm. Social workers can and should take the lead in promoting just social policies that create opportunities for all people to achieve their full potential and gain economic independence.

References

Barker, R. (1995). *The social work dictionary* (4th ed.). Washington, DC: NASW Press.

Besharov, D. J. (1996). Poverty, welfare dependency, and the underclass trends and explanations. In M. R. Darby (Ed.), *Reducing poverty in America: Views and approaches* (pp. 13–56). Thousand Oaks, CA: Sage.

Baugher, E., & Lamison-White, L. (1996). *Poverty in the United States, 1995* (Current Population Reports, Series P60–194). Washington, DC: U.S. Department of Commerce, Bureau of the Census.

Chelf, C. P. (1992). *Controversial issues in social welfare policy, government and the pursuit of happiness.* Newberry Park, CA: Sage.

Children's Defense Fund. (1998). *The state of America's children: Yearbook, 1997.* Washington, DC: Author.

Coulton, C., & Chow, J. (1995). Poverty. In R. Edwards et al. (Eds.), *Encyclopedia of social work* (19th ed., pp. 1867–1878). Washington, DC: NASW Press.

Darby, M. R. (1996). Facing and reducing poverty. In M. R. Darby (Ed.), *Reducing poverty in America: Views and approaches* (pp. 3–12). Thousand Oaks, CA: Sage.

DiNitto, D. M., & Dye, T. R. (1983). *Social Welfare: Politics and public policy.* Englewood Cliffs, NJ: Prentice-Hall.

Gibelman, M., & Schervish, P. H. (1997). *Who are we, a second look.* Washington, DC: NASW Press.

Ginsberg, L. (1998). *Conservatives social welfare policy: A description and analysis.* Chicago: Nelson-Hall.

Institute for Research on Poverty. (1998). *Poverty thresholds and poverty guidelines.* Retrieved from http://www.ssc.wisc.edu/lrp/.

Jansson, B. S. (1993). *The reluctant welfare state: A history of American social welfare policies* (2nd ed.). Pacific Grove, CA: Brooks/Cole.

Johnson, L. C., & Schwartz, C. L. (1988). *Social welfare: A response to human need.* Boston: Allyn and Bacon.

Karger, H., & Stoesz, D. (1994). *American social welfare policy: A pluralist approach.* New York: Longman.

Landrine, H., & Klonoff, E. A. (1997). *Discrimination against women: Prevalence, consequences, remedies.* Newberry Park, CA: Sage.

Lennon, T. (1997). *Statistics on social work education, 1996.* Alexandria, VA: CSWE.

Segal, E., & Brzuzy, S. (1998). *Social welfare policy, programs, and practices.* Itasca, IL: Peacock.

U.S. House Committee on Ways and Means. (1991). *Overview of entitlement programs.* Washington, DC: U.S. Government Printing Office.

Further Reading on Theories about Poverty

Culture of Poverty

Banfield, E. C. & Lewis, O. (1966). *The unheavenly city.* Boston: Little, Brown.

Moynihan, D. P. (1965). *The negro family: The case for national action.* Washington, DC: Office of Policy Planning and Research.

Underclass

Auletta, K. (1982). *The underclass.* New York: Vintage.

Ricketts, E., & Sawhill, I. (1988). Defining and measuring the underclass. *Journal of Policy Analysis and Management, 7*(2), 316–325.

Wilson, W. J. (1987). *The truly disadvantaged.* Chicago: University of Chicago Press.

Eugenics

Jensen, A. R. (1969). How much can we boost IQ and scholastic achievement? *Harvard Educational Review, 39,* 1–23.

Shockley, W. (1976). Sterilization: A thinking exercise. In C. Bahema (Ed.), *Eugenics: Then and now.* Stroudsburg, PA: Doidon, Hutchinson and Ross.

Radical School

Gil, D. (1981). *Unraveling social policy.* Boston: Schenkman.

Piven, F., & Cloward, R. (1971). *Regulating the poor.* New York: Vintage.

Chapter 8

Child Welfare Services

IN 1995, OVER 70 MILLION CHILDREN UNDER AGE 18 MADE UP 26.8 percent of the U.S. population (Baugher & Lamison-White, 1996, p. C-5). Supporting and caring for these millions of children is the single most important investment we an make in the future of our society. In twenty years, people now in their mid-40s will rely heavily on the children of today to keep the United States prosperous.

We cannot overestimate the importance of today's children to tomorrow's society. Don't you want the best and brightest people leading our country? Don't you want competent and self-assured people in the labor force, supporting the retirement of workers of today? We need to start raising these bright and competent people early. Through current investment in support and intervention we can avoid a future in which millions of undereducated and at best minimally competent Americans continue to suffer from personal and social problems deeply rooted in their childhood.

The importance of nurturing children is not a new idea. Indeed, a complex child welfare system exists to give children the opportunity to grow and reach their full potential. Karger and Stoesz have asserted, however, that child welfare programs and services are controversial because "they sanction the intervention of human service professionals in family affairs that are ordinarily assumed to be private matters related to parental rights" (1994, p. 338). As long as some people believe that child welfare is based on intrusion in private matters it will "remain among the more controversial in American social welfare" (Karger & Stoesz, 1994, p. 339).

Most of us can remember being told that being a child should be "fun." Many adults long to return to a simpler time in their lives when cares and responsibilities were few and far between. For many, Norman Rockwell's images of small-town America capture the ideal childhood. Televison too has actively promoted the idea of families as caring groups always having fun—even during hard times. *Father Knows Best, Good Times, The Brady Bunch,* and *The Cosby Show* illustrated life in suburbia and the city within a happy and caring family. When outside help was required, it often came from extended family members, friends, neighbors, religious organizations, and even membership associations.

In this society we expect, and the media encourages us to expect, that *no* child will face the horrors of poverty, homelessness, abuse and neglect, and inadequate

Name: Claire Massey
Place of residence: Longwood, Florida
College/university degrees: B.A., Rhodes College, M.S.W.,
Tulane University School of Social Work
Present position: School Social Worker
Previous work/volunteer experience: Community mental
health worker at state and local levels

What do you do in your spare time? I like to spend time with friends and read.

Why did you choose social work as a career? I was drawn to the field partly because I am
a "people person" by nature. I was also influenced by my mother's work as a school social
worker for about 7 years and her stories about the job.

What is your favorite social work story? I was once working with a young man diagnosed with paranoid schizophrenia. During an interview, he started telling me about a
book he had read called The Three Christs of Ypsilanti. The book was about a psychiatrist
who brought together three patients, all of whom believed they were Jesus Christ. The
book told what the psychiatrist did to try to help these clients see how unrealistic their
beliefs were. It became clear to me as my patient talked that he did not get the contradic-
tion of having three Christs. Instead, the book served to support his own belief that he
himself was in the process of becoming Christ. I learned that when helping clients even
the best intentions may not always work, and individualized assessment and plans to
assist clients are always needed.

*What would be the one thing you would change in our community if you had the power to
do so?* I would rid the community of poverty, inadequate housing, and insufficient medical care, especially for children.

health care, or live in an environment where crime, alcohol, tobacco, and drug abuse are the norm. This is a worthy goal, but we sometimes satisfy these expectations simply by denying that such problems exist. After all, if the media did tell negative stories, ratings would probably plummet. Few sponsors, if any, would want to be the ones to tell America that all is not well with its children. But all is *not* well with America's children. For millions of children life is filled with turmoil. These children repeatedly face crises that may eventually lead to chaos and tragedy.

In this chapter, we look in depth at America's children. We examine what life is like for many of them and explore the laws, programs, and services geared toward helping them. In addition, we discuss how the public and voluntary child welfare systems work together.

CHILD WELFARE DEFINED

Let's begin by looking at how **child welfare** has been defined. The *Social Work Dictionary* defines child welfare as

> that part of human services and social welfare programs and ideologies oriented toward the protection, care, and healthy development of children. Child welfare measures are found in national, state, and local programs, and are usually designed to prevent conditions that interfere with the healthy and positive development of children. (Barker, 1991, p. 35)

Heffernan, Shuttlesworth, and Ambrosino, like Barker, offer a very broad view of child welfare that encompasses "programs and policies that address the needs of children, youth, and families as diverse as the type of needs experienced" (1988, p. 167). Linderman (1995, p. 424) also stresses the formal organizational aspects of child welfare. His definition of child welfare characterizes it as both a public and a voluntary effort to coordinate seven interrelated objectives:

- ◆ Protect and promote the well-being of children
- ◆ Support families and seek to prevent problems that may result in neglect, abuse, and exploitation
- ◆ Promote family stability by assessing and building on family strengths while addressing needs
- ◆ Support the full array of out-of-home care services for children who require them
- ◆ Take responsibility for addressing social conditions that negatively affect children and families, such as inadequate housing, poverty, chemical dependence, and lack of access to health care
- ◆ Support the strengths of families whenever possible
- ◆ Intervene when necessary to ensure the safety and well-being of children

Dobelstein (1996, p. 242), however, omits the voluntary sector from his discussion and concludes that child welfare involves a broad range of public activities undertaken on behalf of children. Mirroring Dobelstein's view, Chelf describes family and child welfare policies as "covering a broad spectrum of public efforts . . .

[and] closely interwoven with several other policy sectors such as health, nutrition, education, and income maintenance, making them somewhat a confusing patchwork of policies and programs" (1992, p. 108).

The work of Kadushin and Martin is especially important in understanding social welfare because they view it from a social work perspective. For them, "child welfare is concerned with the general well being of all children. It encompasses any and all measures designed to protect and promote the bio-psycho-social development of children" (1988, p. 1). Gil gives another straightforward definition of child welfare: "In the simplest terms, as well as in a most profound sense, child welfare means conditions of living in which children can 'fare well,' conditions in which their bodies, minds, and souls are free to develop spontaneously through all stages of maturation" (1985, p. 12).

All these definitions of child welfare have several points in common. First, the child welfare system is firmly established within the public sector. Second, child welfare policy is closely tied to and directly influenced by family policy. Third, the policies, services, and programs included in child welfare cover a broad area, but all aim to provide children the environment they need for positive growth and full development. Taking into account these commonalities, we define the child welfare system as the system of services and programs that protect, promote, and encourage the growth and development of all children in order that they can achieve their full potential and function at their optimal level in their communities.

AMERICA'S DIVERSE CHILDREN AND THEIR FAMILIES

Although there are more white children than any other racial or ethnic group, population increases for blacks and Hispanics have been far greater than for whites (table 1). The Hispanic population in the United States has grown quite dramatically, but it is important to note that these rates may be inflated. The term "Hispanic" is difficult to define. In the U.S. census Latinos can classify themselves as Hispanic, black, or white; in other cases, they might be listed as both Hispanic and black. Part of the growth in the Hispanic population may actually reflect resolution of this confusion as individuals switch affiliations.

Just as American children have become more diverse so too have their families. The family is a critical institution in shaping and transmitting from generation to generation the values and rich traditions of culturally and ethnically diverse

Table 1: Population under Age 18, by Race and Ethnicity (in thousands)

Race/Ethnicity	1995	1990	1985	1980	Percentage Change, 1980–95
Total	70,566	65,049	62,876	62,914	12.2%
White	55,444	51,929	51,031	51,653	7.3
Black	11,369	10,162	9,545	9,368	21.4
Hispanic	10,213	7,457	6,475	5,276	93.6

Source: Baugher and Lamison-White (1996, pp. C-5–C-7).

Child Fact Sheet

- ◆ In 1993, 15.7 million children were poor—the highest number in thirty years.
- ◆ Between 1983 and 1992, the percentage of child support claims for which *any* payments were collected grew from 14.7 to 18.7 percent. At this rate, it will take 180 years for all cases to receive some child support.
- ◆ More than 9.4 million children were without health insurance in 1993, an increase of 800,000 over 1992.
- ◆ About 7 percent of all babies were born at low birthweight (5.5 pounds) in 1992.
- ◆ More than 13 percent of black babies were born at low birthweight, a rate that has not improved in over twenty years.
- ◆ More than 60 percent of married women with children under age 6 are in the labor force.
- ◆ In 1992, only thirty-two states supported prekindergarten programs.
- ◆ A record level of 14.2 million children received food stamps in 1993, up 51 percent over the 1989 level.
- ◆ WIC provided nutritional assistance to 6.5 million women, infants, and children in 1994—only 72 percent of those eligible.
- ◆ Guns killed 5,379 children in 1992, one every ninety-eight minutes.
- ◆ One in four persons reported as homeless are children.
- ◆ Nearly half of poor households pay more than half of their incomes for housing.
- ◆ An estimated 1.2 million families are on waiting lists for public housing.
- ◆ More than one million cases of child abuse and neglect were confirmed in 1993.
- ◆ An estimated 463,000 children were in foster care, group care, and residential treatment centers on an average day in 1993.
- ◆ An estimated 7.7 million children suffer from serious emotional disorders.
- ◆ Of teens who give birth 83 percent come from economically disadvantaged homes.
- ◆ Only one in three teenage mothers received early prenatal care in 1993.
- ◆ Eleven percent of 16–24-year-olds have dropped out of school.
- ◆ Each day about 16,000 thefts and violent crimes occur in or near a school. (Children's Defense Fund, 1996)

Americans. The kaleidoscope of families includes those whose roots are Anglo-European, Native Indian, African, Latino, Asian, and Middle Eastern, to mention a few. American families, whatever their ethnic heritage, are expected to respond to the expectations and norms of this society, even though many have very different cultural traditions, values, beliefs, norms, folkways, and mores. Some families hold their distinctive beliefs so strongly that they refuse to change; instead, they pass the same set of rigid expectations from one generation to the next. The key challenge for families is to balance the rich traditions and customs of their cultural heritage with the values and beliefs of the dominant society.

> *Did You Know...In 1996, 68 percent of American children lived with two parents, down from 85 percent in 1970; about 24 percent lived only with their mothers, 4 percent with their fathers, and 4 percent with neither parent (Brunner, 1997, p. 365).*

Family structures are also becoming more diverse. No longer do families mirror the traditional stereotype of a two-parent household in which the father works and the mother maintains the home. Single-parent households, homosexual parents, and parents who both work are all becoming more common. For many, parents working outside the home, and in some cases having a second job, is not a choice but a necessity.

Divorce rates are increasing, and more children are seeing their parents split up than ever before. In the thirty-two years between 1960 and 1992, the number of divorces tripled from 400,000 to 1,200,000 annually, with nearly 50 percent of all 1992 marriages ending in divorce (Lindsey, 1994, p. 73).

Another significant force shaping family structure is the growth in the number of children born out of wedlock to single parents. Between 1950 and 1991, the number of such births increased almost ninefold from 140,000 to 1,200,000 annually (Lindsey, 1994, p. 74). Although the birthrate for adolescents—that is, the number of children born per 1,000 adolescents—declined in the early 1990s, 518,389 babies were born to teenage mothers in 1994 (Children's Defense Fund, 1998, pp. 81, 82). In that year, 36 percent of children lived with a single parent who had never married the birth partner (Brunner, 1997). Increased divorce rates and high out-of-wedlock birthrates have together fueled an increase in the number of single-parent households.

Have you ever wondered why so many people worry about the growing number of single-parent households? Why does it matter whether a family is single-parent or two-parent? The primary reason is that two-parent families usually have a greater income and therefore greater resources with which to carry out their parenting obligations and responsibilities. Simply stated, by pooling their income two parents have more money for the family to spend on goods and services. Lindsey (1994, p. 87) estimated that the difference between two- and one-parent families is so great that a single parent earns only 25 percent of what two parents can earn. Underlying this figure is the fact that most single parents are women, who have income levels much lower than average.

A two-parent family is also better able to supervise its children. With two adults available, whether taking turns or jointly, more nurturing parent-child time is available. A single parent often has no one to help ease the childcare burden. The single parent thus faces alone enormous challenges, having to manage a lower family income and singlehandedly maintain a safe and nourishing home environment (Lindsey, 1994, p. 87).

A third significant development changing family structure is the rise in "blended families." A blended family is one in which the primary caretakers did not give birth to one or more of the children who live in the household. Such families are most often the result of divorce and remarriage. With the high rate of American divorce and lifestyle adjustment, blended families are becoming more common.

These families often face a difficult task because supportive relations may need to be developed even before they can be nurtured. Becoming a blended family requires adjustment because members may enter and reenter the family at various times throughout their lives. These adjustments intensify the need to establish and maintain family unison and support. Although all family systems need constant negotiation to maintain equilibrium, blended families face the added struggle of keeping their balance as family members come and go.

The growing diversity and changing structure of American families is the focus of much attention. The kind of family situation regarded as "ideal" is often shaped by a **political lens**. Think about political candidates and their campaign rhetoric and advertisements. How often have you seen "the family" play a starring role in a local, state, or national election? The Republican Party's *Contract with America* (Gillespie & Schellhas, 1994) and the Christian Coalition's (1995) *Contract with the American Family* placed the family as the centerpiece of all political activities. Why have children and families become such hot political items? Three reasons come to mind immediately:

Every human being was once a child: Having been a child and had experiences that influenced the way you think and feel about things as you aged helps raise your consciousness in this area. Most of us identify with children's issues simply because of our own experiences. All of us had positive and negative childhood experiences. Most of us cherish the good times and wish we could have avoided the bad ones. Few, if any, adults believe it is in a child's best interest to suffer physical or emotional pain. Therefore, people support and encourage programs and services that prevent and alleviate children's suffering.

Children are vulnerable: Most adults agree that all children should be protected and have a safe environment in which to grow. Adults are responsible for ensuring that children are shielded from various risks.

Everyone has a family: Just as all of us were children once, we were all raised in some kind of family. Our families probably differed vastly. Some had two parents; others come from single-parent homes. Some people were raised with siblings, others without. Some were raised in foster homes or were adopted; others had aunts, uncles, or other relatives as their primary caretakers; and for some, institutions played the family role. No matter what our family background, our experiences mean we have strong feelings about what families should be like.

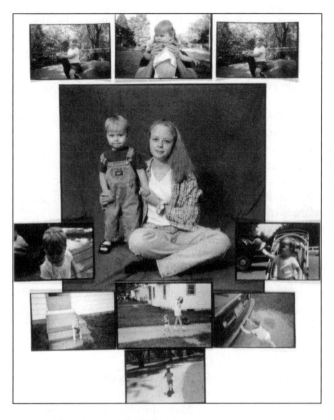

These photographs were developed in an Arts Outreach project for teenage mothers. The program, "My Life, My Lens, My Child," was part of an effort to help the mothers to finish high school. The program, staffed by social workers and teachers, taught photography skills, provided enrichment, and offered a positive school experience. The mothers photographed their children in various settings and created collages.

THE RIGHTS OF CHILDREN

Children have fewer rights than adults (Wineman, 1995, p. 465). In this, two counterbalancing forces are at play. On one hand, we recognize that children generally are not able to make mature decisions. This is not a negative statement about young people but rather refers to their inexperience. For this reason, children's rights are limited, and critical decisions about and responsibility for their lives rests, not with them, but with their caregivers. On the other hand, we also recognize that children need protection—sometimes from their own caretakers. As a result, we have established a complex system of child protective services.

The interesting history of children's rights thus for the most part reflects ambivalence. From a legal standpoint children are treated differently than adults. Children can face "status offenses"—that is, crimes based on status, in this case age. For example, a child can be arrested or detained for drinking alcohol, smoking cigarettes, being truant or being a runaway. An adult cannot be arrested merely for smoking or drinking (unless doing so causes a public disturbance) or for running away from home or being truant.

The overriding principle of *parens patriae*—under which children can become wards of the state—guided interpretations of children's rights. This principle sup-

ported creation of a broad range of juvenile services including parent-child relationships (Crosson-Tower, 1998, p. 270). Taking this basic position, child advocates
were able to argue that children should be viewed in a different light from adults
and offered rehabilitation rather than punishment.

In 1899, the first juvenile court was established in Chicago based on the principle of *parens patriae* and the belief that children could be rehabilitated, which
required a legal system far different from the punishment-based adult system. By
1925, all but two states—Maine and Wyoming—had juvenile courts; by 1945 all
states had such courts. Prosecution took a back seat to treatment as the primary
focus of the juvenile justice system. Hearings were closed to the public to protect
the child's right to confidentiality, and all juvenile legal records were sealed once
the child reached the legal age of maturity, generally age 18. The juvenile court
operated very informally. Attorneys were rarely provided for child offenders, and
trial by jury and the right to appeal a decision were not available options. In these
courtrooms hearsay evidence was admitted. Remember, the court's purpose was
twofold: 1) to identify the problem and 2) to develop and implement an appropriate
treatment plan.

The juvenile court changed dramatically as a result of U.S. Supreme Court
decisions in the 1960s. Juveniles were given many of the legal protections enjoyed
by adults. Courts were required to allow attorneys to be present; witnesses could be
cross-examined; defendants had the right to refuse to incriminate themselves; and
guilty decisions (or, in some states, "not innocent" decisions) had to meet the legal
standard of reasonable doubt.

In recent years, as violent juvenile crime has worsened, people have begun to
ask whether children should also face some of the same penalties as adults. Horrific
crimes committed by children in 1998 alone left many people in shock. Two young
boys, ages 8 and 9, in Chicago, Illinois, murdered a young girl in order to ride her
bicycle; two teenagers in Arkansas shot and killed schoolmates; another teenager
walked into a school hallway and indiscriminately murdered his junior high school
peers. The Chicago youth were released to their parents because state law forbade
the incarceration of a child under age 10; these cases sparked a national debate over
whether the teens should be tried in adult courts and, if found guilty, should serve
their sentences in adult prisons or even be subjected to the death penalty. Is there
an answer? At what age do we stop trying to rehabilitate young people? As you have
probably guessed there are no clear-cut answers to these questions.

In a nutshell, children have few rights, and there is little agreement on what
further rights, if any, they should be granted. The courts have primarily defined
children's rights with regard to criminal proceedings against them. In addition,
children have the right to financial support and education (Gustavsson & Segal,
1994, pp. 4, 6). This is only the situation in the United States, however. Interna-
tionally, the United Nations has brought the rights of children to the forefront. The
UN Convention on the Rights of Children adopted in 1989 a declaration of children's rights. By the mid-1990s, more than 154 nations had ratified the declaration.
But what about the United States? You may be surprised to learn that the United

States, together with Iraq, Somalia, and Singapore, do not support the declaration and, by 1996 had not ratified it. The declaration is very specific about issues facing children:

> Preamble. . . Childhood is entitled to special care and assistance. . . . The child. . . should grow up in a family environment, in an atmosphere of happiness, love, and understanding. . . . The child, by reason of his physical and mental immaturity, needs special safeguards and care, including appropriate legal protection.

> Article 3 (1). In all actions concerning children . . . the best interests of the child shall be a primary consideration.

> Article 18 (1). . . . Both parents have common responsibilities for the upbringing and development of the child. Parents or, as the case may be, legal guardians, have the primary responsibility for the upbringing and development of the child.

> Article 19 (1). State parties (government) shall take appropriate legislative, administrative, social and educational measures to protect the child from all forms of physical or mental violence, injury or abuse, neglect or negligent treatment, maltreatment or exploitation, including sexual abuse, while in the care of parent(s), legal guardian(s) or any other person who has the care of the child (United Nations, 1989)

THE DESIGN OF THE AMERICAN CHILD WELFARE SYSTEM

Formal child welfare programs and services are found in both public and private settings. Government programs—local, state, and federal—are augmented by both for-profit and nonprofit agencies. Together, these programs form a complex system that starts with prenatal care and ranges to opportunities for teenagers.

Programs are varied, but they can generally be categorized as child protective services, family preservation, out-of-home services, and other services.

Child Protective Services

Child protective services (CPS) is probably the best known as well as the most controversial children's program. The intent of CPS is to protect children from abusive situations in order that they can grow and develop.

We've all heard stories about abusive CPS workers responding to unfounded charges, taking children from their parents, breaking up families, and ruining the lives of countless people. In fact, the CPS worker investigates each allegation of abuse or neglect and determines whether the charges are founded or unfounded. A case is opened if the investigation demonstrates that abuse or neglect is indeed occurring. A child is only removed from the home if his life is in immediate danger. An open case may receive direct services from the agency or from other contract agencies, such as a family service agency. The case is reviewed by CPS staff and is closed once all goals are achieved.

All states provide some form of CPS. In 1962, a study of battered children in hospitals recommended that suspected cases be reported so that protective measures could be taken. By 1966 all states had passed legislation concerning abuse (Lindsey, 1994, p. 92).

---

*Did You Know...*Neglect *is maltreatment through the failure to provide needed, age-appropriate care.* Physical abuse *is physical injury resulting from punching, beating, kicking, biting, burning, or otherwise harming a child (National Resource Center on Child Abuse and Neglect).*

The Beginning of CPS: The Case of Mary Ellen

In 1873, Mrs. Etta Angell Wheeler, a church visitor in New York City, learned from people in a neighborhood about a 9-year-old girl, Mary Ellen Wilson, who had been whipped and left alone for hours on end. Neighbors in her apartment building heard the child's cries time and again. The New York City Department of Charities had placed Mary Ellen in this home when she was 18 months old. There had been no followup by the agency to assess the placement. Mrs. Wheeler sought help from a number of charitable organizations and the police to protect Mary Ellen, but no agency was willing to intervene and no CPS organization existed. She turned for help to Mr. Henry Bergh, president of the New York Society for the Prevention of Cruelty to Animals. The society intervened with court action and Mary Ellen was removed from the home.

The court found the home to be abusive. The foster mother, Mrs. Mary Connolly, was arrested and found guilty of assault. The court decided that Mary Ellen was to move to a group home, but Mrs. Wheeler asked that the child be placed in her care. Mary Ellen moved in with Mrs. Wheeler's mother and stayed with her until the mother's death.

Within a few months of the reported abuse, the New York Society for the Prevention of Cruelty to Children was founded, the first such organization in the world. (Watkins, 1990)

In 1966, there were 2,025,956 reports of alleged child abuse or neglect, involving some 3,000,000 children. Of those investigated, 28.3 percent were substantiated, 6.1 percent indicated abuse or neglect, and 57.7 percent were unfounded. According to statistics the most common form of maltreatment was neglect (57.7 percent), followed by physical abuse (22.2 percent), other types of maltreatment (10.5 percent), sexual abuse (12.3 percent), emotional maltreatment (5.9 percent), and other (14.5 percent; U.S. Department of Health and Human Services, 1998, pp. 2-1, 2-3, 2-7–2-8).

Slightly more than half of victims were under age 4, 53 percent were female, and 53 percent were white. About 77 percent of the perpetrators—that is, people who victimized children—were parents, and another 11 percent were other relatives (U.S. Department of Health and Human Service, 1998, pp. 2-8, 2-9, 2-10, 2-14).

According to the Children's Defense Fund the number of abuse and neglect cases continues to rise. It reports that between 1985 and 1995, the number of reports rose by 61 percent and the number of confirmed reports by 31 percent. The Children's Defense Fund also believes that these numbers undercount the true incidence of abuse and neglect, a claim it supports by citing a note that the number of abused and neglected children was actually triple the number reported by the U.S. Department of Health and Human Services (Children's Defense Fund, 1998, pp. 51, 53).

Family Preservation Services

Family preservation services seek to stabilize troubled families in a short period of time (Linderman, 1995, p. 424). They require intensive, direct social services with the entire family. The goal of family preservation is to prevent child removal from the parental home when direct services may avoid the need for such out-of-home placement, keep families together, and strengthen family bonds (Tracy, 1995, p. 973). Gaining popularity in the 1970s and 1980s, these services received a boost in 1980 with the passage of the Adoption Assistance and Child Welfare Act (P.L. 96–272). The 1980 act called for reasonable efforts to be made to keep children within their families and to minimize family disorder.

The Child Welfare League of America (1989) recommended very specific standards for program implementation. Work is intensive, requiring anywhere from six to ten hours of direct worker-family contact each week. The typical case requires four to twelve weeks of contact, and a worker's caseload should range between two and six families. In addition, the worker is on call twenty-four hours a day, providing a mix of services (Edna McConnell Clark Foundation, n.d.).

Research on family preservation has shown some positive outcomes. The first study examined Homebuilders, a program in Washington. The research findings revealed that out-of-home placement was avoided in 97 percent of cases (Lindsey, 1994, pp. 41–43). The Edna McConnell Clark Foundation reported that family preservation workers are extremely positive about this form of intervention. Clients too are strong supporters of family preservation programs: 99 percent are satisfied with services, 87 percent rated services as helpful, and 97 percent would recommend family preservation to other families in similar situations (Edna McConnell Clark Foundation, n.d.). Tracy (1995, p. 978) wrote, however, that not all reports reveal such high success rates, and in fact much more research is needed to establish the validity of family preservation.

Out-of-Home Services

Out-of-home services are programs for children no longer living with their biological or legal guardians, whose parental rights have been or may be terminated. Typical out-of-home programs are foster care, residential care, and adoption.

Foster Care: The *Social Work Dictionary* defines foster care as physical care for children "who are unable to live with their natural parents or legal guardians"

Myths and Facts about Out-of-Home Placements

Myth: Foster care is in the best interests of children who have known the hurt of abuse and neglect.

Fact: In some cases, when the child is at great risk, removal from the home is necessary, but it is not necessarily the solution. The devastating norm for foster children is multiple moves, extended stays, and no stable permanent family ties.

Myth: Foster care is principally a problem of poor and minority families.

Fact: Problems leading to abuse and neglect know no race or class boundaries. Of all children entering foster care and substitute care, almost 55 percent are white, 22 percent are black, and 10 percent are Latino.

Myth: Children placed in foster care are typically younger than 5 years of age.

Fact: Roughly half the children in out-of-home care are over age 10. However, the greatest growth in such placements is for infants under 1 year of age.

Myth: Most children in foster care are placed there because of physical or sexual abuse.

Fact: More than half of child removals are for neglect.

Myth: Child abuse is on the rise.

Fact: While the number of reports has increased, the evidence does not clearly substantiate that the actual incidence is on the rise. The growing number of reports may be a result of the public's growing awareness of child abuse and of resources to contact.

Myth: Parents whose children are removed from the home do not want their children, do not deserve their children, and cannot or will not change their behavior.

Fact: Experts working with troubled families find that their problems are more extreme versions of similar issues confronting any family. Troubled families often lack resources, knowledge, and skills that most take for granted. Most parents want their children and really want to be good parents. Proper help can help many families, but it must be timely.

Myth: Child protective service workers are well-trained professionals but have little authority to protect children.

Fact: The child protective service worker position is an entry-level job requiring minimal education. Most states do not require education in social work and allow a person to work in this position with a degree in music, math, and other non–human service disciplines. Caseloads are usually high, pay and morale low, and employee turnover high. Child protective service workers have a wide range of authority, including the power to remove a child from a home, in some instances without supervisor or court approval. (Edna McConnell Clark Foundation, n.d.)

(Barker, 1995). The goals of foster care include 1) maximum protection for the child, 2) permanency, and 3) family preservation. Foster care is generally organized through state or county social services. It may be provided within foster family homes, residential group homes, or institutions (Everett, 1995, p. 375).

A child is placed in a foster home temporarily. Placement may be made at the start of a CPS investigation if the worker assesses that the child's life is in immediate danger. The family is entitled to a court hearing, in most states within twenty-four to seventy-two hours of the time of removal, if the child was removed without a court order. In other cases, placement may occur after a court hearing, if a CPS investigation finds that this action is in the best interests of the child. Any placement must be in the least restrictive setting. For example, a foster home is less restrictive than a residential treatment center; placement with a relative is less restrictive than removal to a nonbiological foster home.

Children in foster care are provided with certain protections including the following:

◆ A detailed written plan that describes the appropriateness of the placement, the services to be provided to the child, and a plan for achieving permanence
◆ Periodic case review at least once every six months, though a jurisdiction may review a case more often
◆ A state inventory of children who have been in care for more than six months in order to track these children and the goals related to their placement
◆ Procedural safeguards that involve parental input in the development of case plans
◆ Reunification or permanency planning services, which programs include day care, homemaker services, counseling, parent education, adoption services, and followup (Everett, 1995, p. 381).

In 1994, an estimated 468,000 children were in foster care, a 16 percent increase over 1990 (Children's Defense Fund, 1998, p. 53). Most children in foster care are placed in foster family homes; most are boys; about three-quarters have no known physical disabilities; and half are in care for more than two years (Everett, 1995). The Children's Defense Fund (1998, p. 54) has reported that the number of children entering foster care exceeds the number leaving. In other words, the population of children in foster care is growing.

How are foster parents selected? What is their motivation—money? What about reports that children in foster homes are often subjected to more abuse? (Mushlin, 1991, pp. 102–104). Kantrowitz and King (1991, p. 98) defended foster parents by stating that most have a calling, a sense of altruism, for the work. People choose to be foster parents because of their love for children. Their decisions to take children into their homes have to be for something more than the money because reimbursement rates are so low (Kantrowitz & King, 1991, p. 98). At the time daily reimbursement rates ranged from $5.00 to $12.00 (remember, this article was written in 1991, so reimbursement figures are higher today).

We need to keep in mind that children in foster care are coming from terrible home situations. Because permanency planning interventions are preferred, only those children in the most unbearable situations are removed. Most foster children are burdened by a unique set of complex problems that requires understanding and compassion. Being a foster parent is not easy, and it does require a special person.

Residential care: Residential group care, also called institutional care, takes place in physical settings apart from the natural parents or legal guardians. Residential settings include residential treatment centers, state hospitals, detention centers, runaway shelters, and halfway houses. All have a common theme: caring for groups of special needs children, twenty-four hours a day (Whittaker, 1995, p. 451).

Did You Know…The first residential program for children was established in 1729 in New Orleans. The program was developed by Ursuline nuns to care for children orphaned as a result of a battle with Native Americans at Natchez.

A number of trends in residential care have been consistent over time:
- The number of residential facilities is increasing though the actual number of youth in care has declined
- The two main types of new facilities are juvenile delinquent centers and mental health centers
- The average number of children in facilities has declined to fewer than thirty per facility
- One-third of children are in juvenile justice facilities; one-quarter are in mental health settings; and one-fifth are in child welfare facilities (Whittaker, 1995, p. 452).

Did You Know…The terms runaway, throwaway, *and* push-out *describe youths (under age 18), who no longer live at home with their legal guardians. A* runaway *is a person running away from home. A* throw-away *is a person forced or thrown out of home by the caretaker. A* push-out *is a person who with the agreement of the caretaker decides it is in everyone's best interest that he or she leave home.*

Residential programs are also available for children who no longer live with their legal caretakers. Typically such programs are shelters that provide temporary housing and counseling. The purpose of the runaway shelter is to get youths off the streets, provide protection, and attempt to reunite children with their families. Social service providers recognize the importance of getting runaways off the streets and into services as quickly as possible. Colby (1990, p. 282) reported that after living on the streets for two weeks, 75 percent of runaways turn to theft, drugs, prostitution, or pornography for support.

Activity…Contact your local runaway shelter and ask about the rules of admission and length of stay. Ask what happens to youths who leave the shelter but do not return home.

State-established limits on the length of time that young people may reside in shelters generally restricts these settings to homeless youths. Some programs require parental consent for children to remain in shelters. What happens to the youth whose parents do not grant permission for her to remain in the program? And some programs do not allow disruptive youths or youths with mental health problems to enter shelters. What types of community programs, if any, are available for these youths?

Adoption: The *Social Work Dictionary* defines adoption as *"taking a person . . . into one's home and treating the child as though born into the family. A legal as well as a child welfare function and process, it includes changes in court records to show the legal transfer of the individual from the birth parents to the adoptive parents"* (Barker, 1991, p. 5). Adoption creates a *"legal family for children when the birth family is unable or unwilling to parent"* (Barth, 1995, p. 48).

Massachusetts is credited with being the first state to enact an adoption law, in 1851 (Cole, 1985, p. 639), though some cite Mississippi, in 1846, and Texas, in 1850, as having earlier adoption statutes (Crosson-Tower, 1998, p. 356). Whichever state was first, there is consensus that the Massachusetts legislation served as the model for other states (Kadushin & Martin, 1988, p. 535; Crosson-Tower, 1998, p. 639). By 1929 all states had enacted some form of adoption law.

During the nineteenth and much of the twentieth centuries most children in need of homes lived in orphanages. Young people were placed there for any number of reasons: poor parents who couldn't afford to raise their children placed them in orphanages, others were born to unwed mothers, and others were orphaned by death or were abandoned (Crosson-Tower, 1998, p. 357).

Charles Loring Brace, a minister and organizer of the Children's Aid Society in New York City, led one of the more compelling child welfare efforts of the nineteenth century. Brace developed what became known as the Orphan's Train, through which some 50,000 to 100,000 urban orphans were placed on midwestern and western farms (Quam, 1995, p. 2575). The children, picked up on the streets of New York City, were put on a wagon train heading west. In town after town, city after city, the train would stop and put the youths up for adoption. Brace believed that moving waifs off city streets, away from the temptations of urban life, to more rural, tranquil lives of work and family, would allow them to be prosperous and productive (Brace, 1872).

The Orphan's Train was a manifestation of the nation's prevailing belief, no less strong today, that children should live in wholesome environments where caretakers can provide for their needs. Remember the basic child welfare principle: in the best interests of the child? Brace's program and other child-saving programs, including orphanages, were built on this ideal.

Today, adoption takes place in many different ways. These include placing children through child placement agencies and through direct agreements between two parties sanctioned by the courts.

"Agency-based adoption" occurs in government, nonprofit, and for-profit family welfare settings. It entails a rigorous and time-consuming process, which generally includes the following steps:

Name: Lysa Schuller
Place of residence: Orlando, Florida
College/university degrees: B.S.W. & M.S.W. Student, University of Central Florida
Present position: M.S.W. student
Previous work/volunteer experience: Volunteer at several agencies in the areas of health and mental health

What do you do in your spare time? I enjoy snow skiing, water skiing, and reading.

Why did you choose social work as a career? I love working with people and I want to convey to others that they have the capacity and the ability to grow toward their potential. What I love most about social work is that the profession is dedicated to helping people. In this field I am able to assist people in getting the services and resources they need. I enjoy working with diverse individuals.

What is your favorite social work story? At BETA, an agency that assists pregnant and homeless teenage girls and women, I was able to impact a woman's life in a way I will never forget. While the 23-year-old woman was staying at BETA I was able to help her regain her sense of autonomy. I helped her to find a job and a place to live, and I assisted her in achieving reunification with her 5-year-old son. I was so proud of her when she later enrolled in a local community college.

What would be the one thing you would change in our community if you had the power to do so? I would love to get individuals more involved in community service and get recognition for those individuals who do provide valuable service to the community. I would like to change the economic power structure to allow for a redistribution and reward system for professionals such as teachers and other individuals who provide services so essential to the development of our communities.

Identification of suitable children ensures that all children in need of adoptive homes are identified.

Freeing for placement is the legal process by which custody of the child is removed from one set of parents in order that it can be assigned to the adoptive parents.

Preparation for adoption involves working with the child before adoption to prepare him for his new family. Potential adoptive parents are closely scrutinized by the agency to ensure they have the resources needed to raise a child in a loving, caring environment.

Selection of adoptive parents is conducted by the agency after close review of applications and supporting materials. The agency's goal is to match a child with the adoptive parent who can best meet her unique needs.

Placement with adoptive family is characterized by many social workers as one of the most exciting days for worker, family, and child. It is a time of joy as the new family begins its life together. Everyone involved often sheds tears!

Postplacement services include a variety of agency-based supports to the family as it makes the transition to a new system of relations. By placing a child with a specific family, the agency is affirming that the placement is in the best interests of the child. To increase the likelihood of success, the agency offers the family continuing supports ranging from individual and family counseling and support groups to social worker home visits. Again, the agency wants as few disruptions as possible with the adoption. Nevertheless, sometimes the child is removed from the adoptive parent's home. When this happens, the social worker does not blame anyone or refer to the original placement as a failure but instead looks again at what supports are needed for the child and what type of child is best suited for that particular family.

Legal finalization of the adoption takes place after a period of time following initial placement. There is a popular myth that adoption is final when the child is placed with the family. Not so for agency-based adoptions. The final legal assignment of custody is made after an extended period of time. The period varies among agencies; the norm seems to be six months to one year following placement. The court is the final authority in legally assigning custody of the child to the adoptive parent. The court's decision is reached after review of the agency's reports and recommendations.

Postadoption services provide children with any needed supports such as counseling, and parents with educational or ongoing counseling sessions. Agencies recognize that it may be in the best interests of the child for support services to be provided for extended periods beyond the legal adoption phase (Cole, 1985, p. 644).

Have you seen advertisements in your college or local newspaper that read something like this?

> Loving couple with a great deal to give looking to adopt a newborn. Will pay all fees, including prenatal, delivery, hospitalization, legal, and followup costs. Please call . . . .

Some families resort to private sources, also called "independent adoption," rather than use agency-based adoption services. Agreements are reached between the two families involved, and the courts, assisted by attorneys, finalize the legal arrangements. These adoptions can take place much faster and with less red tape than the agency-based process. The prospective adoptive parents usually provide financial support for the pregnant mother and her family, cover all related health costs, and often add a financial stipend—that is, a salary.

Independent adoption is costly, running to tens of thousands of dollars. For-profit adoptions are against the law, but Cole (1985, p. 663) has claimed that the law is little enforced. Recognize that with independent adoptions there is less scrutiny and followup than with agency-based services. Cole suggested that problems with independent adoptions could be reduced if the following steps are taken:

- ◆ Courts require a detailed statement of all monies that change hands relating to the adoption.
- ◆ Violators are vigorously prosecuted and subjected to severe sanctions.
- ◆ Communities provide enough financial support to adoption agencies that they can offer the same level of health and maintenance care that takes place with independent adoption (1985, p. 664).

There are three potential pools for adoption: healthy infants, children with special needs, and children from foreign countries (Kadushin & Martin, 1988). Fewer healthy infants are available for adoption because of the increased availability of birth control and abortion (Crosson-Tower, 1998, p. 374). It is common for a couple to be told the waiting period for a healthy infant may be up to ten years!

A special needs child has unique characteristics that can include race and ethnicity, medical problems, older age (over age 3), attachment to a sibling group, developmental disabilities, and emotional difficulties (Crosson-Tower, 1998, p. 374). Such children are much harder to place because of their special needs and are more available than healthy infants for adoption.

In recent years, more and more people are looking to the international community for children to adopt. Children born in areas of civil strife or extreme poverty are the main subjects of such adoptions. Latin America, Vietnam, Korea, the Philippines, India, and other Asian countries have been the principal nations and regions sending children to the United States (Crosson-Tower, 1998, p. 379).

A final but controversial point about adoption. Our discussion has been framed by the notion of placement in the best interests of the child. Yet one practice in adoption may run counter to this central tenet of child welfare: there is strong pressure to place children with adoptive families of the same race or ethnicity. The justification is that the cultural needs of a child far outweigh other placement considerations. For example, the National Association of Black Social Workers does not support the placement of African American children in nonblack homes. Or consider the 1978 Indian Child Welfare Act, which places responsibility for adoption of Native American children within tribes rather than with traditional public child welfare agencies. The 1978 law requires Native American children to be placed with extended family members as a first option and then with other tribal families, regardless of the wishes of the parents.

Should adoption be constrained by race and ethnicity and other cultural factors? Does the compelling need for permanency override the cultural needs of a child? Can a child develop cultural competence and identity in a home of different racial or ethnic origin? What about religion? In Judaism, for example, the religion's law is that a child born to a Jewish mother is always Jewish. Should a Jewish child always be placed in a Jewish home? Should Catholic children always be placed with Catholic families? Is it best to keep a child in a temporary foster home if no culturally similar family can be found? There are no easy answers to these questions.

Other Services

A number of other child welfare services meet additional needs of children. It is impossible to discuss all of them, but we touch briefly on two important program areas.

Youth programs: Most of us at one time or another have participated in youth programs sponsored by such groups as the YMCA, YWCA, Boys Clubs, Girls Clubs, Blue Birds, Girls Scouts, Boys Scouts, Brownies, Little League baseball, and so on. Many agencies in our communities work with young people through an array of programs ranging from gym-and-swim to therapeutic prevention.

The YMCA, for example, offers parent-child programs called Y-Indian Guide and Y-Indian Princess. The parent and child meet with other parents and children one evening each week. Ostensibly providing recreational opportunities, these programs also ensure that the parent and child have at least one evening each week of quality interaction. In addition, the parent and child carry out tasks and activities in the home between group meetings. These activities strengthen relations when time is limited.

Youth programs have four important functions in our communities:

◆ Youths have positive peer experiences in a formal supervised atmosphere.
◆ Youths learn to interact with others in groups.
◆ Youths are able to develop their own extended networks outside of the family.
◆ Through the programs youths find a safe haven, particularly with after-school, weekend, or evening activities, which take place when caretakers may be at work and unable to supervise their children.

Teen pregnancy prevention: Another major child welfare initiative targets teen pregnancy. Adolescent child bearing declined in the early 1990s, but 1 million teenagers still become pregnant each year: 33 percent have abortions, 14 percent miscarry, and about 50 percent give birth (Children's Defense Fund, 1997, pp. 81, 83–84). The prevalence of young people having babies continues to shock our communities.

Why does the idea of children having children disturb the American public? The reason is that teenagers are indeed still children in many ways. Few have the emotional or intellectual preparation needed to cope with the rigors of combined parenthood and employment. Stability is virtually unknown in the lives of teenage parents. The financial costs to the country are staggering: $13 to $19 billion in welfare payments (Children's Defense Fund, 1998, p. 84).

Numerous federal initiatives have been directed toward reducing teenage pregnancy. The 1996 welfare reform act specifically targeted this problem by requiring teen parents to attend school and to live either at home with their parents or with another custodial adult; otherwise, benefits are not provided to the family. The act also set aside money for the states, $50 billion, to establish abstinence education programs. Finally, the act called for states to receive a fiscal bonus if they are among the top five states to reduce teenage pregnancy between 1999 and 2002.

Note that these initiatives are directed to the states and emphasize the individual behavior of teenagers. No attention is paid to other possible causes of teen pregnancy: educational and schooling programs, and different opportunity structures for the poor that are laced with barriers to success.

SUMMARY

Children are an essential part of our country's future development. What we do with and for them benefits all of us. Homer Folks, in 1940, wrote, "The safety of our democracy depends in large measure upon the welfare of our children" (White House Conference, 1942).

Our nation's history shows a sense of ambivalence toward children. While we want to protect them—even from themselves—we also want to ensure they are provided as many opportunities as possible.

How we care for our children tells us a great deal about our society's beliefs, hopes, and aspirations. We do a great deal to care for our nation's children, but we need to do more. We need to find ways to guarantee every child a healthy, caring home. A stimulating environment that encourages growth and development should be the norm for all children. We can accept nothing less.

Child welfare is an exciting field. It is in constantly flux, though always under the watchful eyes of the public and of policymakers. Social workers have been, are, and will continue to be significant players in child welfare.

References

Barker, R. L. (1991). *The social work dictionary* (2nd ed.). Washington, DC: NASW Press.

Barker, R. L. (1995) *The social work dictionary* (4th ed.). Washington, DC: NASW Press.

Barth, R. P. (1995). Adoption. In R. Edwards et al., (Eds.), *Encyclopedia of social work* (19th ed., pp. 48–59). Washington, DC: NASW Press.

Baugher, E., & Lamison-White, L. (1996). *Poverty in the United States, 1995* (Current Population Reports, Series P60–194). Washington, DC: U.S. Department of Commerce, Bureau of the Census.

Brace, C. L. (1872). *The dangerous classes of New York and twenty years' work among them.* New York: Wynkoop and Hallenbeck.

Brunner, B. (Ed.). (1997). *1998 Information please almanac.* Boston: Information Please.

Chelf C.P. (1992). *Controversial issues in social welfare policy: Government and the pursuit of happiness.* Newbury Park, CA: Sage.

Child Welfare League of America. (1989). *Standards for service to strengthen and preserve families with children.* Washington, DC: Author.

Children's Defense Fund. (1996). *The state of America's children yearbook, 1995.* Washington, DC: Author.

Children's Defense Fund (1998). *The state of America's children yearbook, 1997.* Washington, DC: Author.

Christian Coaliltion. (1995). *Contract with the American family.* Nashville, TN: Moorings.

Colby, I. (1990). The throwaway teen. *Journal of Applied Social Sciences, 14*(2), 227–294.

Cole, E. S. (1985). Adoption: History, policy, and program. In J. Laird & A. Hartman (Eds.), *A handbook of child welfare: Context, knowledge, and practice* (pp. 638–666). New York: Free Press.

Crosson-Tower, C. (1998). *Exploring child welfare: A practice perspective.* Boston: Allyn and Bacon.

Dobelstein, A. W. (1996). *Social welfare: Policy and analysis* (2nd ed.). Chicago: Nelson-Hall.

Edna McConnell Clark Foundation. (N.D.). *Keeping families together: Facts on family preservation services.* New York: Author.

Everett, J. E. (1995). Child foster care. In R. Edwards et al. (Eds.), *Encyclopedia of social work* (19th ed., pp. 375–389). Washington, DC: NASW Press.

Gil, D. (1985). The ideological context of child welfare. In J. Laird & A. Hartman (Eds.), *A handbook of child welfare: Context, knowledge, and practice* (pp. 11–33). New York: Free Press.

Gillespie, E., & Schellhas, B. (Eds.). (1994). *Contract with America.* New York: Times.

Gustavsson, N. S., & Segal, E. A. (1994). *Critical issues in child welfare.* Thousand Oaks, CA: Sage.

Heffernan, J., Shuttlesworth, G., & Ambrosino, R. (1988). *Social work and social welfare: An introduction.* St. Paul, MN: West.

Kadushin, A., & Martin, J. A. (1988). *Child welfare services* (4th ed.). New York: Macmillan.

Kantrowitz, B., & King, P. (1991). Foster care can protect children from abuse. In C. Wekesser (Ed.), *America's children: Opposing viewpoints* (pp. 96–99). San Diego, CA: Greenhaven.

Karger, H. J., & Stoesz, D. (1994). *American social welfare policy: A pluralist approach* (2nd ed.). White Plains, NY: Longman.

Linderman, D. S. (1995). Child welfare overview. In R. Edwards et al. (Eds.), *Encyclopedia of social work* (19th ed., pp. 424–433). Washington, DC: NASW Press.

Lindsey, D. (1994). *The welfare of children.* New York: Oxford University Press.

Mushlin, M. B. (1991). Foster care cannot protect children from physical abuse. In C. Wekesser (Ed.), *American children: Opposing viewpoints* (pp. 100–104). San Diego, CA: Greenhaven.

Quam, J. (1995). Charles Loring Brace (1826–1890). In R. Edwards et al. (Eds.), *Encyclopedia of social work* (19th ed., p. 2575). Washington, DC: NASW Press.

Tracy, E. M. (1995). Family preservation and home-based services. In R. Edwards et al. (Eds.), *Encyclopedia of social work* (19th ed., pp. 973–983). Washington, DC: NASW Press.

United Nations. (1989, November 20). *United Nations convention on the rights of children.* New York: Author.

U.S. Department of Health and Human Services. Children's Bureau. (1998). *Child maltreatment 1996: Reports from the states to the National Child Abuse and Neglect Data System.* Washington, DC: U.S. Government Printing Office.

Watkins, S. A. (1990). The Mary Ellen myth: Correcting child welfare history. *Social Work, 35*(6), 500–503.

White House Conference on Children in a Democracy (1942). *Final Report, Washington, D.C., January 18–20, 1940* (Publication No. 272). Washington, DC: U.S. Government Printing Office. Reprinted in Children and Youth: Social Problems and Social Policy; New York: Arno Press.

Whittaker, J. K. (1995). Children: Group care. In R. Edwards et al., (Eds.), *Encyclopedia of social work* (19th ed., pp. 448–460). Washington, DC: NASW Press.

Wineman, D. (1995). Children's rights. In R. Edwards et al., (Eds.), *Encyclopedia of social work* (19th ed., pp. 465–475). Washington, DC: NASW Press.

Chapter 9

Health Care

OFTEN WE START IN ONE CAREER AND CHANGE TO ANOTHER. THIS was Liz's experience when she began her professional career as a nurse but after several years decided to switch to social work. Liz felt that her knowledge of the medical aspects of a client's condition blended beautifully with mental health considerations.

Liz's belief is not unique; health care social workers know the importance to successful intervention of linking mind and body. Some contend that mind and body cannot be separated and each client must be treated individually with a focus on continued wellness and prevention. At a minimum, the health care social worker, who often works as part of an interdisciplinary team, brings knowledge and understanding of the special relation between the medical and the mental health of the client. In particular, the knowledge and skills used in linking the client to the environment are central to discharge planning and case management.

Health care social workers face great challenges in the new century. Issues of managed care, downsizing and reorganization of hospital social work staffs, services to insured and uninsured populations, and increased demand for brief interventions make health care a formidable setting for creative social work practice. Philosophy often comes into play: Do we provide health care to the homeless—and if so, to what extent? What about people in prison—do we provide health care to those serving life sentences with no possibility of parole? How do we ensure that people in rural and sparsely populated areas have access to high-quality health care? Should we move toward a national health insurance model? Should we finance alternative, nontraditional health interventions?

Health care is costly. You know that from your own experiences buying medication or paying for medical treatment. Health insurance is also costly—one reason why so many Americans, more than 35 million in 2000, have no form of health insurance! And there is no reason to believe that costs will decline or even level off in the near future. Rice (1995) calculated that annual per capital expenditures— that is, what each person on average will spend each year—for health care will grow from $1,740 in 2000 to $3,789 in 2010 and $7,839 in 2020. Another more meaningful figure is annual cost as a percentage of gross domestic product (GDP)—that is, the total cost, or value, of every item and service in the U.S. economy. Put simply, how much of the American economy consists of health care? Rice

Name: Ramsi Wilkes

Place of residence: Birmingham, Alabama

College/university degrees: B.S. Social Work, University of Montevallo

Present position: Admissions Coordinator, Galleria Oaks Guest Home

Previous work/volunteer experience: Discharge planner in a rehab hospital (Healthsouth) and retirement community

What do you do in your spare time? I participate in church activities, and I like music.

Why did you choose social work as a career? It was a way to act compassionately for others and make a difference. I was drawn to geriatrics from personal experience and I believed service in this area represented my Christian beliefs.

What is your favorite social work story? I will never forget working with a terminally ill client who was receiving hospice services. She lived in the supervised housing facility where I worked. I was with her when she was dying, and she told me what she was seeing and experiencing. She told me she saw angels in her room while she breathed her last breaths. She described everything about them and pointed them out. Spine tingling!

What would be the one thing you would change in our community if you had the power to do so? I would encourage more people to work with seniors and to learn to respect them more.

(1995) showed that health care will account for 12 percent of GDP in 2000 and 27 percent in 2020!

In this chapter we introduce the numerous opportunities open to social workers who choose to practice in health care. Health care is one of the more complex arenas for social work. Many external issues and constituencies affect the delivery of health care social work. With all the challenges, however, the rewards from helping others in their time of need can be great.

HEALTH CARE SOCIAL WORK DEFINED

Health care social work, historically called "medical social work" and today "clinical social work" (not to be confused with the work of the private practitioner also referred to as a "clinical social worker"), is one of the oldest, best established fields of professional social work practice. Simply stated, health care social work practice deals with all aspects of general health. It enhances, promotes, and restores the highest level of social functioning for clients, families, and small groups when their abilities to do so are affected by actual or potential stress caused by illness, disability, or injury (Poole, 1995).

In health care practice, as in other areas of social work, the tasks performed are diverse and unique. Social workers serving in health care settings must be well trained in providing services to clients because they are competing in a service provision environment overcrowded with health care professionals. Moreover, today's health care social workers are exposed to all the turbulence and change of managed health care (Dziegielewski, 1998). In this new environment, the insurance company dictates the level of service; no longer are recommendations from physicians or other professionals treated as "written in stone." Pressures to cut costs mean that health care service must be provided in the briefest, most effective manner possible (Dziegielewski, 1996, 1997, 1998). As a result, social work professionals, indeed all health care providers, must work in a versatile, flexible manner to complete tasks with limited resources. The varied tasks coupled with the dynamic environment complicate our simple definition of health care practice.

Did You Know...In 1918, the National Conference of Social Work in Kansas City helped to form the American Association of Hospital Social Workers. This was the first professional social work organization in the United States.

Tom Carlton, a major social work thinker and advocate in health care social work during the 1970s and 1980s, defined health care social work in its broadest sense as "all social work in the health field" (1984, p. 5). Carlton felt that social workers interested in this area must be prepared to do more than engage solely in direct clinical practice. His vision of health care practice includes program planning and administration; preparation, supervision, and continued training for social workers and other health care professionals; and social research.

So, let's complicate our definition. The term "health care social work" has historically been used interchangeably with the term **medical social work,** but this obscures a subtle difference in meaning. In the *Social Work Dictionary*, medical social work is defined as a form of practice that occurs in hospitals and other health care settings. This type of practice facilitates good health, prevention of illness, and aids physically ill clients and their families in resolving the social and psychological problems related to disease and illness (Barker, 1995). Health care social work is more encompassing, indicating a type of practice that can take place in more than one setting.

Health care social workers often serve as members of professional **multidisciplinary** and **interdisciplinary teams**. Their role is essential in sensitizing the other team members to the social-psychological aspects of illness (Barker, 1995). Health care social workers are expected to address the psychosocial aspects of client problems. They are also expected to alert other team members to the psychosocial needs of clients and to ensure adequate service provision within the discharge environment. In performing these functions, social work professionals not only represent the interests of clients but often become the "moral conscience" of the health care delivery team.

The struggle to define exactly what health care social workers are expected to do reflects the changing nature of the health care system. Part of the struggle is trying to establish concrete cost-containing goals and objectives that clearly represent the diverse and often unique service provided. This inability to document a concrete service strategy has long been a thorn in the side of health care administrators, who need this information to justify and compete for continued funding. Nevertheless, simple descriptions of service provision vary, depending on the client population served and the services needed.

Health care social workers practice in a setting where doctors "fix what's broken" and do so with incredible speed and competence. As a result these workers are often expected to do the same. Given the complexity of the human situation, however, this task is not at all straightforward. In adapting to their diverse clients while anticipating changes in the health service environment social work professionals must employ flexible, and constantly updated skills.

A BRIEF HISTORY OF HEALTH CARE SOCIAL WORK

Medical social work can be traced back to the nineteenth-century public health movement. With urban growth, a result of industrialization, came overcrowding and the spread of disease. In Trattner's (1989) graphic words:

American cities were disorderly, filthy, foul-smelling, disease ridden places. Narrow, unpaved streets became transformed into quagmires when it rained. Rickety tenements, swarming with unwashed humanity, leaned upon one another for support. Inadequate drainage systems failed to carry away sewage. Pigs roamed streets that were cluttered with manure, years of accumulating garbage, and other litter. Slaughterhouses and fertilizing plants contaminated the air with an indescribable stench. Ancient plagues like smallpox, cholera, and typhus threw the population into a state of terror

from time to time while less sensational but equally deadly killers like tuber-
culosis, diphtheria, and scarlet fever were ceaselessly at work.

All in all, not a great place or time to live. It soon was evident that public sanitation
programs were needed. The resulting laws and health care efforts helped doctors
and related medical professionals to gain in stature (Segal & Brzuzy, 1998, p. 108).

Hospitals too changed dramatically during this era. Once a haven for the poor,
the hospital became a "scientific center for the treatment of illness" where physicians were in control (Popple & Leighninger, 1990, p. 436). Medical social work was
first practiced in 1900 in Cleveland City Hospital, when the workers helped to discharge from overcrowded wards patients with chronic conditions and homeless
Civil War veterans (Poole, 1995). It subsequently developed as a specialization
through the efforts of Dr. Richard Cabot and shortly thereafter Ida Cannon, a new
graduate from Simmons College. Cabot in 1905 set up the first social service (work)
department in a hospital. Though trained as a physician, Cabot recognized the
unique and important contributions of social workers when he served as director
of the Boston Children's Aid Society. The social worker's skill in linking social environment to disease, thought Cabot, would be extremely helpful in medical diagnosis. The social work department established at Boston's Massachusetts General Hospital is regarded as the debut of medical social work.

*Activity...Have you ever been admitted to a hospital? While you were there did you see
a social worker? If you didn't, would you have liked to? If you did, what services did he provide? Make a brief list of the services that you believe social workers can provide in the hospital setting.*

Health care social work today, as in Cabot's time, takes place in a "host" setting—that is, an organization whose primary purpose is something other than
providing social work services. You'll find social workers in hospitals (a hospital
accreditation requirement), neighborhood health centers, health maintenance
organizations (HMOs), city public health departments, and nonprofit and for-profit
health-related organizations. Our new aspect of today's health care social work is
that it is now team based and interdisciplinary in nature. Social workers are part
of a professional team that may include physicians, nurses, vocational rehabilitation workers, psychologists, and psychiatrists. Today's social worker must therefore understand and value the contributions that other professionals offer. For our
clients and ourselves, we can no longer see matters solely through our individual
professional lens.

UNDERSTANDING THE CURRENT HEALTH CARE ENVIRONMENT

Throughout the last quarter of the twentieth century, spiraling costs and
growing numbers of uninsured people challenged the American health care system. Several reasons for this crisis have been cited:

1. The aging population that has resulted from enhanced technologies
needs more costly health care services.

A daughter is about to give her father a haircut. The father and an adult son who was injured in an auto accident live together. Neither is able to drive and the other adult children take turns dropping by and helping out. Both the father and the son gain a sense of responsibility and accomplishment by taking care of each other.

2. Americans are very resistant to paying additional fees for medical services.

3. The insurance industry is highly fragmented, with managers trained under different environmental conditions.

4. There is excessive pressure to fill an oversupply of hospital inpatient beds.

5. The focus on treating acute illness rather than a more holistic, wellness or preventive perspective leads to more costly treatment.

6. Insufficient medical outcome data impair decision making.

7. Too many heroic attempts are made to implement expensive procedures without regard to quality of continued life.

8. Professionals overcautiously order unnecessary tests and procedures for fear of malpractice suits (Edinburg & Cottler, 1995; Shortell & Kaluzny, 1994).

Did You Know...In 1990 health care costs were estimated at over $640 billion (Shortell & Kaluzny, 1994), and at the current rate of growth will reach $1 to $1.5 trillion by the year 2000 (Hernandez, Fottler, & Joiner, 1994; Skelton & Janosi, 1992).

And the crisis is hardly abating. Researchers, advocates, and politicians alike argue that as the years progress, the cost of health care for aging baby boomers—people born between the end of World War II and the mid-1950s—will be $16 trillion, or 30 percent of GDP! (Bruner, Waldo, & McKusick, 1992). Even though many of the underlying factors are difficult to change, predictions of vastly increased health care urgently require a response of one type or another.

During the early 1990s, politicians were responsive to the American public's demand for health care reform. During the first term of President Clinton, who had made a campaign promise to address this issue, a major task force chaired by his wife, Hillary, began to develop a national health care policy (Mizrahi, 1995). The task force considered numerous proposals for health care reform from single-payer systems to limited forms of universal coverage. The eventual proposal was not a single-payer approach but rather a type of "managed competition" in which purchasing alliances were formed that would have the power to certify health plans and negotiate premiums for certain benefit packages (*President's Health Security Plan*, 1993). Payment for these plans would be financed by employer-employee premiums. The actual consumer out-of-pocket cost would vary based on the benefit package chosen. The Clinton proposal eventually failed after concerted attacks by the health care industry and conservative members of the Congress. Some political commentators felt this had been the last chance to change the health care system, yet during the 2000 presidential campaign, health care resurfaced as a hot topic, with arguments over insurance coverage and a "patient's bill of rights."

Current cost containment strategies, used by managed care plans apply to almost 70 percent of all covered health care expenses (Edinburg & Cottler, 1995). Therefore, health care social workers who participate in these types of reimbursement schemes must deal directly with managed care plans. Such dealings typically involve preauthorization for service by qualified providers; precertification for a given amount of care with concurrent review of treatment and services rendered; continued determination of need for hospitalization through a process of utilization review; and predischarge planning to ensure that proper aftercare services are identified and made available (Hiratsuka, 1990).

We don't want to paint a bleak picture but rather a realistic one. The continual changes and swirling controversies contribute to a turbulent health care environment. Declining hospital admissions, reduced lengths of stay, and numerous other restrictions and methods of cost containment are common threats that unite all health care social workers.

Did You Know...In current health care practice the term "patient" is being replaced. Originally, the adoption of the word "patient" by the medical community caused many social workers to stop using words like "client" when referring to the people they served. The use and acceptance of the term "patient" is obvious when we read articles in the health care social work literature (Alperin, 1994; Coursey, Farrell, & Zahniser, 1991; Cowles & Lefcowitz, 1992).

Today, with the shift away from the "medical sick role model" to the "wellness, concrete service, cost-effective approach," the term "patient" is in conflict with the wholeness and prevention strategy marketed by host health care organizations. Replacement terms include "client" (a term familiar to social work), "consumer" (to represent those receiving a service), and "covered persons" (reflecting those who have some type of medical insurance coverage). Those in favor of the euphemism "covered persons" argue that it is not used just to denote medical coverage but rather to convey a universal care perspective indicative of the security of medical coverage.

ROLES AND TASKS OF THE HEALTH CARE SOCIAL WORKER

According to the *Social Work Dictionary* health care workers can be defined in a generic sense as all "professional, paraprofessional, technical and general employees of a system or facility that provides for the diagnosis, treatment and overall well being of patients" (Barker, 1995, p. 164). Nevertheless, a clear distinction must be made between **health care workers** and **allied health care professionals**. Health care workers are nonprofessional service support personnel such as home health aids, medical record personnel, nurse's aides, orderlies, and attendants (Barker, 1995). Allied health care providers, by contrast, are generally professionals such as social workers, psychologists, audiologists, dieticians, occupational therapists, optometrists, pharmacists, physical therapists, and speech pathologists, among others.

It is as allied health care professionals that you will find social workers practicing in health care settings. Health care social workers appear to serve this area well because of their broad-based training in evaluating based on behavior the biological, psychological, and social factors that can affect a client's environmental situation—that is, the behavioral biopsychosocial approach. The beginning generalist (BSW) and advanced specialist (MSW) levels of education help to make the social work professional an invaluable member of the health care delivery team. The services that health care social workers provide can be divided into two major areas: direct practice and support or ancillary services.

Did You Know...The U.S. Veterans Bureau, now the Department of Veterans Affairs, began hiring social workers to work in its hospitals in 1926.

Where do physicians and nurses—the most recognizable health care providers—fit in? Physicians and nurses are not considered *allied* service providers. Because their services are necessary to any type of medical care, they are called "essential health care providers"—they are the major players in the host environment.

Direct Practice

Today, the role of the health care social worker is clearly established, and they can be found in every area of our health care delivery system. These practitioners typically provide a wide variety of services to clients and their families:

Case finding and outreach: Assist client to identify and secure the services they need

Preservice or preadmission planning: Identify barriers to accessing health care services

Assessment: Identify service needs and screen to identify health and wellness concerns

Direct provision: Secure concrete services such as admission, discharge, and aftercare planning

Psychosocial evaluation: Gather information on client's biopsychosocial, cultural, financial, situational factors for completion of the psychosocial assessment or social history

Goal identification: Establish mutually negotiated goals and objectives that address client's health and wellness issues.

Counseling: Help client and family to deal with their situation and problems related to health interventions needed or received

Short- and long-term planning: Help client and family to anticipate and plan for the services needed based on client's current or expected health status

Service access assistance: Identify preventive, remedial, and rehabilitative service needs and assist client and family to overcome potential barriers to service access

Education: Instruct client and family on areas of concern in regard to their health and wellness

Wellness training: Help client to establish a plan to secure continued or improved health based on a holistic prevention model

Referral services: Provide information about services available and make direct connection when warranted

Continuity of care: Ensure that proper connections are made among all services needed, taking into account the issue of multiple health care providers

Advocacy: Teach and assist clients to obtain needed resources, or on a larger scale advocate for changes in policy or procedure that directly or indirectly benefit the client (Dziegielewski, 1998)

Did You Know…In the 1920s and 1930s the U.S. military started to add social workers to its ranks. Military social workers usually work in mental health, health, and protective service settings

---

The clinical services that health care social workers provide have clearly expanded far beyond the traditional core of **discharge planning**. Health care is a changing environment where even the classic definition of discharge planning has been altered. Social workers not only coordinate discharges, they also oversee the multidisciplinary or interdisciplinary teams of which they are members to be sure that clients are getting the services they need. Since discharges can involve numerous individual, family, and community factors, counseling services often must accompany these placements. Social workers are often called upon to provide this type of service. Furthermore, once the team agrees that a client is ready for discharge, it is often the social worker who is responsible for ensuring that transfer forms are completed, client and family education has been done, and the records that support continued care are ready for transfer (Mankita & Alalu, 1996).

Support Services

Social workers can also provide health-related services that are not considered direct practice. These support or ancillary services include staff supervision, administration, and community-based services:

Direct supervision: Provide direct professional social work supervision through direction, guidance, and education on case services and counseling

Consultation: Provide consultation services to other social workers and multidisciplinary and interdisciplinary teams

Agency consultation: Provide consultation to agency administrators on how to enhance service delivery to clients and organizations

Community consultation: Provide consultation services to communities to assist with the development of community-based services

Policy and program planning: Assist in formulation and implementation of health care policies and programs that will help to meet client needs

Program development: Assist the agency to refine and develop new and improved programs

Quality improvement: Assist the agency to ensure that continuous quality services are provided that meet standards of professionalism and efficiency

Service advocacy: Assist the agency to recognize the needs of clients

Service outreach: Identify unmet needs and services that are not available to clients; advocate for improved programs and services

At-risk service outreach: Identify clients at risk of decreased health or illness; advocate to secure services for them

Health education: Participate and instruct communities on developing and implementing health education programs

Agency liaison: Serve as liaison to the agency on behalf of the client, ensuring connections are made between client, supervisor, and community

Community liaison : Serve as a contact or connection between client, family, and community

Support services go beyond what we generally consider to be the core of health care social work. We must, nevertheless, recognize the importance of all practitioners who do this type of work day in, day out. These tasks and functions cannot be overemphasized, particularly in this era of managed care.

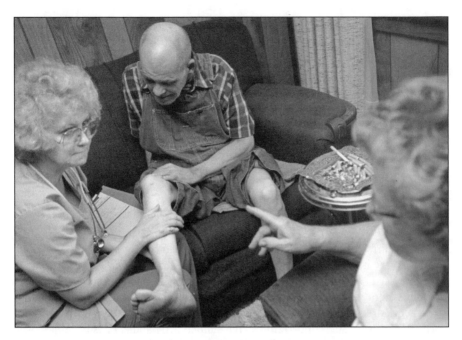

Home healthcare worker examining a developmentally disabled senior who lives with his sister.

Activity...Cultural Diversity in the Medical Setting

Break into groups and discuss the following case. Prepare a plan on how to best assist the client situation described.

The social worker arrives in a client's hospital room to gather some routine admission information when she walks in on a couple having a very heated discussion. Jon, is a 40-year-old Hispanic male who is in the hospital for routine same-day exploratory surgery. Jon's wife is visibly upset and crying. The social worker feels a bit awkward for intruding and asks if the couple would like her to leave. Jon, motions that he would like her to stay, and begins to tell her that he is furious that his wife has decided to go on a trip alone to see her mother. When questioned as to whether he is disappointed because he wants to go with her, he quickly says no. He is angry because she made plans without getting his permission first. His wife states that she is sorry for not asking him first but she felt the decision had to be made quickly. The couple asks the social worker what her opinion is.

Taking into account a respect for cultural diversity and maintaining professional integrity, what types of responses and or assistance could the social worker provide? What types of responses should be avoided?

Direct Supervision: Staff supervision is a major support activity with a long and rich history in health care social work. Supervision requires specialized knowledge that builds on years of practice. As a result, you will find that most social workers performing supervision, in one form or another, have MSWs. On occasion, you may find a BSW worker in a supervisory role, but this is the exception.

Supervision is a complicated activity, but it is necessary for the professional growth of all social workers. Supervisors are mentors, teachers if you will, who can be sounding boards, share practice frustrations, and look at different ways of working with a particular client or group. Kadushin gave a more formal definition:

> An agency administrative staff member . . . is given authority to direct, coordinate, enhance, and evaluate on-the-job performance of supervisees for which work he [or she] is held accountable. In implementing this role the supervisor performs administrative, educational, and supportive functions in interaction with the supervisee in the context of a positive relationship. The supervisor's ultimate objective is to deliver to agency clients the best possible service, both quantitative and qualitatively, in accordance with agency policies and procedures (1976, p. 21).

Kadushin's definition applies to the field of health care social work, though with one very important addition. In health care work *flexibility* must be part of both practice and supervision. Repeated policy changes, and consequent organizational instability, often lead to reorganization, cutbacks, and ultimately reductions in the workforce (Braus, 1996). For the social worker, whether a new or an experienced practitioner, such uncertainty can be difficult to handle. Let's be honest—no one likes to be in an unsure work environment, where the rules may change from one day to the next. In health care, social workers must continually modify details of their practice. For example, they must be flexible in dealing with the varying requirements of different third-party payers, such as insurers, who may refuse to cover services based on such practice issues as length of stay (Shulman, 1993). Supervisors must be sensitive to their staff's ongoing struggles to create proactive client-directed services within the constraints set by payers. Supervisors too must balance the demands of their jobs with those of third-party payers. To say the least, the supervisor's role is difficult.

Flexibility, then, is key to competent supervision as well as good practice. The need to be flexible, however, and the environment that creates this need, is a major source of stress. Stress and its management are, therefore, important issues for both supervisor and staff.

Supportive supervision addresses such issues as stress, staff morale, and work-related anxiety and worry, which if left unattended, can lower job satisfaction and commitment to the agency. Supportive supervision builds worker self-esteem and emotional well-being. In the long run, it can reduce stress levels and thus the dissatisfaction that ultimately results in employee burnout (Resnick & Dziegielewski, 1996; Sheafor, Horejsi, & Horejsi, 1997).

As system uncertainty were not enough for the health care supervisor, let's add another challenge to the job: lack of clarity in staff roles and responsibilities. In particular, what are the differences in the work carried out by BSWs and by MSWs?

Guidelines differentiating practice responsibilities between the BSW and the MSW are rarely clear (Levin & Herbert, 1995). You may find that what BSWs do in one setting is only done by MSWs in another. This lack of clarity about functions means that supervisors must be careful in assigning cases and tasks. Without clear definitions it is possible to assign tasks that are beyond the competence of the social worker, which compromises client care and worker well-being (Levin & Herbert, 1995). Supervisors must ensure that tasks assigned to BSWs are within their scope of practice. That another organization assigns a particular task to BSWs is no guarantee that the activity is appropriate for an entry-level practitioner. Rather, that organization may not be able to assign or even hire an MSW; but the task must be done, so it must be given to a BSW. Though professionally unsound, this task assignment can be made less so if the BSW is given consistent and persistent supervision.

Mediation, Advocacy, and Brokering: The health care social work supervisor also mediates, advocates, and brokers as part of staff supervision (Berkman, 1996). In mediating between supervisees and clients, coworkers, or the larger community, the supervisor remains neutral and does not adopt the opinion of any side (Shulman, 1993). Advice and direction are given on the best way to handle client care for the supervisee, the multidisciplinary or interdisciplinary team, the agency, and the community. Mediation requires the supervisor to recognize that conflicts that are not intentional and to help supervisees to address them in the most ethical, moral, and professional way possible.

The second role, advocacy, requires willingness on the parts of both supervisor and supervisees to assist with the development of needed services for clients, their families, and significant others, while not losing sight of the common ground that links them to administration (Shulman, 1993).

Did You Know...In the early days, hospital nurses generally performed medical social work services. These nurses were convenient choices for this employment because they were easily accessible, already knew agency procedure, and were aware of community resources. Later, however, when it was established that more specialized training in understanding social conditions was needed, the employment of social work professionals began.

Brokering, the third role, requires supervisor and staff to link the client with community services and other agencies. Remember, when most people come into a medical setting, such as a hospital, their stay is limited. The social worker must elicit a great deal of information on the client's environment, including social, emotional, and physical factors and their relation to the illness (remember, this is what Dr. Cabot saw as our great contribution to health care). The social worker may discover that a client needs a variety of follow-up support services to sustain her or his family through the recovery period or through ongoing illness. Brokering is how the social worker seeks out these community-based services and develops a case plan that is tailored to the client.

Health Education and Health Counseling: Social workers were part of the nineteenth-century public health education movement, also called the Sanitation Movement. Therefore, providing education and instruction is not new to social work—though health care counseling was a rarity. Attention wasn't directed toward counseling until training became institutionalized in colleges and moved to an educational model.

Health care counseling is especially important with the increased participation of social work professionals as educators in new health care areas that we might call "nontraditional social work." These include smoking cessation and weight reduction, for example. The worker continues to teach new patterns of behavior but then employs counseling theory and skills to help the client negotiate the period of change. The worker calls on a range of skills and strategies ranging from support to confrontation.

Administration: Administration and related tasks have not been considered a core practice areas of health care social work. In fact, most prospective social workers shy away from studying administration, focusing instead on client-related courses. Don't believe us? Ask your classmates how many of them plan to major in or develop a specialization in administration. You'll probably find that everyone agrees *someone* should study administration "but not me." Yet administration, particularly in health care, directly affects the types of services that are offered in a setting. The role that administration plays in strengthening direct practice cannot be overstated.

Social work administrators, like other health care administrators, must respond to often competing management philosophies. These conflicting styles can affect the provision of client care. For example, the social work administrator may receive a directive from the hospital central administration "to increase the participation of professional staff members in the organization's decision-making processes." The idea behind this directive is that greater involvement will strengthen commitment to the hospital. The social work administrator decides that "quality circles" and "total quality management" (TQM) will best achieve the culture that central administration is seeking. While the social work administrator is attempting to put TQM in place with quality circles among staff members, central administration announces that reimbursement from third-party payers and census data (e.g., patient-bed days) are down. The announcement is an unmistakable signal of financial pressure—remember, a hospital is a business and, like all businesses, needs to make a profit. So now the social work administrator must be concerned with generating significant patient numbers to justify and sustain the department. The goal is now to maximize reimbursement potential. If numbers are not increased, then the department will be forced to cut back on staff while raising workloads for those who stay. A "more with less" mentality takes hold while the edict to develop staff loyalty remains in place.

Sound frustrating? Doesn't make sense? You now understand why so many health care social work administrators feel trapped. Double-edged and conflicting messages sent by central administration or insurance companies make administration the most difficult, frustrating, and challenging aspect of health care work.

But the situation is not as dismal as it seems. Health care social work administrators can balance these pressures and influence the agency's **policy** decisions. Serving on agency committees or boards allows the administrator to help construct new policy directions and provides an opportunity to meet funding bodies in order to explain practice realities and discuss ways to enhance service delivery. This strategy is called *"practice policy."* It reflects the understanding that social work activities are born of policy decisions. As social workers, we must be informed about and involved in the development of organizational policy—our clients are stakeholders in the policy-making process. Our practice, knowledge, advocacy skills, and ability to mediate between conflicting parties are all contributions we social workers can make to the health care policy-making process.

Acute and Long-Term Care Settings

Social work has long been at the forefront in providing health care services to clients in acute care and long-term care settings. Acute care settings are the single largest employer of social workers involved in health care delivery (Poole, 1995). We find that the skills and theory that social workers bring to the workplace—again Dr. Cabot's observation holds true—are needed in today's acute care setting (Berkman, 1996). The health care social worker's roles and responsibilities in the acute care setting are clear:

- Provide assistance with treatment plans and compliance issues
- Assist clients and families with discharge planning and referral
- Provide counseling and support for clients and significant others in the areas of health, wellness, mental health, bereavement, and so forth
- Assist clients and their families ethically to make difficult decisions that can affect health and mental health
- Educate clients, their families, and significant others about psychosocial issues and adjusting to illness; assist in resolving behavioral problems
- Assist in identifying and obtaining entitlement benefits
- Secure nonmedical benefits; assist with risk management and quality assurance activities
- Advocate for enhanced and continued services to ensure client well-being

Did You Know...In 1928, the American College of Surgeons developed and included a minimum standard of service provision for social service—that is, social work—departments.

Long-term and restorative care settings may not be that familiar to you. Let's try some other names that you're more likely to recognize: rehabilitative hospitals and clinics, nursing homes, intermediate care facilities, supervised boarding homes, home health care agencies, hospices, and hospital home care units. These settings are usually multidisciplinary, and social workers provide services within the areas of assessment, treatment, rehabilitation, supportive care, and prevention of increased disability of people with chronic physical, emotional, or developmental impairments. Poole (1995) called for such health services to 1) be provided in the least restrictive environment possible, 2) support clients in autonomous decision making, and 3) maximize a client's level of physical, social, and psychological functioning and subsequent well-being.

Poole's recommendations may seem like common sense, and they are. They reflect the core values and ethics set out in the Code of Ethics, which remind us of how important it is to maintain sensitivity and respect for people served, to be aware of the individual's right and ability to make decisions for himself (in most situations), and to focus on client strengths and resources that can be maximized.

The phrase "long term" indicates that the client has a chronic condition that may affect his abilities. Unfortunately, many chronic conditions are unlikely to improve. But that doesn't mean the social worker and other team members give up hope or stop trying to ensure that the client receives the highest quality of professional treatment. We must be realistic, but optimistic. We should not hide information from clients or discount their feelings. Remember, we are all people who think, feel, and care.

Health care social workers employed in long-term care must develop specialized knowledge of various chronic conditions and learn to identify and assess signs and symptoms of the expected progression of various diseases (Dziegielewski, 1998). Such information is critical to being an effective practitioner with the client, family, and friends. For they—family, friends, and significant others—often need assistance to participate in the care of their loved ones. Many people don't know what to say or how to say it and, as a result, feel overwhelmed and even useless. We should never underestimate the importance of "others" in the healing or sustaining process. Considerable evidence exists that the involvement and support of family and friends contributes greatly to the overall wellness and satisfaction of all involved (Rubinstein, Lubben, & Mintzer, 1994; Dziegielewski, 1990, 1991).

Did You Know...Johns Hopkins Hospital established its first social work program in 1907. The first social worker to be employed there was Helen B. Pendleton (Nacman, 1977).

One last thought about chronic situations: When addressing the needs of a client who suffers from a chronic condition the beginning professional should strive not to be afraid. Rely on what you have learned in school, and always be a compassionate person who uses skills and theory grounded in values and ethics that allow for the celebration of the entire human experience.

WHY DO IT?

By now you may be wondering why anyone would want to work in the changing, often unsettling, health care system. This is a fair question, so let's try to find an answer.

Social workers are among the many allied health professional groups that make up the health care "army." Given the interdisciplinary nature of today's work, it is incumbent for the social work profession to promote a clear understanding of its purpose and role in order to maintain a place in health care delivery. What we bring to the health care arena is vital. History shows this. Nevertheless, we must always define our role and be players in this process. Social workers cannot afford to let others decide what we can do with and on behalf of clients and their families.

The roots of health care social work, as part of the social work profession, lie in serving the poor and disenfranchised. As the medical arena has changed over the years so too has the role of the health care social worker.

And now, as the social environment changes, expectations for health care are becoming clouded. Is health care a right or a privilege? Should the government guarantee a minimum standard of health care for all people? Who would establish such a standard? What role should the insurance industry have in such deliberations? Should we develop a "patient's bill or rights" as a new initiative? (FYI: In New York City taxi cabs you will find a "rider's bill or rights." Interesting that taxi cab riders are provided certain guarantees but not people in the health care system!) While the public debates these issues the day-to-day work of the social worker in health care is daunting. Flexibility is a prerequisite for helping our clients and for adjusting to the constantly renegotiated health care environment.

All health care social workers—whether in the role of clinical practitioner, supervisor, or administrator—face the challenge of understanding and anticipating health care trends. Each worker's skills must therefore be current, flexible to change, and proactive with clients. And yes, all health care social workers must also understand macroeconomics and its influence on health care delivery. The current economic environment is characterized by a shifting tension between quality of care and cost containment. While the goal of the social work profession is to provide high-quality care, these services are shadowed and ultimately influenced by cost containment strategies. Health care social workers are expected to include cost containment among their practice principles whether they serve as direct practitioners, professional supervisors, administrators, or community organizers (Caper, 1995).

The viability of health care social work rests on two points. First, medical settings must place greater emphasis on the macroperspective in health care. The social work profession must work actively to help the larger community understand its responsibility to create a cradle-to-grave health care system. Believing that the health care system will eventually solve its own problems is ludicrous. Health care social workers, whatever roles they choose for practice delivery, must take the lead in developing a more humane health care system that meets the needs of all people, regardless of their financial capabilities.

The second point that must be ingrained into all areas of health care social work practice is that advocacy leads to client empowerment. Health care social workers must change the mindset that managed care and the policies dictated by it are all bad. Social workers must recognize that there are benefits in a managed care system for both clients and providers. The strengths of managed care include enhanced and accountable mental health treatment; more positive client outcomes through concentration on specific goals and objectives in therapeutic treatment; time limits that can force emphasis on identifying external and environmental supports to allow continued therapeutic gains; avoidance of long-term therapy, with resulting decreases in long-term medication supplementation; and reduced health care costs for American businesses, which can only benefit the larger society (Browning & Browning, 1996).

We must recognize, however, that managed care also has many pitfalls. Health care social workers are therefore needed to advocate for clients. Workers must always stress development of new and needed services within the managed care framework. They must also teach clients how to obtain needed resources and help them to do so. On a larger scale, social workers are required—by our Code of Ethics—to advocate changes in policies or procedures that will directly or indirectly benefit clients.

Health care social work is far from easy. If you decide, nonetheless, that it's the area for you, the question is: How do you best respond to the challenge? You will often be tempted to switch areas and collect a paycheck in a less volatile setting. Health care social work is suited to people who will relish the changing environment, want to maximize resources for clients, look to serve on boards and committees to influence policy and practice, and enjoy the idea that every day will be different. If that's you, the health care setting is worth considering.

SUMMARY

Health care social work is a dynamic, exciting, constantly changing field of practice. The past ten years have brought things never seen before. Experienced social workers are forced to address specific issues in an environment where the "rules" are evolving. Health care social work's history is an extensive one, deeply rooted in the activities of pioneers such as Ida Cannon and Richard Cabot. These early practitioners directly linked social work practice to the "medical model" considered the core of health care practice.

Today health care social workers continue to strive to restore the highest level of functioning for each client, family, small group, and community served. The settings these workers occupy vary from acute short-term settings to extended care long-term settings. Regardless of the type of clientele served, or the area of practice, health care social work is a challenging and essential area of practice.

References

Alperin, R. M. (1994). Managed care versus psychoanalytic psychotherapy: Conflicting ideologies. *Clinical Social Work Journal, 22* (2), 137–148.

Barker, R. L. (1995). *The social work dictionary* (3rd ed.). Washington, DC: NASW Press.

Berkman, B. (1996). The emerging health care world: Implications for social work practice and education. *Social Work, 41* (15), 541–549.

Braus, P. (1996, February). Who will survive managed care? *American Demographics, 18,* 16.

Browning, C. H., & Browning, B. J. (1996). *How to partner with managed care*. Los Alamitos, CA: Duncliffs International.

Burner, S. T., Waldo, R. R., & McKusick, D. R. (1992). National health expenditures: Projections through 2030. *Health Care Financing Review, 14,* 1–29.

Caper, P. (1995). The next shift: Managed care. *Public Health Reports, 110,* 682–683.

Calrton, T. O. (1984). *Clinical social work in health care settings: A guide to professional practice with exemplars*. New York: Springer.

Coursey, R. D., Farrell, E. W., and Zahniser, J. H. (1991). Consumers' attitudes toward psychotherapy, hospitalization and after-care. *Health and Social Work, 16*(3), 155–161.

Cowles, L. A. & Lefcowitz, M. J. (1992). Interdisciplinary expectations of medical social worker in the hospital setting. *Health and Social Work, 17*(1), 58–65.

Dziegielewski, S. F. (1996). Managed care principles: The need for social work in the health care environment. *Crisis Intervention and Time-Limited Treatment, 3*(2), 97–110.

Dziegielewski, S. F. (1997). Time limited brief therapy: The state of practice. *Crisis Intervention and Time-Limited Treatment, 3*(3), 217–228.

Dziegielewski, S. F. (1998). *The changing face of health care social work: Professional practice in the era of managed care.* New York: Springer.

Edinburg, G. M., & Cottler, J. M. (1995). Managed care. In R. Edwards et al. (Eds.), *Encyclopedia of social work* (19th ed., Vol. 2, pp. 1199–1213). Silver Spring, MD: NASW Press.

Hernandez, S. R., Fottler, M. D., & Joiner, C. L. (1994). Integrating strategic management and human resources. In M. Fottler, S. Hernandez, & C. L. Joiner (Eds.), *Strategic Management of human resources in health service organizations* (2nd ed., pp. 3–25). Albany, NY: Delmar.

Hiratsuka, J. (1990). Managed care: A sea of change in health. *NASW News, 35*, 3.

Kadushin, A. (1976). *Supervision in social work.* New York: Columbia University Press.

Levin, R., & Herbert, M. (1995). Differential work assignments of social work practitioners in hospitals. *Health and Social Work, 20*(1), 21–30.

Mankita, S., & Alalu, R. (1996, Spring). Hospital social work: Challenges, rewards. *New Social Worker*, pp. 4–6.

Mizrahi, T. (1995). Health care: Reform initiatives. In R. Edwards et al. (Eds.), *Encyclopedia of social work* (19th ed., Vol. 2, pp. 1185–1198). Silver Spring, MD: NASW Press.

Nacman, M. (1977). Social work in health setting: A historical review. *Social Work in Health Care, 2*(4), 407–418.

Poole, D. (1995). Health care: Direct practice. In R. Edwards et al. (Eds.), *Encyclopedia of social work* (19th ed., Vol. 2, pp. 1156–1167). Washington, DC: NASW Press.

Popple, P., & Leighninger, L. (1990). *Social work, social welfare and American society.* Needham, MA: Allyn and Bacon.

The President's health security plan. (1993). New York: Times Books/Random House.

Resnick, C., & Dziegielewski, S. F. (1996). The relationship between therapeutic termination and job satisfaction among medical social workers. *Social Work in Health Care, 23*(3), 17–35.

Rice, D. (1995). Health care: Financing. In R. Edwards et al. (Eds.), *Encyclopedia of social work* (19th ed., Vol. 2, pp. 1168–1175). Washington, DC: NASW Press.

Ross, J. (1993). Redefining hospital social work: An embattled professional domain [Editorial], *Health and Social Work, 18*(4), 243–247.

Rubinstein, R. L., Lubben, J. E., & Mintzer, J. E. (1994, March). Social isolation and social support: An applied perspective. *Journal of Applied Gerontology, 13*(1), 58–72.

Segal, E., & Brzuzy, S. (1998). Social welfare policy, programs, and practice. Itasca, IL: Peacock.

Sheafor, B. W., Horejsi, C. R., & Horejsi, G. A. (1997). *Techniques and guidelines for social work practice* (4th ed.). Needham Heights, MA: Allyn and Bacon.

Shortell, S. M., & Kaluzny, A. D. (1994). Foreward. In S. M. Shortell & A. D. Kaluzny (Eds.), *Health care management: Organizational behavior and design* (3rd ed., p. xi). Albany, NY: Delmar.

Skelton, J. K., & Janosi, J. M. (1992). Unhealthy health care costs. *Journal of Medicine and Philosophy, 17*, 7–19.

Trattner, W. (1989), *From poor law to welfare state: A history of social welfare in America* (4th ed.). New York: Free Press.

Chapter 10

Mental Health

SOCIAL WORKERS ARE THE NATION'S LARGEST PROVIDERS OF MENtal health services. Furthermore, these professionals are often the only mental health care providers serving residents of the poorest, most rural communities (NASW, 1998).

In mental health practice social workers are essential service providers helping individuals meet their daily needs. Social workers practicing in this area engage in numerous services and functions, including mental health counseling in community mental health centers, private practice, psychiatric hospitals and psychiatric units, long-term care facilities, courts, and prisons; case management; discharge planning; intake or admission evaluation; high social risk case finding; patient education; support and advocacy; crisis intervention; and interdisciplinary collaboration. Services are provided to all clients and their families, and all the major psychiatric disorders are addressed, including schizophrenia, affective and mood disorders such as depression, neuropsychiatric disorders, eating disorders, personality disorders, phobias, substance abuse, childhood disorders, and organic psychoses (NASW, 1990).

The mental health social worker has either a baccalaureate or a master's degree from an accredited school of social work. Social work in general is not a highly paid profession, but of all the practice areas workers in mental health fare well. Social workers at the BSW level who work in mental health earned about $20,000 to $30,000 a year; those with MSWs earned a median salary of approximately $47,500 in 1995 (NASW, 1998).

Did You Know...Massachusetts General Hospital in Boston pioneered hospital and psychiatric social work, starting a social service department in 1905, and hiring social workers to work with patients who suffered from mental illness in 1907 (NASW, 1998).

When a social worker employed in a local mental health clinic outside of Orlando, Florida, was asked how she felt about her job, she said she could describe it best as "challenging, rewarding, and most of the time quite frustrating." She believed that the role of the mental health social worker is complicated because allegiances must be divided, and always placing the needs of the client first forced her to maintain a delicate balance between the needs of the family, the society, and the agency. Clients who are mentally impaired often cannot handle their own

Name: Carolyn Heymann
Place of residence: Indiana
College/university degrees: Indiana University, M.S.W.
Present position: Mental Health and Addiction Specialist
Previous work/volunteer experience: Worked with clients that suffer from addictive disorders

What do you do in your spare time? Flower/landscape gardening, writing, family

Why did you choose social work as a career? I believe that "if you give a person a loaf of bread you feed them a meal, teach that person how to plant wheat and bake bread, you feed them for a lifetime." That model assumes the recipient is physically and mentally able to sow the grain, follow instructions, and has an oven available. I chose to assist those who cannot and do not.

What is your favorite social work story? One Friday afternoon I was working in the Crisis department when a lady came in with a bag of clothing stating her doctor had told her to get over to the Psychology Pavilion as soon as possible. She didn't know why, except that she had told him she finally had to confess that she hadn't been taking her anxiolytics and painkillers as prescribed. "He was in the process of writing another prescription, and I just had to tell him." I asked if she had been abusing prescription narcotics. She explained that what she had been trying to tell the doctor for months that he was prescribing too many meds in excessive dosages and she had been decreasing intake to the point that she no longer needed them. "I don't know why he sent me here. I haven't been taking any meds and I am fine."

What would be the one thing you would change in our community if you had the power to do so? Within the social work community I would like to see social workers apply principles of acceptance, tolerance, compassion, and nondiscrimination to those with brain disease or addictions.

affairs, making it essential for the social worker to ensure that the client's rights are not violated.

The mental health social worker must also be well aware of "duty to warn." If a client is perceived as a "danger to self or others," action is taken to protect any person or persons who may be at risk. "Duty to warn" may force a social worker to violate the confidence of the client in order to protect others in the immediate environment or, if threatening suicide, to protect the client.

Therefore, mental health social work practitioners must always strive for balance between the *rights* of the client and the *needs* of the client and her family. Social workers must be advocates for clients who are mentally impaired; these clients will often be provided services through facilitation and referral because they are rarely capable of representing themselves.

Many beginning social work professionals are attracted to the area of mental health because they aspire to do therapy with the clients they serve. NASW (1990) described the essential components of psychosocial psychiatric services as 1) the completion of timely psychosocial screenings, 2) timely psychosocial assessments, 3) comprehensive psychosocial assessments, 4) timely contacts with family and significant others, 5) teamwork on interdisciplinary or multidisciplinary teams. These highlight how important it is for the social work professional to understand diagnosis and assessment, particularly because most social workers serve as advocates, facilitating and ensuring as part of the interdisciplinary team that the client gets the services needed.

In this chapter we introduce the role of social worker in mental health. In particular, we concentrate on the method of psychosocial assessment. A comprehensive psychosocial assessment begins the helping process in mental health and allows the social worker to gather information needed to understand the client and his environment.

MULTIDIMENSIONAL PSYCHOSOCIAL ASSESSMENT

Over the years the concept of taking a psychosocial history and formulating a clinical assessment that might lead to a psychiatric label or formal diagnosis for the client has been a subject of serious debate within the profession. Carlton (1984) and Dziegielewski (1998) concurred that the debate stems primarily from the fact that social work has not always separated the process of diagnosis from the process of assessment. Whatever its source, it should not induce social workers to shy away from assessment, a critical professional duty.

In the area of mental health the profession of social work did not develop in isolation. In order to survive and compete in the mental health practice environment many social workers have adapted to the dominant culture. This means that the practice approaches and methodologies employed by social workers at all levels meet the same expectations as other mental health professionals address. These expectations generally relate to reimbursement for service. For example, outcome measures, which dictate service reimbursement, have become almost mandatory.

Mental Illness Can Strike Anyone and the Consequences Can Be Devastating: A True Case Story

Forth Worth—Jane fell so far so fast. A woman of education with a soft spot for the underdog, Jane combined a master's degree in social work with a compassion for the homeless that propelled her into Austin's power circles. She drove an expensive car, lived a full life, and was devoted to a loving family.

And she lost it all—a victim of mental illness.

The petite, blue-eyed blonde who once turned heads was beaten to death Saturday, left alone on a dirty sidewalk among those she once helped. At age 43, she died penniless and homeless—all her worldly goods in two plastic grocery bags.

For those who knew Jane, the tragic end was no surprise. Jane suffered from bipolar and personality disorders that left her without a family, unable to work, and on the street. "It is sad to say, but we feared something like this would happen," said her friend for 12 years. "She was so out of control, and no matter how hard we tried to help, she wouldn't take it."

Early Saturday, Jane was found slumped over in front of Mental Health–Mental Retardation Services day resource building. An autopsy showed she died from blunt force injuries to her head. Her killer remains a mystery, and there are no new leads in the case. Witnesses told police they saw Jane talking to an unidentified man about an hour before she was found dead, said the homicide detective.

A composite of the man has been posted on fliers and tacked up around the shelters and known hangouts for local indigents. "He could be a witness or a suspect, and right now we just want him for questioning."

Jane's daughter said the fact that her mother wouldn't accept help from loved ones adds to her sadness. "A lot of people ask me, 'Why didn't you help? Why didn't you do anything?' Well, what they don't know is that it is harder than that," her daughter said.

Jane's former social work professor, who taught and served as a mentor, said Jane is proof that mental illness can tear apart lives. "I don't think the general public knows just how vicious mental illness is. It can destroy you. . . It destroyed her to the end."

Her daughter stated that most of her family hadn't seen Jane for two years. Her mother had avoided seeing loved ones but managed to keep in touch through phone calls and letters. She described her mother as someone who had inner and outer beauty, a person with a great sense of humor who was articulate and who made sure the family went to church. "During the summer she used to make me volunteer. She was just that way. She really cared about others. But the mental illness tore our relationship apart," her daughter said.

"I had a real good conversation with her, a week ago," her daughter continued. "It was the best we had in a long time. I was beaming for days afterward. . . I think, since it was the last time we talked that is was a gift from God."

News about Jane's slaying unnerved the night shelter residents, who expressed fear that the killer might be among them.

"Women who are street-wise know how to protect themselves," said the executive director of the shelter. "Unfortunately, Jane didn't. Jane did not fit the stereotypes of a homeless person. She was educated and not addicted to drugs or alcohol. But the mental illness left her destitute. Jane didn't say anything to anybody. She kept to herself and roamed all over the city. I was really crushed when I heard what happened to her. She didn't deserve this."

"About 60 percent of the homeless in this country suffer from some form of mental illness, and about 40 percent have a substance abuse problem," said the chief of mental health and addiction services. Jane was first diagnosed with depression when she was about 18, relatives and friends said. She was in and out of treatment facilities much of her life, beating the illness long enough to fall in love, get married and raise a family.

At some point, Jane, who was adopted, sought out her birth mother. The reunion proved devastating when her mother rejected her, friends said. The illness resurfaced and her marriage failed. She divorced her husband and lost custody of her daughter.

She remarried and enrolled in college while in her 30s. Her friend remembered the days when they went to the state capitol to lobby for welfare reform and how easily Jane fit into the social work community and the jobs that followed.

But Jane left the work she loved in 1993, when she learned she was pregnant with her second child. After the birth, manic depression took its toll, relatives and friends said. The marriage failed and her second husband took custody of her son, who is now 4.

Those close to her said those events may have triggered her depression and mood swings. And by the spring of 1996, Jane found comfort living on the streets, traveling between Forth Worth, Las Vegas, and San Diego.

Her friend tracked her down at a psychiatric facility in Forth Worth and found Jane staring blankly at daytime television through a fog of medication. She said, "Hi, what are you doing here?" And I said, "To see you. What are you doing here?" And she said, "Well, this is where I belong." This memory left her friend feeling helpless and frustrated.

"Jane used to work hard to help people who had fallen through the cracks and were unemployed or near homeless," her friend said. "She was a good person who took everything to heart. . . . To me, this is proof that if it can happen to Jane, it can happen to the rest of us." (Modified from Craig, 1998; names were either deleted or changed and text was abridged.)

Moreover, it is not uncommon for social workers to feel forced to reduce services to some clients, focusing their efforts instead of those covered by insurance or able to pay privately. For those who cannot pay, services may be terminated if they seem too costly (Ethics Meet Managed Care, 1997). Accurate psychosocial assessment is therefore a critical tool for all mental health and health care social workers because it documents a client's needs and can support the efficiency of a chosen intervention. Such assessments not only open the door for services, they determine who will receive them and what will be provided.

Did You Know...Social workers have actively supported President Clinton's creation of a commission to review changes in health care and make recommendations for consumer protection and health care quality (Steps Taken to Watchdog Managed Care, 1997). This support is just one example of the ways health care and mental health social workers can not only assist in developing a comprehensive strategy to help clients but also ensure that high-quality service is made available and obtainable.

Currently, many social workers work with clients who suffer from mental illness—from the BSW-level practitioner who is active in case management, initial assessment, and discharge planning to the master's-level social worker who is an active participant in completing assessments and diagnoses. Whatever his level of practice a social worker must be aware of the tools and expectations characteristic of the field. The importance of the initial psychosocial assessment should not be underestimated; it provides the foundation and the framework for any future intervention.

Starting a Psychosocial Assessment

The information presented here does not cover everything involved in assessment in the mental health setting. We outline the basics in order to make you aware of the tasks of the mental health social worker and how the process of professional helping in this area begins.

Assessment is defined as "the process of determining the nature, cause, progression and prognosis of a problem and the personalities and situations involved therein; the social work function of acquiring an understanding of a problem, what causes it, and what can be changed to minimize or resolve it" (Barker, 1995, p. 27). Social workers assume that any type of assessment begins with the first client-worker interaction. The information that the social worker obtains determines the requirements and direction of the helping process. The mental health social worker gathers information about the present situation, elicits history about the past, and anticipates service expectations for the future. This assessment should always include creative interpretations of alternatives to best assist the client to get the services needed.

In mental health assessment, as in all social work assessments, the client is regarded as the primary source of data. In most cases, the client is questioned directly either verbally or in writing. Information about the client is also derived

This woman was previously hospitalized for schizophrenia. With family support she was able to live outside of an institution, enjoy her grandneice, and live a fuller life.

from direct observation of verbal and physical behavior or interaction patterns between the client and other interdisciplinary team members, family members, significant others, or friends. Viewing and recording these patterns of communication can be extremely helpful in later identifying and developing strength and resource considerations. In addition, background sheets, psychological tests, and tests to measure health status or level of duty functioning may be used.

Furthermore, in keeping with social work's traditional emphasis on including information about other areas, the worker talks with family members and significant others to estimate planning support and assistance. It might also be important to access secondary sources such as client's medical record and other health care providers.

To facilitate assessment, the social worker must be able to understand the client's medical situation or at least know where to go for information and help. Knowledge of certain mental health conditions, as well as common accompanying conditions, can only help the social worker to provide needed services or to decide when and where to refer the client to other health professionals for continued care. A key point: no social worker should ever be afraid to ask others to clarify concepts in regard to a client's care, especially when unsure about how the information may enhance understanding of the client.

Five expectations guide the initiation of assessment in the health and mental health setting (Dziegielewski, 1998).

1. Clients must be active and motivated in the treatment process: As in almost all forms of intervention, the client is expected to be active. The client must often expend serious energy in attempting to make behavioral changes. Clients therefore must not only agree to participate in the assessment process but must be willing to embark on the intervention plan that will produce behavioral change. Social workers usually practice verbal therapy; however, clients who are unmotivated or unwilling to talk or discuss change strategies may require more concrete goals and objectives to bring about specific behavior change.

2. The problem must guide the approach or method of intervention used: Social workers need to be aware of different methods and approaches to practice. No preferred approach should guide the choice of intervention. Sheafor, Horejsi, and Horejsi (1997) also warned about the opposite extremes, however: social workers becoming overinvolved and wasting valuable time in trying to match a particular problem to a particular theoretical model or approach. Health and mental health social workers must never lose sight of the ultimate purpose of the assessment process—that is, to complete an assessment that helps to establish a concrete service plan that addresses the client's needs.

Activity...Review the definition of assessment, and look at the reasons given for social workers to participate in this function. Discuss these issues with your classmates and decide where you believe it is essential for social workers in health care and mental health to participate in assessment. Explain both what you see as reason for participation and what you see as problems that might be caused by taking this active stance as a member of an interdisciplinary team.

3. The influence of values and beliefs should be made apparent in the process: Each one of us, professional or not, is influenced by her own values and beliefs. These beliefs are the foundation of who we are. In the professional practice of social work, however, it is essential that these personal beliefs and values do not affect the assessment and subsequent intervention process. A social worker must clearly identify from the onset of treatment those of his individual values, beliefs, and practices that can influence treatment outcomes. For example, what if an unmarried client in a psychiatric hospital has tested positive for pregnancy. The social worker assigned to her case personally believes that abortion is wrong, and even though the client does not have the capability to be a parent the worker cannot in good conscience recommend abortion as an option. The client is unsure about what to do yet knows her own limitations and wants to explore every possible alternative. For the social work professional this can be a difficult case, but the ultimate assessment and intervention strategy must be based on the client's needs and desires, not the social worker's. Therefore, guided by the profession's Code of Ethics the social worker tells the client of his prejudice and refers her to someone who can be more objective in exploring abortion as a possible course of action.

Most social work professionals agree that clients have the right to make their own decisions. Clients exercise this right especially when they are aware of their situation and want to participate in their own health care plans. Whatever their own feelings mental health social workers must do everything possible to ensure this right and to keep their personal opinions from impairing a proper assessment.

In addition, the beliefs and values of the members of the interdisciplinary team must be considered. Social workers need to recognize value conflicts that arise among the other team members and make team members aware of how their personal feelings and opinions might keep them from exploring all possible options for a client. This is not to suggest that social workers are more qualified to address this issue or that they always have an answer; it means that social workers should *strive* to assist these professionals and should always keep before the team the goal of best serving the client.

4. Issues of culture and race should be addressed openly in the assessment and treatment: The social worker needs to be aware of his own cultural heritage as well as the client's to create the most open and receptive environment possible. Dziegielewski (1997) suggested that the social work professional:

1. Be aware of her cultural limitations
2. Be open to cultural differences
3. Recognize the integrity and the uniqueness of the client
4. Use the client's learning style, including his own resources and supports
5. Implement a behavior biopsychosocial approach to practice within an integrated, nonjudgmental format.

Did You Know…The fourth edition of the Diagnostic and Statistical Manual of Mental Disorders *(DSM-IV), the major reference for the diagnosis of mental disorders and related mental health conditions, stresses that cultural factors must be considered before establishing a diagnosis. DSM-IV emphasizes that delusions and hallucinations may be difficult to separate from general beliefs or practices related to a client's culture or lifestyle. Social workers do not take behavior arising from a client's cultural beliefs—however "socially inappropriate" it may seem—as evidence of mental disorder. To help professionals to deal with the cultural aspects of mental health, an entire appendix of the DSM-IV describes and defines culturally bound syndromes that might affect the diagnosis and assessment process (American Psychiatric Association, 1994). All social workers must know how cultural and ethnic factors can affect assessment.*

---

5. Assessment must focus on client strengths and highlight the client's own resources: Clients have enormous difficulty identifying and planning to use their own strengths. People in general tend to focus on the negative and rarely praise themselves for the good they do. In today's high-pressure health and mental health environments social workers cannot spend time exploring issues that don't contribute to the client's well-being. They must quickly help the client to identify her own strengths. Most treatment is time limited these days, so individual resources are essential for continued growth and maintenance of wellness after the formal treatment period has ended. Although there are many different time-limited

Members of the Berrien County Association of Retarded Citizens (ARC) gather for a photo after a Fourth of July field trip with a social worker to a town on Lake Michigan. These citizens live either in group homes or with families.

approaches to practice most social workers agree that their first task is to clearly identify the client's strengths to use them as part of the treatment planning process. Focusing on a client's strengths helps to empower the client to make changes in her life.

Completing a Psychosocial Assessment

There are four primary steps in completing the assessment process.

1. Problem Recognition: The social worker must be active in uncovering problems that affect daily living and in engaging the client in self-help or skill-changing behaviors. It is important for the client to acknowledge that the problem exists, because once this happens "the boundaries of the problem become clear, and exploration then proceeds in a normal fashion" (Hepworth, Rooney, & Larson 1997, p. 205).

2. Problem Identification: The problem of concern is the problem the client thinks is important. After all, the client is the one who is expected to change his behavior. In assessment and planning, the end goal should always be identified and accepted by the client.

3. Problem Strategy and Developing an Intervention Plan: According to Sheafor, Horejsi, and Horejsi, the plan is the "bridge between the assessment and the intervention" (1997, p. 135). Here the social worker must help the client to focus on the goals and objectives to be achieved in the intervention process. In this initial planning stage, emphasis on the desired outcome is essential.

Tips on Information Recording and Documentation
Social workers must document their assessment plans clearly. Although it is beyond the scope of this book to discuss documentation techniques in detail, the following tips introduce the most important aspects of accurate and timely record keeping.

1. Always document justification for the "service necessity" of what you do.

2. Be sure to document clearly purpose, content, and outcome in every note you write—regardless of the type of note or reason for making the entry.

3. Always sign your name, credentials, and so forth, at the end of every note you write. Be sure to include the date and time the service was provided in every note. Don't forget to put in the record the amount of time spent with the client.

4. All those who review records for billing say that the biggest problems are lack of information and inaccurate information in the record.

5. Always document problem behaviors in terms of frequency, intensity, and duration.

6. Always be able to benchmark progress.

7. Use a black pen (whose ink does not run), and never reproduce notes for others.

8. If you do not document it, it did not happen.

4. Implementation: The outcome is a plan that will guide and enhance the course of treatment to be implemented. With the complexity of human beings and the problems they encounter a properly prepared multidimensional assessment is the first step in ensuring high-quality service delivery.

Person-in-Environment: A Systematic Approach to Assessment

In mental health practice today many forms of formal assessment can assist in the development of a treatment plan. One system of assessment that has recently gained favor with social workers is the **Person-in-Environment Classification System,** also known as the PIE. Designed primarily for advanced MSW-level practice, the PIE was underwritten by an award given to the California chapter of NASW from the NASW Program Advancement Fund (Whiting, 1996). Knowledge of the PIE is relevant for all mental health social workers regardless of educational level because of its emphasis on situational factors.

In the PIE the process of assessment is built around two major premises that are basic to all social work practice: recognition of social considerations and the person-in-situation stance. The PIE responds to the need to identify the problems of clients in a context that mental health and health professionals can easily understand (Karls & Wandrei, 1996a, 1996b):

[It] calls first for a social work assessment that is translated into a description of coding of the client's problems in social functioning. Social functioning is the client's ability to accomplish the activities necessary for daily living (for example, obtaining food, shelter and transportation) and to fulfill major social roles as required by the client's subculture or community. (Karls & Wandrei, 1996a, p. vii)

The PIE provides the following:

◆ A common language with which social workers in all settings can describe their clients' problems in social functioning
◆ A common capsule description of social phenomena that can facilitate treatment or ameliorate problems presented by clients
◆ A basis for gathering data to be used to measure the need for services and to design human service programs to evaluate effectiveness
◆ A mechanism for clearer communication among social work practitioners and between practitioners, administrators, and researchers
◆ A basis for clarifying the domain of social work in human service fields (Karls & Wandrei, 1996a)

The PIE is an excellent tool for advanced social workers; beginning professionals are not ready nor will they be expected to use this complex assessment tool. As you progress through human behavior and practice courses you will become more familiar with this technique, its advantages, and its uses in mental health practice. It's enough now to observe that PIE provides an important vehicle to understanding the many factors that affect a client's behavior, which is an important part of the assessment process.

The PIE system is user friendly because it classifies clients' problems into four distinct categories, or "factors." For the purpose of this chapter we have presented an abbreviated version of this assessment system. This information is not meant to be all inclusive; rather it is intended to help introduce beginning social work professionals to the knowledge base underlying the use of the PIE and to its relevance to formalized mental health assessment.

DSM-IV: Just to make sure you're aware of it, another important tool for social workers in the mental health arena is the *Diagnostic and Statistical Manual of Mental Disorders* (DSM-IV; American Psychiatric Association, 1994). The DSM is considered an advanced tool for social work practice. Its use is covered in graduate courses, and in some schools, entire courses are devoted to the study of the DSM. For a more detailed explanation of the DSM-IV and its relation to the PIE in practice see Dziegielewski (1998).

THE BEHAVIORAL BIOPSYCHOSOCIAL APPROACH TO SOCIAL WORK PRACTICE

Social work practice in assessment and intervention should recognize three factors: the *bio*medical, the *psycho*logical, and the *social* (Carlton, 1984; Dziegielewski, 1998). A social worker who understands the **biopsychosocial**

approach to health and mental health practice strives to ascertain for each client the appropriate balance among biomedical, psychological, and social considerations. "Balance" doesn't mean that these factors are treated as equal for every client, however. The particular situation experienced by the client determines where emphasis must be placed and what area must be addressed first. In today's practice environment, with its insistence on observable, measurable outcomes, the mental health social worker addresses the biopsychosocial factors in the client's life through the *behavioral* aspects of the client's condition.

For example, if a client is newly assessed as having schizophrenia while also being HIV positive, many issues must be addressed. At first the emphasis may be placed on the biomedical or biological area. The client needs immediately to be told that the medical test for HIV is positive and to be given information about what a positive test means. The task can be complicated by the client's mental condition. The schizophrenia may produce periodic breaks from reality, such as hallucinations and delusions, that keep him from accurately interpreting medical information. The client may have difficulty understanding how far the disease has progressed and what can be expected medically, for example. Nevertheless, every attempt must be made to help the client to understand the medical aspects of his condition and what being infected with this virus actually means. It is critical to ensure the client understands terms such as "t-cell count" and how important future self-protection from illness and opportunistic infectious disease is.

Once the biomedical area is addressed, emphasis may shift to the social and psychological aspects of the client's condition. Since HIV is clearly communicable, the client must realize quickly that his behavior could have significant effects on people in his support system. Early education about how the virus is transmitted can be critical. Since HIV is most often sexually transmitted, the client's past and present sexual partners must be considered. Himself or with help, the client must face telling loved ones about what has happened and what it will mean for future social relations.

Biomedical or Biological Factors to Be Considered in Mental Health Assessment

Area	Explanation
General medical condition	Describe the physical illness or disability from which the client is suffering.
Overall health status	Client is to evaluate her self-reported health status and level of functional ability.
Overall level of functioning	Describe what the client is able to do to meet her daily needs. Concrete tasks are assessed and documented for focus on future change effort.
Maintenance of continued health and wellness	Measure the client's functional ability and interest in preventive medical intervention.

Social Factors to Be Considered in Mental Health Assessment

Area	Explanation
Social/societal help-seeking behavior	Is the client open to outside help? Is the client willing to accept help from those outside her immediate family or the community?
Occupational participation	How does the client's illness or disability impair or prohibit functioning in the work environment? Is the client in a supportive work environment?
Social support system	Does the client have support from neighbors, friends, or community organizations (church membership, membership in professional clubs, etc.)?
Family support	What support or help can be expected from relatives of the client?
Support from significant other	Does the significant other understand and show willingness to help and support the needs of the client?
Ethnic or cultural affiliation	If the client is a member of a certain cultural or religious group, will affiliation affect medical treatment and compliance issues?

Furthermore, the client may be frightened by the changes in his mental status and be unsure of how to control the symptoms related to schizophrenia. First, the client must understand what is happening. Second, the client must be helped to realize what schizophrenia means for him and for those he comes in contact with. Important information must be shared with family and friends. The social perspective of the biopsychosocial approach focuses on the individual client together with his family, significant others, and friends—on how best to protect them but also to involve them in problem solving. The psychological perspective focuses directly on the fears and concerns of the individual, on how to help him to understand his mental health and the emotions he exhibits.

As you can see, if a client is dual diagnosed helping can become very complicated. In our example, the dual diagnosis of HIV and schizophrenia means that the client may be losing touch with reality and how his behaviors can harm others at a time when this knowledge is especially important.

Once the immediate needs of the client and his family have been addressed, the focus of intervention should shift to the *functional/situational* factors affecting the individual client. A functional assessment allows the social worker to determine the level at which the client is capable of responding to a concrete intervention-based plan.

Psychological Factors to Be Considered in Mental Health Assessment

Area	Explanation
Life stage	Describe the development stage in life at which the individual appears to be functioning.
Mental functioning	Describe the client's mental functioning. Complete a mental status measurement. Can the client participate knowledgeably in the intervention experience?
Cognitive functioning	Does the client have the ability to think and reason about what is happening to her? Is the client able to participate and make decisions in regard to her own best interest?
Level of self-awareness and self-help	Does the client understand what is happening to her? Is the client capable of assisting her level of self-care? Is the client capable of understanding the importance of health and wellness information? Is the client open to help and services provided by the health care team?

It is essential that assessment and intervention be related to the needs and abilities of the client. The social worker expects assessment to help the client better understand himself, and the factors identified during the procedure are shared with the client to assist in self-help or continued skill building. At first, the assessment process is used to examine the situation and initiate the helping process; later it contributes to an intervention plan.

FORMULATING A TREATMENT PLAN IN MENTAL HEALTH SOCIAL WORK

In the practice of mental health social work, taking the assessment and on that basis formulating a treatment or intervention plan is considered the next logical step. Often it is done by a multidisciplinary or interdisciplinary team that includes the social worker as a member. The first step in developing the treatment plan is helping the client to look concretely at what goals and objectives can be completed during the time available. These goals and objectives should always be set at the beginning of treatment; they will be essential when you measure the outcome of your treatment efforts.

When clients present with multiple problems, as they often do, first identify primary and secondary problems to give the treatment plan some focus. Ask the client what she sees as the most important problems to address. Remember that you will be asked to measure the effectiveness of your interventions and this generally begins with showing how mutually negotiated goals and objectives have been met. In addition, goals need to be specific, clear, verifiable, and measurable.

Functional/Situational Factors to Be Considered in Mental Health Assessment

Area	Explanation
Financial status	How does the health condition affect the financial status of the client? What income maintenance efforts are being made? Do any need to be initiated? Does the client have savings or resources to draw from?
Entitlements	Does the client have health, accident, disability, or life insurance benefits to cover her cost of health service? Has insurance been recorded and filed for the client to assist with paying of expenses? Does the client qualify for additional services to assist with illness and recovery?
Transportation	What transportation is available to the client? Does the client need assistance or arrangements to facilitate transportation?
Placement	Where will the client go after discharge? Is there a plan for continued maintenance when services are terminated? Is alternative placement needed?
Continuity of service	If the client is to be transferred to another health service, have the connections been made to link services and service providers appropriately? Based on the services provided has the client received the services she needs during and after the treatment period?

Always try to make them concrete and behavior specific. The specific objectives should be designed to further quantify the goals.

Once the goals and objectives have been outlined, attention turns to the contracting process. Many social work professionals question whether "working alliances" between clients and practitioners should really be referred to as contracts. But whatever we call these professional agreements we must be aware of them and know how to use them. The details of contracting and the specific treatment process that results are beyond the scope of this book; however, it's useful to consider some simple rules for contracting in the mental health setting: 1) Always put contracts in writing; verbal contracts are generally not recommended. 2) Be very clear about what you are going to do and what rewards the client will gain with compliance. 3) If you make your written contract part of the client's record be aware that it can be introduced into legal proceedings should a difficulty arise.

Activity…Here is a sample treatment plan for a client who is suicidal. Taking a behavioral biopsychosocial approach, what do you think of this plan? What are its strengths and its limitations for the client being served?

Sample Treatment Plan for Suicidal Ideation/Behavior

Definition: a human act of self-inflicted, self-intentional cessation. Simply stated, it is the wish to be dead with the act that carries out the wish.
Suicide ideation: thinking about suicide. Suicide verbalization: talking about suicide.
Parasuicide: attempting suicide.

Signs and Symptoms to Note in the Record (be sure to document any of these signs in the record):
Changes in eating and sleeping; changes in friends and social programs.
Changes in grades, job status, or love relationships; changes in usual daily activities.
Constant restlessness or unshakable depression; neglected appearance or hygiene.
Increase in drug or alcohol use; giving away of material possessions.
Recurrent thoughts or preoccupation with death; recent suicide attempt.
Ongoing suicidal ideation and any previous or present plans; history of suicide attempts in the family.
Sudden change in mood that is not consistent with life events; past suicide attempts and what was done.
History of drug abuse.

Goals:
1. Stabilize suicidal crisis.
2. Place client at appropriate level of care to address suicidal crisis.
3. Reestablish a sense of hope to deal with the current life situations.
4. Alleviate suicidal impulses and intent and return to higher (safer) level of functioning.

Objective	Intervention	Time Frame*
Client will report no longer feeling the need to harm self.	Assess for suicidal ideation and concrete plan of execution. Then make appropriate disposition/referral.	
Client will discuss suicidal feelings and thoughts.	Assist client to develop awareness of negative self-talk patterns and encourage positive images and self-talk.	
Identify positives in current life situation.	Complete no-suicide contract. Address behaviors to complete when having suicidal thoughts or impulses.	
Help client to identify consistent eating and sleeping patterns.	Educate client in deep-breathing and relaxation techniques. Assist clients in developing coping strategies.	
Take medications as prescribed and report any inconsistencies or side effects.	Monitor for medication use and misuse, and confer with treatment team on a regular basis.	
Complete assessments of functioning.	Arrange or complete administration of the test. Determine level of depression or suicide precaution. Assess and monitor suicide intervention.	

*Time frame is to be individualized to the client.

Three Types of Contracts

Service contract: This type of contract usually outlines steps that must be completed prior to any service provision. It provides information to the client and tells the client what can be expected.

Initial contract: This is usually a very short range contract made to ensure that client and worker are in agreement. It usually deals with assessment, problem definition, and goal setting.

Therapeutic contract: This is the most individualized of the three kinds of contracts; it defines the goals, objectives, and interventions to be used. This is the contract generally used for insurance reimbursement, and it establishes the basis for assessing and evaluating client-worker progress.

SUMMARY

Whatever we call them, psychosocial assessments performed by mental health and health care social workers are essential. Assessment is the critical first step in formulating a plan for intervention. It thus sets the tone and framework for the entire mental health social work process.

Mental Health Social Work Practice in the New Millennium: Questions to Guide Assessment and Intervention Success

1. Are you able to document a DSM-IV multiaxis diagnosis?
2. Can you show that the identified condition is treatable with a realistic chance of success?
3. Have you developed specific goals and objectives for the treatment of the client?
4. Do you provide a clear rationale for the level of care, modality, types of intervention, and duration of treatment?
5. Is there a process for updating and periodic review of goal and objective attainment?
6. Is the client involved in the treatment development process?
7. If treatment is to be longer than originally expected, is a rationale for extension provided?
8. What specific things will happen to indicate that treatment goals and objectives have been met?
9. Is the intervention plan utilized consistent with social work values and ethics?

In order to compete in today's mental health environment social work professionals must play a twofold role: 1) to ensure that high-quality service is provided to the client and 2) to ensure that the client has access and is given an opportunity to see that her mental health needs are addressed. Neither of these tasks is easy, nor will they make a social worker popular in today's environment. Mental and other health services must now be delivered with limited resources, and the pressure to reduce services is intense. Social workers must know the assessment and treatment planning tools that are used in the field and be able to use them. Assessment and treatment planning are together the first step in providing services, a step that social work professionals cannot afford to neglect.

Numerous tools and methods exist to assist social workers in the mental health assessment process. The PIE is only one example of what is available. These forms of systematic assessment can provide social workers with frameworks for practice. We should always use such systems cautiously, however; as you will learn in practice courses yet to come, many social workers fear that these methods can place **labels** on clients that are very difficult to remove. These fears are well founded, but they shouldn't cause social workers to shun assessment. Indeed, the fact that social workers are aware of such dangers makes their participation in assessment essential. In addition, the social worker brings a wealth of information to the interdisciplinary team about a client's environment and family situation. Social workers, who focus on building on the skills and strengths of the client, are well equipped to help design a treatment plan that is realistic and effective.

Although assessments completed today appear to have a more narrow focus, it is essential that utility, relevance, and salience be maintained (Mitchell, 1991). Because social workers practice in numerous health and mental health settings and perform many different duties, it is not surprising that the processes of assessment and treatment planning show great diversity. Assessment and subsequent treatment plan development depend on a multiplicity of factors, including client need, agency function, practice setting, service limitations, and coverage for provision of service. Many times the scope of assessment and intervention must be narrowed in response to reductions in economic support (Mitchell, 1991). Therefore, overall practice in the mental health setting must continually be examined to ensure high quality. If the process of helping is rushed, superficial factors may be highlighted and significant ones overlooked. All social workers—whether in health care or mental health, or any other area—must, above all, establish that the services provided are quality driven, no matter what the administrative and economic pressures may be.

Questions to Think About

1. Based on the information provided in this chapter, what do you see as the future role for mental health social workers in the assessment process?

2. Do you believe that the PIE will continue to gain in popularity in health and mental health settings with practitioners other than social workers?

3. Do you believe that a complete assessment and treatment planning framework is needed to guide social work practice and will continue to be required for reimbursement of social work services to increase?

References

American Psychiatric Association. (1994). *Diagnostic and statistical manual of mental disorders* (4th ed.). Washington, DC: Author.

Barker, R. L. (1995). *The social work dictionary* (3rd ed.). Washington, DC: NASW Press.

Carlton. T. O. (1984). *Clinical social work in health care settings: A guide to professional practice with exemplars*. New York: Springer.

Craig, Y. (1998, August 19). Victim dived from La Madeline lunches to homeless. Star-Telegram.com.

Dziegielewski, S. F. (1997). *Clinical, advanced, intermediate: Preparation for the clinical licensure exam*. Tuscaloosa, AL: Siri Productions.

Dziegielewski, S. F. (1998). *The changing face of health care social work: Professional practice in the era of managed care*. New York: Springer.

Ethics meet managed care. (1997, January). *NASW News, 42*(1), 7.

Hepworth, D. H., Rooney, R. H., & Larsen, J. (1997). *Direct social work practice: Theory and skills* (5th ed.). Pacific Grove, CA: Brooks/Cole.

Karls, J. M., & Wandrei, K. M. (Eds.). (1996a). *Person-in-environment system: The PIE classification system for social functioning problems*. Washington, DC: NASW Press.

Karls, J. M., & Wandrei, K. M. (1996b). *PIE manual: Person-in-environment system: The PIE classification system for social functioning problems*. Washington, DC: NASW Press.

Mitchell, R. W. (1991). *Documentation in counseling records*. Washington, DC: American College Association.

NASW. (1990). NASW clinical indicators for social work and psychosocial services in the acute psychiatric hospital [Pamphlet]. Washington, DC: Author.

NASW. (1998). Centennial information: Celebrating 100 years of social work practice [Pamphlet]. Washington, DC: Author.

Sheafor, B. W., Horejsi, C. R., & Horejsi, G. A. (1997). *Techniques and guidelines for social work practice* (4th ed.). Needham Heights, MA: Allyn and Bacon.

Steps taken to watchdog managed care. (1997, January). *NASW News, 42*(1), 12.

Whiting, L. (1996). Foreword. In J. M. Karls & K. M. Wandrei (Eds.), *Person-in-environment system: The PIE classification system for social functioning problems* (pp. xiii–xv). Washington, DC: NASW Press.

Further Reading

Adkins, E. A. (1996). Use of the PIE in a medical social work setting. In J. M. Karls & K. M. Wandrei (Eds.), *Person-in-environment system: The PIE classification system for social functioning problems* (pp. 67–78). Washington, DC: NASW Press.

Dziegielewski, S. F. (1996). Managed care principles: The need for social work in the health care environment. *Crisis Intervention and Time-Limited Treatment, 3*(2), 97–110.

Fischer, J., & Corcoran, K. (1994). *Measures for clinical practice: A sourcebook* (2nd ed.). New York: Free Press.

Chapter 11

The Elderly

LET'S BEGIN BY EXPLORING YOUR THOUGHTS ABOUT AGING. TRY TO answer these questions about getting older (Garner et al., 1997):
1. For me, getting older means. . .

2. Close your eyes and imagine yourself at various ages. What do you see?
   a) At age 60, I am . . .
   b) At age 70, I am . . .
   c) At age 80, I am . . .
   d) At age 90, I am . . .
   e) At age 100, I am . . .

3. Name a person age 65 or older whom you admire or have admired.
   What is so special about this person?
   How can this person be a role model for you?

No one escapes the aging process. In fact, from the moment we're born we all begin to age. During the aging process, as in all phases of human growth and development, people must adjust to changes in their life circumstances. Unfortunately, many of these changes are viewed negatively in our society. Declines in physical functioning, changes in physical appearance, loss of income, retirement, and loss of partner and social supports are all associated with aging. But not everyone experiences these shifts. Most professionals agree that to understand aging, we must look at more than just a person's chronological age—that is, how old he is. The study of the elderly therefore embraces varied life circumstances and issues and must consider physical and psychosocial factors (Brieland, Costin, & Atherton, 1980; Strawbridge, Camacho, Cohen, & Kaplan, 1993; Segrin, 1994).

> *Did You Know...One myth about aging is that "all older people are alike" and should therefore display predictable patterns of age-related behavior. However, this has not been proved; if anything, the opposite appears true: "as people get older they are less alike" (Peterson, 1994, p. 46).*

Over the years, however, use of a chronological age cutoff has been the most common way to decide who is "elderly." You may know people who shortly after their 50th birthdays began to receive retirement information from various groups. A number of major airlines offer "senior discounts" to people age 55 or older. The

Name: Maryann Petri

Place of residence: Palm Bay, Florida

College/university degrees: B.S.W., M.S.W., University of Central Florida

Present position: Counselor/Educator, Prevent! of Brevard

Previous work/volunteer experience: Alzheimer's Association, Case Management and Guardianship Services

What do you do in your spare time? I enjoy playing water sports, bowling, and karaoke.

Why did you choose social work as a career? I chose social work because I enjoy engaging in social change activities and advocating for better conditions for the aged. Many times elderly individuals may be left to feel helpless and useless and I enjoy helping them and their families to prepare for the future and adapt to existing social conditions.

What is your favorite social work story? My favorite social work story is one that involved a homeless man suffering from pneumonia. The man was admitted to a nursing home for short-term care while he recovered. Although he did not need long-term care, he remained at the facility for approximately 3 years because he had no one able to support his return to the community. He had a married daughter who lived out of state with her new husband. Her husband felt that the responsibility of caring for his elderly father-in-law was overwhelming and awarded power of attorney and limited guardianship to the agency where he resided. I worked for many months to reunite my client with his family. I advocated for his veteran benefits and helped the family work through the issues that were preventing reunification. He was later reunited with his daughter and son-in-law.

What would be the one thing you would change in our community if you had the power to do so? I would acquire a state-mandated allotment of funds to provide parenting classes to all pregnant mothers- and fathers-to-be.

Senior Golf Tour minimum age is 50 as is the entry age to various states' "senior games," that is, athletic contests. Most professionals agree that the definition of "senior" status began with the Economic Security Act of 1935 and was based on the German precedent, which established 65 years as the appropriate age for benefits to begin (Brieland et al., 1980). And indeed, this simple definition is administratively useful because it establishes clear eligibility standards for programs such as social security.

Did You Know...When the Economic Security Act was passed in 1935, age 65 marked the 95th percentile of the U.S. age distribution. By 1986, age 65 marked the 76th percentile (Wolinsky & Arnold, 1988). Therefore, the share of the U.S. population age 65 and over has increased, and it is expected to continue growing dramatically.

Although looking at chronological age is the simplest approach for administrators and policy planners, it is deficient when used alone because it cannot reflect changes in the composition of the aged population. These changes have made the elderly a much less homogeneous group. One long-term change is based on gender. As Americans continue to enjoy longer and longer life spans and lower death rates, elderly women in particular have benefitted. About fifty years ago there were equal numbers of men and women age 65 and over, since then, however, the proportion of men in this population has declined (Rhodes, 1988). Population projections suggest that this trend will continue: by the year 2000, there will be 64 males per 100 females (Rhodes, 1988) and the estimated life expectancies for people who reach age 65 will be approximately 83 for women and 80 for men (Morgan & Kunkel, 1998).

Another factor that undermines any simple definition of "elderly" is the wide range of ages of people who can be included in this designation (Belsky, 1988). Some people, for example, live well into their 90s and even beyond. Unfortunately, these elderly individuals tend to have significantly more health problems than the younger elderly in their 60s and 70s, and it is almost impossible to compare the two groups. To address this problem, the elderly population can be divided into the young-old, the medium-old, and the old-old (Rhodes, 1988). For purposes of simplicity we will use the terms "elderly" and "aged" to refer to all people age 65 or older.

In this chapter we introduce you to the topic of aging, a normal and universal stage of human development. As the number of elderly citizens rises today, so does the need for social work services. Fortunately, many services provided to the aged are considered human rights and are not subject to the means testing so common elsewhere in the social service arena. We highlight issues and trends essential to an understanding of the elderly population.

AGING: WE CANNOT ESCAPE IT

The number of aged people is rising. Three reasons have been suggested for this increase. The first is simply the large portion of the population that will be reaching old age. Prior to World War II, large numbers of young immigrants came to America—most legally, and as such reflected in the national statistics, and others illegally, and therefore not counted. Many of these immigrants (legal and illegal) are now reaching retirement age. This group will be augmented as people born after World War II between 1945 and 1955—often called "baby boomers"—age into retirement (Rhodes, 1988). The baby boom generation is now estimated at 70 million Americans (Butler, 1994).

In terms of sheer numbers, in 1950 there were 12.4 million individuals over age 65; by 1980 this group had more than doubled in size. Projections for the year 2020 predict 70 million people age 65 and over, making up 20 percent of the population. This means that one in every five individuals will be 65 years or older (Morgan & Kunkel, 1998). In particular, the proportion of the total population that is age 75 and over is expected to grow well into the twenty-first century. The increase in the numbers of elderly people is evident throughout the American population: for example, between 1992 and 2040 the nonwhite elderly population is expected to grow from 3.3 to 14.1 million (Lilienfeld & Perl, 1994). Currently, the elderly make up the fastest growing age group in the United States.

Activity...Explore the concept of aging by visiting the Census Bureau web site www. census.gov/population/www/socdemo/age.html. Compare trends on the national level and in your home state or county. For information from an international perspective try www.census/gov/ipc/www/idbnew.html.

The second factor underlying the growth in the number of aged individuals is the number of births in relation to the number of deaths. The trend in recent years has been fewer births and longer and healthier lives resulting in lower death rates (Rhodes, 1988; Morgan & Kunkel, 1998). It is predicted that death rates will continue to decline, leaving more aged individuals in society, especially among the old-old, or those over age 75.

The third, most obvious reason for growth in the elderly population is the strides made by the scientific community in understanding and promoting the factors that support longer and healthier life spans (Belsky, 1988; Rhodes, 1988; Mosher-Ashley, 1994). The study of aging did not become popular until the end of the 1930s (Shock, 1987). This increased attention to the elderly was related to three major events: 1) the implementation of the Economic Security Act, 2) the development of a scientific basis for the study of the aged, and 3) the dramatic population trends involving elderly people.

By the late 1930s, the United States was experiencing the aftermath of many major social changes. As World War I had ended many people were thrust into poverty. The Great Depression made destitute so many people who had never been poor before. Faced with these newly and "unusually" impoverished fellow citizens, American society showed increased willingness to help certain disadvantaged groups. This sentiment was felt particularly toward older people and young children (Frank, 1946). At the same time, the country still held a strong work ethic; regardless of age or circumstances every person was expected to be a productive

Rosa is an older woman who lives with her daughter and receives help from a visiting social worker.

part of society. It was during this period that the public, among whom social workers were active, began to insist that government take the necessary steps to ensure that the elderly and children did not, through their inability to work, become burdens on society (Axinn & Levin, 1982).

The Economic Security Act of 1935 was a societal response to the problem of widespread unemployment caused by the Great Depression. The act mobilized an unprecedented redistribution of income within society. As a result of this legislation, elderly citizens were provided with a government-assisted income, because they were officially designated as unemployable (Axinn & Levin, 1982). Their new guaranteed income helped to make this "worthy" group prosperous enough to command additional professional and societal attention.

Also in the 1930s, an improved scientific basis for the study of the aged developed. The year 1942 saw the publication of *Problems of Aging* by E. Cowdry, a collection of papers by eminent scientists from many disciplines that represented the first compilation of "scientific data on aging" (Shock, 1987, p. 34). Following Cowdry's publication, the first issue of the *Journal of Gerontology* appeared in January 1946. This journal claimed to be the first in the field of gerontology designed "to provide a medium of communication and of interpretation in our efforts to gain a much surer knowledge of human growth and development" (Frank, 1946, p. 3). It represented the Gerontological Society, whose primary interest was to assist the elderly "against the present almost brutal neglect of the aged, by which many have been misused" (Frank, 1946, p. 3). These two publications highlighted the point that that science and technology could assist in preventing the loss of this valuable resource. Now, a half-century later, a large body of literature reflects the popularity of aging as a subject of study. Numerous books, textbooks, and classes are offered in this area. Furthermore, such professionals as chemists, physicians, economists, dentists, psychologists, and social workers have all contributed to existing knowledge about the aging population.

Did You Know…The social work profession has a long-standing interest in aging. This interest was expressed as early as 1947 at the National Conference of Social Work. Issues in aging were also included in the 1949 Social Work Yearbook *(Lowry, 1979).*

Finally, the third reason for increased attention to the concept of the elderly in the late 1930s lay in population trends within this group. The late 1930s saw growing numbers of elderly individuals (Axinn & Levin, 1982; Morgan & Kunkel, 1998), which caused much concern because these people were not considered capable of contributing to the national economy in terms of work (Frank, 1946; Axinn & Levin, 1982). Many people now worry that programs created under the Economic Security Act to assist this population may no longer suffice. This fear is inspired primarily by expected increases in the elderly population and the extended life spans that these elderly people will enjoy. Given the open advocacy and concern expressed for the elderly today, a sense of cautious optimism has developed; yet resistance continues to new programs to address the needs or our elderly population (Morris, 1993).

THEORETICAL FRAMEWORKS FOR PRACTICE WITH THE ELDERLY

A cornerstone of all social work programs is the acknowledgment of the influence of human growth and development theory. This theoretical framework became popular in the 1970s because its broad approach takes into account the benefits and challenges that individuals encounter as they mature in life. The personality of an individual is assumed to be consistent with the way life tasks are developed and managed throughout his lifetime (Rhodes, 1988). For social workers borrowing from this psychological theory, the most comprehensive and widely used work is that of Erikson (1959). Erikson described eight different stages of human development:

> Basic trust vs. mistrust
>
> Autonomy vs. shame and doubt
>
> Initiative vs. guilt

Industry vs. inferiority

Identity vs. identity diffusion

Intimacy vs. self-absorption

General activity vs. stagnation

Integrity vs. despair

He believed that once an individual had completed all of these stages successfully, she would accept her self and take responsibility for her own life. In the last developmental stage, integrity versus despair, an individual's life goals reach finalization, and reflection and contemplation become important tasks. Ryff (1982), among others, expanded on Erikson's last developmental stage by including such tasks as adjusting to no longer gaining an identity through work, accepting the physical limitations imposed by the aging process, and learning to cope with the concept of death and accepting spirituality.

Social workers must help elderly people to maximize the positive experiences in their lives while minimizing the negative ones. Creating an environment where successful aging can occur is essential. Unfortunately, we all have to face objective losses in the body and the mind, but the way we feel about and react to these losses helps to lay the foundation for future acceptance (Marsiske, Franks, & Mast, 1998).

Disengagement Theory

Disengagement theory was introduced by Cumming and Henry (1961) and focused on the "normal" process of withdrawal from the social environment to which an aging person belonged. The aging person initiates withdrawal from the usual life events and acknowledges his impending death, reduced physical energy, or poor health. The process of disengagement is considered beneficial to both the individual and society. According to proponents of this theory, the role of the social worker is to help the client to disengage from mainstream society. This allows a natural transition by physically separating the individual from mainstream life, thus fostering an adjustment period to his absence. Disengagement is viewed as an inevitable process that every aging individual must undergo. Further, if a person resists this natural process of "letting go," then problems in adjustment to the elderly years would develop (Cumming & Henry, 1961).

To date, most social workers, although aware of this theoretical perspective, do not embrace it wholeheartedly. This is especially true since the research on disengagement theory has been controversial and contradictory. The relationship between disengagement and the activity level the elderly individual will engage in after leaving mainstream society is unclear (Rhodes, 1988). Previous studies suggested that the role elderly individuals assume after disengagement depends on the behavior patterns they had established over their lifetimes (Maddox, 1964; Sills, 1980). Furthermore, some individuals do not separate but instead stay engaged by changing the focus of their activities. In closing, more research is needed to determine whether disengagement really is a natural part of the aging process.

Activity Theory

Activity theory assumes that the elderly have the same social and psychological needs as middle-aged people. The concepts of activity theory were introduced before disengagement theory, but activity theory was not formalized until 1972 with the work of Lemon, Bengston, and Peterson. These authors were among the first to test activity theory in relation to reported life satisfaction. They hypothesized that as activity increased, life satisfaction would also increase; and conversely, as role loss increased, life satisfaction would decrease. Basically, getting older is characterized by the desire to remain middle aged. Therefore, in order for aging to be successful, the elderly individual needs to continue activities similar to those that were important in middle age (Lemon, Bengston, & Peterson, 1972).

Proponents of this theoretical framework believe that professional intervention involves helping the client to continue an active existence. For example, a social worker might encourage an elderly person to do volunteer work as a way to replace previously paid employment. To date, most social workers working with the elderly are aware of this theory and of its influence on ideas about the aging process; however, most agree that more research is needed before activity theory can be used as a framework for practice. In particular, additional research is needed to establish a direct link between level of activity and life satisfaction (Hoyt, Kaiser, Peters, & Babchuk, 1980; Rhodes, 1988).

Whatever theoretical practice framework is used, more empirical research is needed to establish the utility of developmental theories in working with the elderly (Rhodes, 1988). Ryff (1982) argued that research must attempt to isolate the factors that result in accomplishment of Erikson's developmental stages and to examine the factors that actually allow elderly individuals to achieve optimal levels of performance. It is important to add another caution about these theories, namely, their apparent middle-class and sexist biases.

Human growth and development theories have largely displaced older theories about how the elderly adjust to their changing societal role. Historically, in our quest to understand the aging process and the milestones that elderly people attain, social workers entertained the concepts of disengagement and activity. These theories postulate that activity and disengagement from traditional life experiences are normal and natural parts of the aging process. While research has not proved these theories to be comprehensive enough to explain all life changes experienced by the elderly (Rhodes, 1988), their influence on social work practice remains. Social workers need to be aware of these perspectives on aging and how they can affect elderly clients. Whether these theories are valid or not, the fact that many professionals and lay people believe them may strongly affect their expectations and behavior. Uncritical adherence to these ideas may keep practitioners from thinking about alternative explanations for clients' behavior and from trying innovative problem-solving techniques.

The Pain in My Elbow

A 90-year-old man visits a physician for pain in the elbow joint of his right arm. After the client explains his symptoms to the physician, the physician says, "You are 90 years old. It's possible that the pain is merely related to your age, and there may be no plausible medical explanation for your pain." After hearing this theory the patient thought for a moment and asked, "If your idea is tenable, why doesn't my other elbow hurt? After all, it's the same age."

HEALTH, MENTAL HEALTH, AND THE ELDERLY

How often have you heard someone describe an aged loved one as dying "of old age"? How often have you heard professionals encourage this notion? How often have you seen or heard of an elderly person who consulted a physician about a certain ache or pain only to be told that the pain was simply related to old age?

Dying of old age is a myth that should not be propagated. Social work professionals must give elderly clients the respect they deserve, allowing them to state their concerns in a nonjudgmental atmosphere. *No one ever died of old age.* There are many causes of illness in the elderly, including such serious conditions as heart disease, cancer, and stroke (Rhodes, 1988), but death due to these or other medical conditions should never be dismissed as dying of old age. This attitude can lead to actual diseases going undetected because symptoms characteristic of disease may be attributed by both client and physician to the aging process itself (Anderson & Williams, 1989). The elderly deserve the same professional treatment as any other age group, and social work professionals have a role in educating and helping elderly individuals to secure the specific health services they need.

Did You Know...In an archival study of records on 298 clients treated by a mental health center, three types of issues predominated among elderly clients: 1) family conflicts, 2) poor physical health, and 3) feeling that they were not in control of their lives (Mosher-Ashley, 1994).

The U.S. Senate Special Committee on Aging (1981) reported that 45 percent of elderly people experience limitation of activity due to some type of chronic condition. "In 1980, approximately 10.7 million persons over age 65 experienced some limitation. By the year 2000, this number will increase to 16.3 million and will reach 31.7 million by 2050" (Maldonado, 1987, p. 99). As a result the elderly are important consumers of health care. They account for at least 30 percent of the nation's health expenditures even though they make up only 12 percent of the total U.S. population (McCullough & Cody, 1993). It is the elderly individual who is most frequently hospitalized with the most costly hospital stays (Specht & Craig, 1982).

Hospital use by the elderly received a strong boost in 1965 with the initiation of Title XVIII (Medicare), which provided health insurance for the elderly, a high-risk group in terms of vulnerability to illness and poverty (Axinn & Levin, 1982). Medicare was one of the amendments to the Economic Security Acct of 1935. Obviously, as people get older they are more likely to need health care services; yet since 1965 and the implementation of Title XVIII, the increase in health care consumption at age 65 has been dramatic. The Medicare program brought health care within the means of many elderly people who could not afford it otherwise; physicians and hospitals also benefitted from the greater assurance of payment for providing needed health care services. The benefits to health care recipients and providers, however, came at a particularly high price for the federal government. As the cost of services continued to escalate, the government became determined to control Medicare expenditures (Starr, 1982).

In 1983, Congress mandated a radical change in the payment structure for hospital care to rescue the Hospital Insurance Trust Fund from imminent bankruptcy (Lee, Forthofor, & Taube, 1985). The original system required Medicare to pay whatever hospitals charged for a particular service. Faced with these various and fluctuating costs the government wanted to achieve uniformity and predictability. To control costs and develop an equitable payment system, Diagnostic Related Groups (DRGs) were developed (Begly, 1985).

The DRG system groups together individuals who have similar diagnoses, regardless of age or general health status. Each diagnostic category is assigned a particular standard of care, including length of stay, for which the government is willing to pay—for example, gallbladder removal is allowed seven days of hospital treatment. This new system thus has a fixed payment schedule and hospitals know how much money they will receive for each individual. Unfortunately, for elderly people, who are more fragile and often have chronic or complicating conditions, this system is problematic. Little incentive exists for hospitals to accept patients who might require extended stays. When hospitals do accept elderly patients, many social workers here noted that they are discharged as quickly as possible. Quick discharges are problematic because many of the sick elderly have low incomes and few supports in the community for extended care assistance (Blazyk & Canavan, 1985). Facilities such as nursing homes are often reluctant to take these recently discharged individuals, in their less medically stable conditions. Nursing home professionals are strained when these new patients require much more care and observation; in many cases an increase in staff to accommodate the additional needs of these new patients never occurs. The result in the long run can be readmission, which is costly for the individual and for the hospital (Berkman & Abrams, 1986).

Medicare—and insurance reimbursement in general—is of particular interest to social workers because they are the ones who generally handle the discharge and placement of elderly clients in both nursing home and hospital settings. Social workers must be aware of community supports for discharge back into the community and the availability of any special treatment or services. Discharging elderly people home may place great stress on the family and extended care staff. In dis-

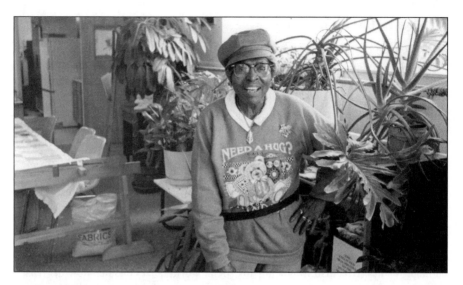

An 80-year-old at the ecumenical social center after an exercise class. This is a drop-in center that offers seniors lunch and a variety of activities.

charges back to the community, family stress is often a major contributing factor to long-term care admission (Pratt, Wright, & Schmall, 1987). Measures should be taken to allow families to communicate needs, problem solve, and participate in support groups. Social workers provide an excellent entry point for supportive and educational services to both elderly clients and caregivers. Similarly, placing an elderly client who needs a great deal of individual care into a long-term care facility can create great stress for the staff. Support groups and regular inservice training on how to treat these clients is mandatory. If additional staff are needed to facilitate placement, social workers should recommend such support.

From the individual perspective, developing a chronic health condition is generally an elderly person's worst fear because it can impair activity and unaided mobility (Rhodes, 1988). The chronic conditions from which the elderly often suffer are either physical (biological or physiological) or mental (psychological) in nature. We make this distinction only for simplicity's sake; it is important to note that physical and mental health conditions are often related and interdependent. For example, a physical event such as a stroke may develop into the mental health condition dementia.

Did You Know...A "chronic" condition is generally defined as a disease of long duration, following a long, drawn-out progression (Taber's Cyclopedia Medical Dictionary, 1977). An "acute" condition, on the other hand, generally has a rapid, severe onset and a short duration (Taber's Cyclopedia Medical Dictionary, 1977). Elderly people are affected more often by chronic than by acute conditions.

Physical Health Conditions

"Probably no factor is of more immediate concern to older people than physical health" (Maldonado, 1987, p. 99). Many elderly people fear the loss of individual, unaided activity or perceived independence. Of all physical health conditions, heart disease is the leading cause of death among those age 65 or older (Anderson & Williams, 1989), followed closely by cancer and stroke, respectively (Rhodes, 1988, p. 23). Although these conditions (excluding cancer) are considered acute, patients often gradually fall prey to chronic conditions such as paralysis and mental impairment resulting in some type of dementia (Crichton, 1987). Arthritis and hypertensive diseases are the most prominent chronic conditions among men and women age 65 or older (Maldonado, 1987). Other major chronic conditions that result in the restriction of activity include rheumatism and hearing and vision impairments.

Among vision conditions, cataracts and glaucoma are most common. Social workers should always encourage elderly clients suffering from vision impairments to receive regular check-ups to aid in detecting such conditions before permanent damage results. It is also important for social workers to consider how decreased vision can affect the counseling relationship. For example, an elderly client may not want to admit that he cannot easily read written material or navigate in a particular setting.

Special attention should also be paid to possible hearing loss in clients. Someone who seems withdrawn and unresponsive to conversation may simply be suffering from hearing loss and may be hearing only part of what is said and hypothesizing the rest. If the response is not appropriate, it can seem like confusion. Family members, in particular, may believe their aged relative is becoming confused or simply ignoring them, and confusion in the elderly tends to increase the stress felt by family members about their aged relative (Smallegan, 1985).

In closing, social work professionals should always be aware that the elderly are often shocked and embarrassed by changes in their health, and these feelings may lead to denial. All of us can understand reluctance to admit individual inadequacy. Counseling and interviewing should include initial assessment to determine whether health concerns are affecting the interview process.

Mental Health Process

Elderly individuals suffer many life circumstances that can affect their mental health. It is virtually impossible to age and not have traumatic life-changing experiences. Common stressful life events include widowhood, social and occupational losses, and physical health problems. Taking the sheer number of life tragedies that elderly people have faced, it would seem logical that they would seek more mental health services than other population groups; however, this is not the case (Maldonado, 1987; Rhodes, 1988). The elderly use mental health services at less than half the rate of the general population (Maldonado, 1987). One reason is the method of delivery. When living in the community elderly psychiatric clients generally go to community mental health centers for check-ups and medication; many of the elderly refuse these services because they don't want to leave their homes (Sherwood, Morris, & Ruchline, 1986).

Depression: Depression is a common mental health problem of the elderly, one frequently associated with physical symptoms and illness (Rhodes, 1988; Marsiske et al., 1998). There is little consensus among researchers, however, regarding the prevalence of this condition and how to recognize it in the aged (Ban, 1987; Reynolds, Small, Stein, & Teri, 1994). According to Belsky (1988), who interpreted the results of various community surveys, anywhere from 5 to 50 percent of the elderly population suffer from some level of depression; a finer estimate is 5 to 20 percent of the elderly who reside in the community (Reynolds et al., 1994). The existence of depression among the elderly is especially unfortunate, because although it is often treatable, few of the elderly actually seek treatment for this or any other mental health condition (Maldonado, 1987; Belsky, 1988). Furthermore, depression is believed to be related to the disproportionately high suicide rate among the aged population (Ban, 1987; Perkins & Tice, 1994).

Commons signs and symptoms of depression include feelings of sadness, loneliness, guilt, boredom, marked decrease or increase in appetite, lack or increase in sleep behavior, and a sense of worthlessness (American Psychiatric Association, 1994). When depression arises in response to life circumstances, it is called "situational." Situational depression is a particular risk for the elderly because they generally endure many tragedies including loss of loved ones, jobs, status, and independence and other personal disappointments. Feelings of depression can be triggered by such experiences as bereavement for a deceased loved one or frustration with a medical condition (Marsiske et al., 1998).

Social work intervention and counseling can help elderly clients to deal with situational depression and achieve greater life satisfaction. For example, social workers can teach elderly people how to control the frequency of their depressive thoughts and to use relaxation techniques, such as imagery and deep muscle relaxation, to calm down during anxious times. Concrete problem solving and behavioral contracting can be used to help the elderly client change problem behaviors. Whenever possible, family members should be included in treatment contracting because they can provide support and assist in recording and observing behaviors that the elderly client is seeking to change.

Caution should always be used, however; not all cases of depression in the elderly are situational. Some cases of depression may arise directly from internal causes; this is called "endogenous" depression. Furthermore, the etiology of depression in the elderly is not always distinct; depression may be the result of a combination of situational and endogenous factors. For example, many chronic medical conditions are often accompanied by depression. These include hypothyroidism, Addison's Disease, Parkinson's disease, Alzheimer's disease, and congestive heart failure. It is also possible that symptoms of depression are by-products or side effects of medication taken for another condition (Belsky, 1988;

Dziegielewski & Leon, 1998) or are, in fact, symptoms of something else. The American Psychiatric Association (1994) has warned that the diagnosis of depression in the elderly can be particularly problematic because the symptoms of dementia in its early stages and those of depression are very similar. Symptoms such as loss of interest and pleasure in usual activities, disorientation, and memory loss are common to the two conditions. There is one big difference, however. Although many signs and symptoms are the same, the person in the early stages of dementia will rarely improve as a result of treatment.

For the beginning social work professional, working with clients who are depressed can be frightening. You may feel very uncertain about what to do and also worry greatly that the client might try to harm herself. This makes it a practice necessity to gather as detailed a social, medical, and medication history as soon as possible. In addition, depressed elderly clients should always be referred for medical examination in order to rule out any physical reasons for depressive symptoms. Depression is most dangerous when it is unrecognized. When implemented, treatment for depression in the elderly is as effective as with other age groups (Reynolds et al., 1994).

Discharge Options: The current trend is for many mentally impaired elderly who cannot be handled at home or in the community to be discharged to long-term care facilities. This practice has increased as a result of the deinstitutionalization that over the past thirty-three years has shrunk state mental health hospitals to one-third their former capacity, and thus reduced one important placement option (Talbott, 1988). In response to the consequent need for more constricted placement many privately run long-term care facilities, including adult congregate living facilities (boarding homes) and intermediate- and skilled-level care nursing homes, have been opened. In the past thirty years the number of nursing homes alone has tripled in the United States (Morgan & Kunkel, 1998). These homes provide a discharge option for mentally impaired elderly clients that other population groups do not have. Most patients admitted to long-term care facilities are over age 65.

Several authors (Dobelstein & Johnson, 1985; Lusky, 1986; Diamond, 1986) have contended that long-term care facilities, although convenient, are inappropriate placement options for the mentally impaired elderly because they generally do not provide mental health services (Swan, 1987). Talbott (1988) argued that according to the President's Commission on Mental Health, very few long-term care facilities provide psychosocial interventions, and medication is often the sole method of treatment. Beginning social work professionals must exercise caution when placing a client in a long-term care facility, especially if the client needs mental health services. Each facility is different. Social workers need to be aware not only of what long-term facilities exist in an area but which services these different facilities offer to the mentally impaired elderly client.

Many elderly people fear functional activity loss. Social workers must be aware of this fear, regardless of whether such loss has actually occurred. Such worries have a real foundation. Since many elderly individuals suffer from chronic conditions, the probability that their condition will improve is low.

Our society tends to deny that problems may be terminal. Family members, and some professionals, may tell aged people that they'll get better, rather than helping them to develop ways to cope. It is important for social work practitioners to be knowledgeable about common chronic conditions, their signs and symptoms, their expected progression, and when and where to refer clients for additional treatment. Furthermore, there is considerable evidence that the involvement and support of family members is important in creating a general sense of well-being in the elderly (Rubinstein, Lubben, & Mintzer, 1994; Dziegielewski, 1990, 1991). Therefore, the role of the social worker is essential in educating aged clients and their family members to cope with and understand changes that will occur. A comprehensive assessment of the individual, taking into account health conditions and environmental factors, is critical.

EMPLOYMENT CHANGES OF THE ELDERLY AND SOCIAL WORK PRACTICE

Today, problems associated with unemployment in the United States are inspiring social work professionals to look seriously at the social and economic consequences of being without a job (Rife & Belcher, 1994). At the same time, a growing abundance of low-paying and minimum wage jobs are not being filled. Having to address these problems has brought to the attention of the public the specific experiences of certain groups such as older adults. Currently, the trend toward early retirement, in conjunction with the diminishing number of youths entering the workforce (as a result of lower birthrates), has created interest in the elderly as a potential source of labor to help fill this gap. Elderly people, who are living longer and healthier, are an underutilized labor pool that should not be ignored (Mor-Barak & Tynan,1993). In addition to societal need, many elderly individuals who enjoy good health see continued employment as desirable. For example, an archival study conducted by Mosher-Ashley (1994) on 298 mental health outpatient records found that elderly men between ages 60 and 98 described loss of "work role" as a major area of personal concern. Furthermore, with today's economic turbulence and changes in traditional family structure, elderly people may be expected to take more active roles in supporting their extended families (Duke, Barton, & Wolf-Klein, 1994).

The Working Elderly

Sadly, if an elderly person does decide to return to work there is no guarantee that a job will be obtainable. Even with the protective legislation that exists, such as the ban on mandatory age-based retirement, age discrimination can and does take place (Sterns, Barrett, Czaja, & Barr, 1994). Many times it occurs when prospective employers refuse to make necessary adjustments for elderly employees (Sterns et al., 1994; Mor-Barak & Tynan, 1993).

Social Security Retirement Benefits

At one time people used to talk about retiring at age 65. Well, retirement age has increased for most people, as seen in this table. Can you retire at any age? Sure, but if you retire earlier than "full retirement age" your monthly social security check will be reduced. An eligible person may begin receiving retirement checks at age 62 or delay receiving checks while working past retirement age. Note that the longer you wait to collect your benefits, the larger your monthly checks will be.

Year of Birth	Full Retirement Age (years)	Total Reduction of Benefits If Retire Early[a]
1937 or earlier	65	20%
1940	65.5	22.5
1943–54	66	25
1960 and later	67	30

Source: See www.ssa.gov.

[a]Early retirement is age 62. An advantage of early retirement is that you collect your benefit for a longer period (if you live). The disadvantage is that your monthly check is permanently reduced by some percentage for the remainder of your life.

Until recently, social security rules created an unnecessary barrier for seniors who wished to work. Seniors who worked full or part time and earned income over a certain level were penalized for working by having their social security checks reduced. The U.S. Congress hopes to pass legislation that eliminates this penalty and allows seniors to earn as much as they can while maintaining their retirement checks.

To assist elderly clients returning to the workforce social work professionals strive to perform the following three tasks. First, social workers must encourage elderly clients to update or learn new skills so that they can remain competitive throughout their careers. This consideration is especially important with the rapid technological advances occurring today, as well as the use of computer and automation technologies in most occupational settings. For an elderly client learning and maintaining these types of skills can be frightening. This apprehension creates the need for the next point of social work intervention.

Second, social workers must work with employers to make job sites more worker friendly while linking elderly clients to larger support systems. Programs are often needed to accommodate older workers. These may include work schedule modifications such as sharing one job between two or more workers, flextime schedules, and reduced work weeks. Furthermore, programs that are designed to build worker skills, motivation, and self-confidence need to be made available either by the employer through in-house programs or in community through community-based programs (Mor-Barak & Tynan, 1993). Assistance programs such as the "job club" described by Rife and Belcher (1994), which utilized a specialized job assistance strategy, provide an excellent practice environment in which social workers can help older workers to become reemployed.

This couple has just celebrated their 50th wedding anniversary. It is often difficult for them to make Social Security income cover all their expense and they get help from their children.

Lastly, social workers must be aware that caregiving assistance may be needed to allow elderly clients to leave the home and continue working. Caregiving can be as serious an issue for elderly couples as for younger couples. However, although several major companies have altered their benefit packages to include eldercare provisions, most have not (Tennessee Commission on Eldercare, 1993; Sterns et al., 1994; Mor-Barak & Tynan, 1993). At a workshop sponsored by the Tennessee Commission on Eldercare (1993), the need for adult daycare was voiced as a major concern of families who maintain employment outside the home. In addition, recent studies have found that such services are valuable in easing the burden on caregivers (Dziergielewski & Ricks, 2000). For all extended families, the need for eldercare services will become a reality. Provision of elder daycare services similar to child daycare services can help these families. Social workers should advocate for companies to consider adding eldercare as a standard option in employee benefit packages.

The Elderly in Retirement

Retirement from the workforce has been viewed in different ways over the years. Attitudes toward retirement have changed with changes in social, emotional, political, and cultural climates. To illustrate how the view of retirement has changed, we present a brief history of the role of the aged in the labor force, drawn from Dziegielewski and Harrison (1996).

Activity...Go to the Social Security Administration web page www.ssa.gov and using the on-line retirement planner estimate your monthly social security benefit check. What do you find? Is this what you thought you would get? Can you live on this amount of money?

The early twentieth century saw a shift from an agrarian to an urban industrial economy in the United States (Axinn & Levin, 1982). In agrarian society, all family members were viewed as contributing members of a cohesive unit. The family was responsible for meeting all the needs of its individual members, including elderly family members. Industrialization, however, changed this perspective, establishing different expectations and roles. The decline in individual business and farm ownership meant that many people had to obtain incomes from outside sources (Atchley, 1976).

During these years (1890–1912), one member's income was not enough to support the entire family, and often work outside of the home by all family members, including women, children, and the aged, became mandatory (Axinn & Levin, 1982). The participation of all these groups in the labor force did not last long, however. Family members left the workforce for primarily two reasons: 1) With industrialization fewer workers were needed in the production of output. 2) An influx of new immigrants made far more workers available (Morrison, 1982). Women, children, and the elderly were therefore no longer needed in the workforce. It was in this era that elderly people began to receive attention from the public. Morrison (1982) attributed this increased interest to the growth in the elderly population and to worries that this large population might compete for limited jobs with younger workers.

The Economic Security Act of 1935 was the first time the government had acknowledged responsibility for providing the elderly with an income that did not depend on continuing participation in the labor market. "The Social Security Act . . . set up a national system of old age insurance . . . which legitimized retirement at age 65" (Morrison, 1982, p. 9). This act supported limited, although permanent, economic guarantees to elderly individuals. Social security helped to ensure that retirement benefits would moderate the reduction in income that workers faced when they left the labor market, and it helped to establish 65 years as the encouraged or expected retirement age (Morrison, 1982).

The lives of the aged have not changed radically over the past fifty years; what had changed, however, is our view of the elderly and how society acts upon this view. In working with elderly clients, social workers need to be aware of the following aspects of retirement, and how they can affect the lives of the aged. Over the short span of forty years, retirement has become an important concern of the American people; almost every day, articles and commentaries appear in publications throughout the country on the economic, social, and psychological conse-

Activity...Retirement involves both endings and beginnings. Take a look at your own retirement and think about your endings and beginnings.

Endings: *What will your life be like when you retire? Think about your paycheck, alarm clock, commute . . .*

What Will End	Will You Miss It?	
	Yes	No
1. _____	_____	_____
2. _____	_____	_____
3. _____	_____	_____
4. _____	_____	_____

Beginnings: *What will you miss from your work environment and what can you replace with it? For example, you might miss managing projects, and replace it with volunteering in a program that requires management skills.*

Miss	Replace
1. _____	_____
2. _____	_____
3. _____	_____
4. _____	_____
5. _____	_____

Source: Garner et al. (1997).

quences of retirement. It is clear that this interest in retirement has been heightened by the rising costs of public and private retirement benefits and by doubts as to whether these costs can be sustained in the future (Morrison, 1982; Dziegielewski & Harrison, 1996). As the baby boomers approach retirement age, concern centers specifically on the ability of the social security system to handle the inevitable growth in the number of beneficiaries.

Helpful Point...When working with clients approaching retirement have them contact the Social Security Administration to get a copy of their lifetime earnings report. They should do this each year to verify the amount earned and credited toward their retirement. Any problems can be corrected with documentation of salary. But it's best to catch errors early rather than waiting until retirement.

Social work intervention can be critical in helping an aged client make a successful transition from the role of worker to the new role of retiree. It is important, however, that the social worker clearly communicate to elderly clients what role he will play in the delivery of services, because the provision of such services may be poorly understood (Scharlach, Mor-Barak, & Birba, 1994). For example, preretirement planning is just one of the services a social worker can provide to assist in the transition process. Through counseling and more specific assistance the social worker can help aged clients to plan for the role adjustment they will face. It is important to remember that many people gain their status or identity through working (Mosher-Ashley, 1994). They enjoy the work they do and don't want to give up the internal and external rewards they derive from it. Some elderly people can afford to retire but choose not be because of the value placed on working for money in this society (Davidson & Kunze, 1979). Ekerdt (1986) concurred that the importance of the work ethic in our society should not be underestimated. He recommended that elderly people reaching retirement plan their leisure time as carefully as they planned their work time; otherwise, their self-esteem may suffer. Social workers need to be sensitive to this aspect of work in order to help elderly individuals to find other activities that they will find fulfilling.

In planning leisure time, the degree and type of activity that a client can perform (and afford) must be considered. Worker and client can together create a list of possible options and discuss each option in a problem-solving, decision-making manner. Once they have chosen an appropriate leisure activity they can develop an individual contract. The contracting of leisure time activity can give the client "permission" to engage in something that's not work and can provide structure to an otherwise ambiguous period in life.

Finances are another factor that may deter an elderly individual from entering retirement (Davidson & Kunze, 1979). Fear of not having enough income or of being inundated with medical bills and having difficulty securing health insurance may cause an elderly person to avoid facing retirement. A social worker must be aware of the resources available to his elderly client and must help the client to obtain adequate financial counseling. Places of employment often will provide such counseling on request. Insurance brokers can be consulted about health and life insurance. These brokers are usually able to discuss numerous policy options because they represent several different companies.

Always remember when conducting retirement counseling that people often resist change and avoid what they cannot predict. Many people approaching retirement have grown comfortable in their careers and established job patterns that are integral parts of their lives. Elderly clients need to be made aware of the options available to them in retirement, especially in regard to leisure activities.

Preretirement services offered to prospective retirees is an area of social work intervention that should probably be expanded because currently many people preparing to retire avoid or do not engage in this type of planning (Rhodes, 1988) and social work practice offers few preretirement services (Montana, 1985). Most social work interventions in this area come after the fact and are supportive in nature. Montana (1985) stated that preretirement counseling is necessary because it can help elderly people to decrease their anxiety about what retirement will bring. Social workers can take a more active role in preretirement counseling by telling clients about its importance, as well as about how to plan for the future and what to expect in the way of benefits and activities. Attitude toward retirement can be very important in determining life satisfaction during retirement (Rhodes, 1988).

Did You Know...Two general terms are often used in the medical community to describe the process of getting older. The first, "aging," is defined as the condition of growing older regardless of chronological age; the second, "senescence," is used to characterize the later years in a life span (Peterson, 1994).

Furthermore, normal aging can be divided into two types: "intrinsic aging," which refers to the characteristics and processes common to all elderly people of a given gender, and "extrinsic aging," which refers to the factors that influence aging in varying degrees and that can affect individuals differently—for example, lifestyle patterns and exposure to environmental influences. "Normal aging is defined as the sum of intrinsic aging, extrinsic aging, and idiosyncratic or individual genetic factors in each individual" (Peterson, 1994, p. 46).

DIVERSITY TOPIC: ASSESSING SUICIDE AND PLANNING FOR DEATH IN PRACTICE WITH THE ELDERLY

Today, suicide rates among the elderly are on the rise, particularly among elderly men, and some authors believe these rates are underreported.

Among the general population, the suicide rate is 12.4 per 100,000 persons; the suicide rate for older people is higher than in the general population with a rate of 20 per 100,000 being recorded in 1990. Persons aged 65 and older compromise 12.5 percent of the population and account for 20.9 percent of the suicides annually. (Perkins &Tice, 1994, p. 438)

Did You Know...Suicide is the eighth leading cause of death in the United States and accounts for over 30,000 deaths each year.

There is probably no conclusive reason for these trends, but one possibility is that stress levels among the elderly are so high that usual methods of coping and problem solving are ineffective (Canetto, 1992). Furthermore, the elderly appear to be more dissatisfied with their functional abilities because of ill health and its effects (Reynolds et al., 1994). Finally, the tremendous number of life stressors that the elderly may experience in a short amount of time—for example, death of spouse, relatives, or friends and changes in social status and employment status—cannot be overemphasized.

Suicide rates are usually considered indicative of the mental health, satisfaction, and well-being of a population. But society doesn't always view suicide among the elderly in the same way as suicide involving young people. For example, the increase in suicide rates among adolescents has raised much alarm and led many to a call for solutions. At the same time, however, suicide is sometimes accepted as an understandable option for elderly people who feel lost, trapped, and alone (Kastenbaum & Coppedge, 1987). Indeed, Kastenbaum and Coppedge (1987) have suggested that suicide for the frail and sick elderly may even be encouraged by the reduction of health care benefits and the rationing of "limited health care options" to aged individuals.

A No-Suicide Contract

Social work professionals often help clients to complete these contracts even when clients have no actual plans to harm themselves. This is not a legal contract; it is merely done to help the client feel that there is a plan and that the plan is being monitored.

I _____ agree that I will not harm myself in any way and that I do not have any plans to do so. If I start to feel as though I might want to try to harm myself, I agree to immediately call [insert the name and number of a 24-hour hotline or emergency room the client can call].

Signed [client's name signed here]

Witness [Social worker's name here] [Phone number for agency/social worker]

Family Witness [if possible get a family member to witness]

The death of a partner presents a particular coping problem because it may require the elderly survivor to assume new, unfamiliar duties: balancing a checkbook, driving, shopping for groceries, and so forth. These new tasks and the adjustments they imply, in conjunction with the loss of a life partner, can place unbelievable stress on the elderly. They may feel isolated from married friends and fear possible dependence on family or friends. Widowhood particularly affects elderly women because they generally outlive men by approximately fifteen years (Belsky, 1988). Female widowhood may not be directly linked to suicide, however, because suicide rates are higher for elderly men than for elderly women (Specht & Craig, 1982). Nevertheless, Wan (1985) warned, widowhood is likely to have negative effects on the survivor, including impairment of physical, psychological, and social well-being. Suicide among the elderly is almost always a result of major life stresses and accumulated losses; therefore, widows and widowers have a high probability of committing suicide. Research indicates that the first year after the death of a spouse is the hardest time of adjustment (Wan, 1985; Belsky, 1988). During this especially stressful period, social workers should keep aware of a client's abilities or problems in coping with grief.

The social worker plays an essential role with potentially suicidal elderly clients. First, if a client, young or old, expresses a wish to commit suicide and has a concrete plan, steps to ensure hospitalization must be taken immediately. The person needs to be in a safe place. Unfortunately, criteria for hospital admission are not always clear, and the social worker may not know how likely the client is to turn thoughts into actions (Dziegielewski & Harrison, 1996). In any case, some type of counseling must take place. For dealing with aged clients Perkins and Tice (1994) emphasized a counseling strategy that focuses on client strengths. In this method client and social worker identify the client's preexisting coping and survival skills in order to help the client to accept the role of survivor. This approach, in conjunction with crisis services and bereavement counseling, can help the elderly client to regain control of her life.

Much of the confusion in our society regarding death can be linked to the atmosphere of denial, secrecy, and fear that we have created around this inevitable part of life (LaRue, 1985). Many people attempt to ignore or avoid this fact, at least until it affects them indirectly. For example, have you prepared for your own death? Do you have a will? Is your family aware of your wishes? For most of us the answer is no. Our reasons vary from "I'm too young to worry about that now" to "I have plenty of time." Now consider, if you the helping professional said no, what do you think your clients will answer? By the way, if you did say no, you're not alone; but don't take too much comfort in this—it's evidence that you need to address these issues in your own life.

No one rationally desires to be dying or to have a terminal illness. Indeed, most people resist even the idea of being ill. (For some people, however, regardless of age, there comes a time when they truly do want to die; High, 1978). Among the elderly, many fear the chronic conditions that can make them dependent on family and or friends. Family members too fear this new relation, daunted by the prospect of making decisions about a loved one, especially in regard to continuing or terminating life. The elderly person and family members often turn to science and medicine for the answers. Physicians, as representatives of the scientific and healing community, are sought out and expected to supply answers and make decisions. Unfortunately, many physicians, taught from the day they enter medical school to preserve life, may feel unprepared to deal with the psychosocial aspects of dying (Nolan, 1987). Trained to be "rescuers from pain . . . many times these physicians (and other health professionals) see themselves as arch rivals from death" (LaRue, 1985, p. 11). It is the social worker, often as part of an interdisciplinary team, who will be asked to help the client or family to cope with death.

Before a social worker can successfully help a client and her family to deal with death, several issues should be addressed. First, the social worker must explore his own feelings about death. Many social work practitioners, like their medical counterparts, are uncomfortable with the subject of dying (LaRue, 1985). It may help for the social worker to discover how death is viewed in other countries and religions (Dziegielewski & Harrison, 1996). The Roman Catholic Church, for example, has been very responsive in helping individuals to prepare for death (LaRue, 1985). By examining alternative conceptions of death and the legitimization of the role of death, social workers can disperse some of the mysticism that surrounds death in this country. Once the social worker feels comfortable talking about death these concepts need to be discussed with the client as well as family members.

Second, the social worker must know what resources and services available in the community might assist elderly clients in preparing for death. One example is the Hospice program. Hospice, which is funded by Medicare, offers services to people suffering from terminal illnesses who are expected to live six months or less (Crichton, 1987). This and similar programs do not focus on prolonging life beyond its natural end. In providing services through such programs the social worker serves on an interdisciplinary team designed to help the client and family members to prepare for natural death.

Finally, the social worker should learn about living wills and decide whether such a measure is appropriate for the client. Most people are aware of the need for, and some do complete, a will that declares who is to receive their money, property, and other possessions. However, the concept of a living will is less familiar (Paterson, Baker, & Maeck, 1993). Simply stated, a living will allows a person to document, in advance, her preferences relating to the use or avoidance of life-sustaining procedures, in the event of a terminal illness. This type of documentation is especially helpful to family members burdened with making such decisions when an elderly relative is mentally incapacitated. Without it, they may avoid making any decision because they feel that doing so gives them too much control and responsibility.

SUMMARY

We all face the prospect of growing old. Yet the elderly often suffer as the result of societal attitudes that devalue old age. Our society fears aging and promotes any number of attempts to beat the effects of old age on the human body and the mind. Such prejudices spring from both rational and irrational fears. Rational fears about worsening health, the loss of loved ones, and declining social status can be intensified by negative stereotypes of the elderly. And irrational fears about changes in physical appearance, loss of masculinity or femininity, and perceived mental incompetence are not unusual. For elderly people, misinformation and myth, as well as real biological, psychological, social, and economic challenges, can impede self-help and the pursuit of individual contentedness.

Aging in today's society creates complexities both in policy and in the human experience. Advances in medicine allow people to live longer. You will find many families that have three generations of "seniors": the granddaughter in her late 50s, the father in his early 80s, and the grandmother in her 100s. Talk about perplexing family dynamics!

As we age and live longer, we will spend more years in retirement. Once a short period of time, maybe ten to fifteen years, retirement now can last forty and even fifty years. Income, health care, socialization, loneliness and happiness, and support are among the many areas that policymakers and senior advocates struggle with today.

At a minimum, social workers need to examine their own attitudes about aging and how these attitudes can affect their practice with elderly clients and their families. We should be keenly aware of the types of discrimination that can occur, and we must never contribute, directly or indirectly, to any discriminatory practices based on age. All helping professionals need to recognize that each aged person is a valuable resource in our society. Our role is to provide services and advocacy that will help the elderly to maximize their life satisfaction and well-being.

References

American Psychiatric Association. (1994). *Diagnostic and statistical manual of mental disorders* (4th ed.). Washington, DC: Author.

Anderson, F., & Williams, B. (1989). *Practical management of the elderly.* Boston: Blackwell.

Atchley, R. (1976). *The sociology of retirement.* New York: Halsted.

Axinn, J., & Levin, H. (1982). *A history of the American response to need.* New York: Harper and Row.

Ban, T. A. (1987). Pharmacological perspectives in therapy of depression in the elderly. In G. L. Maddox & E. W. Busse (Eds.), *Aging: The universal experience* (pp. 127–131). New York: Springer.

Begly, C. (1985). Are DRGs fair? *Journal of Health and Human Resources Administration, 8,* 80–89.

Belsky, J. (1988). *Here tomorrow: Making the most of life after fifty.* Baltimore: Johns Hopkins University Press.

Berkman, B., & Abrams, R. (1986). Factors related to hospital readmission of elderly cardiac patients. *Social Work, 31*(2), 99–103.

Besdine, R. W. (1994, February). Successful aging for all? *Patient Care,* pp. 7–8.

Blazyk, S., & Canavan, M. (1985). Therapeutic aspects of discharge planning. *Social Work, 30,* 489–495.

Brieland, D., Costin, L. B., & Atherton, C. R. (1980). *Contemporary social work* (2nd ed.). New York: McGraw-Hill.

Brody, E. M., Brody, S. J. (1987). Aged: Services. In A. Minahan (Ed.), *Encyclopedia of social work* (pp. 106–126). Silver Spring, MD: NASW Press.

Butler, R. N. (1994). Baby boomers: Aging population at risk. *Geriatrics, 49*(2), 13–14.

Canetto, S. S. (1992). Gender and suicide in the elderly. *Suicide and Life Threatening Behavior, 22,* 80–97.

Cowdry, E. V. (Ed.). (1942). *Problems of aging: Biological and medical aspects.* Baltimore: Williams and Wilkins.

Crichton, J. (1987). *The age care source book: A resource guide for the aging and their families.* New York: Simon and Schuster.

Cumming, E., & Henry, W. (1961). *Growing old: The process of disengagement.* New York: Basic Books.

Davidson, W. R., & Kunze, K. (1979). Psychological, social and economic meanings of work in modern society: Their effects on the worker facing retirement. In W. C. Sze (Ed.), *Human life cycle* (pp. 690–717). New York: Jason Aronson.

Diamond, T. (1986). Social policy and every day life in the nursing home: A critical ethnology. *Social Science Medicine, 23,* 1287–1295.

Dobelstein, A., & Johnson, B. (1985). *Serving older adults: Policy, programs and professional activities.* Englewood Cliffs, NJ: Prentice-Hall.

Duke, W. M., Barton, L., & Wolf-Klein, G. P. (1994). The chief complaint: Patient caregiver and physician's perspectives. *Clinical Gerontologist, 14*(4), 3–11.

Dziegielewski, S. F. (1990). *The institutionalized dementia relative and the family member relationship.* Unpublished Ph.D. dissertation. Florida State University, Tallahassee.

Dziegielewski, S. F. (1991). Social group work with family members of elderly nursing home residents with dementia: A controlled evaluation. *Research on Social Work Practice, 1*(4), 358–370.

Dziegielewski, S. F. & Harrison, D. F. (1996). Counseling the aged. In D. F. Harrison, B. A. Thyer, & J. Wodarski (Eds.), *Cultural diversity in social work practice* (2nd ed.). Springfield, IL: Thomas.

Dziegielewski, S. F. & Leon, A. M. (1998). Psychopharmacology and the treatment of major depression. *Research on Social Work Practice, 8*(4), 475–490.

Dziegielewski, S. F. & Ricks, J. (2000, July–September). Adult daycare for mentally impaired elderly and measurement of caregiver satisfaction. *Activities, Adaption and Aging, 24*(4), 51–64.

Ekerdt, D. J. (1986). The busy ethic, moral continuity between work and retirement. *Gerontology, 26*, 239–244.

Erikson, E. (1959). Identity and the life cycle. In *Papers by Erik H. Erickson*. New York: Universities Press.

Frank, L. (1946). Geronotology. *Journal of Gerontology, 1*, 1.

Garner, J., et al. (1997). *Ernst & Young's' retirement planning guide*. New York: Wiley.

High, D. (1978). Quality of life and care of the dying person. In M. Blaes & D. High (Eds.), *Medical treatment and the dying: Moral issues* (pp. 65–84). Salem, MA: Hall.

Hoyt, D. R., Kaiser, M. A., Peters, G. R., & Babchuk, N. (1980). Life satisfaction and activity theory: A multi-dimensional approach. *Journal of Gerontology, 35*, 935–981.

Kasterbaum, R., & Coppedge, R. (1987). Suicide in later life: A counter trend among the old-old. In G. L. Maddox & E. W. Busse (Eds.), *Aging: The universal human experience*. New York: Springer.

LaRue, G. A. (1985). *Euthanasia and religion*. Eugene, OR: Hemlock Society.

Lee, E., Forthofor, R., & Taube, C. (1985). Does DRG mean disastrous results for psychiatric hospitals? *Journal of Health and Human Services Administration, 8*, 53–78.

Lemon, B. L., Bengston, V. L., & Peterson, J. A. (1972). An exploration of activity of aging: Activity types and life satisfaction among in-movers to a retirement community. *Journal of Gerontology, 27*, 511–583.

Lilienfeld, D. E., & Perl, D. P. (1994). Projected neurogenerative disease mortality among minorities in the United States. *Neuroepidemiology, 13*, 179–186.

Lowry, L. (1979). *Social work with the aging: The challenge and promise of later years*. New York: Harper and Row.

Lusky, R. (1986). Anticipating the needs of the U.S. elderly in the twenty-first century: Dilemmas in epidemiology, gerontology and public policy. *Social Science Medicine, 23*, 1217–1227.

Maddox, G. (1964). Disengagement theory: A critical evaluation. *Gerontologist, 4*, 80–82.

Maldonado, D. (1987). Aged. In A. Minahan (Ed.), *Encyclopedia of social work* (pp. 95–106). Silver Spring, MD: NASW Press.

Marsiske, M., Franks, M. M., & Masat, B. T. (1998). Psychological perspectives on aging. In L. Morgan & S. Kunkel (Eds.) *Aging: The social context* (pp. 145–182). Thousand Oaks, CA: Pine Forge Press.

McCullough, P. K., & Cody, S. (1993). Geriatric development. In F. S. Sierles (Ed.), *Behavioral science for medical students* (pp. 163–167). Baltimore: Williams and Wilkins.

Montana, P. (1985). *Retirement programs: How to develop and implement them*. Englewood Cliffs: NJ: Prentice-Hall.

Mor-Barak, M. E., & Tynan, M. (1993). Older workers and the work place: A new challenge for occupational social work. *Social Work, 38*, 45–55.

Morgan, L., & Kunkel, S. (1998). *Aging: The social context*. Thousand Oaks, CA: Pine Forge Press.

Morris, R. (1993). Do changing times mean changing agendas for the elderly? *Journal of Aging and Social Policy, 5*(3), 1–6.

Morrison, M. (1982). *Economics of aging: The future of retirement.* New York: Van Nostrand Reinhold.

Mosher-Ashley, P. M. (1994). Diagnoses assigned and issues brought up in therapy by older adults receiving outpatient treatment. *Clinical Gerontologist, 15*(2), 37–64.

National Council on Aging. (1981). *Aging in the 80s: America in transition.* Washington, DC: Author.

Nolan, K. (1987). In death's shadow: The meanings of withholding resuscitation. *Hastings Center Report, 17*, 9–14.

Paterson, S. L., Baker, M., & Maeck, J. P. (1993). Durable powers of attorney: Issues of gender and health care decision making. *Journal of Gerontological Social Work, 21*, 161–177.

Perkins, K., & Tice, C. (1994). Suicide and older adults. The strengths perspective in practice. *Journal of Applied Gerontology, 13*, 438–454.

Peterson, M. (1994). Physical aspects of aging: Is there such a thing as normal? *Geriatrics, 49*(2), 45–49.

Pratt, C., Wright, S., & Schmall, V. (1987). Burden, coping and health status: A comparison of family caregivers to community dwelling institutionalized Alzheimer's patients. *Social Work, 10*, 99–112.

Reynolds, C. F., Small, G. W., Stein, E. M., & Teri, L. (1994, February). When depression strikes the elderly patient. *Patient Care*, pp. 85–101.

Rhodes, C. (1988). *An introduction to gerontology: Aging in American society.* Springfield, IL: Thomas.

Rife, J. C., & Belcher, J. R. (1994). Assisting unemployed older workers to become reemployed: An experimental evaluation. *Research of Social Work Practice, 4*, 3–13.

Rubinstein, R. L., Lubben, J. E., & Mintzer, J. E. (1994). Social isolation and social support: An applied perspective. *Journal of Applied Gerontology, 13*, 58–72.

Ryff, C. D. (1982). Self-perceived personality change in adult-hood and aging. *Journal of Personality and Social Psychology, 42*, 108–115.

Scharlach, A. E., Mor-Barak, M. E., & Birba, L. (1994). Evaluation of a corporate sponsored health care program for retired employees. *Health and Social Work, 19*, 192–198.

Segrin, C. (1994). Social skills and psychological problems among the elderly. *Research on aging, 16*, 301–321.

Sherwood, S., Morris, J., & Ruchline, H. (1986). Alternate paths to long-term care, nursing home, geriatric day hospital, senior center and domiciliary care options. *American Journal of Public Health, 76*, 38–44.

Shock, N. W. (1987). The International Association of Gerontology: Its origins and development. In G. L. Maddox & E. W. Busse (Eds.), *Aging: The universal experience* (pp. 21–43). New York: Springer.

Sills, J. S. (1980). Disengagement reconsidered: Awareness of finitude. *Gerontologist, 20*, 457–462.

Smallegan, M. (1985). There was nothing else to do: Needs for care before nursing home admission. *Gerontologist, 25*, 364–369.

Specht, R., & Craig, G. T. (1982). *Human development: A social work perspective.* Englewood Cliffs, NJ: Prentice-Hall.

Starr, P. (1982). *The social transformation of American medicine.* New York: Basic Books.

Sterns, H. L., Barrett, G. V., Czaja, S. J., & Barr, J. K. (1994). Issues in work and aging. *Journal of Applied Gerontology, 13*, 7–19.

Strawbridge, W. J., Camacho, T. C., Cohen, R. D. & Kaplan, G. A. (1993). Gender differences in factors associated with change in physical functioning in old age: A six-year longitudinal study. *Gerontologist, 33*(5), 603–609.

Swan, F. (1987). The substitution for nursing home care for in-patient psychiatric care. *Community Mental Health Journal, 23,* 1.

Taber's cyclopedia medical dictionary. (1977). Philadelphia: Davis.

Talbott, J. (1988). Taking issue. *Hospital and Community Psychiatry, 39,* 115.

Tennessee Commission on Eldercare. (1993). *Workers in eldercare: Issues in practice* (pp. 1–25). Conference proceedings, National Association of Social Workers Eldercare Conference, Nashville, TN.

U.S. Senate Special Committee on Aging. (1981). *Development in aging, 1981* (Vol 1). Washington, DC: U.S. Government Printing Office.

Wan, T. (1985). *Well-being for the elderly: Primary preventive services.* Lexington, MA: Lexington Books.

Wolinsky, F. D., & Arnold, C. L. (1988). A different perspective on health and health services utilization. In G. L. Maddox & M. P. Lawton (Eds.), *Annual review of gerontology and geriatrics* (Vol. 8, pp. 77–94) . New York: Springer.

Chapter 12

Domestic Violence

CONSIDERABLE ATTENTION HAS BEEN PAID TO THE FACT THAT OUR society is "violent." Recently, *Time* magazine reported that women are as likely to be killed by their partners as by any other kind of assailant (July 4, 1994, p. 21). Nevertheless, numerous studies on the abuse of women by partners indicate that only a very small percentage of all cases of domestic violence are reported to police, and of those reported, less than half result in charges being pressed against the abuser (Siegler, 1989). Although domestic violence is not purely a crime against women, millions of women are affected by this cyclic pattern of abuse. The numbers are astounding: each year 2,000 to 4,000 women are beaten to death, and more than half the women in the United States report that at some point in the love relationship they have been abused either physically or emotionally by their partners (Liutkus, 1994).

> *Did You Know...It is estimated that approximately 12 million women are abused by their partners each year (Mancoske, Standifer, & Cauley, 1994) and 2 million to 4 million women are abused in their homes each year (Roberts, 1996b).*

Studies indicate that in any given year anywhere between one-third and one-half of women murdered in the United States have been killed by a boyfriend, spouse, or ex-mate (Schneider, 1994; Litsky, 1994) whereas 10 percent of the men murdered in America have been killed by a female partner, usually in self-defense (Statman, 1990). As many as half of the couples living in the United States are estimated to have experienced violence in their relationship (Gelles, 1979). Finklehor (1988) reported that 12 percent of spouses surveyed stated that they had experienced at least one violent incident with their mates in the past year and 28 percent reported experiencing violence throughout the course of the marriage. Approximately 20 percent of female visits to emergency rooms are the result of battering, and more generally, assault by a partner—domestic violence, date rape, and so forth—accounts for 70 percent of all admissions (Statman, 1990). With abuse being addressed more and more in emergency rooms, many states now allow the police to arrest a suspected abuser without a warrant when evidence exists of an injury serious enough to require emergency medical care (Statman, 1990). The legal treatment of domestic violence can be complicated because laws in regard to domestic violence vary from state to state and often differ between municipalities in the same state (Statman, 1990). Over the past fifteen years the problem of domestic violence

Name: Dianne Harrison Montgomery
Place of residence: Tallahassee, Florida
College/university degrees: B.A., M.S.W., University of
Alabama; Ph.D., Washington University
Present position: Associate Vice President for Academic
Affairs, School of Social Work, Florida State University
Previous work/volunteer experience: Former Dean of the
School of Social Work, Florida State University; social
worker in mental health settings; social work researcher
and academician; certified sex educator; designed HIV prevention interventions; member
of numerous community agency boards (telephone crisis hotline, women's prison, teen
pregnancy program, local high school)

What do you do in your spare time? Aside from watching both of my kids play soccer, I
read, watch movies, play tennis, and cook.

Why did you choose social work as a career? I did not really know much about social
work but I knew I wanted to work with people. I went into a graduate program in social
work basically because they offered me a scholarship. Once I experienced the courses and
my first internship (in a mental hospital), I knew I had found a career that would be
incredibly interesting and rewarding.

What is your favorite social work story? As a dean, I spent a lot of my time talking with
social work alumni about their education and careers. On occasion, I would talk with
both men and women who received their social work degrees but who never practiced
social work. To a person, they each claimed that their social work education was a key to
their success in their chosen career (whether it was law, banking, real estate, or parenting). Why? Because as social work students, they had all learned good communication,
problem-solving, and people skills.

*What would be the one thing you would change in our community if you had the power to
do so?* I would eliminate prejudices that are based on race, gender, physical ability, or
socioeconomic differences. These kinds of biases and subsequent discrimination are a
waste of our human energy.

and legal system intervention, as well as the roles of assessment and social work practice, have gained wide recognition within the social work profession.

Domestic violence has deep roots. Women have historically been characterized as subordinate to men. Numerous theological teachings, Judeo-Christian as well as Moslem, foster the belief that women must submit to men. Roman law defined the status of women as subject to the wishes and desires of their husbands because women were regarded as personal possessions of men (Siegler, 1989). Throughout history father-to-son transmission of wealth has been common, and a woman's property has fallen under the control of her husband after marriage. Under English common law, a woman had no legal existence apart from the relation with her spouse. For example, if a woman was raped, only her father or her husband could claim compensation from the perpetrator (Siegler, 1989).

Did You Know...In 1883 the state of Maryland outlawed wife abuse after acknowledging that violence against women was assault. In 1910 thirty-five states followed this lead and adopted the view that the battering of women is equivalent to assault (Siegler, 1989).

The advent of the feminist movement in the 1960s and 1970s greatly altered the perception of violence perpetrated against women. The prevailing psychoanalytic view, which asserted that battered women were masochistic and gained sexual excitement from beatings, was challenged (Costantino, 1981; Gelles & Harrop, 1989). Recent theories of violence toward women take the view that battering is rooted in patriarchal society (Srinivasan & Davis, 1991) and that imbalances in power between men and women leave women vulnerable to abuse. The problem is thus redefined as a social issue rather than an individual pathology. Sociological perspectives investigate domestic violence in the context of social stress, learned violent response, and cycles of perpetuated family violence (Gutierrez, 1987). Feminist perspectives identify battering as a means of obtaining social control and maintaining social oppression (Gutierrez, 1987). Indeed, it wasn't until the feminist movement of the 1970s that the battering of women was recognized as a problem that required attention (Siegler, 1989).

In this chapter we discuss the problems of domestic violence. We emphasize that social workers must not—and must teach others not to—blame those involved in domestic abuse. It is a nationwide problem that can affect anyone, of any age, race, creed, or income. Interventions with survivors of domestic violence must be interdisciplinary in nature. Social workers must cooperate closely with other service providers, including members of the criminal justice system.

DOMESTIC VIOLENCE DEFINED

What exactly is domestic violence? We use the word "violence" because "this is not a question of minor arguments or disputes but, rather, intentional hostile and aggressive physical or psychological acts" (Dwyer, Smokowski, Bricout, & Wodarski, 1996). Definitions of violence range from "the use of physical force by one person against another" (Siegler, 1989) to "pushing, slapping, punching, kicking, knifing, shooting, or the throwing of objects at another person" (Gelles, 1987, p. 20). In its most simple form **domestic violence** is defined as any physical act of violence directed at one partner or the other (Edleson, 1991).

A broader concept, **abuse** refers to any behavior that harms the target, including psychological, emotional, and nonviolent sexual abuse (Siegler, 1989). Although the magnitude and severity of domestic abuse varies, it generally also involves violent acts perpetuated against a partner in a relationship, in the presumed safety and privacy of the home (Dwyer et al., 1996).

CHARACTERISTICS OF THE ABUSED AND THEIR ABUSERS

In discussing survivors of abuse two points must be emphasized. First, social workers must be careful never to blame the victim for domestic violence. Unfortunately, both society at large and the abuser may assert that the violence itself is evidence that the victim must have done something wrong. It is important to ensure that both the victim and her family understand that blaming the victim for what is happening simply reinforces the problem. Second, social workers need to be aware that female abuse survivors may blame themselves for the abuse. The may have illusions of being able to control the abuser's behavior and so feel great shame at allowing themselves to be abused (Dziegielewski & Resnick, 1996).

Several studies—admittedly on small samples—indicate that women who are battered have experienced childhood family violence, witnessed parental abuse, and were often abused as children (Siegler, 1989; Gelles & Cornell, 1990; Tolman & Bennett, 1990). Characteristics of women who feel trapped in abusive relationships include 1) low self-esteem, 2) lack of self-confidence, 3) a tendency to withdraw from marital disputes and stress, 4) increased feelings of depression, hopelessness, and frustration, 5) proneness toward drug and alcohol abuse and dependency, and 6) suicide attempts and successful suicidal and homicidal behavior (Liutkus, 1994).

Blaming The Victim and the Case of Hedda Nussbaum

Societal contempt was clear in the case of Hedda Nussbaum, who made the cover of *Newsweek* in 1988. Her live-in boyfriend, Joel Steinberg, charged with murdering the couple's adopted 6-year-old daughter, had beaten her face and body. The abuse in this relationship was documented as beginning in March 1978 and ending November 1987, when Hedda asked Steinberg for permission to get help for their abused child. Unfortunately, the child was already dead from the beating she had received. In the aftermath many people blamed Hedda for her failure to save the child. The *Washington Post* described as sickening that the state and its key witness could collude to use "victimization" as an excuse for Hedda's lack of judgment and inaction (Jones, 1994, p. 175). Many people could not believe that the beatings that Hedda received and the fear she developed as a result of the abuse left her incapable of intervening for the life of her daughter, let alone her own.

No one knows exactly why a woman stays in a violent relationship, but numerous reasons have been postulated. The abused woman may believe that her spouse will reform. She may doubt her ability to manage alone. She may fear the stigma of divorce and of being left "alone." She may worry about what will happen to her and her children if she leaves—poor employment options and the possibility of homelessness (half of homeless women in this country are fleeing from domestic violence; Mullins, 1994), as well as difficulty finding adequate daycare for her children (Dziegielewski & Resnick, 1996; Dziegielewski, Resnick, & Krause, 1996; Gelles & Cornell, 1990).

Among all these possibilities, it has been speculated that the greatest deterrent for women is the fear of economic hardship and inadequate care for their children. For women this fear is very well founded. Many women, by accepting primary responsibility for home and children, place themselves at a disadvantage as wage earners. Their economic dependence can serve to preserve abusive situations by reducing opportunities for leaving them. On average for all women—not just abused women—marital separation leads to a 73 percent drop in a woman's standard of living within the first year. Nearly 70 percent of child support payments are not made regularly, and consistent alimony payments are rare even when they are awarded (Davidson & Jenkins, 1989). Economic disparity alone amply explains why women stay in abusive relationships. Social and economic factors overall clearly indicate the need for therapeutic intervention that is progressive and addresses protection, prevention, and economic support.

A high correlation exists between substance abuse and domestic violence (Liutkus, 1994; Siegler, 1989; Tolman & Bennett, 1990; Stith, Williams, & Rosen, 1990). It is important to note that in such cases spouse abuse is very often mutual. Husbands and wives have both been found to initiate repetitive, violent interactions; however, the consequences of male physical violence are usually more profound (Siegler, 1989; Stith et al., 1990). Men who physically abuse their partners expect their partners to be subordinate to them (Stith et al., 1990). Abusive males generally adhere to traditional, stereotypic gender or sex roles and use violence to maintain power and control over the family (Petretic-Jackson & Jackson, 1996).

Men who abuse have low self-esteem, low assertiveness, and a low sense of self-efficacy and have often been exposed to childhood family violence (Tolman & Bennett, 1990). These men are especially prone to feelings of helplessness, powerlessness, and inadequacy. Abusers are often pathologically jealous, prone to addiction, and passive, dependent, and antisocial (Gelles & Cornell, 1990). Histories of sexual aggressiveness and violence toward others, poor impulse control, isolation, and poor relationship skills are also common traits (Finklehor et al., 1988). Educational level, occupational status, and income are customarily low, and in fact, unemployment or underemployment increases the likelihood of battering (Siegler, 1989; Gelles & Cornell, 1990). Pregnancy can put a tremendous stress on a relationship, and is it indeed also a factor that increases the rate of battering (Siegler, 1989; Rizk, 1988). Liutkus (1994) reported that 37 percent of pregnant women seeking obstetrical care reported battering during the term of their pregnancies.

Did You Know...Although there is no consensus about the causes of domestic violence, Straus (1980) identified the following characteristics in cases of spousal abuse:
- *Husband employed part time or unemployed*
- *Spousal concerns about economic security*
- *Two or more children*
- *Spousal disagreements over children*
- *Spouses from violent families*
- *Couples married less than ten years*
- *Spouses under 30 years of age*
- *High levels of family and individual stress*
- *Spouses verbally aggressive*
- *Frequent alcohol use*
- *Residence in a neighborhood less than two years*
- *Family not part of an organized religion*
- *Wife a full-time homemaker*

Those who abuse often tell social workers that they were provoked to violence (Edleson & Tolman, 1992; Pence, 1989). Although claims that "she drove me to it" are often made to justify abusive behavior, research suggests that such provocation is rare (Ganley, 1989). Many professionals believe that these claims likely reflect the abuser's denial of responsibility for his actions and must be challenged and refuted in order for him to progress in treatment (Edleson, 1991).

HELPING SURVIVORS OF ABUSE

To this point we have stressed that domestic abuse is a societal and a family problem and thus needs attention from social workers trained in both macro- and micropractice. However, no practitioner should forget that "a domestic violence incident [is also] a crime and, as with other crimes, the responsibility of taking legal action against an offender should rest with the justice system" (Goolkasian, 1986, p. 3). To best help survivors of abuse social workers must be skilled in cooperating and coordinating with representatives of the criminal justice system— from police officers to prosecutors and judges.

The Criminal Justice System

To understand how the legal system treats survivors of abuse three major areas merit consideration (Parker 1985, presented in Siegler, 1989). The first is the ideology of privacy, whereby an individual's home is viewed as a private place. Acts that happen in the home are considered to have occurred in a sacred place. As long as the couple stay together in the same house the husband cannot be ordered to change his behavior (Siegler, 1989). Many judges will not evict a man from his home because they believe the old adage that "a man's home is his castle" and they believe that evicting him from his home would leave him homeless (Abbott, 1996; Mullins, 1994).

Did You Know…A woman could not legally refuse her spouse conjugal rights until the 1970s, when some states legally recognized the concept of marital rape.

The second area is the gap between written law and contemporary practice. Traditionally, the justice system has been unwilling to intercede or intrude in family matters, and society has preferred it that way. Survivors of abuse can feel helpless trying to persuade police officers and the courts to take action to control their partners; police officers, for their part, are often frustrated by women who refuse to press charges when incidents occur. In recognition of this weakness in the law the federal **Violence Against Women Act** of 1994 (VAWA) was designed to improve the response of the criminal justice system to violent crimes against women (National Resource Center, 1994).

The purpose of the VAWA is to create policies to prevent domestic violence. The VAWA treats domestic violence as a major law enforcement priority and funds improved services to victims of domestic violence. Title II of the bill, the Safe Homes Act, will increase federal funding for battered women's shelters and related programs. It also establishes a new federal crime statute for spouse abuse committed during interstate travel (Mullins, 1994). By creating emergency and long-term solutions for battered women's housing and survival needs, the VAWA is an important step in the government's commitment to preventing domestic violence.

The third area is the complexity and lack of integration of existing legal remedies. The laws that currently exist are complex, contradictory, and at times unenforceable. The law regards property division, divorce, child custody, financial obligations, and criminal culpability as separate matters. In domestic violence cases, however, many of these issues overlap, yet because they must be addressed separately important considerations are overlooked. Although new domestic violence statutes have reduced this confusion and increased integration between jurisdictions, an abuse survivor should still have a legal representative to successfully negotiate the system (Siegler, 1989).

Police discretion in the assistance they provide used to be the most essential part of police work at the domestic violence scene. Today, however, this is changing; in many states police are now required to process charges. Policies that favor the arrest of abusers continue to spread even though the short-term effects of arrest on getting abusers to stop abusive behavior in the future are unknown (Roberts, 1996c). Frisch and Caruso (1996) warned, however, against the opposite extreme: even the most complete legal plan to address an abused woman's needs is useless if those responsible for carrying it out have no enforcement power.

The Role of the Social Worker

Mullarkey (1988) identified five areas in which social workers can join the criminal justice system and prosecutors to assist domestic violence survivors.

Mandatory arrest policies and warrantless arrests can detain the abuser, but they do not address the entire problem (Roberts, 1996c). First, the social worker can help the system to understand the client by completing a detailed and accurate assessment thus providing more information about the type of abuse, the history of abuse, and the circumstances and repercussions of the abuse. Using this additional information the social worker can attempt to identify the most dangerous cases, screen survivors for treatment, and evaluate and predict potential treatment outcomes (Saunders, 1992). The social worker can also help the client to understand the system. Abused women have varied needs for legal services, social services, and psychological services. A well-documented community-wide approach, coordinated by the social worker, can help to integrate the efforts of mental health, social service, judicial, and law enforcement agencies for the benefit of abused women (Roberts, 1996c).

The second type of assistance the social worker can provide is education. Social workers have an obligation to educate, and to be educated by, system participants such as police telephone operators and dispatchers, police officers and staff, prosecutors, judges, and those directly involved such as the survivors, the abusers, and family and support system members. They need to be aware of pro-arrest and mandatory arrest policies and what they involve, as well as the potential of electronic monitoring as part of a coordinated community effort (Roberts, 1996c).

Social workers need to educate and train police telephone operators, dispatchers, and police officers. Operators and dispatchers are the first to receive the call for help and the officer is usually the first on the scene. This education and training should include telephone training for screening and assessment, basic techniques of police safety, and dispute management and crisis intervention techniques, as well as the ability to provide referral links with the social service worker (Fusco, 1989). Training sessions in these skills can influence police officers to take seriously their role in protecting the abused woman (Roberts, 1996c).

When conducting training the social worker is responsible for creating an atmosphere for a team intervention that reflects respect, support, cooperation, and feedback. Moreover, the social worker plays a crucial role in advocating for the rights of the client, particularly in ensuring equality of access, discouraging sex-role stereotyping, explaining the social and emotional effects of discrimination, and identifying the dynamics of victimization and other relevant psychosocial factors (Martin, 1988).

In addition to training frontline workers, education and training also should be provided to court clerks, case managers, legal advocates, and judges (Roberts, 1996a). Professionals in the legal system often focus on conviction as the primary means for accomplishing justice. The pain that the abuser has caused the female survivor, her children, and her family may be overlooked. The social worker therefore has a twofold task: the social worker needs, first, to educate people in the legal system about the dynamics and issues within the abusive situation and, second, to remind everyone to address the psychosocial effects that have occurred regardless of the legal outcome.

Activity...It is important to understand the difference between physical and psychological abuse and how best to handle the two types of situations. Break into groups and take the two case examples below. Decide whether they involve physical abuse or psychological abuse. As a social worker presented with this situation, how would you best intervene to help? What referrals would you make in each situation and for whom would the referral be made?

Scenario 1: A verbal dispute between a husband and wife resulted in the husband threatening to get a knife and stab the wife if she tried to leave the house with the children. For fear that her husband might act on the threat, the wife did not leave.

Scenario 2: During an altercation a husband and wife yelled and pushed each other repeatedly. Upon being pushed down the husband hit his head, cutting it on an end table, and the wife later developed bruises on her shoulder and arms where her husband had grabbed her in anger.

The third role that the social worker can assume is to be a "safe individual" whom the survivor can trust and feel comfortable with. One dynamic in abusive relationships is for women to become isolated from their family and friends. They have often been taught to fear and avoid contact with others outside the abusive relationship. This isolation is problematic even when a woman has started to receive relief from the legal system. This woman must face her abuser and others who may threaten retaliation if the abuser faces conviction and possible incarceration. Anticipating this outcome of the legal process may leave the survivor feeling a mixture of relief and guilt, and these contradictory emotions can hamper her testimony and make her look like an unreliable witness. To represent herself in the best possible light the survivor needs to feel supported in this process. The prosecutor is usually rushed, however, and cannot build the rapport needed to get the survivor to trust her; therefore, the social worker can be a critical bridge between the prosecutor and the survivor.

The fourth role the social worker embraces is that of advocate. This role has always been critical for social work professionals, and advocating for the survivor within the legal system through all stages of the criminal process is essential. Social workers have the right to serve as advocates for the survivor, even before an arrest is made or while a case is awaiting trial or on appeal (Mullarkey, 1988). The role of the survivor's advocate (a.k.a. victim's advocate) is to assist the client in acting as her own representative whenever possible (Martin, 1988). When it is not possible—perhaps because the survivor is too distraught or is incapacitated by the fear of retribution—the advocate can speak with the client's permission. Many states now permit the survivor or the survivor's advocate to address the judge at sentencing (Mullarkey, 1988).

The successful advocate for a domestically abused woman must address two important tasks. The first is recognizing and preparing for the complexities of the legal system. The social worker needs to make himself aware of the variety of system components that are involved—in particular, law enforcement procedures, prosecution, and corrections. The second task is advocacy with family members and the support system to which the client will return. Many myths and beliefs about the survivors of domestic violence are ingrained in our society (Roberts, 1996b), and clients may be forced to confront myths subscribed to by family and friends.

The social worker can assist the survivor in this by telling people in the support system 1) about the strengths of the survivor, 2) the reason it was necessary for her to leave the abusive relationship, and 3) the reason she should put a formal end to abuse and request legally sanctioned punishment for the abuser.

The fifth role the social worker plays is expert witness. The social worker can provide professional information to clarify the meaning of the survivor's behavior (Saunders, 1992; Martin, 1988). Although social workers welcome any opportunity to assist their clients, they may worry that acting as a witness will compromise their duty to protect their client's legal rights. Counseling sessions and written notes may contain information that the social worker does not want to share because its disclosure might harm the survivor's case. For example, many times the survivor is angry with the abuser and voices this anger in an attempt to gain emotional distance from the abuser. The social worker should nevertheless always take careful case notes, though well aware that these notes can be subpoenaed by a court of law. "The constitutional guarantee to confront accusers provided by the sixth amendment can be interpreted by any competent court to override any privacy statute or shield law" (Mullarkey, 1988, p. 49).

Without a court order, social workers are not required to speak to defendants, attorneys, or investigators outside of the courtroom. Mullarkey (1988) recommended that when social workers are summoned to court they recognize the importance of 1) appearing and being professional and nonpartisan, 2) answering all questions directly or fully, 3) immediately asking for clarification of unclear questions, 4) going over possible questions with the prosecutor before testifying, and 5) ensuring that every note, professional conversation, and report they have prepared is discoverable by the defendant and his legal representatives.

Activity...In the classroom, break into small groups of three or more students. As a group look at the six goals for domestic violence programs listed below and choose the three most important goals. Compare your group's choices with those of the other groups. Was it difficult for your group to agree? Why? Why not?

Goals for Domestic Violence Programs

1. To ensure safe surroundings for survivors and their children
2. To increase access to material resources—income, housing, food, etc.
3. To establish and enhance legal supports
4. To build social contacts and support networks for survivors and their children
5. To change societal beliefs about domestic violence
6. To create a model for relationships of shared power and leadership (adapted from Roche & Sadoski, 1996).

These are photographs taken in a shelter for women and children who are victims of domestic abuse. The bedroom with two beds and two bunk beds may be used for one or two families. The women are cleaning up after lunch in the communal kitchen. The child is in a play area. The center is staffed by childcare workers who care for the children while mothers go to work, look for work, or go to counseling.

PRACTICE APPLICATION: THE ROLE OF THE WOMEN'S SHELTER SOCIAL WORKER

Susan and her husband have been together for ten years. During that time she has been beaten severely and treated in the local hospital emergency room. Much of the abuse between the couple is reported to be mutual; however, Susan's husband has never been hospitalized for her return attacks. On several occasions Susan has called the police to intervene, but when they arrived on the domestic violence scene, she usually refuses to press charges. Susan has stated that she once began to press charges but soon dropped them when her husband called from jail to tell her that he loved her and to beg her forgiveness. The police are being dispatched to the scene so often that they refer to Susan and her husband by their first names.

Susan has tried to leave her husband several times but he always tracks her down and persuades her to return. Susan's family is well aware of the abuse. Both Susan's mother and her sister have started to refuse her calls asking for help. Susan often calls them when she and her husband are fighting, asking for an "understanding ear or a safe place to stay." Her family is frustrated because no matter what they do Susan always seems to return to the abusive situation. Also, whenever they do take Susan in, her husband arrives and tries to intimidate her mother. Susan's mother doesn't think her health is strong enough to handle the repeated stress.

On a referral from her employer, Susan has confided in a shelter social worker that she feels lost and abandoned. During the second session Susan tells the social worker that she wants to kill her husband. When asked how she would do it, Susan immediately breaks down and cries that she would probably be better off killing herself. The event that precipitated Susan's crisis is a fight that she and her husband had the previous night. Susan's husband insisted that she climb a ladder and help him paint the house. Susan refused because she is four months pregnant and is afraid of heights. Her husband then hit her with the ladder across her back.

Based on the information Susan provides the social worker is able to make the following assessment. First, Susan is being beaten regularly. Second, she fears for her life and is threatening to take the life of another. Third, Susan has alienated her family and has no support system available to her. Last, she is threatening to take her own life. The social worker feels that immediate intervention is essential to help Susan to adjust to her current situation without violence to herself or others. First, the social worker explores the possibility of inpatient admission. Since Susan has no medical insurance and none of the local facilities have an empty bed, the worker forms another plan.

The social worker helps Susan gain admission to the local shelter for abused women. Shelter personnel are notified of Susan's possible desire to end her life and a suicide watch is implemented. Intensive individual and group counseling resources are made available. With the help and support of the social worker an order of protection is filed. Susan decides to press charges against her husband, and asks the social worker to help her to state her case to an attorney; the social worker agrees. Susan does press charges this time and her husband is sentenced to two years in prison with the possibility of parole in six months. After she regains the recognition and assistance of her family, Susan moves to another city and stays with her aunt. Before leaving, Susan has started making plans to give up her child for adoption.

Discussion: In this case the social worker played a twofold role. First, the social worker found a safe environment where the client received help in dealing with her crisis. The social worker also provided counseling and supportive services. Second, the social worker helped the client to create and carry out a plan of action in her dealings with the legal system. Women who have been abused by their spouses or partners need supportive services. In addition, they need the assistance of this country's legal institutions. These women need to know the following: 1) that legal services are available to them, 2) that supportive services such as those provided by a social worker are available, and 3) that the combined use of these services will alleviate and eventually resolve the situation. The role of the social work professional is crucial. Whether working within the criminal justice system itself or outside the system in an ancillary agency, the social worker can make a true difference for a survivor of domestic abuse.

SUMMARY

Women who survive abuse need all the services and protection that law enforcement can provide. They also need to be treated with respect. Social workers play a crucial role by providing the following services to survivors of abuse. First, they complete detailed assessments that give information about the type of abuse, the history of abuse, and the circumstances and repercussions of the abuse. Second, they actively educate and are educated by law enforcement and justice system participants and people directly involved, such as survivors, abusers, and family and support system members. Third, they act as safe individuals whom survivors can trust. Fourth, they advocate for survivors through all stages of the criminal prosecution. Last, they assist prosecutors and aid survivors by acting as expert witnesses.

Social workers must strive to develop a team approach with the legal professionals involved. These professionals must be trained to view domestic assault situations as appropriate and routine targets of police intervention. Representatives of the legal system and social workers can work together, each an integral part of the intervention team.

The criminal justice system can be an effective force in decreasing violence against women. Both short-term emergency support and long-term support services are needed (Davis, Hagen, & Early, 1994). Counseling, social service assistance, and protection must be carefully coordinated and available to the abuse survivor twenty-four hours a day (Fusco, 1989; Roberts, 1996c). Morning or next-day referrals are a poor substitute for an immediate response to the crisis. Social work professionals need to be available to work directly with police and to start intervention services at the crisis scene or as soon after the incident as possible. Our current system of referral "after the fact" is not meeting the needs of many survivors of abuse.

The domestic violence shelter can offer an "immediate" safe place for women who wish to escape an abusive situation. Unfortunately, however, the number of existing shelters is far from adequate (Dziegielewski et al., 1996). There are few shelters convenient for women in rural areas, and attempts to establish emergency shelters for battered women in cities still meet a variety of obstacles. Before a facility is granted approval a review of proposed property use by community boards and city planners is required in many cities. However, this requirement may compromise the confidentiality of the women and children who depend on the emergency shelter for services and so risk their safety. In addition, many community residents object to having emergency shelters in their neighborhoods because they believe such facilities are disruptive (Mullins, 1994).

Social workers must participate in and help to establish brief time-limited practice strategies (Dziegielewski, 1996, 1997). The purpose of these programs and policies is to immediately ease the severity of domestic violence as well as to develop long-term solutions to the need for emergency housing and financial support systems. One advance in this direction was the 1994 Violence Against Women Act.

Until recently, our society and our laws have treated the preservation of the family as paramount. Fortunately, this is changing. We must break from our history of preserving the family at any cost—even the cost of exposing women to abuse. Because social workers practice across the public and private sectors, they have enormous potential for influencing approaches to the problem of violence against women (Martin, 1988). The profession must demand changes in our laws and legal system that will prevent domestic violence. Social workers clearly recognize the importance of counseling and supportive services. However, to plan for the future, they must never lose sight of the importance of social policy change in assisting the survivors of domestic violence.

References

Abbott, A. A. (1996). Epilogue: Helping battered women. In A. R. Roberts (Ed.), *Helping battered women: New perspectives and remedies* (pp. 235–239). New York: Oxford University Press.

Constantino, C. (1981). Intervention with battered women: The lawyer social worker team. *Social Work, 26*(6), 456–460.

Davis, L., Hagen, J., & Early, T. (1994). Social services for battered women: Are they adequate, accessible, and appropriate? *Social Work, 39*(6), 695–704.

Dwyer, D. C., Smokowski, P. R., Bricout, J. C., & Wodarski, J. S. (1996). Domestic violence and woman battering: Theories and practice implications. In A. R. Roberts (Ed.), *Helping battered women: New perspectives and remedies* (pp. 67–82). New York: Oxford University Press

Dziegielewski, S. F. (1996). Managed care principles: The need for social work in the health care environment. *Crisis Intervention and Time-Limited Treatment, 3*(2), 97–110.

Dziegielewski, S. F. (1997). Time-limited brief therapy: The state of practice. *Crisis Intervention and Time-Limited Treatment, 3*(3), 217–228.

Dziegielewski, S. F., & Resnick, C. (1996). Crisis intervention in the shelter setting. In A. R. Roberts (Ed.), *Crisis management and brief treatment* (pp. 123–141). Chicago: Nelson Hall.

Dziegielewski, S. F., Resnick, C., & Krause, N. B. (1996). Shelter based crisis intervention with abused women. In R. Roberts (Ed.), *Helping battered women: New perspectives and remedies* (pp. 159–171). New York: Oxford University Press.

Edleson, J. L. (1991, June). Note on history: Social worker's intervention in woman abuse, 1907–1945. *Social Service Review*, pp. 304–313.

Edleson, J. L., & Tolman, R. M. (1992). *Intervention with men who batter: An ecological approach*. Newbury Park, CA: Sage.

Finkelhor, D. (1988). *Stopping family violence*. Newbury Park, CA: Sage.

Frisch, L. A., & Caruso, J. M. (1996). In A. R. Roberts (Ed.), *Helping battered women: New perspectives and remedies* (pp. 102–131). New York: Oxford University Press.

Fusco, L. J. (1989). Integrating systems: Police, courts and assaulted women. In B. Pressman, G. Cameron, & M. Rothery (Eds.), *Intervening with assaulted women: Current theory, research and practice* (pp. 125–135). Hillsdale, NJ: Erlbaum.

Ganley, A. L. (1989). Integrating feminist and social learning analyses of aggression: Creating multiple models for intervention with men who batter. In P. L. Caesar & L. K. Hamberger (Eds.), *Treating men who batter.* New York: Springer.

Gelles, R. J. (1979). Violence in the American family. *Journal of Social Issues, 35*(1), 15–39.

Gelles, R. J. (1987). *The violent home.* Thousand Oaks, CA: Sage.

Gelles, R. J., & Cornell, C. P. (1990). *Intimate violence in families.* Thousand Oaks, CA: Sage.

Gelles, R. J., & Harrop, J. W. (1989). Violence, battering, and psychological distress among women. *Journal of Interpersonal Violence, 4*(4), 400–420.

Gutierrez, L. M. (1987, Summer), Social work theories and practice with battered women: A conflict-of-values analysis. *Affilia,* pp. 36–52.

Jones, A. (1994). *Next time she'll be dead: Battering and how to stop it.* Boston: Beacon.

Litsky, M. (1994). Reforming the criminal justice system can decrease violence against women. In B. Leone, B. Szumski, K. de Koster, K. Swisher, C. Wekesser, & W. Barbour (Eds.), *Violence against women.* San Diego, CA: Greenhaven.

Liutkus, J. F. (1994, April). Wife assault: An issue for women's health. *Internal Medicine, 7,* 41–53.

Mancoske, R. J., Standifer, D., & Cauley, C. (1994). The effectiveness of brief counseling services for battered women. *Research on Social Work Practice, 4*(1), 53–63.

Martin, M. (1988). A social worker's response. In N. Hutchings (Ed.) *The violent family: Victimization of women, children, and elders.* New York: Human Science Press.

Mullarkey, E. (1988). The legal system for victims of violence. In N. Hutchings (Ed.), *The violent family: Victimization of women, children, and elders* (pp. 43–52). New York: Human Science Press.

Mullins, G. P. (1994). The battered woman and homelessness. *Journal of Law and Policy, 3*(1), 237–255.

National Resource Center on Domestic Violence and the Battered Women's Justice Project. (1994, September). The Violence Against Women Act 1994. Available from the National Resource Center, 6400 Flank Drive, Suite 1300, Harrisburg, PA 17112-2778.

Petretic-Jackson, P. A., & Jackson, T. (1996). Mental health interventions with battered women. In A. R. Roberts (Ed.), *Helping battered women: New perspectives and remedies* (pp. 188–221). New York: Oxford University Press.

Rizk, M. (1988, April). Domestic violence during pregnancy. In *Proceedings Family Violence: Public Health Social Work's Role in Prevention* (pp. 19–31). Pittsburgh, PA: Department of Health and Human Services, Bureau of Maternal and Child Health.

Roberts, A. R. (1996a). Court responses to battered women. In A. R. Roberts (Ed.), *Helping battered women: New perspectives and remedies* (pp. 96–101). New York: Oxford University Press.

Roberts, A. R. (1996b). Introduction: Myths and realities regarding battered women. In A. R. Roberts (Ed.), *Helping battered women: New perspectives and remedies* (pp. 3–12). New York: Oxford University Press.

Roberts, A. R. (1996c). Police responses to battered women: Past, present and future. In A. R. Roberts (Ed.), *Helping battered women: New perspectives and remedies* (pp. 85–95). New York: Oxford University Press.

Roche, S. E., & Sadoski, P. J. (1996). Social action for battered women. In A. R. Roberts (Ed.), *Helping battered women: New perspectives and remedies*. New York: Oxford University Press.

Saunders, D. G. (1992). Woman battering. In R. T. Ammerman & M. Hersen (Eds.), *Assessment of family violence: A clinical and legal source book*. New York: Wiley.

Schneider, E. M. (1994). Society's belief in family privacy contributes to domestic violence. In B. Leone, B. Szumski, K. de Koster, K. Swisher, C. Wekesser, & W. Barbour (Eds.), *Violence against women*. San Diego, CA: Greenhaven.

Siegler, R. T. (1989). *Domestic violence in context: An assessment of community attitudes*. Lexington, MA: Heath.

Srinivasan, M., & Davis, L. V. (1991). A shelter: An organization like any other? *Affilila, 6*(1), 38–57.

Statman, J. B. (1990). *The battered woman's survival guide: Breaking the cycle*. Dallas: Taylor.

Stith, S. M., Williams, M. B., & Rosen, K. (1990). *Violence hits home: Comprehensive treatment approaches to domestic violence*. New York: Springer.

Straus, M. (1980). A sociological perspective on the causes of family violence. In M. R. Green (Ed.), *Violence and the family* (pp. 7–31). Boulder, CO: Westview.

Tolman, R. M., & Bennett, L. W. (1990). A review of quantitative research on men who batter. *Journal of Interpersonal Violence, 5*(1), 87–118.

Chapter 13

The Political Arena

THINK FOR A MOMENT ABOUT POLITICS AND THE GLAMOUR OF being an elected politician. Think about the movie *Mr. Smith Goes to Washington*, in which Jimmy Stewart plays a young, idealistic politician who goes to Washington to represent the people and do what is right. As he embraces this mission he truly believes that government is the friend of all the people, works for all the people, and represents all the people. He believes that elected leaders are simply an extension of our neighbors who act on our behalf and place the community's need above their personal interests. Their overriding purpose is to help achieve what is best for the country. Do you hold this view of politics and the government? We suspect not. It's likely that few people today believe that Mr. Smith's idealistic vision accurately depicts the motivations of politicians in the late twentieth and early twenty-first centuries.

For many of us the political arena is not an enticing place. Politics may conjure up ideas of backroom deal making, abuses of rank and power, payoffs, and other unethical activities. Political scandals and allegations of wrongdoing over the past few years have reached every level of political office and branch of the government. It's not surprising if you hold politics in low esteem.

Before going any further, let's clarify what we mean by politics. Certainly, politics and the political arena include all elected offices and the officials who fill them, at the local, county, state, and federal levels. This arena is often referred to as "electoral politics." This classification, however, doesn't include what some would call "informal politics," which involves politically charged or motivated behavior in organizations, agencies, and even on social work practice teams. How often have you heard someone say "the politics here stink" or "they're just playing politics" or "you have to understand the politics of the situation"? Therefore, what we refer to as "politics" is diverse and embraces many of our day-to-day activities. Indeed, Haynes and Mickelson (1991) have gone further, contending that "all social work is political" (p. 21). In this chapter we look at electoral politics and its relation to social work practice. Our discussion examines political strategies and we hope can serve as a primer for social workers on politics and political activities.

WHY POLITICS AND SOCIAL WORK?

First, let's take a brief look at the political arena and its relation to social service agencies. What guides the activities of social workers in agencies? Workers are

Name: Susan Hoechstetter

Place of residence: Washington, D.C.

College/university degrees: B.A., M.S.W., University of Pittsburgh,

Present position: Legislative Representative for a coalition of social work organizations (NADD, BPD, GADE, NASW, SSWR, and CSWE) called the Action Network for Social Work Education and Research (ANSWER).

Previous work/volunteer experience: Since 1997 I have worked both as a lobbyist for nonprofit organizations and as a catalyst to foundations supporting nonprofits' advocacy work. As Foundation Advocacy Director at the Alliance for Justice, I developed training, technical assistance, and publications for foundations seeking to give their grantees more leeway to do public policy work. From 1984 to 1997 I directed the National Association of Social Workers' government relations program.

What do you do in your spare time? In my spare time I care for my two-year-old daughter, Kalia, whom I adopted in Guatemala when she was a few months old. I enjoy swimming and the outdoors. A favorite pastime of mine is lending my support to activist causes.

Why did you choose social work as a career? I chose social work as my career because I wanted to provide mental health therapy to individuals. During graduate school I discovered that working for change by influencing public policy suited me very well. It has been particularly satisfying for me to experience the connection between working to help individuals change and working to help society change.

What is your favorite social work story? In the mid-1980s, as the lead lobbyist for NASW, I asked members of Congress to allow social workers to be reimbursed for mental health services under the Federal Employees Health Benefit Program without requiring physician supervision. A key senator asked, "why do you want that when all your people do is hand out welfare checks?" Two months later the senator placed language in his bill that gave social workers status of independent mental health providers. The bill subsequently became law.

What would be the one thing you would change in our community if you had the power to do so? What would be the one thing you would change if you had the power to do so? I would change social workers' mindsets so that they understood how powerful they could be in influencing public policy and how much better the lives of their clients would be if all social workers included policy advocacy in their work.

not able to take liberties in their practice and provide any type of service they see fit. An agency's function clearly dictates what the practitioner can do with and on behalf of a client. Let's say, for example, that a practitioner in a child welfare agency wants to offer group therapy to senior citizens in a local housing project. The intervention may be worthy, but the agency is likely to decide that a senior's group falls outside its purpose and function.

An agency's function is set forth in its mission statement and operationalized by its policies. Policies do not just spring forth; rather they are the result of a political process, be it an agency board of directors or an elected body such as a state legislature. And who are these people? Are they social workers? Are they really expert enough in human services that they should be shaping social work practice? Unfortunately, many people who develop social policies have little, if any, direct social work experience, and few have an educational background in social work. When professional social workers choose to avoid the political aspects of the field, one outcome is inevitable: people who are not social workers will govern social work practice.

Activity...Find out how many social workers there are in your state legislature, both the house and senate. You can do this by checking with your state's secretary of state's office. Then look at the house and senate committees that oversee social problems; they may have titles like Committee on Health and Human Services. Now, look to see how many committee members are social workers. Now look at their staffs—how many staff members are social workers? What do your findings tell you about the development of social policies in your state?

SOCIAL WORK VALUES AND POLITICAL ACTIVITY

Some social workers allow negative images of politics and political activity to outweigh their responsibility to engage in the political arena. Yet the NASW Code of Ethics clearly states our obligations and political responsibilities in two separate places in section 6, "The Social Worker's Ethical Responsibilities to Society":

Social workers should facilitate informed participation by the public in shaping social policies and institutions. (sec. 6.02)

Social workers should . . . advocate for changes in policy and legislation to improve social conditions in order to . . . promote social justice. (sec. 6.04(a))

CSWE accreditation standards also support the profession's political involvement. To be accredited BSW and MSW programs must include in their curricula such political content as knowledge of political systems, including how policies are formulated and how their content can be influenced. The Curriculum Policy Statement states specifically:

Students must be taught to analyze current social policy within the context of historical and contemporary factors that shape policy. Content must be presented about the political and organizational processes used to influence policy, the process of policy formulation, and the framework for analyzing policies in light of the principles of social and economic justice. (CSWE, 1994, pp. 102, 141)

Why do the Code of Ethics and the CSWE accreditation standards emphasize practitioner involvement in the political arena? First, and foremost, remember that the definition of social work includes working to bring about a just community built on the tenets of social and economic equality. Second, many of the problems experienced by clients are created by forces external to the client and can be remedied only through amended social policy or additional funding for social services. Third, the best advocates for change are those who deal with problems day in and day out. Through direct practice, social workers see firsthand the debilitating effects of problems on clients.

A HISTORICAL OVERVIEW OF POLITICAL ACTIVITY BY SOCIAL WORKERS

Social work has had three separate but significant waves of political involvement: the Progressive Era of the nineteenth century, the 1930s New Deal, and the 1960s War on Poverty. In each of these periods, social work's involvement in politics mirrored the profession's growth and internal conflict over mission, scope, and function. In all three periods, leaders disagreed about the causes of social problems and how best to solve them. The Progressive movement was attractive to many social workers and provided a political focus for their philosophical beliefs and commitments. Jane Addams and Florence Kelley, among others, used the political system to address social problems. Settlement house workers seemed to be more partisan than other social workers. Weismiller and Rome (1995, p. 2306) have noted that settlement workers ran political campaigns, organized neighborhoods to support particular candidates, lobbied, and worked on welfare reform. On the other hand, Mary Richmond, a leader in the COS movement, believed that social workers should be nonpartisan and confine their efforts to helping clients to resolve their individual issues (Weismiller & Rome, 1995, p. 2307).

The Great Depression of the 1930s created ample opportunity for social workers to again venture into the political arena. Schools of social work were more organized than their forerunners during the Progressive Era and macrocontent, which touched on political concerns, was included in the curriculum. The federal government's Children's Bureau and Women's Bureau provided social workers with a setting in which to address social issues. In fact, many parts of the Economic Security Act of 1935 were written by social workers (Weismiller & Rome, 1995, p. 2307). The profession was beginning to accept political activism as an appropriate response to crisis; however, it still did not embrace political activity as an appropriate long-term social work methodology (Haynes & Mickelson, 1991, p. 8).

The third wave of political activism by social workers came in the 1960s. With the emergence of the Peace Corps and VISTA, a domestic version of the Peace Corps program, and the burgeoning civil rights movement, social workers actively promoted a political agenda. Community organization, both as a practice and an educational specialization, took shape in the late 1950s and 1960s. This activity challenged social workers to view systems from the much broader macroprospective. Federal dollars were funneled to initiatives that encouraged neighborhoods and local people to engage in problem solving and community action.

Within the profession, debate continued on the role and scope of political activity. Weismiller and Rome (1995, p. 2308) have reported that NASW members in one study agreed to pay increased dues if it brought about greater political activity by members. Yet the zeal didn't nearly affect the entire profession, and members continued to debate the merits of efforts at the political level, particularly in light of the massive problems facing individuals and families.

Did You Know...A social worker, Senator Barbara Mikulski (D-Maryland), was a keynote speaker during the 1992 Democratic National Convention

In 1976, NASW organized its first conference on politics, in Washington, DC. Aimed primarily at social work political activists, the meeting gathered NASW members from around the country for a political training institute. NASW then supplemented this national meeting with regional institutes. NASW continues to sponsor these meetings approximately every two years.

The 1990s seemed to be a watershed decade for social workers involved in electoral politics. Never before in the profession's history were social workers and their professional organizations as active in political campaigns as in the last decade of the twentieth century. "Life Up America" was the NASW's 1992 Presidential Project theme, augmented by numerous national, regional, and state election activities (Landers, 1992,); and NASW's political action committee, Political Action for Candidate Election (PACE), endorsed more than one hundred candidates for national office (Hiratsuka, 1992) and contributed approximately $200,000 to national campaigns while state PACE committees dispensed in excess of $160,000 to state and local candidates (D. Dempsey, personal communication, November 30, 1992; Dempsey, 1993).

In 1991, NASW reported that 113 social workers held elected office (Weismiller & Rome, 1995, p. 2309); by 1992, 165 known social workers in forty-three states had won a variety of races (NASW, 1992); and by 1998, there were more than 200 known social workers holding political office in the nation! They held elected office at all levels of government from city council to the U.S. Senate. With each succeeding election, individual social workers and their professional associations gained new experiences, built on previous knowledge, and strengthened themselves as active players in the political arena.

ELECTORAL AND LEGISLATIVE POLITICS

Political social work has two sides that are intricately related and both of which are important to the social work profession's realization of its goals. First, social workers identify and support candidates who are friends of the profession and support our issues. By making contributions and working in candidates' cam-

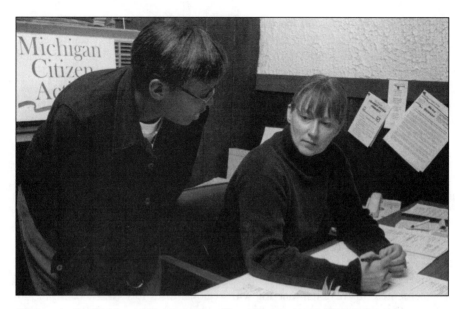

Workers in the Michigan Citizens Action office. This is a nonprofit policy group.

paigns, social workers are able to help pro–human service candidates to win elections. We call this phase "electoral politics." Second, social workers collaborate with elected officials on policy proposals during the legislative process. We call this phase "lobbying."

Political activity is generally viewed through the lobbying lens. Richman (1991), Haynes and Mickelson (1991), Mahaffey and Hanks (1982), and Wolk (1981), among others, emphasize the lobbying side of politics. Little attention is paid to electing candidates to public office. Deemphasizing electoral politics violates two important legislative lessons, however:

Lesson 1: Lobbying is much easier with supporters and friends of social work than with its detractors and antagonists.

Lesson 2: Lobbying for prevention proposals is a much better use of energy than lobbying against negative proposals and rectifying previous legislative errors.

You might view the political process as a cycle (see box 1). In a rational model, the political life cycle begins with candidate identification, then progresses through participation in electoral politics, educating the candidate on social work issues and advocating certain positions, lobbying the candidate to support the profession's stance, and back to candidate identification and reelection. The real-life political cycle is not so rational, and you may in fact enter the process and begin your efforts at any given point. Suppose, for example, that legislation regarding abortion is up

Box 1: Political Life Cycle
Candidate identification, endorsement, education
Electoral politics
Issue education
Advocacy
Lobbying
Candidate identification, endorsement, education
Electoral politics

.

.

.

for debate in the state senate. First, you attempt to educate your legislator on the issue from a social work perspective; the representative decides not to support your view. You soon realize that a new elected official is needed to better serve the interests of your district and the profession, and you begin to seek an alternative candidate for the next election. And the cycle continues.

Elected officials, while primarily responsible to their constituencies, are also open to input from their campaign supporters. Active campaign support establishes a positive relation between the office holder and the social work community. When this is achieved, rather than having to adopt a defensive lobbying posture—protecting what we have from social work antagonists—social workers are able to influence the development and enhancement of social services through public policy. Conversely when we don't have friends in the legislative body, social workers must put most of their efforts into attempting to block of modify coercive public policies.

Social Work Organizations and Electoral Politics

Education Legislative Network: In 1971, the *Education Legislative Network* (ELAN) was organized by NASW as a vehicle to bring together divergent and often contentious social work groups, in particular, clinical and macrolevel social workers. The premise of ELAN was that a united work community would strive together for the good of the whole and as it did so separate groups would become more friendly toward each other, thus creating broader support for each group's issues.

As a beginning effort, ELAN was successful in educating NASW members on a number of national policy issues. ELAN used a progressive strategy in which NASW members were 1) informed on issues and 2) encouraged to lobby their elected representatives in Washington. It became obvious, however, that more friendly elected leaders were needed. Concurrent with the association's first organized political efforts, political action committees took on greater importance in American politics overall. In 1976, NASW organized PACE, which served as the association's national effort to raise money and endorse candidates for national office who supported the profession's agenda.

Michigan Citizen *Action*

Together we can protect:

℞ Our HEALTH

- fighting for real patients' rights for all
- safeguarding Social Security and Medicare
- covering prescription-drug costs for seniors

♨ Our POCKETBOOKS

- working against abuse of utility monopolies
- [open access *OR* other consumer issue #2]
- [consumer issue #3 – sales tax/living wage?]

☑ Our DEMOCRACY

- promoting genuine campaign-finance reform
- getting candidates & issues more time on TV
- putting the public back in public education

430 West Paterson
Kalamazoo, Michigan   49007
(616) 349-9170 phone / (616) 349-9271 fax
Web site: *www.michcitizenaction.org*

Linda Teeter, Executive Director
e-mail: *linda902@aol.com*

Michigan's largest independent, issue-based citizens' lobby

Flier urging political action to change social and economic policies.

Political Action for Candidate Election: PACE has a threefold purpose. First, it endorses those candidates who are most supportive of social work issues. Second, PACE sometimes makes campaign contributions to endorsed candidates. And third, PACE educates NASW members about candidates and encourages electoral participation.

National PACE is limited to endorsing and contributing to national candidates—that is, candidates for the presidency, the U.S. House of Representatives, and the U.S. Senate. A board of trustees, each of whom is appointed by the national NASW president, governs PACE. The board, with consultation from NASW members and state chapters, screens candidates for national elections, endorses candidates, and in some but not all instances makes financial contributions. Following endorsement of a candidate, NASW members in the candidate's state or district are encouraged to work in the candidate's campaign and make additional campaign contributions.

Even as the national PACE effort grew in strength, NASW recognized the truth of former House Speaker Tip O'Neil's (D-Massachusetts) statement "All politics is local." NASW therefore encouraged state chapters to organize their own PACE units to endorse local and statewide candidates and raise funds for their campaigns.

By 1998, every state had a PACE unit working to help candidates who support social work positions. The state PACE units are structured in a manner similar to the national PACE: each has a board of trustees, appointed by the state chapter president, and each screens and endorses candidates. The efforts and activities of the state PACE units are separate from each other and from the national PACE; there is no formal mechanism or means for accountability to the national professional association.

In theory, a state PACE unit could work against the interests of NASW by endorsing candidates who do not support the social work positions outlined at the national level. If this happened there would be no recourse for the NASW or the chapter membership. As trustees, the board members are ultimately responsible for all endorsements and for disbursements of campaign contributions, and they are accountable only to themselves. Nevertheless, the nationwide network of social work PACE units provides an important opportunity to identify, support, and work to elect individuals who can be advocates for social work issues and friends of the profession.

According to the Political Affairs Office of NASW, 1992 national PACE contributions placed PACE in the top ten of the more than 2,000 PACs contributing to that year's election (D. Dempsey, personal communication, November 30, 1992; Dempsey, 1993). While the national PACE's level of activity seems impressive, Colby and Buffum (1998) did not find the NASW membership to be especially active or concerned with PACE activities, and few dollars were raised by the association outside of the money collected as part of membership dues. (PACE dollars are raised by a "negative dues check-off" that requires NASW members to check off on their annual dues bills that they *do not* want $10.00 of their dues to be donated to PACE. If the box is left unchecked, $10.00 is transferred to PACE.)

Did You Know...A number of graduate and undergraduate academic programs offer courses focusing on politics and social work. The University of Houston School of Social Work implemented a graduate specialization in politics *and* social work, *and the University of Connecticut sponsors an institute on political social work.*

PACE Endorsement Process: Each state unit as well as the national PACE develops its own endorsement process and procedures. Remember that the state PACE units are not tied to each other or to the national PACE; they are separate entities, each with its own set of by-laws. A state's PACE unit is separate even from the state's NASW chapter.

Colby and Buffum (1998) found what seems to be a typical format for state endorsement (but recognize that not all states follow this procedure). The board puts together a survey that is distributed to all candidates (see box 2). Candidates are given a specified period in which to respond; if a survey is not returned a telephone call to the candidate's office is made asking to have the survey completed. If the candidate is seeking reelection, the board will also review the incumbent's voting record. Finally, members of local NASW units are asked to provide input to the process. Some state PACE units also hire professional lobbyists to help assess candidates. Professional lobbyists work the legislative halls every day, attempting to convince legislators to vote one way or another on specific legislation. As a result they often have a more detailed understanding of candidates than PACE trustees.

Based on the information it accumulates from the survey, the board decides which candidates to endorse. Once endorsements are made, the board then determines whether a financial contribution will be made. The board looks at many issues in deciding whether to make a contribution: Is the candidate opposed in the election? Does the candidate need the money? If unopposed, does the candidate need help in retiring a campaign debt? There are no correct answers to these questions; they simply serve as discussion points to help the trustees to make a final decision.

Financial contributions are governed by state law. Typically states cap the amount an organization may contribute to a candidate for a specific election or election cycle. Also, the level of office—for example, state representative versus governor—affects the limits on contribution size.

Did You Know... "Bundling" *is a campaign loophole that allows organizations to get around legal financial caps on contributions. For example, a state PACE unit may contribute the maximum amount for a person running for the state house, say $500.00. When presenting the PACE check, additional checks* from individual *NASW chapter members are given at the same time (thus the idea of a bundle of checks). So a candidate may receive $500.00 from the organization and, say, thirty checks each for $50.00, for a total of $2,000. In effect, the organization, with member support, has increased its level of financial support to the candidate. And the candidate is more likely to remember a $2,000 contribution than individual $50.00 checks.*

Once endorsements are made and the level of contributions determined, NASW members are informed of the PACE decisions. Checks are presented directly to the candidate by social workers from the candidate's district; this provides an opportunity for local social workers to make a direct connection with the candidate and to strengthen the relations for future lobbying efforts.

Activity...Contact your state PACE unit through NASW. Find out who serves on the PACE board of trustees. What is the track record of PACE endorsements? Do endorsed candidates get elected? How many Republicans, Democrats, or candidates from other political parties were endorsed in the last election? How much money was contributed to the candidates?

Social Workers and Political Campaigns

Volunteers and paid campaign staff provide critical support to a candidate's electoral bid. Commitments to a candidate and her ideas is the only prerequisite. It doesn't matter where the individual's competence lies: a campaign has room for a volunteer to perform an array of tasks—answering phones, preparing bulk mailings, putting up yard signs, and canvassing neighborhoods.

Social workers, in particular, can contribute many skills typical of their profession to a political campaign. These include planning decision making, consensus building, group management, research, assessment, relationship building, crisis intervention, and communication. In terms of roles, or functions, that social workers perform, eight are appropriate for political campaigns:

Role	Tasks
Advocate	Speaks on behalf of the candidate and represents his position to various constituent groups
Teacher/educator	Instructs staff and volunteers about campaign strategy and issues; in conjunction with advocacy, educates potential supporters about the candidate
Mobilizer	Energizes staff and volunteers; prioritizes and assigns individuals to needed campaign activities
Consultant	Provides expertise in problem solving and strategizing; helps candidate and staff to develop strategies for the campaign
Planner	Identifies key community players and activities; assesses strengths of potential relationships and overall prospects for electoral victory
Caregiver	Provides emotional support to candidate, his family, friends, staff, and supporters (relations can become strained)
Data manager	Develops and implements a data structure that allows for quick and *easy* access; designs a user-friendly system for staff, volunteers, and candidate
Administrator	Develops and implements a well-operating campaign structure that is functional and not overwhelming; keeps the structure simple, efficient, and consistent with the candidate's best interests

The following are a few simple things that social workers can do to strengthen the presence of the social work profession in a political campaign.

Spend time at a campaign office: Traditionally a campaign begins on Labor Day and concludes with the general election in November, generally a ten- to eleven-week period. A campaign relies on volunteers to staff an office, with much of the work taking place during evenings and on weekends. Organize ten to fifteen social workers and commit to providing a volunteer for one night each week at the campaign office for the duration of the campaign. Say you selected Tuesday evening;

Box 2: Examples of Candidate Survey

Currently, Texas is ranked 49th of the 50 states and the District of Columbia in the delivery of health and human services. At the same time, Texas also ranks near or at the top of all states in terms of severity of many health and social problems, including teen pregnancy, school dropouts, the number of AIDS cases, infant mortality, and the lack of rural health care.

The Texas legislature will be as asked to take action on a number of bills that will have an impact on these problems.

Do you support or oppose the following initiatives?

Support   Oppose

_____   _____   1. Legislation that would allow parents to take up to three months' leave without pay from their jobs to care for a seriously ill child, spouse, or parent or for the birth or adoption of a child.

_____   _____   2. Increased funding for Aid to Families with Dependent Children (AFDC).

_____   _____   3. Legislation ensuring that all at-risk students have access to pupil services (including school social workers, school psychologists, and counselors).

_____   _____   4. Legislation that would prohibit the use of corporal punishment in Texas public schools.

_____   _____   5. Legislation that would ensure that pregnant women have full access to prenatal care.

_____   _____   6. Legislation that would ensure that children in need receive regular preventive health care and treatment.

_____   _____   7. Include funding in Texas' budget to supplement federal funds for Head Start.

_____   _____   8. Include funding to supplement federal funds for the Supplemental Food Program for Women, Infants and Children (WIC).

_____   _____   9. Legislation increasing the availability of affordable, quality childcare, preschool, and early childhood development programs.

_____   _____   10. Legislation that opposes mandatory HIV testing of all health care workers who perform invasive procedures.

_____   _____   11. A state income tax in order to adequately fund state services.

this can become known as Social Work Night to the candidate and key staff. The potential value to future lobbying efforts of even such a brief commitment is incalculable. The candidate will be much more open and sympathetic to a group that worked throughout the campaign.

_____   _____   12. Increased funding for the Texas Department of Human Services Child Protective Services Unit to hire professional social workers in order to provide higher quality services to children at risk and raise the minimum standards of training and qualifications for frontline workers.

_____   _____   13. In the event the Supreme Court overturns _Roe v. Wade_, legislation protecting the freedom of choice and access to reproductive health care for women and families.

_____   _____   14. Legislation that increases the availability of affordable housing in the state.

_____   _____   15. Legislation amending the Texas Commission on Human Rights Act of 1991 and requiring state agencies to implement Affirmative Action programs and workforce diversity programs.

_____   _____   16. Making a substantial investment in initiatives to reform and improve services to children and families involved in protective services, mental health, and the juvenile justice system.

On a separate piece of paper, please answer the following questions:

1. If elected, (a) what would be your main legislative priorities, and (b) what committee assignments would you seek?
2. Are you, any member of your family, or a close personal friend a professional social worker?
3. Many of the health care licensing and certification acts are under Sunset Review, and the legislature will have to re-enact these laws during the next regular session. Social work certification is one of the laws under Sunset Review. NASW/Texas is interested in strengthening this law by refining the definition of social work practice and regulating under the law only those practitioners who hold BSW and MSW degrees. Will you support the continued regulation of social workers? Would you support the narrowing of the law to only regulate social workers who hold professional degrees? Would you support a license for social workers?
4. Why are you seeking our endorsement? If endorsed, how would you use our endorsement?

Source: National Association of Social Workers/Texas PACE Candidate Questionnaire, 1992.

Use buttons and t-shirts: Make a modest investment to purchase buttons or t-shirts printed with a simple slogan. Social workers for (Candidate's Name)—what an effective message! Be sure to wear the buttons or t-shirts on Social Work Night/Day at the campaign office. Let others know who you are and where you stand.

Host a fundraiser: All candidates need money to run a campaign. A bare-bones, efficient run for the state house costs at least $25,000. Plan a fundraising event with other social workers. Be sure to coordinate the event with the candidate's campaign staff—there is usually one person who is responsible for scheduling the candidate's time. Make the event brief—the candidate has no extra time during the heat of a campaign and often needs to be in four places at once. Try to make the event fun as well. Be creative. For example, one interesting fundraiser was a "non-event fundraiser" that people donated $25.00 *not* to attend! If you host an event with the candidate present, be sure to wear your buttons or t-shirts.

Realize the importance of election day: Election day is the longest day in the campaign. With polls opening as early as 6:00 A.M. in some states and closing as late as 8:00 P.M., campaign volunteers work up to eighteen hours! Volunteers are needed to work near the polling places, passing out candidate literature; put up last-minute candidate yard signs; provide voters with transportation to the polls (be sure to wear your buttons or t-shirts and to talk about your candidates with those you are driving); and staff the campaign office answering phones and dealing with last-minute glitches and crises. When the polls close, go to the candidate's headquarters or wherever the party is being held. You deserve to celebrate after all the energy you've put into the campaign. And be sure to wear your buttons or t-shirts.

Lobbying for Social Work Legislation

Lobbying is an act of persuasion in which you educate someone about an issue with the goal of gaining their active support. Recognize one key principle of lobbying: you are the expert with key information.

Lobbying takes many different forms. Typical activities include writing letters, making telephone calls, making personal visits, and giving public testimony. Each is an effective and important part of the lobbying process. With computer technology, letter writing is not very easy—a mass mailing to the legislature doesn't take too much longer to compose than a single letter. Telephone calls may be more costly, especially if you don't live in the state capital, but they take far less time. Personal visits are expensive if you don't live in or near the state capital, and they also require a great deal of time for what are generally brief meetings; but face-to-face meetings are effective. No matter which form of lobbying you select be sure to be brief, dignified, sincere, and, most important, respectful.

Letter writing: Write early, before the legislator has made up her mind. Make the letter one page or less—legislators don't have time to read dissertations! Get to the point quickly and be concise. Attach handouts to support the key points. Make sure you educate, educate, and educate the legislator on the issue. If you are writing about a specific bill, be sure to include the bill number. Note how the legislation will affect the legislator's district, mention the names of key supporters of your position from the district or from the legislator's campaign, provide reasons to support the bill, and request an answer to your letter indicating how she plans to vote on the issue. Be sure to say thank you at the beginning and the end of the letter, and be sure to use the appropriate salutation (see box 3).

Box 3: Salutations for Letter Writing

Governor
1. Writing:
   The Honorable (full name)
   Governor of (State)
   Address

   Dear Governor (last name)

2. Speaking: "Governor (last name)"

Lieutenant Governor
1. Writing:
   The Honorable (full name)
   Lieutenant Governor of (state)
   Address

   Dear Lieutenant Governor (last name)

2. Speaking: "Lieutenant Governor (last name)"

Speaker of the House
1. Writing:
   The Honorable (full name)
   Speaker of the House
   Address

   Dear Mr./Madame Speaker:

2. Speaking: "Mr./Madame Speaker"

State Senator
1. Writing:
   The Honorable (full name)
   The (State) State Senate
   Address

   Dear Senator (last name)

2. Speaking: "Senator (last name)"

State Representative
1. Writing:
   The Honorable (full name)
   The (State) House of Representatives
   Address

   Dear Mr./Ms. (last name)

2. Speaking: "Representative (last name)" or "Mr./Ms. (last name)"

Telephone calls: You'll probably talk with a legislative aide, so don't take it personally if you don't speak with the legislator. Also, if there is a phone blitz on the bill you're calling about, the aide may be rather short with you and may cut you off in the middle of your presentation. Again, don't take it personally.

Be brief and to the point; try to take less than three minutes. Make notes before you call and practice what you want to say. Introduce yourself and mention your address, especially if you are from the legislator's home district. Follow the same principles as in letter writing: identify the bill number and describe how it will affect legislator's district. Ask how the legislator plans to vote on the issue; if the person you speak to doesn't know, ask when you can call back to learn of the decision. End by thanking the legislator or aide for his time and support.

Personal visits: Personal visits are probably the most time-consuming, frustrating, and potentially the most effective form of lobbying. Meetings are as a rule very brief, lasting from a few to no more than fifteen minutes. They usually take place in the legislator's office, but don't be surprised if you find yourself walking down the hall accompanying the representative or senator to a meeting while you lobby for a few short minutes. Most often you'll meet with an aide, but if you have a good relationship with the legislator—in particular, if you were a good campaign volunteer—you'll probably be able to meet with the elected official. You'll need to be pleasant, brief, concise, and convincing. Discuss only one legislative issue during your meeting. Be sure to follow up with a phone call and a letter of appreciation.

These meetings may be short in time, but many a social worker has found that they have been able to change a politician's stance on an issue as a result of a face-to-face meeting. Your sincerity, knowledge, and compassion about the issue speak volumes to politicians.

Public testimony: In general, when considering legislation a committee must allow opportunities for public input. Such testimony usually lasts less than five minutes per speaker. The committee will have rules that govern the testimony's length—check them out beforehand by contacting the committee's staff person in the legislative offices.

Be sure your testimony is typewritten; distribute copies to the committee members, and be sure to have a few extra copies available for others who are interested in your comments. Make sure your name, address, and phone numbers are easily found on the cover page of your testimony in case someone wishes to get in touch with you after the hearing.

Don't be surprised if the legislators ask you no questions after your presentation. There may be twenty to thirty people offering testimony, each speaking three to five minutes. Asking questions only prolongs the process. If a question is asked, be sure of your answers. Don't make up an answer; if you aren't sure what the answer is, tell the committee you'll find out and get back to their staff person within twenty-four hours. And be sure you do! Nothing is more damaging to your credibility in the legislature than to give inaccurate or misleading information or to make a promise and not follow up.

Finally, *don't argue with the legislators!* You are a guest in their workplace. You are there to convince and make friends, not to argue and make enemies. Your legislative opponent today may be your key supporter tomorrow on another issue. Don't burn your bridges.

SUMMARY

"Despite residual skepticism about the appropriateness of political work, there has been a resurgence of political action in recent years" among social workers (Weismiller & Rome, 1995, p. 2312). Courses in schools of social work, ongoing efforts by national and state PACE units, direct participation in political campaigns, and the election of social workers to political office are among the many ways social workers are developing much-needed political savvy.

We have learned through many, often painful, experiences that attempts to influence the development of public policy must begin well before the legislative process. Identifying and working for the election of people who are in favor of human services initiates the lobbying effort; having the right people in place makes lobbying that much easier.

Moreover, elected officials are influenced by groups that "vote regularly and are active in the electoral process" (Parker & Sherraden, 1993, p. 27). Social workers and their membership organizations are making significant contributions to political campaigns. As campaign workers, social workers are able to translate their agency-based practice expertise to the political arena.

Social work practice is directly affected by politics. Who can call themselves social workers and practice as such, program eligibility requirements, and the types and levels of services are but a few of the critical decisions made by elected politicians. Every two years, more than 450,000 offices are up for election, involving some one and a half million candidates (Beaudry & Schaeffer, 1998, p. xv). These elected officials are for the most part not social workers. While the number of social workers holding elected office increased by over 90 percent in the 1990s, decisions made by non–social workers continue to have enormous impact on social workers and clients alike. Social workers face a simple choice: remain on the sidelines while others make decisions that determine how the social service community operates, or participate aggressively at all levels of political activity in order to open the door for progressive lobbying efforts. Simply put, social workers can sit in the audience watching others or can be pivotal actors who build on the rich experiences of political campaigns.

References

Beaudry, A., & Schaeffer, B. (1986). *Winning local and state elections: The guide to organizing your campaign.* New York: Free Press.

Colby, I., & Buffum, W. (1998). Social work and political action committees. *Journal of Community Practice, 5*(4), 87–103.

CSWE Commission on Accreditation. (1994). *Handbook of accreditation standards and procedures.* Washington, DC: CSWE.

Dempsey, D. (1993, March 10). Letter to chapter presidents. Washington, DC: NASW.

Haynes, K., & Mickelson, B. (1991). *Affecting changes* (2nd ed.). New York: Longman.

Hiratsuka, J. (1992). 114 more races backed. *NASW News, 37*(9), 1, 10.

Landers, S. (1992). NASW steps up efforts to elect Clinton. *NASW News, 37*(9), 1.

Mahaffey, M., & Hanks, J. (Eds.). (1982). *Practical politics and social work and political responsibility.* Silver Spring, MD: NASW

NASW Political Affairs Office. (1992, April). *The political social worker.* Washington, DC: NASW.

Parker, M., & Sherraden, M. (1992). Electoral participation of social workers. *New England Journal of Human Services, 11*(3), 23–28.

Richman, W. (1991). *Lobbying for social change.* New York: Haworth.

Weismiller, T., & Rome, S. H. (1995). Social workers in politics. In R. L. Edwards et al. (Eds.), *Encyclopedia of social work* (19th ed., pp. 2305–2313). Washington, DC: NASW Press.

Wolk, J. (1981). Are social workers politically active? *Social work, 26*(4), 283–288.

Part **IV**

Expanding Horizons for Social Work

Chapter 14

International Social Welfare

OUR WORLD IS A GLOBAL COMMUNITY. WE MUST THINK ON A LARGE scale about our interests, concerns, influences, and obligations, for the community in which we live stretches far beyond the confines of our geographic neighborhood. Today, we call this phenomenon globalization, the creation of an international system that affects domestic economies, politics, and cultures (Midgley, 1997, p. 59).

Most of us would agree that we live in a global neighborhood. Twentieth-century history has shown how regional conflicts and disasters can quickly escalate into global ones. The Great Depression of the 1930s, for example, was felt worldwide and not only in the United States where the early effects were concentrated.

Later in the 1930s, after the German and Japanese war machines had conquered many of their neighbors, the United States, which had originally assumed an isolationist position, became one of the leading allied nations. The collapse of the Berlin Wall in November 1989 signaled upheavals in many communist bloc nations that have had significant social and economic consequences around the world. In 1998, weakening in the Asian and Russian economies led to stock market gyrations in the financial centers of the world. Certainly, other examples of global effects exist, and the message is clear: what happens across the oceans affects all of us, no matter where we live.

Did You Know…According to the World Bank, 3 billion people in the world live on less than $2.00 each day.

We also can learn from other societies and cultures about how to strengthen our own approach to social living. We can study how other countries approach social problems and think about how their successes may work in our communities. Some people believe that the United States has nothing to learn from the rest of the world about technology, education, and other social advancements. But this is not true! "Social scientists agree that knowledge can be increased by investigating phenomena in other societies and by testing propositions in different social, economic, and cultural contexts" (Midgley, 1995, p. 1490). The study of international social welfare is an imperative that will move us beyond our many self-imposed barriers and allow all of us to be better off in a cooperative, world community.

Name: Matthew Colton

Place of residence: Swansea, Wales, United Kingdom

College/university degrees: B.A. with honors (First Class) in Applied Social Studies, Diploma in Applied Social Studies, Certificate of Qualification in Social Work, Keele University; D.Phil., Oxford University.

Present position: Professor and Head of Applied Social Studies (Social Work), University of Wales, Swansea

Previous work/volunteer experience: Social work teacher and researcher, social worker mainly with children and families

What do you do in your spare time? I don't have any spare time as such. Outside of my work, most of my time is spent with my wife, two children, and extended family. I really enjoy family activities and take an active interest in my children's hobbies and interests.

Why did you choose social work as a career? From an early age, my parents nurtured and encouraged me to have respect and concern for others, particularly those who are troubled or oppressed. My mother died when I was 9 years old. I think that this experience deepened my compassion and empathy for those whose lives are especially difficult, and my concern for social justice.

What is your favorite social work story? There are so many! For example, I was once called to the home of a client who wished to make a complaint about her social worker. Having introduced myself on the doorstep, I was beckoned in by the old woman whom I was there to see. The house was dimly lit and overrun with cats.

"How can I help?," I asked when we were seated.

"She [the social worker] doesn't like my cats," complained the woman. "Wants me to kill them all. Told me to hit them with a spade."

"Hit them with a spade?" I asked, somewhat puzzled. Then it dawned on me. My colleague had, in fact, advised the woman to have the cats spayed.

What would be the one thing you would change in our community if you had the power to do so? I would like to see a genuine commitment to tackling social exclusion. This would include practical measures to reverse the increasing polarization in British society between the poor and the affluent as well as measures to combat child poverty—which has tripled over the past two decades—and institutional racism.

Yet American social workers have been ambivalent in their commitment to the international arena. In fact, Midgley (1997, p. 63) has contended that the profession is not "fully prepared" to meet international challenges and opportunities and must be more aggressive in benefitting from international opportunities. In other words, just as the world experiences globalization, so too must the social work profession.

In this chapter we touch on the many international facets of social work. Though we cannot delve into details of cultural differences and economic and demographic trends, we hope to raise your awareness of these issues. By the end of the chapter you'll recognize that social work is a global profession, facing the persistent challenge of promoting social and economic justice.

HOW DO WE COMPARE DIFFERENT NATIONS?

When making international comparisons, it is helpful to have a framework for grouping nations based on similarities. Otherwise, comparisons may not be meaningful. For example, very little can be learned from comparing the economic systems of the United States and Nepal. The vast political, economic, social, and cultural differences between these two nations makes such a comparison virtually impossible.

One framework is based on a nation's technological level. Three levels are identified: preindustrial, industrial, and postindustrial (Bell, 1973). This framework can be visualized as a core with circles, or "concentric zones," surrounding the core. Core nations include western Europe and North America; a semiperiphery surrounds the core; and the semiperiphery is then encircled by the periphery (Chatterjee, 1996, p. 48). The semiperiphery includes former communist nations and selected nations in Asia and South America. The periphery includes the remaining Asian and South American countries and Africa. Chatterjee called these three groups of nations the first world, the second world, and the third world (see box 1).

The World Bank, an international organization that promotes economic development and productivity to raise the standard of living in less developed nations, uses a different framework. The World Bank categorizes nations into six regions: South Asia, Middle East and North Africa, Latin America and the Caribbean, Europe and Central Asia, East Asia and the Pacific, and the Africa Region (see box 2).

We've described two frameworks here, but there are a number of alternative approaches to comparing nations. The purpose of our work is to be able to organize the world's countries in order that our discussions are consistent and appropriate. In other words, we want to compare apples with apples, not apples with peaches!

Let's use Chatterjee's classification to demonstrate how a framework can be applied to make international comparisons. As shown in box 3, Chatterjee identified social issues and then tabulated how the first, second, and third worlds respond to them. Chatterjee also took the application a step further by asking the

---

Box 1: The World System

First World: Also known as the core, it includes North America, western Europe, Australia, and Japan. It is wealthy, capitalist, industrial, and based on the traditions of a market economy and individualism.

Second World: Somewhat outside the core, it consists of eastern Europe, central and northern Asia, and Cuba. It is neither wealthy nor poor, socialist, selectively industrial, and based on the traditions of a planned economy and collectivism. A substantial part of the second world has been attempting to convert to a market economy since 1991.

Third World: It includes nations mostly in Africa, southern and Southeast Asia, and South America. It is mostly poor, often nationalist, selectively industrial to preindustrial, and based on a mixed economy and regional loyalty.

Source: Chatterjee (1996, p. 46).

---

following questions about the three worlds and then compiling responses, listed in box 4.

1. Once a person has been socially defined as not employable, can he/she ask the state for help?

2. Once a person has been socially defined as employable but is unemployed, can he/she ask the state for support?

3. Once a person has been socially defined as employed but is marginally employed, can he/she ask the state for support?

4. If the state is providing support, is it means tested?

5. If the state is providing support, it is related to past or potential future earnings?

6. If the state is providing support, it is a flat rate or with a minimum or maximum, or is it linked to an index of fluctuating living costs?

7. Is the state committed to seeing that each citizen receives a basic package of health care, or has it engaged other qualified parties to do so?

8. Is the state committed to seeing that each citizen receives a basic education? If so, has it set up a formal structure to provide such education itself, or has it engaged other qualified parties to do so?

9. Is the state committed to seeing that each citizen receives basic housing? If so, has it set up a formal structure to provide such housing, or has it engaged other parties to do so?

10. Is the state committed to providing protection to various vulnerable groups (children, elderly, developmentally disabled, and mentally ill)? If so, has it set up a formal structure to provide such protection, or has it engaged other qualified parties to do so?

11. Have one or more occupational groups emerged within the state, which are self-appointed advocates for vulnerable groups and are seeking increased professionalization? (1996, p. 78)

Box 2: Regions of the World as Defined by the World Bank

South Asia: Afghanistan, Bangladesh, Bhutan, India, Maldives, Nepal, Pakistan, Sri Lanka.

Middle East and North Africa: Algeria, Bahrain, Egypt, Iran, Jordan, Kuwait, Lebanon, Morocco, Oman, Qatar, Saudi Arabia, Syrian Arab Republic, Tunisia, Yemen, United Arab Emirates.

Latin America and the Caribbean: Antigua and Barbuda, Argentina, Belize, Bolivia, Chile, Colombia, Costa Rica, Dominica, Dominican Republic, Ecuador, El Salvador, Grenada, Guatemala, Guyana, Haiti, Honduras, Jamaica, Mexico, Nicaragua, Panama, Paraguay, Peru, St. Kitts and Nevis, St. Lucia, St. Vincent and the Grenadines, Suriname, Trinidad and Tobago, Uruguay, Venezuela.

Europe and Central Asia: Albania, Armenia, Azerbaijan, Belarus, Bosnia and Herzegovina, Bulgaria, Croatia, Czech Republic, Estonia, Georgia, Hungary, Kazakhstan, Kyrgyz Republic, Latvia, Lithuania, Former Yugoslav Republic of Macedonia, Moldova, Poland, Romania, Russian Federation, Slovak Republic, Slovenia, Tajikistan, Turkey, Turkmenistan, Ukraine, Uzbekistan.

East Asia and the Pacific: Cambodia, China, Fiji, Indonesia, Kiribati, Korea, Lao People's Democratic Republic, Malaysia, Marshall Islands, Federated States of Micronesia, Mongolia, Myanmar, Palau, Papua New Guinea, Philippines, Samoa, Solomon Islands, Thailand, Tonga, Vanuatu, Vietnam.

Africa: Angola, Benin, Botswana, Burkina Faso, Burundi, Cameroon, Cape Verde, Central African Republic, Chad, Comoros, Congo, Democratic Republic of Congo, Republic of Côte d'Ivoire, Djibouti, Equatorial Guinea, Eritrea, Ethiopia, Gabon, The Gambia, Ghana, Guinea, Guinea-Bissau, Kenya, Lesotho, Liberia, Madagascar, Malawi, Mali, Mauritania, Mauritius, Mozambique, Namibia, Niger, Rwanda, São Tomé and Principe, Senegal, Seychelles, Sierra Leone, Somalia, South Africa, Sudan, Swaziland, Tanzania, Togo, Uganda, Zambia, Zimbabwe.

Question: What countries are missing from the list and why? Connect with the World Bank's web page (www.worldbank.org) for additional information and read the organization's purpose for the answer.

Source: www.worldbank.org.

THE WORLD TODAY

The astronauts who first circled the moon took one of the most exciting pictures of the planet Earth. The photograph shows a beautiful globe hanging just above a stark lunar landscape. For the first time, we were able to see our planet from outside—our planet that beforehand had seemed so large, but looked so fragile as it was suspended in the darkness of space.

Box 3: Welfare Trends on Selected Issues in the Three Worlds

Issue	First World	Second World	Third World
Housing	Public housing for the poor; some rent control or subsidy	Rationed housing for all	No such concept
Education	State supported; uneven in the United States	State supported	State efforts do not reach all
Income maintenance	Almost all countries	Almost all countries	Almost none except in Singapore, South Korea, Taiwan, and Hong Kong
Health care	Almost all countries except the United States; rising costs	Almost all countries; supplies and equipment problematic	Crisis-based care to the poor from charitable clinics or hospitals

Did You Know…The World Bank estimates that 900 million adults worldwide are illiterate. Four hundred million 6–17-year-olds are not in school and 225 million of them are girls

But from our perspective, the earth is a very large home. If anything, we find great diversity among the earth's people, governments, and experiences. And yet within this great diversity are common social problems that afflict people day in

Box 4: Comparison of Eleven Welfare State Variables

Question	First World	Second World	Third World
1.	Yes	Mostly yes	Mostly no
2.	Yes	Mostly yes	No
3.	Mostly yes	Mostly yes	No
4.	Mostly yes	Mostly yes	Does not apply
5.	Mostly yes	Mostly yes	Does not apply
6.	Mostly yes	Mostly yes	Does not apply
7.	Yes except in US	Yes	No
8.	Mostly yes	Mostly yes	No
9.	Mostly yes	Yes	No
10.	Yes	Mostly yes	No
11.	Yes	Partially yes	Partially yes

Source: Chatterjee (1996, p. 80).

and day out. Poverty, homelessness, mental illness, inadequate housing, hunger, poor health care, physical violence, and neglect are among the many problems that know no geographic borders.

Social problems are enormous from a worldwide perspective. Although poverty, for example, has declined in parts of South Asia and the Middle East and North Africa, three billion people live on less than $2 each day. About one-third of the world's developing population is poor. In 1996, 132 of every 1,000 African children died before age 5, and 91 of every 1,000 before age 1. In 1995, over nine million children in developing countries under age 5 died of avoidable causes. Adult literacy is approximately 70 percent. In most countries, social exclusion is closely linked to economic, health, and educational disparities.

Did You Know...The World Bank estimates that 70 percent of women infected with HIV are between ages 15 and 25.

The infant mortality rate is an indicator of a nation's health care—in particular, of its comprehensiveness and ability to cover the poor and nonpoor alike. It counts the number of children under age 1 who die per 1,000 live births. The U.S. rate in 1997 was 6.6—that is, 6.6 infants died for every 1,000 born (Brunner, 1997, p. 181). Infant mortality was lower in seventeen nations than in the United States (see table 1).

Table 1: National Infant Mortality Rates Lower than U.S. Rate, 1998

Nation	Infant Mortality Rate (per 1,000)
United States	6.6
Australia	5.4
Austria	6.1
Belgium	6.3
Canada	6.0
Denmark	4.8
Finland	4.9
France	6.0
Germany	5.9
Ireland	6.3
Japan	4.4
Netherlands	4.8
New Zealand	6.5
Norway	4.9
Spain	6.1
Sweden	4.5
Switzerland	5.4
United Kingdom	6.3

Source: Brunner (1997).

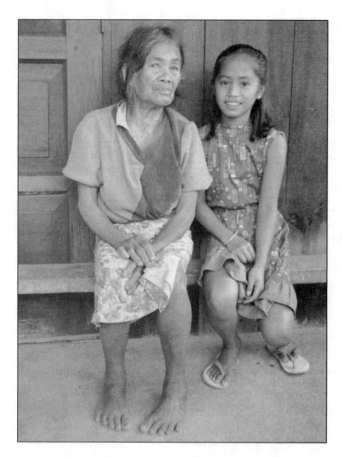

Chona and her grandmother at their home in the mountains of Northern Luzon in the Philippines. They live with the bare necessities and medical help is scarce. The grandmother's feet show the effects of a lifetime of work in the rice fields.

At the other extreme, infant mortality exceeding 50 per 1,000 live births can be found in Bangladesh (100), Pakistan (95.1), India (69.2), Kenya (55.2), Brazil (53.4), South Africa (53.2), and Iran (50.8) (Brunner, 1997, p. 182).

Life expectancy is a second indicator of a nation's well-being. Life expectancy is a numerical estimate of the average age a group of people will reach. U.S. life expectancy in 1997 was 76 years; eighteen nations have higher expectancies (see table 2).

Many other indicators show that the United States lags behind other countries. While some people may be surprised at how the United States ranks worldwide in these areas, the findings suggest that nations can both learn a great deal from and assist each other.

HOW DO WE LOOK AT INTERNATIONAL SOCIAL WELFARE?

The literature detailing international social welfare issues is, to say the least, interesting and stimulating. Themes that you'll find consistently in international

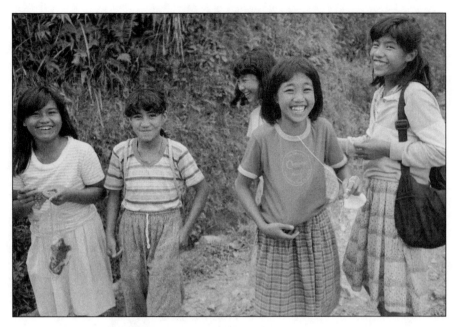

Girls on their way home from school in a remote mountain area of the Philippines where the New People's Army is rebelling against the government. Roads are almost nonexistent in this part of the country.

social welfare journals include peace and social justice, human rights, and social development. These areas are critical for all social workers to understand. In fact, CSWE accreditation standards require that these topics be included in both baccalaureate and graduate social work programs. Our fascination with international issues transcends our educational mandates, however, and is evident in our day-to-day conversations. How often have we heard people compare the United States with other countries? Typically, the conversation will include a statement such as "The poor in the United States have it easy compared with the poor in India." Statements of this sort form the basis of comparative social welfare discussions.

Did You Know...Each day, according to the World Bank, 6,000 girls are subjected to genital mutilation in twenty-eight nations around the world.

Midgley identified five basic types of international social welfare studies:
◆ Comparative studies of social need
◆ Comparative studies of social policies and human services
◆ Typologies of welfare states
◆ Studies of the genesis and functions of social policy
◆ Studies of the future of the welfare state (1995, p. 1491).

Table 2: National Life Expectancies Greater Than U.S. Expectancy, 1998

Nation	Life Expectancy (years)
United States	76.0
Australia	79.6
Austria	76.7
Belgium	77.2
Canada	79.3
Cyprus	76.5
Denmark	77.4
France	78.6
Germany	76.1
Greece	78.3
Israel	78.2
Italy	78.2
Japan	79.7
Netherlands	77.9
New Zealand	77.3
Norway	77.0
Spain	78.5
Sweden	78.2
Switzerland	77.8
United Kingdom	76.6

Source: Brunner (1997).

Comparative studies of social need are reports that collect and assess a variety of social and economic data from different countries. These reports are usually quantitative in nature and present tabular data on a variety of topics. Typical studies include data on income, education, birthrates, poverty, and migration.

Comparative studies of social polices and human services are most often qualitative or descriptive presentations of issues. The topics explored are similar to those addressed by comparative studies of social needs, but the discussion includes analysis of political issues, funding patterns, eligibility standards, types of services, and provision or delivery of services.

Typologies of welfare states discuss the ideological and philosophical bases for the welfare systems of different countries. Typology studies, which are generally qualitative or descriptive, can shed light on a nation's view of people and social issues and, at the same time, provide important insight into the direction of its social welfare program. According to Midgley (1995, p. 1493), the most common typology is the Wilensky and Lebeaux conceptual model of residual versus institutional social welfare (see chapter 2 for a discussion of this framework).

Studies of the genesis and functions of social policy are closely related to welfare typology studies. They focus on three areas: how welfare organizations emerged,

Japanese students in a school for persons with developmental disabilities. Like most Japanese students, they wear uniforms. The school teaches trade skills (woodworking, plumbing, bricklaying) as well as life skills. Art, music, and physical education are taught. The school has a large gym and swimming pool. Many of the students train for the Special Olympics.

what forces affect the development of social policy, and what are the functions of social policy in the society (Midgley, 1995, p. 1493). Such studies may be either quantitative or qualitative. They form the theoretical basis for social welfare endeavors.

Studies of the future of the welfare state have become more common recently. Midgley (1995, p. 1493) believed this happened in response to international criticism of social welfare and worldwide attempts to rethink national social welfare commitments and responsibilities. Such reports integrate the other four types of welfare studies and forecast the future.

INTERNATIONAL SOCIAL WELFARE ASSOCIATIONS

Many social work practitioners and students are surprised to learn that numerous, long-standing social welfare associations exist around the world. The number of international social welfare associations greatly expanded following World War II, primarily to help rebuild war-torn countries and to assist poor countries in gaining greater economic stability (Healy, 1995, p. 1499). Healy (1995, p. 1499) classified international associations into three groups: 1) United Nations structures, 2) U.S. government agencies, and 3) private voluntary bodies.

United Nations Structures

The United Nations was originally organized in 1945 to provide a forum to help to stabilize and maintain international relations and to give peace among nations a more secure foundation. By 1998, 185 nations were members (www.un.org). The United Nations is probably most recognized for its peacekeeping forces, which have been deployed throughout the world to help mediate conflict. In addition to its peacekeeping mission, however, the United Nations conducts a variety of activities, with 80 percent of its work taking place in developing nations. Typical of these services are programs for children, environmental protection, human rights, health and medical research and services, poverty and economic development, agricultural development, family planning, emergency and disaster relief, air and sea travel, use of atomic energy, and labor and workers' rights.

Did You Know...The U.S. share of the 1998 regular budget for the United Nations is $298 million, the equivalent of $1.11 per American. San Marino, another member nation, pays $4.26 per citizen to the UN.

While the United Nations is involved in an array of activities, seven specific agencies address social welfare issues:

United Nations Children's Fund: Probably the best known UN social welfare program, it provides a variety of child-directed services in such areas as health, child abuse, neglect and exploitation, child nutrition, education, and water and sanitation. UNICEF received the Nobel Peace Prize in 1965 for its efforts on behalf of children.

World Health Organization: This specialized UN agency focuses on worldwide health issues. It works to establish international health standards in a variety of areas, including vaccines, research, and drugs; it monitors and attempts to control communicable diseases; and it has a special focus on primary health care.

UN High Commission for Refugees: The commission oversees protection, assistance, and resettlement aid. In 1981, it was awarded the Nobel Peach Prize for its work with Asian refugees.

Economic and Social Council: The council coordinates a number of economic and social activities, with specific commissions for focusing on social development, human rights, population, the status of women, and drugs.

Department of Policy Coordination and Sustainable Development: Under the auspices of the UN Secretariat, the leading body of the United Nations, this department coordinates the development of welfare policies and activities.

UN Developmental Program: This program provides technical assistance grants to developing member nations. Its primary area of support is in agriculture, though grants also support health, education, population, employment, and other related human service programs.

UN Fund for Population Activities: This agency collects worldwide population data and implements family programs, including education and contraception.

Did You Know...The United Nations and its organizations have been awarded the Nobel Peace Prize on five separate occasions—1954, 1965, 1969, 1981, and 1988. In addition, six people affiliated with the United Nations have received the Nobel Peace Prize— 1945, 1949, 1950, 1957, 1961, and 1974.

The United Nations provides many other social welfare services. Typical activities include conferences and conventions, as well "special years" dedicated to a specific issue. Conferences focus on very specific themes. In 1990, for example, the United Nations sponsored the World Summit for Children; in 1992, the UN Conference on the Environment (Brazil); and in 1995 the Fourth World Conference on Women (Beijing). Special years included the 1994 International Year of the Family and the 1999 International Year of Older Americans.

U.S. Government Agencies

The United States carries out a variety of international social welfare efforts through federal agencies:

Administration for Children and Families: A subsection of the Office of Public Affairs, this agency is the primary conduit for international affairs and social work. Activities include meetings, research, professional exchanges, and cosponsorship of welfare programs. (See www.acf.dhhs.gov.)

Office of Refugee Resettlement: This office coordinates resettlement of refugees in the United States. Since 1975 over two million people have been assisted in the United States because of persecution in their homelands due to race, religion, nationality, or political or social group membership. (See www.acf.dhhs.gov/programs/orr/.)

Social Security Administration: This agency examines social insurance programs worldwide. (See www.ssa.gov.)

U.S. International Development Corporation: This corporation has two responsibilities: international private investment and operating the Agency for International Development (AID). AID provides funding for international projects and is very concerned about AIDS, child welfare, population growth, and basic education. AID has given money to welfare groups, including NASW, to sponsor international programs. (See www.info.usaid.gov.)

Peace Corps: First organized in 1961, the Peace Corps sends American volunteers to different nations to assist in a variety of social, economic, and agricultural projects. (See www.peacecorps.gov.)

U.S. Information Agency: This agency sponsors international leaders from around the world to participate with their colleagues in the United States. The agency also sponsors Americans to study abroad. (Healy, 1995, p. 1503).

Private Voluntary Bodies

Private or nongovernmental groups provide a variety of services and activities throughout the world. Human service organizations such as the YMCA and YWCA sponsor direct services and programs. In addition, nonprofit organizations consult with international agencies and groups about human service issues.

INTERNATIONAL PROFESSIONAL SOCIAL WELFARE ORGANIZATIONS

There are a variety of international social welfare organizations around the world. Some are social work membership associations, similar to the NASW. Others are national and regional educational associations, similar in purpose and function to CSWE.

Three primary worldwide organizing bodies cross national boundaries and encourage partnerships: the International Federation of Social Workers, the International Association of Schools of Social Work, and the International Council on Social Welfare.

International Federation of Social Workers

The International Federation of Social Workers (IFSW) was founded in 1956 to promote social work on the world stage. IFSW is divided into five geographical regions: Africa, Asia and the Pacific, Europe, Latin America and the Caribbean, and North America. Membership is open to one professional social work association in each country. In 1998, seventy national member associations represented more than 460,000 social workers (see box 5 and appendix F). Individuals and organiza-

---

Box 5: Member Nations of IFSW, 1998

Albania	Egypt	Latvia	Romania
Argentina	Faeroe Islands	Luxembourg	Russian Federation
Australia	Finland	Macedonia	Singapore
Austria	France	Malaysia	Slovak Republic
Bahrain	Germany	Malta	South Africa
Belarus	Ghana	Mauritius	Spain
Belgium	Greece	Mongolia	Sri Lanka
Benin	Hong Kong	Netherlands Antilles	Sweden
Bolivia	Hungary	New Zealand	Switzerland
Brazil	Iceland	Nicaragua	Tanzania
Bulgaria	India	Niger	Thailand
Canada	Ireland	Nigeria	Uganda
Chile	Israel	Norway	Ukraine
China	Italy	Pakistan	United Kingdom
Colombia	Japan	Philippines	United States
Cyprus	Kenya	Poland	Former Yugoslavia
Czech Republic	Korea	Portugal	Zimbabwe
Denmark	Kuwait		

---

tions may join IFSW as well as take part in the Friends Program. As a friend, a social worker receives the IFSW newsletter, published three times annually, policy papers, and a discount on registration for IFSW international and regional conferences.

IFSW sponsors meetings throughout the world (see box 6). In addition to its biennial international meetings, IFSW sponsors regional meetings that focus on specific area issues; participant costs are much lower for these meetings. Between 1966 and 2002, there have been sixteen regional meetings in Europe, eleven meetings in Asia and the Pacific, and four meetings in Africa. Both regional and worldwide gatherings provide social workers from around the world with a chance to share research findings as well as program ideas.

IFSW also provides critical leadership in the pursuit of human rights for individual social workers, social work students, and social service workers. In 1988, IFSW established a Human Rights Commission with members representing each region. The commission works with a number of international human rights groups including Amnesty International.

Did You Know...The headquarters for IFSW is located in Oslo, Norway, and can be contacted through its web page www.gen@ifsw.org. The national office of the International Association of Schools of Social Work is located in Vienna, Austria.

Another noteworthy activity of IFSW is its research and publication of policy papers that explore social issues that social workers face day in and day out. In addition to the following issues, policy papers are planned to explore indigenous people and international adoptions:

Advancement of women	Welfare of elderly people
Child Welfare	Health
HIV-AIDS	Human rights
Migration	Peace and disarmament
Protection of personnel	Refugees
Rural communities	Self-help
Youth	

Box 6: Meetings Sponsored by IFSW

1966	Helsinki	1988	Stockholm
1970	Manila	1990	Buenos Aires
1974	Nairobi	1992	Washington, DC
1976	Puerto Rico	1994	Colombia
1978	Tel Aviv	1996	Hong Kong
1980	Hong Kong	1998	Jerusalem
1982	Brighton	2000	Montreal
1984	Montreal	2002	Harare
1986	Tokyo		

International Association of Schools of Social Work

As the name suggests, the International Association of Schools of Social Work (IASSW) is the focal point for social work education around the world. IASSW does not set international accreditation standards for social work education, rather it promotes social work education and the development of high-quality educational programs around the world. In a 1928 worldwide meeting, attended by more than 3,000 people from forty-two different nations, the participants agreed that social work was a mechanism that could professionalize and achieve better outcomes from charitable activities (Hokenstad & Kendall, 1995, p. 1513). The following year IASSW was organized, and today membership is open to national associations, such as CSWE, and their specific educational programs. By 1995 IASSW membership totaled 450 schools from 100 countries (Hokenstad & Kendall, 1995, p. 1514). Member schools are divided into six regions—Asia, Africa, Europe and Middle East, Latin America and Caribbean, North America, and Oceania—which facilitates development of regional educational initiatives.

Did You Know...The journal International Social Work *is sponsored jointly by the International Association of Schools of Social Work, the International Federation of Social Workers, and the International Council on Social Welfare.*

IASSW sponsors a biennial meeting, the International Conference of Schools of Social Work, and supports a variety of educationally directed projects. In addition, the association publishes a newsletter and texts. IASSW has also published, with CSWE, a very useful guide to social work programs around the world. The guide—Rao and Kendall (1984)—lists social work programs in different countries, admission standards, and an overview of curricula. While this publication is out of date, it does provide an interesting look at the diversity of social work education around the world. For example, in some African countries you'll find a "certificate" or "state diploma" awarded after the completion of three years of postsecondary study. In Asia, undergraduate and graduate programs are similar in structure to those in America. Hokenstad and Kendall (1995, p. 1516) have written that national traditions and ideologies make it impossible to generalize about social work education in Europe. Structures differ greatly, from length of time to complete a degree program to the content studied.

International Council on Social Welfare

The International Council on Social Welfare (ICSW) is a "global non-governmental organization which represents a wide range of national and international member organizations that seek to advance social welfare, social justice and social development" (www.icsw.org). The primary thrust of the council is to promote social and economic development activities that will reduce poverty, hardship, and vulnerability. The council was founded in Paris in 1928, and today its office is located in Montreal, Canada. Like IFSW and IASSW, the council holds a biennial conference as well as regional meetings.

ICSW is subdivided into five regions—Africa, Asia and Pacific, Latin America and Caribbean, North America, and Europe. In 1995 ICSW was active in more than seventy countries (Healy, 1995, p. 1506).

NASW AND CSWE INTERNATIONAL INITIATIVES

National Association of Social Workers

NASW is active in pursuing and promoting international relations. The association is guided by its International Activities Committee, which was formed in 1986. The international committee seeks to adopt a variety of mechanisms to increase the globalization of NASW.

As part of its international outreach activities, NASW has sponsored international meetings and travel opportunities. For example, in 1992 NASW, as part of that year's annual meeting, cohosted the World Assembly, the biannual international conclave of social workers, in Washington, D.C. During the 1980s and 1990s, many state NASW chapters forged partnerships with social workers and associations in other countries. In fact, by 1992 twenty-one state chapters had formal relationships with other associations around the world. In addition, the national association and a number of state chapters have sponsored study tours in various countries around the world.

Council on Social Work Education

CSWE is also extremely active in international circles. Organizationally, the council includes an International Commission, which was established in 1978. The

---

Box 7: Sample of International Social Welfare Organizations and Their Web Sites

HelpAge International	www.helpage@dial.piper.com
Inclusion International	www.incluit@skynet.be
International Catholic Migration Commission	www.admin@icmc.dpn.ch
International Council of Jewish Women	www.hg@icjw.demon.co.uk
International Council on Jewish Social and Welfare Services	(no web; phone: 011 44 171387 3925)
International Federation of Aging	www.ifa@citenet.net
International Federation of Red Cross and Red Crescent Services	www.secretariat@frc.org
International Federation of Settlements and Neighborhood Centers	www.ifs@mcll.poprel.org.uk
International Organization for Migration	www.info@geneva.iom.ch
International Planned Parenthood Federation	www.info@ippf.org
International Social Service	www.plan-ih@plan.geis.com
Salvation Army	www.websa@salvationarmy.org

Please note that web site addresses may change over time. If you are unable to connect because a URL is out of date, conduct a search using the organization's name.

International Acronyms

EC	European Community
ECE	Economic Commission of Europe
EFTA	European Free Trade Association
EU	European Union
Eurostat	European Statistical Office
FAO	Food and Agriculture Organization
GATT	General Agreement on Tariffs and Trade; succeeded by WTO
IBRD	International Bank for Reconstruction and Development; usually called the World Bank
IDA	International Development Association
IFAD	International Fund for Agricultural Development
IFC	International Finance Corporation
IMF	International Monetary Fund
NATO	North Atlantic Treaty Organization
OPEC	Organization of Petroleum Exporting Nations
UNDP	United Nations Development Programme
Unesco	United Nations Educational, Scientific, and Cultural Organization
UNICEF	United Nations Children's Fund
UNIDO	United Nations Industrial Development Organization
USAID	United States Agency for International Development
WFP	World Food Programme
WHO	World Health Organization
WTO	World Trade Organization

commission's focus is on enhancing international opportunities in the social work curriculum. While linking CSWE with international groups, such as IASSW, the commission strongly advocates that schools internationalize curricula and provide students with worldwide opportunities. In 1998 CSWE, its International Commission, and a number of schools of social work sponsored an international meeting that primarily examined issues related to the Caribbean Basin.

A number of social work programs offer international student exchanges, field placement opportunities, and study tours. These opportunities are usually announced through *NASW News*, state NASW newsletters, or flyers sent to departments and schools. The following list is just a small sample of the activities that social work programs have undertaken; check directly with your own social work program about any international opportunities it offers:

> *University of North Carolina–Chapel Hill*: study tour of Ireland, Wales, and Scotland

> *University of Central Florida*: summer course in Mexico

> *Florida State University*: summer course in London, England

East Carolina State University: summer course in Bristol, England

University of South Carolina: study tour of Greece

SUMMARY

Problems of substance abuse, child abuse and neglect, spouse battering, poverty, inadequate mental health and health care, and the "isms" of race, age, and gender are found in every region of the world. And social workers too are found throughout the world, helping individuals, families, and communities to confront these and other social issues.

We experience globalization every day. We can cross the oceans in a matter of hours; we can talk to a friend in another nation simply by dialing a telephone. Through e-mail we can send messages around the world to any number of people in mere milliseconds.

Social work and social welfare are part of this fast-paced, ever-changing world. Yet social work students in the United States have limited exposure to international issues (Hokenstad & Kendall, 1995, p. 1520). Certainly, CSWE and NASW encourage, in a variety of ways, exposure to the international scene as part of the professional experience. But should we be doing more? And if so, how?

The social work educational curriculum is already packed with required content. It is easy to say "International content is required in all social curricula," but at what expense? Will existing content need to be dropped or modified? Are social work educators and practitioners willing to decide whether international content, while important in our world today, is *necessary* for effective social work practice?

Social work practitioners often claim that they are stretched to the limit by work obligations and wonder how they could continue to manage the rigors of work if required to move into the international arena. As one practitioner stated:

> Don't get me wrong, I'm very concerned about poverty in India and the clear mistreatment of people based on a caste system. BUT I just don't have enough time in a day to do what needs to be done for my child welfare clients. What is important for me is that my kids are able to get back with their families and no longer feel the pain of abuse and neglect.

Attending an international meeting is often a surprise for the American social worker. It's not uncommon to hear social workers from around the world speak in negative terms about the American social work community. Many believe that American social workers do not value the international experience. Whether true or not, they perceive that American social welfare journals discriminate against international authors by declining to publish their manuscripts. They feel that U.S. social work programs do not value international journals and texts, an idea reinforced by the absence of international materials among required readings in social work courses.

There is some truth to allegations that American social workers are ignorant of the international social welfare arena. We are surprised to learn that there are social work organizations similar to NASW and CSWE throughout the world. Yes, we are surprised to discover that social work extends beyond the borders of North America and some parts of Europe.

But rather than berate the profession and each other, we need to commit ourselves to professional globalization. In the classroom, we need to look at issues and conduct discussions in an international context. That doesn't mean that the focus of all efforts should be international, but it does mean that we should consider topics through an international lens, when appropriate.

But what are some specific things we can do? First, we can support NASW in its organizational efforts on a national level as well as in the state chapters and local units. Dedicating one monthly meeting to an international issue with either a guest speaker or a film will enhance our efforts. Second, while more ambitious than looking for a guest speaker, we can try to organize with NASW or utilize a study-travel tour offered by a social work program. Third, we can work to develop a sister program with an international social welfare association or school that can lead to professional exchanges for practitioners and students alike. Fourth, each year most colleges sponsor an "international week" on their campuses. The local social work student group, with help from NASW, can sponsor an activity that highlights international social welfare.

What we do is only limited to our creativity. But before doing anything we must first commit to the belief that we live in a global community. We need to embrace the notion that our work influences and is influenced by the global community. Then, and only then, will we be able to confront the social ills that plague the world and have any chance of achieving social justice for all people no matter where they live or what their social and economic status.

References

Bell, D. (1973). *The coming of post-industrial society.* New York: Basic Books.

Brunner, B. (Ed.). (1997). *1998 Information please almanac.* Boston: Information Please.

Chatterjee, P. (1996). *Approaches to the welfare state.* Washington, DC: NASW Press.

Healy, L. (1995). International social welfare: Organizations and activities. In R. L. Edwards et al. (Eds.), *Encyclopedia of social work* (19th ed., pp. 1499–1510). Washington, DC: NASW Press.

Hokenstad, M. C., & Kendall, K. A. (1995). International social work education. In R. L. Edwards et al. (Eds.), *Encyclopedia of social work* (19th ed., pp. 1511–1520). Washington, DC: NASW Press.

Midgley, J. (1995). International and comparative social welfare. In R. L. Edwards et al. (Eds.), *Encyclopedia of social work* (19th ed., pp. 1490–1499).

Midgley, J. (1997). Social work in international context: Challenges and opportunities for the 21st century. In M. Reisch & E. Gambrill (Eds.), *Social work in the 21st century* (pp. 59–67). Thousand Oaks, CA: Pine Forge Press.

Rao, V., & Kendall, K. (Eds.). (1984). *World guide to social work education.* New York: CSWE.

Chapter 15

Conclusions

YOU CAN TELL A GREAT DEAL ABOUT SOME BOOKS JUST FROM THEIR titles. Margaret Truman's *Murder at the CIA,* for example, is a murder mystery set within the government. Woodward and Bernstein's *All the President's Men* is a work exploring a president—Nixon in this case—and his staff. On the other hand, titles may mislead you. *Hunt for Red October* is not a story about fall in New England. Salinger's classic *Catcher in the Rye* is not a baseball story about the exploits of Yankee legend Yogi Berra.

In social work, you can also tell a lot from book titles. Look at the following titles and think about what they say to you:

◆ *Social Work, a Profession of Many Faces* (Morales & Sheafor, 1997)
◆ *The Professional Altruist* (Lubove, 1965)
◆ *Social Work, the Unloved Profession* (Richan & Mendelsohn, 1973)
◆ *The Drama of Social Work* (Bloom, 1990)
◆ *Unfaithful Angels* (Specht & Courtney, 1994)

Each title should tell you something about the authors' view of the profession. Morales and Sheafor find social workers involved in a number of settings providing an array of services. Lubove recognizes social workers as people who want to help others but looks beyond the philanthropic model, to someone who is professionally trained in this important art and science. *Social Work, the Unloved Profession* depicts the somewhat negative view that the larger community holds of social work, one in which the profession's activities are not held in high regard. Finally, *Unfaithful Angels* is a critical look by two social workers at the social work profession in which the authors strongly assert that professionals have abandoned advocacy efforts on behalf of the poor in favor of for-profit and private psychotherapeutic services.

These titles taken collectively—each viewed as part of a whole—can inspire an interesting, though provoking discussion. And while the main purpose of a text is to educate and inform, a text should also get its readers to think about the subject matter in a more critical, insightful manner.

So, what does the title of our book suggest? After reading the chapters, have you learned something new about the social work profession? Do you have a better understanding of the profession, its varied practice methodologies, and the issues faced by today's practitioners?

Name: Donald W. Beless

Place of residence: Oakton, Virginia

College/university degrees: B.A., Wheaton College, Illinois; A.M., Ph.D., School of Social Service Administration, University of Chicago

Present position: Executive Director, Council on Social Work Education

Previous work/volunteer experience: Assoc. Prof. and Dean of Students, School of Social Service Administration, University of Chicago; Professor and Director, Kent School of Social Work, University of Louisville; consultant to numerous professional organizations; member of boards of directors of several local, national, and international social service and educational organizations

What do you do in your spare time? I like to run, and I enjoy traveling.

Why did you choose social work as a career? Social work appealed to me as the profession most clearly focused on helping improve the lives of people through a wide range of interventions, such as direct practice with individuals, groups, and families; community organization, and social policy development.

What is your favorite social work story? My favorite social work story is not a single event, but the history of the profession itself. From its roots over a century ago in the organization and training of "friendly visitors," to an empirically based, officially recognized profession, the story of social work is one of making a positive difference for individuals, families, and communities. While not without its missteps, it is a remarkable and inspiring story of over 100 years of people dedicated to social justice and the development of a scientifically based approach to social problem solving.

What would be the one thing you would change in our community if you had the power to do so? I would eliminate prejudice, discrimination, and social and economic oppression.

The primary purpose of this book is to help you, the reader, to develop a better understanding of social work as a profession. While we've certainly tried to highlight the many exciting and intriguing areas of social work for the beginning social work professional, this presentation is based on reality and we've been as realistic as possible about the state of the profession as it enters its second century.

THE TIME TO DECIDE IS APPROACHING

From the outset, we've made some assumptions about you as the reader of this text and as a beginning social work professional. First, we believe you are reading this book because it's assigned for a class. We realize this isn't the evening, weekend, or vacation book of choice! Second, we think you are taking a social work course that's called "Introduction to Social Work," or something similar, because you're interested in learning more about the field. Actually, whatever the course title may be, the class you are taking is probably one of the first social work courses in a series of prospective majors. Third, we've assumed that while you or some of your classmates may have had some experience with social work professionals, for the most part you agreed when we said that most people do not really have a detailed understanding of the social work profession, including its mission, purpose, and function. Fourth, some of you are seriously exploring social work as a possible career and have registered for this course with that purpose in mind. For others of you, however, this may have been the course that was available at the time or you may have heard that the instructor was really interesting.

Trying to address all of the needs implicit in these assumptions was sometimes daunting, but it was an effort we enjoyed making. It feels good to have put together a text that meets the social work accreditation standards, helps people to gain a clear understanding of the social work profession, supports the faculty member's direction in a course, and helps the individual student to make a career decision: is social work for me?

Making a career decision is not easy, nor should it be. We'll be very forthright with our advice to you: Don't make yourself miserable with worry. What you decide today doesn't obligate you for the rest of your life, or even through next week! You can change your mind at any time about your career goals. It's not unusual for college students to change majors a number of times before completing their baccalaureate studies.

To be fair, it's true that family, friends, and college teachers and counselors put unnecessary pressure on today's students. Why is it so important to select a major by the end of your sophomore year? When you say that you're going to college, why is the first question you hear "What's your major?"

The reasons vary. Family and friends are probably excited that you're pursuing a college education, and naturally they're interested in what courses you plan to take and what career path you'll follow. Those of us who teach in higher education see the potential major as a means to sustain the field. Academic programs are under constant pressure, in many institutions intense pressure, to maintain student enrollments. Declining student enrollments jeopardize continuation of a major. Look at what happened to sociology at a number of colleges in the 1980s: it was discontinued as a major, nontenured faculty were released from their jobs, and tenured faculty members were moved to other departments.

While there is pressure on faculty and programs to recruit students for academic survival, there is also a counterpressure to have students graduate within a specified period of time. In Florida, a public university is penalized if a student takes more than a certain number of credit hours toward graduation. If a student exceeds this number, his tuition costs are increased while the university's funding is reduced!

Only a few years ago, the preference was for a student to get a liberal arts education as an undergraduate. To be considered educated a person must have studied a variety of subjects in the arts, sciences, and humanities in an effort to develop a broad, worldly view of people and their settings. The idea was that a liberal thinker, in the literal rather than the political sense, is better suited to participate in society. Some occupations were satisfied with this broad-based education. People could get good jobs without having majored in a specific area. Training for a specific position or workplace happened on the job. People who chose to continue their studies in a specialized field did so in graduate programs.

By contrast, today undergraduate students, some even at the time of application, are asked to declare their majors. Is it fair to ask someone who is just beginning her college education to select a career? Well, we could argue the merits and drawbacks of this practice till we're all blue in the face. The fact is that you must select a major or be cast into the land of the general major (different colleges have different terms for this group; it usually captures all students who haven't chosen a career path).

Most readers of this text have probably made some decisions about social work by this point. We won't take sole credit for influencing the decision-making process. In your course, class discussions, guest speakers, and other instructional strategies, in addition to this text, have helped you to make your decision, or at least a partial decision.

The Non–Social Work Major

We want to offer a few words to those of you who have decided that social work is not for you. First, we're glad you've made a decision that is right for you at this time. Don't be disappointed that social work is not your profession of choice as you may have thought originally. By looking at yourself in the light of information gleaned from this course, you are taking a very important step in your life. And you can always revisit your decision. In career choices the door never closes for good: you can always reconsider your options.

We hoped you have a better understanding and appreciation of social work and the issues that drive our profession. While you feel social work is not your

This woman has suffered serious physical illness and can no longer live at home. Her care needs were more than the staff at a nursing home could provide and she was moved to a hospital. Her grandniece and other family members visit her in the hospital.

career choice, you can nevertheless help to strengthen the social welfare system. You are better informed about a number of social issues and a number of myths that shroud public policy. When you hear others attack social welfare, listen carefully to what is being said and respond with accurate information. You can be part of the myth-busting squad that dispels misinformation. Let people know the facts about poverty, child welfare, mental health, and the many other areas discussed in the text. Stay informed about the issues: read the daily newspapers and visit social welfare web sites for updated information. Information and facts are among the most powerful tools you can have at your disposal. You can also be invaluable as a social service volunteer. The vast majority of social agencies need people of one kind or another. All it takes is one phone call to a specific agency asking if it needs help. Or if you just want to volunteer a few hours a week and the agency setting doesn't matter, call your local volunteer service agency. They will place you in the most needy agency at which your skills and expertise can make a contribution.

The Social Work Major

Well, you are about to enter a very structured educational experience. Remember what we learned about CSWE accreditation demands in chapter 2? (If not, you may want to reread that chapter, especially before your final examination!) Your academic schedule is pretty much set for the remainder of the program. Courses are sequenced by semester or quarter. You can look at your program's student handbook or ask the course instructor or your academic advisor to review the academic program.

A few features of your program are set in granite, with little room for modification or negotiation. We also want to raise some considerations you need to keep in mind.

1. The program will take two years of full-time study. You will not be able to graduate in one year. We have found over the years that some students spend an inordinate amount of time challenging and trying to change a structured educational program. They often become angry with the faculty and program, calling them inflexible. Before signing on the dotted line as a social work major be sure to check the curriculum model and its specific requirements, including length of time to complete the program. Can you meet these structural requirements? If not, meet with a social work advisor and determine whether your needs can be accommodated. Don't select the major without first checking all possible scenarios. Plan your schedule carefully and make any necessary arrangements, such as childcare or employment, in order that you can complete all the program requirements (see item 3 below on field placement). Check whether your program has a part-time option in which you can take longer to complete your course of study.

2. Academic credit will not be given for any life experiences, according to CSWE accreditation standards. There are no ifs, ands, or buts on this point. Academic credit is awarded for successful completion of specific college courses. It doesn't matter if you were in the Peace Corps for two years or worked in an agency for five years—no credit can be awarded for these activities.

3. You will have a field placement, which is strategically scheduled in your academic program to allow demonstration of specific knowledge and skills learned in the classroom. You will not be able to take the field course any sooner in the program. Nor can your field course be waived in recognition of previous work experience. Remember, the CSWE life credit requirement applies to all facets of the educational program, including field placement. Check with the field coordinator to discuss any worries you may have; if you aren't able to work in any agency or require some special situation, it is best to let the field coordinator know this as early as possible in order to find a site that meets your needs. You'll need to be flexible in field placement selection. A program will work with you to find the best site to meet your academic needs, but the final field assignment rests with the social work program.

We've heard students say that their placement *must* be in a certain agency, in order to get a job. While programs are concerned about employment, the primary issue in field assignment is your learning—employment comes later.

Some programs may have limited resources to meet all or even some of your field placement needs. Some students haven't received BSW degrees simply because they did not complete field placements because the placements were not during the evening when the students were able to work.

4. Remember: Your peers in social work courses are in the same place you are. Although everyone's circumstances are different—some are older or younger, some have agency experience while others have none—these differences really have minimal importance: all of you are evolving as you begin the process of becoming a professional social worker. No one is better off than anyone else as a result of life experiences. Don't be intimidated by what others say or do or how they come across in class.

5. The purpose of your educational program is to prepare you for entry-level generalist social work practice. It is not to prepare you for a specialization. Nor is it the program's purpose to get you into a graduate program. Your course instructor and academic advisor care primarily about your development as a beginning social worker.

6. Don't approach an instructor and say that you need an A in the course in order to get into graduate school. There's a saying in Texas that fits this type of situation: That dog won't hunt! You certainly have the right to talk with a faculty member about a grade and how it was reached, but it doesn't do any good to be argumentative. The instructor's responsibility is to assess your answers and summarize the quality of your responses with a grade. Grading is not easy—to say the least—and many teachers struggle to ensure that their grades are fair and consistent. Rather than arguing your position, be a social worker: clarify the situation and seek a remedy if you feel one is needed. Can you redo the assignment? Is there extra credit work you can do for the course? And so on. If you feel that your grade is incorrect, check out the student grievance policy in the program. But, we emphasize, use this only as a last resort.

Remember that your faculty members were once students and, like you, at one time or another felt that an instructor had graded them unfairly. We also know that the vast majority of the time, the instructor's assessment is correct; it's just that as students we don't like to get negative information. The key is to look at what the assessment is saying: What didn't you do on the assignment? What could you have done to get your point across more clearly?

Remember, your goal should be the same as your faculty's goal for you: to develop competence and expertise in entry-level generalist social work practice. Your energy should be directed toward developing critical knowledge and skills necessary for effective practice.

Two questions, then, to ask around grades: 1) How will my challenging a grade for a paper, test, or final exam make me a better social work practitioner? 2) Is there an error in the grading that I can demonstrate to the course instructor that justifies the assignment of another grade?

THE FUTURE AND YOU

We are now in a new century and the second hundred years of social work practice. As an up-and-coming social worker, the foundation for the twenty-first century will be laid by your efforts. What you do and say will shape the profession for years to come.

As we bring the text to a close, we want to spend our remaining time looking at two questions. First, knowing what you do about social work, what do you want the profession to look like in the years to come? And second, what changes do you foresee in the social welfare system?

Social Work as a Profession: Future Considerations

You've seen how social work evolved from volunteer effort geared toward the poor to a multifaceted profession working with a variety of client groups. Education was initially limited to on-the-job training, with no oversight of work other than the agency's internal safeguards. Men were the supervisors while women were the caseworkers. Today, education is formal, for some too rigid, and set within colleges and universities. There is public regulation in every state for some, but not all, levels of social work practice. And women, throughout the first hundred years of the profession, made critical contributions to the theory, practice, and politics that make social work what it is today. In the twenty-first century, we find women holding critical positions, leading the profession in academic, professional associations, and in social welfare agencies.

The profession's first century required commitment, passion, and vision in order to achieve its current stature. While we've come a long way, as the poet Robert Frost wrote, we have miles to go before we sleep.

So what are some areas the profession should move into more aggressively? Let's put forth a few ideas to consider:

1. Social work in the twenty-first century is in a pivotal position to create positive social change. Social workers hold elective office at the local, state, and national levels. But we need more of our colleagues to run for office. Who better to write laws about families, children, the poor, the sick, and those at risk, but social workers? Why should lawyers hold a monopoly on political office? Let our opponents call us "bleeding heart liberals." If being a bleeding heart means that we stand for health care for all people, shelter for the homeless, food for the hungry, and education for all children, then call us bleeding hearts. Wouldn't you love to run against an opponent who claims to oppose care of sick children, to want homeless seniors to live unprotected on the streets, to want people, in particular children, to starve, and to oppose mak-

ing all of our children the best educated in the world? In other words, the profession must use its assets. Our assets are people skills and knowledge.

2. The profession must somehow work together and present a unified front. We need special interest groups and membership associations in order to focus on specialized practice matters. But we are fast approaching, if we haven't already reached, a crossroads where practice membership associations are in conflict with each other and with the overall interests of the profession. A case in point is public regulation of social work practice. NASW is a staunch advocate of regulation for BSW and MSW levels of practice. The national and state clinical social work membership groups oppose licensing of practice other than clinical practice. Why? Because clinical practitioners fear losing fee-paying clients. They will deny this and point to other factors, but they oppose licensing that will protect all members of the public, not just those who are insured.

How do we bridge the gulf between these two groups? NASW, nationally and in the states, is an important power than can help clinical social worker membership societies achieve their goals. Tension between members of these two groups is not healthy for the profession or, more important, for the public and the clients we serve. Social work membership groups must find common ground if we are to become even more effective in our public efforts.

3. We must seek out more BSWs to join NASW. There are too few BSW members in the association. As a result, BSW practice interests are not fully represented at all levels of the association. Annual membership dues certainly are expensive—in particular, for lower paid BSWs—and NASW has taken this into account in the dues structure. But efforts to attract BSWs must go far beyond lower dues. MSWs must make BSWs feel like accepted and important members of the profession. Elitism and professional ethnocentrism will only weaken our efforts.

Social work programs can play a critical role by involving BSW students in NASW. First, programs can promote membership. Student dues are relatively inexpensive and are far outweighed by the association's benefits. Second, social work programs, together with state chapters and local units, can look at developing student units that hold meetings on campus. Third, social work programs can work with local NASW units to hold meetings on campus—many students are place bound and have no way to get to a meeting.

The key is for NASW and social work programs to be aggressive in recruiting students, then to value BSW students as future members, and finally to involve them in association activities.

4. In chapter 14, we spent time exploring the international social welfare arena. Social work is a worldwide profession that helps people, families, communities, and social systems to deal with issues that cut across national boundaries.

As practitioners in the twenty-first century, your work, more than at any other time in the world's history, will influence and be influenced by the international community. The phrase "think globally, act locally" probably best captures the direction we must go. Yet social workers, for the most part, have little exposure to international social welfare. International course content is sparse in both undergraduate and graduate programs. There are exceptions, of course; some schools sponsor study-abroad programs, offer educationally directed travel programs, or have a greater international emphasis. Yet most social work programs do little more than offer brief mentions as part of a course or courses.

Professional associations also work to promote international issues. Again through study tours and publications, we become more aware of the international community. But is this enough? We don't think so. We support the goal of global understanding and activism. Expanding our understanding will help us to be knowledgeable members of the world community. Our global learning and understanding of others will help us to better appreciate the strength and potential of seemingly different people while developing greater awareness of the struggles that will need to be engaged. Global activism builds on knowledge. Once we understand others we are in a better position to offer effective assistance and support.

There are many mechanisms we can implement to pursue the goal of global understanding and activism. Obviously, the expansion of BSW and MSW curriculum content would help us toward this goal. International content in each course and an additional specific international course would help enhance our knowledge base. We can also become more creative in our approach. Social work educational programs can sponsor annual activities that highlight one or two aspects of international social welfare. Professional associations, both at the national and state levels, can sponsor international activities each year. Hosting continuing education workshops, dedicating parts of association newsletters to international issues, and developing dedicated international handouts and brochures will help us to become more global.

The American Social Welfare System: The Future

What a fascinating history we have in social welfare! The overview in chapter 2 was just that, an overview. Even from that brief foray, we could see emerge the beliefs that underpin the current U.S. social welfare system.

First, the poor and people in need are "different" from the rest of us. Some say the poor are morally inferior and lazy; others might say the poor are poorly educated and lack the motivation to change. Second, welfare services are best organized by nongovernmental entities. Americans have always been reluctant to support federal involvement in the social welfare system. Social agencies, churches, volunteer associations, and informal networks are more acceptable vehicles for social welfare. Third, social welfare is not an entitlement but rather a temporary support given only to the most worthy. Over time, women, infants, children, the aged, and people with disabilities have fallen into the category of the "worthy" poor.

Fourth, work is the primary way to achieve self-sufficiency. All anyone needs is a job, not even a good-paying job at first, because the early experience will lead to future, higher paying jobs.

Now, these views are not necessarily those of most social workers, but they do express the expectations of much of the American public. In chapter 2 we discussed the modern welfare system and in chapter 7 the 1990s welfare reform package. Both these discussions showed how well ingrained into the American welfare system these four beliefs are.

So, where does the American welfare system go? Is the current system working? Here are some proposed changes to the welfare system:

1. The welfare system must be just and treat all people with respect and dignity. How do we explain compassion for the less fortunate when we have a welfare program that only allows a maximum of five years of assistance in a lifetime? Some people, no matter what we do, just won't be able to care for themselves. Why do we penalize an unborn baby by denying it welfare benefits because the mother was already on assistance. What kind of life are we promising that child? A comprehensive welfare system embraces people and their strengths. We should move away from a punitive system to one based on hope.

2. American welfare carries an enormous stigma. Every day politicians, radio talk show hosts and callers, and newspaper columnists, among others, rail against the poor. With this constant barrage, it would be a wonder if welfare clients didn't hide from the general public. Being poor and receiving public assistance is not the fulfillment of a lifelong ambition. We should work to remove the stigma associated with public aid.

3. The goal of the welfare system should be to help all people with adequate benefits and supports. If the system works, then people who are capable of doing so will move to sustainable work. The purpose of the welfare system's benefits and supports is simple: help clients to meet their daily needs in order to focus their energies on becoming self-sufficient. The welfare system should concentrate on meeting basic needs: food, shelter, and protection. The level of these benefits must be sufficient. A second tier of services, which includes high-quality health care and childcare, supports adults in their efforts to work. A third tier of programs focuses on developing knowledge and skills necessary to become self-sufficient in a technological society. Transportation and education and training programs are the two principal components of this tier. Reliable transportation is needed to ensure that people can get to the training programs; not everyone has a car and not all cities and towns have public transportation. The fourth and final tier of the welfare system includes access to permanent, good-paying jobs that offer upward mobility and self-sufficiency. Once employed, the client is able to receive workplace benefits and no longer needs public welfare support.

4. A comprehensive welfare system is expensive. But if we care for the poor and less fortunate, the price tag should not matter. Funding decisions for pro-

grams are made in a political context. The decision to fund roads and highways at one level and after-school childcare at a much lower level is a statement about our beliefs. Funds are available to support a comprehensive welfare system, either by changing governmental spending patterns or by raising taxes. Throughout the text we have referred directly and indirectly to the influence of the political system on social welfare, and in chapter 13 we outlined the role that social workers can assume in politics. As we consider the role of politics in social welfare and questions related to funding, we must first answer two questions: What is the goal of our welfare system? What commitments are we willing to make to achieve that goal?

SOCIAL WORK PRACTICE

In the new environment of cost containment and manage care social workers must either accept this challenge for change or lose the opportunity to be players in this era of competition for the provision of outcome-based services. Social workers must be able to show that what they do is necessary and effective while maintaining their own ethical and moral standards for the helping relationship.

All social workers must take a PROACTIVE stance regardless of their practice area. This book is designed to serve as a practical guide for understanding and applying this philosophy in our social work practice environment. Simply stated, all social workers need to embrace the following imperatives at all levels of practice:

P PRESENT and POSITION themselves as competent professionals with POSITIVE attitudes in all service settings, whatever the type of practice.

R RECEIVE adequate training and continuing education in the current and future practice area of social work
RESEARCH time-limited treatment approaches that can provide alternatives for social workers struggling to provide high-quality services while cutting costs

O ORGANIZE individuals and communities to help themselves to access safe and affordable services
ORGANIZE other social workers to prepare for the changes that are occurring and develop strategies to continue to provide ethical, cost-effective service

A ADDRESS policies and issues that are relevant to providing ethical, effective, efficient service

C COLLABORATE with other helping professionals to address client concerns and needs utilizing an interdisciplinary team approach
COMPLEMENT orthodox practices by utilizing holistic practices and alternative strategies that can help clients achieve increased well-being

T TEACH others about the value and the importance of including social work services and techniques

TAKE TIME to help ourselves holistically by preventing professional burnout thus remaining productive and receptive and serving as good role models for clients and other professionals

I   INVESTIGATE and apply INNOVATIVE approaches to client care problems and issues

INVOLVE all social workers in the change process that needs to occur in traditional social work

V   VISUALIZE and work toward positive outcomes for all clients and potential clients

VALUE the roles of all other helping professionals and support them as they face similar challenges and changes

E   EXPLORE supplemental therapies and strategies that clients can self-administer at little or no cost to preserve and enhance well-being

EMPOWER clients and ourselves by stressing the importance of EDUCATION for self-betterment as well as individual and societal change (adapted from Dziegielewski, 1998)

We will need to face the many changes that are in store for helping professionals, and we need to remember that in this area of budget cutting and cost containment we can be viable players. The NASW Code of Ethics directs us to charge reasonable fees and base our charges on ability to pay. This means that the fees social work professionals charge are very competitive with those of psychiatrists, psychologists, family therapists, psychiatric nurses, and mental health counselors, who provide similar services. This fact could entice managed care agencies to contract with social workers instead of other professionals to provide services that have traditionally fallen in the domain of social work practice. In this era of managed care, no aspect of taking a proactive stance can be underestimated.

SPECIAL TOPIC: REGULATION OF PROFESSIONAL SOCIAL WORK PRACTICE

The government regulates all professions throughout the United States. Regulation is important to ensure that the public is protected from harm caused by unqualified persons. Regulation includes licensing, registration, and certification and confers credentials recognized by the public (Biggerstaff, 1995, p. 1617). According to Biggerstaff, a credential is evidence that the practitioner meets minimum standards for providing specific services to the public.

Why do we regulate occupations? What does credentialing do for us in the long run? First, a regulated occupation's activities are such that the average citizen may be harmed physically, emotionally, or financially if he is exposed to the practice of an unqualified person. Second, credentialing suggests that a specific educational background is needed to make a person qualified to carry out the tasks in a regulated occupation. Third, the public is assured that all regulated persons meet minimum standards of competence as set forth by the state. Finally, the public is assured that mechanisms are available for the pursuit of grievances against regulated workers.

Activity...Contact your state's social work licensing board or regulatory body and ask for information about the regulation of social work practice. Are all levels of social work practice licensed? Does the board seem to reflect the social work profession's broad range of work, or is its membership restricted to one or two types of practice? Attend a licensing board meeting (they are open to the public), and determine how the board protects the public interest. Finally, how does the local social work community perceive licensing? (Check this out at a local NASW unit meeting.)

Think for a moment about the types of occupations that are regulated by the government. Decisions to regulate professions are left to state governments, so you'll find that some occupations are licensed in one state but not in another. Even when a profession is regulated by more than one state, the criteria that must be met for certification may differ. Types of educational degrees and years of experience required and the use of exams to test competence vary by state and occupation.

The list of occupations that states regulate seems endless. The state of Florida, for example, regulated 189 different occupations in 1998! Box 1 lists less than a quarter of the occupations regulated by the Florida state government. You'll note that the state oversees a wide array of occupations that can affect people's lives for good or bad.

The profession of social work is regulated in all fifty states. By that we mean that some form of social work practice is licensed or certified by each state government. For the most part, regulation does not have two levels that mirror the two levels of social work practice, the BSW (generalist practice) and the MSW (specialist practice). For example, some states license both BSW and MSW practitioners together, while other states limit licensing to MSW practitioners who specialize in clinical social work. Most, but not all, states require passage of a written examination; and most, but not all, states require ongoing continuing education after being licensed.

Box 1: Partial List of Occupations Regulated by the State of Florida, 1998

Architect	Interior designer	Barber
Public Accountant	Pool contractor	Solar contractor
Building Contractor	Chiropractor	Nail specialist
Cosmetologist	Hair braiders	Dental hygienist
Dentist	Electrical contractor	Alarm system contractor
Embalmer	Talent agency	Physician
Optometrist	Podiatrist	Veterinarian
Nurse	Auctioneer	Athletic trainer
Respiratory therapist	Midwife	Nutrition counselor
Surveyor and mapper	Audiologist	School psychologist
Mental health counselor	Asbestos contractor	Physical therapist
Occupational therapist	Liquor salesperson	Building inspector

Current and Future Perspectives on Licensing and Credentialing

We must first recognize that social workers cannot be forced to subscribe to voluntary credentialing. In other words, a social worker does not have to join NASW to be held accountable to the association's Code of Ethics or thereby qualify for credentialing in the field. Credentialing needs to take place in the public domain, which through law would require that all social workers meet minimum educational and practice standards and be held accountable for their work. Then, and only then, will the public have an opportunity to be protected from incompetent and unethical practitioners. The differences that currently exist in licensure and certification requirements among the different states appears to mirror the ongoing ambivalence that continues to plague social work licensure and certification in the social work profession. Two inaccurate yet strong beliefs remain prominent and these beliefs continue to influence the social work profession. First, is the erroneous belief that anyone can do social work and that the work doesn't require a professional education or specialized training. Second, is the misconception that the tasks and functions that most social workers perform cannot place the public at-risk so therefore they can indeed be performed by non-social work professionals. As a profession, it is important to note that we are not above our own internal disagreements and conflicts. Yet, we must rise above them and continue to actively debate and struggle with answering such questions as "should we license all levels of social work practice?" For now, we certainly do not have professional consensus on that question and there are some social workers, particularly some MSW practitioners, that do not agree. Further, there are some MSWs and special interest organizations that believe that licensing should be restricted to only certain social work activities, such as the practice of clinical social work. Given that NASW continues to limit its credentialing and certification process to MSWs and no longer sponsors a voluntary BSW form of certification, this inadvertently supports the continued debate between practice levels within the profession.

The research shows that different types of social work practice are regulated. Some states regulate only clinical practice while other states do not specify a practice methodology but license based on the degree. Even so, indications are that more and more states are moving toward multi-level licensure.

Just as problematic is the fact that the practice of social work is so diverse that it has no specific domain. For the most part, there is no national label or title for our work. Given that states establish their own licensing laws, each state has also developed its own titles for social work practitioners. Given that there are 39 different titles nationwide for social workers, it is no wonder that people are confused about the profession!

There is a clear-cut need to adopt a national model licensing law. The American Association of State Social Work Boards proposes one. Prior to the AASSW 1997 proposal, NASW, in 1973, also put forth a model law (NASW, 1973). A model law adopted by all states will accomplish a number of important tasks and benefit the public and the profession alike.

1. All states will regulate the same types of social work practice.
2. All states will maintain similar education and continuing education standards.
3. All states will use similar titles for professionals.
4. There will be less confusion among the public concerning the function and activities of social workers.
5. All social workers will be held accountable for their activities.
6. The public, in particular the poor and clients of public social services, will be assured that their social workers meet minimal educational and practice competencies.
7. Mechanisms will be in place for clients to pursue incompetent and unethical social work practice.

Overall, regulation is a positive step for ensuring quality service provision for the public and the profession alike. It is not surprising that it remains difficult to achieve and maintain order to protect the public. Public regulation should be comprehensive and include all levels of social work practice. Finally, state licensing should be augmented and supported by membership associations' internal voluntary credentialing programs. Together, voluntary association credentialing and state licensing can put forth a strong shield of protection for the public.

The regulation of social work practice is subject to a number of complications. First, it is tied to the intricacies of the political process. As with any law passed by a state legislature, it reflects political interests. What seems to be a logical, straightforward piece of legislation may end up being defeated for any number of reasons. Some social workers are against formal licensure for the profession, but if we license and regulate hair braiders and surveyors (as listed in box 1), doesn't it make sense also to regulate a profession that is concerned with the emotional and psychological well-being of people?

Second, licensing requires social work professionals to overcome their own biases and act in the best interests of the profession. Unfortunately, this is easier said than done. Many social work special interest groups are most concerned with protecting their own members. Once a group feels its interests are enhanced and not compromised, it will support the legislation. You can imagine what happens to a licensing bill that must satisfy any number of social work interest groups, and what can result when ten or more interest groups are all actively lobbying at any given time.

Third, once the profession has pieced together a compromise proposal, it must then meet the demands of other human service professions and organizations. Typically, these groups feel that their activities will be affected by the social work licensing act. As a result, these groups work to ensure that the final legislation will not interfere with their day-to-day activities or finances.

FINAL THOUGHTS

You should be writing this chapter. As future social workers and members of the global community, you will ultimately be responsible for the social welfare system of the twenty-first century. The types of programs, levels of assistance, and the clients eligible for benefits will all be issues that you will address.

The social work profession will always be part of our community as long as complex human social problems remain. As social workers, our challenge is to remain relevant to our nation's goals and our clients' needs. We can do this by vigorously pursuing competence in practice, by discovering and validating innovative interventions, and by ensuring that our educational and training programs continue to excel.

As you tackle social welfare issues be passionate in your convictions, ethical in your actions, knowledgeable about your information, and, above all, committed to the view that social justice is due to all people. Our community will be a better place because of people like you.

References

Biggerstaff, M. (1995). Licensing, regulation, and certification. In R. L. Edwards et al. (Eds.), *Encyclopedia of social work* (19th ed., pp. 1616–1624). Washington, DC: NASW Press.

Bloom, M. (1990). *The drama of social work*. Itasca, IL: Peacock.

Dziegielewski, S. F. (1998). *The changing face of health care social work: Professional practice in the era of managed care*. New York: Springer.

Lubove, C. (1965). *The professional altruist.* Cambridge, MA: Harvard University Press.

Morales, A., & Sheafor, B. (1997). *Social work: A profession of many faces* (8th ed.). Boston: Allyn and Bacon.

NASW (1973). *Legal regulation of social work practice.* Washington, DC: Author.

Richan, W., & Mendelsohn, A. R. (1973). *Social work, the unloved profession.* New York: Franklin Watts.

Specht, H., & Courtney, M. (1994). *Unfaithful angels.* New York: Free Press.

Glossary

absolute poverty   qualitative measure of poverty that compares a person's situation with a numerical standard that usually reflects bare subsistence; cf. *relative poverty*.

abuse   improper behavior that can result in physical, psychological, or financial harm to an individual, family, group, or community. In social work the term is most often related to acts against children, the elderly, the mentally impaired, or spouses or used in relation to drug or other substance abuse.

accreditation   professional recognition that a social work program meets explicit standards; voted on by the CSWE Commission on Accreditation after it reviews the program's self-study documents, the site visitors' written report, and the program's written response to the site visit.

advocacy   professional activities aimed at educating, informing, or defending and representing the needs and wants of clients through direct intervention or empowerment.

agency   organization that provides social services and is typically staffed by social service professionals, including social workers. Public, private, and not-for-profit agencies provide an array of services, usually to a target population. Policy is set by a board of directors and is implemented by administrators.

agency-based   occurring in an agency. Agency-based practice can include a few specific practice methodologies or can span the continuum of social work practice, depending on the agency's size, mission, and purpose.

Aid to Families with Dependent Children (AFDC)   a means-tested program that provided financial aid to children in need due to parental disability, absence, or death. It was administered nationally through the Administration for Children and Families division of the U.S. Department of Health and Human Services; state and county departments of public welfare provided local administration. AFDC ended in 1996 with the creation of Temporary Assistance for Needy Families.

almshouse (also know as poorhouse)   place of refuge for the poor, medically ill, and mentally ill of all ages; considered the forerunner of the hospital.

assessment   process of determining the nature, cause, progression, and prognosis of a problem and identifying the personalities and situations involved; process of reasoning from facts to tentative conclusions about their meaning.

at-risk populations (also known as vulnerable populations)   groups with increased exposure to potential harm due to specific characteristics. Examples are infants born to drug-using mothers, who are at risk for birth defects; minorities, who are at risk for oppression; and poor children, who are at risk for malnutrition.

biopsychosocial approach approach to social work practice, especially in health care and mental health, that assesses and places appropriate emphasis on the biological, psychological, and social or environmental aspects of the client's situation.

block grant lump sum of funds given to a state by the federal government. The state has authority over expenditure of block grants and may supplement them with state funds.

BSW (baccalaureate in social work) undergraduate degree in social work from a CSWE-accredited program; the entry-level social work qualification. BSSW and BA or BS in social work are equivalent degrees.

candidacy preaccreditation status for a social work program, which generally lasts two years; signifies that an educational program meets general criteria to conduct a self-study for accreditation.

charity assistance aid given to the poor in the 1600s; viewed as a mechanism that reinforced dependent lifestyles.

charity organization society (COS) privately or philanthropically funded agency that delivered social services to the needy in the mid- to late nineteenth century; considered the forerunner of the nonprofit social service agency.

child welfare series of human service and social welfare programs designed specifically to promote the protection, care, and health development of children; found at the national, state, and local levels.

client individual, couple, family, group, or community that is the focus of intervention.

Commission on Accreditation CSWE committee of twenty-five social work educators and practitioners who oversee the accreditation process. The commission establishes educational standards and reviews programs to ensure that they meet the standards.

continuing education training acquired after the completion of a degree program. NASW and state licensure boards require specified hours of continuing education in order to maintain a license or certification.

Council on Social Work Education (CSWE) sole national accreditation board for schools of social work; founded in 1952 from the merger of the American Association of Schools of Social Work (founded 1919) and the National Association of Schools of Social Administration (founded 1942).

Curriculum Policy Statement (CPS) written document that outlines the purpose and framework of social work education programs. The CSWE Commission on Accreditation is responsible for oversight of the CPS.

diagnosis process of identifying a problem—social, mental, or medical—and its underlying causes and formulating a solution.

disadvantaged term used to describe individuals, groups, communities, and the like, that are unable to access the resources and services needed to maintain a minimal standard of living.

discharge planning service provided by health care social workers to assist clients in, for example, securing placement and services to support a timely transition from a health care facility to home or to another less restrictive environment.

domestic violence violent acts toward another person perpetrated in a domestic situation.

DSM-IV (*Diagnostic and Statistical Manual*, 4th edition)   manual that presents a classification system designed to assist in reaching formal diagnoses. It uses five "axes": Axis I, the first level of coding, records such categories as major clinical syndromes, pervasive developmental disorders, learning disorders, motor skills disorders, communication disorders, and other disorders that may be the focus of clinical treatment. Axis II records personality disorders and mental retardation. Axis III records general medical conditions that can affect mental health. Axis IV records psychosocial and environmental problems/stressors. Axis V records level of functioning.

DSW (doctor of social welfare or social work)   highest social work degree; typically requires two years of full-time post-master's course work, passage of comprehensive examinations, and successful completion of a dissertation.

empirically based social work practice   type of intervention in which the professional social worker uses research as a practice and problem-solving tool. Data are collected systematically, and problems and outcomes are stated in measurable terms.

ethics   system of moral principles used in decision making to discern right from wrong or to choose between two or more seemingly equal alternatives.

field placement   work in an agency during the BSW or MSW educational experience, supervised by a social worker. Students are trained and monitored by the agency and the educational institution jointly.

food stamp program   program that distributes to people in need "stamps" that can be used to purchase basic food items; implemented in 1964 and administered by the U.S. Department of Agriculture until 1996; now administered by states under the Personal Responsibility and Work Opportunity Reconciliation Act of 1996.

friendly visitor   volunteer from a charity organization society who visited poor families to offer aid and to serve a role model.

generalist practice   practice underpinned by knowledge and skills across a broad spectrum and by comprehensive assessment of problems and their solutions; includes coordination of activities of specialists.

Head Start   program intended to help preschool children of disadvantaged families to overcome or offset problems related to social deprivation; established in 1965 and administered by Child Youth and Families within the U.S. Department of Health and Human Services.

hospital social worker   social worker who practices in hospitals and health care facilities; focuses on assessments, discharge planning, preventive services, interdisciplinary coordination, and individual and family counseling.

indoor relief   assistance provided during colonial times to the "unworthy" poor in poorhouses.

in kind   benefit in the form of food, clothing, education, and so forth, in place of, or in addition to, cash.

institutional social welfare   social programs available to all as a part of well-being in the modern state; cf. *residual social welfare.*

interdisciplinary team   variety of health care professionals brought together to provide a client with effective, better coordinated, and improved quality of services.

International Federation of Social Workers (IFSW)   international association of social workers comprising members through their national organizations; founded in 1928 in Paris; promotes social work, establishes standards, and provides a forum for exchange among associations throughout the world.

intervention   treatment, services, advocacy, mediation, or any other practice action, performed for or with clients, that is intended to ameliorate problems.

label   clinical diagnosis of a client that stays with the client indefinitely, possibly to the client's detriment.

macrosystem   community, administrative, and environmental forces that affect the human condition. Political action, community organizing, and administration of large public welfare agencies are examples of macropractice.

Meals on Wheels   delivery of meals to the homes of people unable to meet their own nutritional needs, usually due to physical or mental impairment. Service is usually provided by community agencies, such as senior citizen councils, local human service departments, and private agencies.

Medicaid   program established in 1965 that funds hospital and other medical services to people who meet means tests; administered by the federal Health Care Financing Administration.

Medicare   national health insurance program established in 1965. Eligibility is universal, with attainment of age 65 the criterion for most people; however, there are allied programs for the disabled among others. Medicare is funded through employee and employer contributions and administered by the Social Security Administration and the Health Care Financing Administration.

mezzosystem   system that connects micro- and macrosystems.

microsystem   individual, family, or small group. Direct intervention and casework are examples of micropractice.

MSW (master of social work)   degree requiring approximately sixty hours of postbaccalaureate education, including 900 hours of field placement, in a CSWE-accredited program. MSSW and MA or MS in social work are equivalent degrees.

multidisciplinary team   mix of health and social welfare professionals, with each discipline working, for the most part, on an independent or referral basis.

National Association of Social Workers (NASW)   world's largest social work membership association with approximately 160,000 members in 1999; established in 1955 through the merger of five special interest organizations; chapters exist in all fifty states and the District of Columbia, New York City, Puerto Rico, and the Virgin Islands, in addition to an international chapter.

New Deal   set of social welfare programs and legislation implemented during President Franklin D. Roosevelt's administration in response to the Great Depression. Examples include the Economic Security Act of 1935, Works Progress Administration, and Federal Emergency Relief Act.

outdoor relief   minimal assistance provided during the colonial period to the "worthy" poor in their own homes.

overseer of the poor   individual responsible during colonial times for identifying the poor, assessing their needs, and coordinating a community reponse by levying and collecting taxes; considered a colonial version of a social worker.

parens patriae   principle under which children can become wards of the state. The basic legal tool for carving out children's rights, this principle has allowed children's advocates to argue that children should be viewed differently from adults. It has been cited to support the creation of a range of juvenile services.

Person-in-Environment Classification System (PIE)   systematic approach to classifying social functioning. It employs four levels to aid in the systematic collection of data about clients and in planning interventions. Level I is social functioning problems. Level II is environmental problems. Level III is mental disorders—DSM-IV Axes I and II. Level IV is physical health problems.

person-in-situation (also called person-in-environment)   casework concept that focuses on the interrelation between problem, situation, and the interaction between them.

Ph.D. (doctorate in philosophy)   highest social work degree, emphasizing research, knowledge expansion, and advanced clinical practice; similar, often identical to, DSW. See *DSW* for requirements.

policy   plan that an agency, organization, or governmental institution follows as a framework; includes formal written policies and unwritten (informal) policies.

political lens   political context—often candidates for public office and their campaigns—that influences how society defines a term, for example, "family."

poor laws   codified in 1601; redefined welfare as no longer a private affair but rather a public governmental responsibility.

poverty   general term used to describe a state of deprivation. See *absolute poverty* and *relative poverty.*

poverty threshold   level of income below which a person is living in poverty. This level is based on the cost of securing the basic necessities of living.

psychosocial history   systematic compilation of information about a client; encompasses family, health, education, spirituality, legal position, interpersonal relations, social supports, economic status, environment, sexual orientation, and culture.

reaffirmation   confirmation of CSWE accreditation, for which an accredited program must undergo the self-study and review process every seven years.

relative poverty   subjective measure of poverty that compares a person's situation with a normative standard; cf. *absolute poverty.*

residual social welfare   social programs activated only when normal structures of family and market are not sufficient; cf. *institutional social welfare.*

sanction   1) formal or informal authorization to perform services; 2) penalty imposed for noncompliance with policies and procedures. NASW sanctions members who have violated the Code of Ethics with membership suspension or removal of certification.

selective eligibility (also called means-tested eligibility)   eligibility based on demonstrating need or inability to provide for one's needs; cf. *universal eligibility.*

site visit visit to a social work educational program by a site team composed of social work educators and, for graduate programs, an MSW practitioner. The site team makes a written report to the CSWE Commission on Accreditation that is considered during the commission's deliberations on the program's accreditation.

social welfare 1) society's specific system of programs to help people to meet basic health, economic, and social needs; 2) general state of well-being in society.

specialist practice practice focused in approach and knowledge on a specific problem or goal or underpinned by highly developed expertise in specific activities.

stigma negative connotation attached to individuals, or groups of individuals, based on characteristics that may include economic status, health, appearance, education, sexual orientation, and mental health.

Temporary Assistance for Needy Families (TANF) program established in 1996 to replace AFDC; subject to strict eligibility requirements, which mandate employment, and to a lifetime limit on benefits of five years; funded through federal block grants to states, which administer the program.

universal eligibility availability to all people regardless of income or social support; cf. *selective eligibility.*

unworthy poor see *worthy poor.*

Violence Against Women Act (VAWA) passed in 1994; a comprehensive federal response to the problems of domestic violence that promotes preventive programs and victim's services.

worthy poor category of people "deserving" of public aid introduced by the 1601 poor laws; included the ill, the disabled, orphans, the elderly—people viewed as having no control over their life circumstances—as well as people who were involuntarily unemployed. The unworthy poor consisted of the vagrant or able-bodied who, while able to work, did not seek employment.

Appendix A

National Association of Social Workers, Code of Ethics

Approved by the 1996 NASW Delegate Assembly and revised by the 1999 NASW Delegate Assembly.

Preamble

The primary mission of the social work profession is to enhance human well-being and help meet the basic human needs of all people, with particular attention to the needs and empowerment of people who are vulnerable, oppressed, and living in poverty. A historic and defining feature of social work is the profession's focus on individual well-being in a social context and the well-being of society. Fundamental to social work is attention to the environmental forces that create, contribute to, and address problems in living.

Social workers promote social justice and social change with and on behalf of clients. "Clients" is used inclusively to refer to individuals, families, groups, organizations, and communities. Social workers are sensitive to cultural and ethnic diversity and strive to end discrimination, oppression, poverty, and other forms of social injustice. These activities may be in the form of direct practice, community organizing, supervision, consultation, administration, advocacy, social and political action, policy development and implementation, education, and research and evaluation. Social workers seek to enhance the capacity of people to address their own needs. Social workers also seek to promote the responsiveness of organizations, communities, and other social institutions to individuals' needs and social problems.

The mission of the social work profession is rooted in a set of core values. These core values, embraced by social workers throughout the profession's history, are the foundation of social work's unique purpose and perspective:

–service
–social justice
–dignity and worth of the person
–importance of human relationships
–integrity
–competence.

This constellation of core values reflects what is unique to the social work profession. Core values, and the principles that flow from them, must be balanced within the context and complexity of the human experience.

PURPOSE OF THE NASW CODE OF ETHICS

Professional ethics are at the core of social work. The profession has an obligation to articulate its basic values, ethical principles, and ethical standards. The NASW Code of Ethics sets forth these values, principles, and standards to guide social workers' conduct. The Code is relevant to all social workers and social work students, regardless of their professional functions, the settings in which they work, or the populations they serve.

The NASW Code of Ethics serves six purposes:

1. The Code identifies core values on which social work's mission is based.
2. The Code summarizes broad ethical principles that reflect the profession's core values and establishes a set of specific ethical standards that should be used to guide social work practice.
3. The Code is designed to help social workers identify relevant considerations when professional obligations conflict or ethical uncertainties arise.
4. The Code provides ethical standards to which the general public can hold the social work profession accountable.
5. The Code socializes practitioners new to the field to social work's mission, values, ethical principles, and ethical standards.
6. The Code articulates standards that the social work profession itself can use to assess whether social workers have engaged in unethical conduct. NASW has formal procedures to adjudicate ethics complaints filed against its members.[1] In subscribing to this Code, social workers are required to cooperate in its implementation, participate in NASW adjudication proceedings, and abide by any NASW disciplinary rulings or sanctions based on it.

The Code offers a set of values, principles, and standards to guide decision making and conduct when ethical issues arise. It does not provide a set of rules that prescribe how social workers should act in all situations. Specific applications of the Code must take into account the context in which it is being considered and the possibility of conflicts among the Code's values, principles, and standards. Ethical responsibilities flow from all human relationships, from the personal and familial to the social and professional.

Further, the NASW Code of Ethics does not specify which values, principles, and standards are most important and ought to outweigh others in instances when they conflict. Reasonable differences of opinion can and do exist among social workers with respect to the ways in which values, ethical principles, and ethical standards should be rank ordered when they conflict. Ethical decision making in a given situation must apply the informed judgment of the individual social worker and should also consider how the issues would be judged in a peer review process where the ethical standards of the profession would be applied.

Ethical decision making is a process. There are many instances in social work where simple answers are not available to resolve complex ethical issues. Social workers should take into consideration all the values, principles, and standards in this Code that are relevant to any situation in which ethical judgment is warranted. Social workers' decisions and actions should be consistent with the spirit as well as the letter of this Code.

In addition to this Code, there are many other sources of information about ethical thinking that may be useful. Social workers should consider ethical theory and principles generally, social work theory and research, laws, regulations, agency policies, and other relevant codes of ethics, recognizing that among codes of ethics social workers should consider the NASW Code of Ethics as their primary source. Social workers also should be aware of the impact on ethical decision making of their clients' and their own personal values and cultural and religious beliefs and practices. They should be aware of any conflicts between personal and professional values and deal with them

[1]For information on NASW adjudication procedures, see *NASW Procedures for the Adjudication of Grievances.*

responsibly. For additional guidance social workers should consult the relevant literature on professional ethics and ethical decision making and seek appropriate consultation when faced with ethical dilemmas. This may involve consultation with an agency-based or social work organization's ethics committee, a regulatory body, knowledgeable colleagues, supervisors, or legal counsel.

Instances may arise when social workers' ethical obligations conflict with agency policies or relevant laws or regulations. When such con-flicts occur, social workers must make a responsible effort to resolve the conflict in a manner that is consistent with the values, principles, and standards expressed in this Code. If a reasonable resolution of the conflict does not appear possible, social workers should seek proper consultation before making a decision.

The NASW Code of Ethics is to be used by NASW and by individuals, agencies, organizations, and bodies (such as licensing and regulatory boards, professional liability insurance providers, courts of law, agency boards of directors, government agencies, and other professional groups) that choose to adopt it or use it as a frame of reference. Violation of standards in this Code does not automatically imply legal liability or violation of the law. Such determination can only be made in the context of legal and judicial proceedings. Alleged violations of the Code would be subject to a peer review process. Such processes are generally separate from legal or administrative procedures and insulated from legal review or proceedings to allow the profession to counsel and discipline its own members.

A code of ethics cannot guarantee ethical behavior. Moreover, a code of ethics cannot resolve all ethical issues or disputes or capture the richness and complexity involved in striving to make responsible choices within a moral community. Rather, a code of ethics sets forth values, ethical principles, and ethical standards to which

professionals aspire and by which their actions can be judged. Social workers' ethical behavior should result from their personal commitment to engage in ethical practice. The NASW Code of Ethics reflects the commitment of all social workers to uphold the profession's values and to act ethically. Principles and standards must be applied by individuals of good char-acter who discern moral questions and, in good faith, seek to make reliable ethical judgments.

Ethical Principles

The following broad ethical principles are based on social work's core values of service, social justice, dignity and worth of the person, importance of human relationships, integrity, and competence. These principles set forth ideals to which all social workers should aspire.

Value: Service

Ethical Principle: Social workers' primary goal is to help people in need and to address social problems.

Social workers elevate service to others above self-interest. Social workers draw on their knowledge, values, and skills to help people in need and to address social problems. Social workers are encouraged to volunteer some portion of their professional skills with no expectation of significant financial return (pro bono service).

Value: Social Justice

Ethical Principle: Social workers challenge social injustice.

Social workers pursue social change, particularly with and on behalf of vulnerable and oppressed individuals and groups of people. Social workers' social change efforts are focused primarily on issues of poverty, unemployment, discrimination, and other forms of social injustice. These activities seek to promote sensitivity to and knowledge about oppression and cultural and ethnic diversity. Social workers strive to ensure access to needed information, services, and resources; equality of opportunity; and meaningful participation in decision making for all people.

Value: Dignity and Worth of the Person

Ethical Principle: Social workers respect the inherent dignity and worth of the person.

Social workers treat each person in a caring and respectful fashion, mindful of individual differences and cultural and ethnic diversity. Social workers promote clients' socially responsible self-determination. Social workers seek to enhance clients' capacity and opportunity to change and to address their own needs. Social workers are cognizant of their dual responsibility to clients and to the broader society. They seek to resolve conflicts between clients' interests and the broader society's interests in a socially responsible manner consistent with the values, ethical principles, and ethical standards of the profession.

Value: Importance of Human Relationships

Ethical Principle: Social workers recognize the central importance of human relationships.

Social workers understand that relationships between and among people are an important vehicle for change. Social workers engage people as partners in the helping process. Social workers seek to strengthen relationships among people in a purposeful effort to promote, restore, maintain, and enhance the well-being of individuals, families, social groups, organizations, and communities.

Value: Integrity

Ethical Principle: Social workers behave in a trustworthy manner.

Social workers are continually aware of the profession's mission, values, ethical principles, and ethical standards and practice in a manner consistent with them. Social workers act honestly and responsibly and

promote ethical practices on the part of the organizations with which they are affiliated.

Value: Competence

Ethical Principle: Social workers practice within their areas of competence and develop and enhance their professional expertise.

Social workers continually strive to increase their professional knowledge and skills and to apply them in practice. Social workers should aspire to contribute to the knowledge base of the profession.

Ethical Standards

The following ethical standards are relevant to the professional activities of all social workers. These standards concern (1) social workers' ethical responsibilities to clients, (2) social workers' ethical responsibilitie to colleagues, (3) social workers' ethical responsibilities in practice settings, (4) social workers' ethical responsibilities as professionals, (5) social workers' ethical responsibilities to the social work profession, and (6) social workers' ethical responsibilities to the broader society.

Some of the standards that follow are enforceable guidelines for professional conduct, and some are aspirational. The extent to which each standard is enforceable is a matter of professional judgment to be exercised by those responsible for reviewing alleged violations of ethical standards.

1. Social Workers' Ethical Responsibilities to Clients

1.01 Commitment to Clients

Social workers' primary responsibility is to promote the well-being of clients. In general, clients' interests are primary. However, social workers' responsibility to the larger society or specific legal obli-gations may on limited occasions supersede the loyalty owed clients, and clients should be so advised. (Examples include when a social worker is required by law to report that a client has abused a child or has threatened to harm self or others.)

1.02 Self-Determination

Social workers respect and promote the right of clients to self-determination and assist clients in their efforts to identify and clarify their goals. Social workers may limit clients' right to self-determination when, in the social workers' professional judgment, clients' actions or potential actions pose a serious, foreseeable, and imminent risk to themselves or others.

1.03 Informed Consent

(a) Social workers should provide services to clients only in the context of a professional relationship based, when appropriate, on valid informed consent. Social workers should use clear and understandable language to inform clients of the purpose of the services, risks related to the services, limits to services because of the requirements of a third-party payer, relevant costs, reasonable alternatives, clients' right to refuse or withdraw consent, and the time frame covered by the consent. Social workers should provide clients with an opportunity to ask questions.

(b) In instances when clients are not literate or have difficulty understanding the primary language used in the practice setting, social workers should take steps to ensure clients' comprehension. This may include providing clients with a detailed verbal explanation or arranging for a qualified interpreter or translator whenever possible.

(c) In instances when clients lack the capacity to provide informed consent, social workers should protect clients' interests by seeking permission from an appropriate third party, informing clients consistent with the clients' level of understanding. In such instances social workers should seek to ensure that the third party acts in a manner consistent with clients' wishes and interests. Social workers should take reasonable steps to enhance such clients' ability to give informed consent.

(d) In instances when clients are receiving services involuntarily, social workers should provide information about the nature and extent of services and about the extent of clients' right to refuse service.

(e) Social workers who provide services via electronic media (such as computer, telephone, radio, and television) should inform recipients of the limitations and risks associated with such services.

(f) Social workers should obtain clients' informed consent before audiotaping or videotaping clients or permitting observation of services to clients by a third party.

1.04 Competence

(a) Social workers should provide services and represent themselves as competent only within the boundaries of their education, training, license, certification, consultation received, supervised experience, or other relevant professional experience.

(b) Social workers should provide services in substantive areas or use intervention techniques or approaches that are new to them only after engaging in appropriate study, training, consultation, and supervision from people who are competent in those interventions or techniques.

(c) When generally recognized standards do not exist with respect to an emerging area of practice, social workers should exercise careful judgment and take responsible steps (including appropriate education, research, training, consultation, and supervision) to ensure the competence of their work and to protect clients from harm.

1.05 Cultural Competence and Social Diversity

(a) Social workers should understand culture and its function in human behavior and society, recognizing the strengths that exist in all cultures.

(b) Social workers should have a knowledge base of their clients' cultures and be able to demonstrate competence in the provision of services that are sensitive to clients' cultures and to differences among people and cultural groups.

(c) Social workers should obtain education about and seek to understand the nature of social diversity and oppression with respect to race, ethnicity, national origin, color, sex, sexual orientation, age, marital status, political belief, religion, and mental or physical disability.

1.06 Conflicts of Interest

(a) Social workers should be alert to and avoid conflicts of interest that interfere with the exercise of professional discretion and impartial judgment. Social workers should inform clients when a real or potential conflict of interest arises and take reasonable steps to resolve the issue in a manner that makes the clients' interests primary and protects clients' interests to the greatest extent possible. In some cases, protecting clients' interests may require termination of the professional relationship with proper referral of the client.

(b) Social workers should not take unfair advantage of any professional relationship or exploit others to further their personal, religious, political, or business interests.

(c) Social workers should not engage in dual or multiple relationships with clients or former clients in which there is a risk of exploitation or potential harm to the client. In instances when dual or multiple relationships are unavoidable, social workers should take steps to protect clients and are responsible for setting clear, appropriate, and culturally sensitive boundaries. (Dual or multiple relationships occur when social workers relate to clients in more than one relationship, whether professional, social, or business. Dual or multiple relationships can occur simultaneously or consecutively.)

(d) When social workers provide services to two or more people who have a relationship with each other (for example, couples, family members), social workers should clarify with all parties which individuals will be considered clients and the nature of social workers' professional obligations to the various individuals who are receiving services. Social workers who anticipate a conflict of interest among the individuals receiving services or who anticipate having to perform in potentially conflicting roles (for example, when a social worker is asked to testify in a child custody dispute or divorce proceedings involving clients) should clarify their role with the parties involved and take appropriate action to minimize any conflict of interest.

1.07 Privacy and Confidentiality

(a) Social workers should respect clients' right to privacy. Social workers should not solicit private information from clients unless it is essential to providing services or conducting social work evaluation or research. Once private information is shared, standards of confidentiality apply.

(b) Social workers may disclose confidential information when appropriate with valid consent from a client or a person legally authorized to consent on behalf of a client.

(c) Social workers should protect the confidentiality of all information obtained in the course of professional service, except for compelling professional reasons. The general expectation that social workers will keep information confidential does not apply when disclosure is necessary to prevent serious, foreseeable, and imminent harm to a client or other identifiable person. In all instances, social workers should disclose the least amount of confidential information necessary to achieve the desired purpose; only information that is directly relevant to the purpose for which the disclosure is made should be revealed.

(d) Social workers should inform clients, to the extent possible, about the disclosure of confidential information and the potential consequences, when feasible before the disclosure is made. This applies whether social workers disclose confidential information on the basis of a legal requirement or client consent.

(e) Social workers should discuss with clients and other interested parties the nature of confidentiality and limitations of clients' right to confidentiality. Social workers should review with clients circumstances where confidential information may be requested and where disclosure of confidential information may be legally required. This discussion should occur as soon as possible in the social worker-client relationship and as needed throughout the course of the relationship.

(f) When social workers provide counseling services to families, couples, or groups, social workers should seek agreement among the parties involved concerning each individual's right to confidentiality and obligation to preserve the confidentiality of information shared by others. Social workers should inform participants in family, couples, or group counseling that social workers cannot guarantee that all participants will honor such agreements.

(g) Social workers should inform clients involved in family, couples, marital, or group counseling of the social worker's, employer's, and agency's policy concerning the social worker's disclosure of confidential information among the parties involved in the counseling.

(h) Social workers should not disclose confidential information to third-party payers unless clients have authorized such disclosure.

(i) Social workers should not discuss confidential information in any setting unless privacy can be ensured. Social workers should not discuss confidential information in public or semipublic areas such as hallways, waiting rooms, elevators, and restaurants.

(j) Social workers should protect the confidentiality of clients during legal proceedings to the extent permitted by law. When a court of law or other legally authorized body orders social workers to disclose confidential or privileged information without a client's consent and such disclosure could cause harm to the client, social workers should request that the court withdraw the order or limit the order as narrowly as possible or maintain the records under seal, unavailable for public inspection.

(k) Social workers should protect the confidentiality of clients when responding to requests from members of the media.

(l) Social workers should protect the confidentiality of clients' written and electronic records and other sensitive information. Social workers should take reasonable steps to ensure that clients' records are stored in a secure location and that clients' records are not available to others who are not authorized to have access.

(m) Social workers should take precautions to ensure and maintain the confidentiality of information transmitted to other parties through the use of computers, electronic mail, facsimile machines, telephones and telephone answering machines, and other electronic or computer technology. Disclosure of identifying information should be avoided whenever possible.

(n) Social workers should transfer or dispose of clients' records in a manner that protects clients' confidentiality and is consistent with state statutes governing records and social work licensure.

(o) Social workers should take reasonable precautions to protect client confidentiality in the event of the social worker's termination of practice, incapacitation, or death.

(p) Social workers should not disclose identifying information when discussing clients for teaching or training purposes unless the client has consented to disclosure of confidential information.

(q) Social workers should not disclose identifying information when discussing clients with consultants unless the client has consented to disclosure of confidential information or there is a compelling need for such disclosure.

(r) Social workers should protect the confidentiality of deceased clients consistent with the preceding standards.

1.08 Access to Records

(a) Social workers should provide clients with reasonable access to records concerning the clients. Social workers who are concerned that clients' access to their records could cause serious misunderstanding or harm to the client should provide assistance in interpreting the records and consultation with the client regarding the records. Social workers should limit clients' access to their records, or portions of their records, only in exceptional circumstances when there is compelling evidence that such access would cause serious harm to the client. Both clients' requests and the rationale for withholding some or all of the record should be documented in clients' files.

(b) When providing clients with access to their records, social workers should take steps to protect the confidentiality of other individuals identified or discussed in such records.

1.09 Sexual Relationships

(a) Social workers should under no circumstances engage in sexual activities or sexual contact with current clients, whether such contact is consensual or forced.

(b) Social workers should not engage in sexual activities or sexual contact with clients' relatives or other individuals with whom clients maintain a close personal relationship when there is a risk of exploitation or potential harm to the client. Sexual activity or sexual contact with clients' relatives or other individuals with whom clients maintain a personal relationship has the potential to be harmful to the client and may make it difficult for the social worker and client to maintain appropriate professional boundaries. Social workers—not their clients, their clients' relatives, or other individuals with whom the client maintains a personal relationship—assume the full burden for setting clear, appropriate, and culturally sensitive boundaries.

(c) Social workers should not engage in sexual activities or sexual contact with former clients because of the potential for harm to the client. If social workers engage in conduct contrary to this prohibition or claim that an exception to this prohibition is warranted because of extraordinary circumstances, it is social workers—not their clients—who assume the full burden of demonstrating that the former client has not been exploited, coerced, or manipulated, intentionally or unintentionally.

(d) Social workers should not provide clinical services to individuals with whom they have had a prior sexual relationship. Providing clinical services to a former sexual partner has the potential to be harmful to the individual and is likely to make it difficult for the social worker and individual to maintain appropriate professional boundaries.

1.10 Physical Contact

Social workers should not engage in physical contact with clients when there is a possibility of psychological harm to the client as a result of the contact (such as cradling or caressing clients). Social workers who engage in appropriate physical contact with clients are responsible for setting clear, appropriate, and culturally sensitive boundaries that govern such physical contact.

1.11 Sexual Harassment

Social workers should not sexually harass clients. Sexual harassment includes sexual advances, sexual solicitation, requests for sexual favors, and other verbal or physical conduct of a sexual nature.

1.12 Derogatory Language

Social workers should not use derogatory language in their written or verbal communications to or about clients. Social workers should use accurate and respectful language in all communications to and about clients.

1.13 Payment for Services

(a) When setting fees, social workers should ensure that the fees are fair, reasonable, and commensurate with the services performed. Consideration should be given to clients' ability to pay.

(b) Social workers should avoid accepting goods or services from clients as payment for professional services. Bartering arrangements, particularly involving services, create the potential for conflicts of interest, exploitation, and inappropriate boundaries in social workers' relationships with clients. Social workers should explore and may participate in bartering only in very limited circumstances when it can be demonstrated that such arrangements are an accepted practice among professionals in the local community, considered to be essential for the provision of services, negotiated without coercion, and entered into at the client's initiative and with the client's informed consent. Social workers who accept goods or services from clients as payment for professional services assume the full burden of demonstrating that this arrangement will not be detrimental to the client or the professional relationship.

(c) Social workers should not solicit a private fee or other remuneration for providing services to clients who are entitled to such available services through the social workers' employer or agency.

1.14 Clients Who Lack Decision-Making Capacity

When social workers act on behalf of clients who lack the capacity to make informed decisions, social workers should take reasonable steps to safeguard the interests and rights of those clients.

1.15 Interruption of Services

Social workers should make reasonable efforts to ensure continuity of services in the event that services are interrupted by factors such as unavailability, relocation, illness, disability, or death.

1.16 Termination of Services

(a) Social workers should terminate services to clients and professional relationships with them when such services and relationships are no longer required or no longer serve the clients' needs or interests.

(b) Social workers should take reasonable steps to avoid abandoning clients who are still in need of services. Social workers should withdraw services precipitously only under unusual circumstances, giving careful consideration to all factors in the situation and taking care to minimize possible adverse effects. Social workers should assist in making appropriate arrangements for continuation of services when necessary.

(c) Social workers in fee-for-service settings may terminate services to clients who are not paying an overdue balance if the financial contractual arrangements have been made clear to the client, if the client does not pose an imminent danger to self or others, and if the clinical and other consequences of the current nonpayment have been addressed and discussed with the client.

(d) Social workers should not terminate services to pursue a social, financial, or sexual relationship with a client.

(e) Social workers who anticipate the termination or interruption of services to clients should notify clients promptly and seek the transfer, referral, or continuation of services in relation to the clients' needs and preferences.

(f) Social workers who are leaving an employment setting should inform clients of appropriate options for the continuation of services and of the benefits and risks of the options.

2. Social Workers' Ethical Responsibilities to Colleagues

2.01 Respect

(a) Social workers should treat colleagues with respect and should represent accurately and fairly the qualifications, views, and obligations of colleagues.

(b) Social workers should avoid unwarranted negative criticism of colleagues in communications with clients or with other professionals. Unwarranted negative criticism may include demeaning comments that refer to colleagues' level of competence or to indi-viduals' attributes such as race, ethnicity, national origin, color, sex, sexual orientation, age, marital status, political belief, religion, and mental or physical disability.

(c) Social workers should cooperate with social work colleagues and with colleagues of other professions when such cooperation serves the well-being of clients.

2.02   Confidentiality

Social workers should respect confidential information shared by colleagues in the course of their professional relationships and transactions. Social workers should ensure that such colleagues understand social workers' obligation to respect confidentiality and any exceptions related to it.

2.03   Interdisciplinary Collaboration

(a) Social workers who are members of an interdisciplinary team should participate in and contribute to decisions that affect the well-being of clients by drawing on the perspectives, values, and experiences of the social work profession. Professional and ethical obligations of the interdisciplinary team as a whole and of its individual members should be clearly established.

(b) Social workers for whom a team decision raises ethical concerns should attempt to resolve the disagreement through appropriate channels. If the disagreement cannot be resolved, social workers should pursue other avenues to address their concerns consistent with client well-being.

2.04   Disputes Involving Colleagues

(a) Social workers should not take advantage of a dispute between a colleague and an employer to obtain a position or otherwise advance the social workers' own interests.

(b) Social workers should not exploit clients in disputes with colleagues or engage clients in any inappropriate discussion of conflicts between social workers and their colleagues.

2.05   Consultation

(a) Social workers should seek the advice and counsel of colleagues whenever such consultation is in the best interests of clients.

(b) Social workers should keep themselves informed about colleagues' areas of expertise and competencies. Social workers should seek consultation only from colleagues who have demonstrated knowledge, expertise, and competence related to the subject of the consultation.

(c) When consulting with colleagues about clients, social workers should disclose the least amount of information necessary to achieve the purposes of the consultation.

2.06   Referral for Services

(a) Social workers should refer clients to other professionals when the other professionals' specialized knowledge or expertise is needed to serve clients fully or when social workers believe that they are not being effective or making reasonable progress with clients and that additional service is required.

(b) Social workers who refer clients to other professionals should take appropriate steps to facilitate an orderly transfer of responsibility. Social workers who refer clients to other professionals should disclose, with clients' consent, all pertinent information to the new service providers.

(c) Social workers are prohibited from giving or receiving payment for a referral when no professional service is provided by the referring social worker.

2.07   Sexual Relationships

(a) Social workers who function as supervisors or educators should not engage in sexual activities or contact with supervisees, students, trainees, or other colleagues over whom they exercise professional authority.

(b) Social workers should avoid engaging in sexual relationships with colleagues when there is potential for a conflict of interest. Social workers who become involved in, or anticipate becoming involved in, a sexual relationship with a colleague have a duty to transfer professional responsibilities, when necessary, to avoid a conflict of interest.

2.08 Sexual Harassment

Social workers should not sexually harass supervisees, students, trainees, or colleagues. Sexual harassment includes sexual advances, sexual solicitation, requests for sexual favors, and other verbal or physical conduct of a sexual nature.

2.09 Impairment of Colleagues

(a) Social workers who have direct knowledge of a social work colleague's impairment that is due to personal problems, psychosocial distress, substance abuse, or mental health difficulties and that interferes with practice effectiveness should consult with that colleague when feasible and assist the colleague in taking remedial action.

(b) Social workers who believe that a social work colleague's impairment interferes with practice effectiveness and that the colleague has not taken adequate steps to address the impairment should take action through appropriate channels established by employers, agencies, NASW, licensing and regulatory bodies, and other professional organizations.

2.10 Incompetence of Colleagues

(a) Social workers who have direct knowledge of a social work colleague's incompetence should consult with that colleague when feasible and assist the colleague in taking remedial action.

(b) Social workers who believe that a social work colleague is incompetent and has not taken adequate steps to address the incompetence should take action through appropriate channels established by employers, agencies, NASW, licensing and regulatory bodies, and other professional organizations.

2.11 Unethical Conduct of Colleagues

(a) Social workers should take adequate measures to discourage, prevent, expose, and correct the unethical conduct of colleagues.

(b) Social workers should be knowledgeable about established policies and procedures for handling concerns about colleagues' unethical behavior. Social workers should be familiar with national, state, and local procedures for handling ethics complaints. These include policies and procedures created by NASW, licensing and regulatory bodies, employers, agencies, and other professional organizations.

(c) Social workers who believe that a colleague has acted unethically should seek resolution by discussing their concerns with the colleague when feasible and when such discussion is likely to be productive.

(d) When necessary, social workers who believe that a colleague has acted unethically should take action through appropriate formal channels (such as contacting a state licensing board or regulatory body, an NASW committee on inquiry, or other professional ethics committees).

(e) Social workers should defend and assist colleagues who are unjustly charged with unethical conduct.

3. Social Workers' Ethical Responsibilities in Practice Settings

3.01 Supervision and Consultation

(a) Social workers who provide supervision or consultation should have the necessary knowledge and skill to supervise or consult appropriately and should do so only within their areas of knowledge and competence.

(b) Social workers who provide supervision or consultation are responsible for setting clear, appropriate, and culturally sensitive boundaries.

(c) Social workers should not engage in any dual or multiple relationships with supervisees in which there is a risk of exploitation of or potential harm to the supervisee.

(d) Social workers who provide supervision should evaluate supervisees' performance in a manner that is fair and respectful.

3.02   Education and Training

(a) Social workers who function as educators, field instructors for students, or trainers should provide instruction only within their areas of knowledge and competence and should provide instruction based on the most current information and knowledge available in the profession.

(b) Social workers who function as educators or field instructors for students should evaluate students' performance in a manner that is fair and respectful.

(c) Social workers who function as educators or field instructors for students should take reasonable steps to ensure that clients are routinely informed when services are being provided by students.

(d) Social workers who function as educators or field instructors for students should not engage in any dual or multiple relationships with students in which there is a risk of exploitation or potential harm to the student. Social work educators and field instructors are responsible for setting clear, appropriate, and culturally sensitive boundaries.

3.03   Performance Evaluation

Social workers who have responsibility for evaluating the performance of others should fulfill such responsibility in a fair and considerate manner and on the basis of clearly stated criteria.

3.04   Client Records

(a) Social workers should take reasonable steps to ensure that documentation in records is accurate and reflects the services provided.

(b) Social workers should include sufficient and timely documentation in records to facilitate the delivery of services and to ensure continuity of services provided to clients in the future.

(c) Social workers' documentation should protect clients' privacy to the extent that is possible and appropriate and should include only information that is directly relevant to the delivery of services.

(d) Social workers should store records following the termination of services to ensure reasonable future access. Records should be maintained for the number of years required by state statutes or relevant contracts.

3.05   Billing

Social workers should establish and maintain billing practices that accurately reflect the nature and extent of services provided and that identify who provided the service in the practice setting.

3.06   Client Transfer

(a) When an individual who is receiving services from another agency or colleague contacts a social worker for services, the social worker should carefully consider the client's needs before agreeing to provide services. To minimize possible confusion and conflict, social workers should discuss with potential clients the nature of the clients' current relationship with other service providers and the implications, including possible benefits or risks, of entering into a relationship with a new service provider.

(b) If a new client has been served by another agency or colleague, social workers should discuss with the client whether consultation with the previous service provider is in the client's best interest.

3.07 Administration

(a) Social work administrators should advocate within and outside their agencies for adequate resources to meet clients' needs.

(b) Social workers should advocate for resource allocation procedures that are open and fair. When not all clients' needs can be met, an allocation procedure should be developed that is nondiscriminatory and based on appropriate and consistently applied principles.

(c) Social workers who are administrators should take reasonable steps to ensure that adequate agency or organizational resources are available to provide appropriate staff supervision.

(d) Social work administrators should take reasonable steps to ensure that the working environment for which they are responsible is consistent with and encourages compliance with the NASW Code of Ethics. Social work administrators should take reasonable steps to eliminate any conditions in their organizations that violate, interfere with, or discourage compliance with the Code.

3.08 Continuing Education and Staff Development

Social work administrators and supervisors should take reasonable steps to provide or arrange for continuing education and staff development for all staff for whom they are responsible. Continuing education and staff development should address current knowledge and emerging developments related to social work practice and ethics.

3.09 Commitments to Employers

(a) Social workers generally should adhere to commitments made to employers and employing organizations.

(b) Social workers should work to improve employing agencies' policies and procedures and the efficiency and effectiveness of their services.

(c) Social workers should take reasonable steps to ensure that employers are aware of social workers' ethical obligations as set forth in the NASW Code of Ethics and of the implications of those obligations for social work practice.

(d) Social workers should not allow an employing organization's policies, procedures, regulations, or administrative orders to interfere with their ethical practice of social work. Social workers should take reasonable steps to ensure that their employing organizations' practices are consistent with the NASW Code of Ethics.

(e) Social workers should act to prevent and eliminate discrimination in the employing organization's work assignments and in its employment policies and practices.

(f) Social workers should accept employment or arrange student field placements only in organizations that exercise fair personnel practices.

(g) Social workers should be diligent stewards of the resources of their employing organizations, wisely conserving funds where appropriate and never misappropriating funds or using them for unintended purposes.

3.10 Labor-Management Disputes

(a) Social workers may engage in organized action, including the formation of and participation in labor unions, to improve services to clients and working conditions.

(b) The actions of social workers who are involved in labor-management disputes, job actions, or labor strikes should be guided by the profession's values, ethical principles, and ethical standards. Reasonable differences of opinion exist among social workers concerning their primary obligation as professionals during an actual or threatened labor strike or job action. Social workers should carefully examine relevant issues and their possible impact on clients before deciding on a course of action.

4. Social Workers' Ethical Responsibilities as Professionals

4.01 Competence

(a) Social workers should accept responsibility or employment only on the basis of existing competence or the intention to acquire the necessary competence.

(b) Social workers should strive to become and remain proficient in professional practice and the performance of professional functions. Social workers should critically examine and keep current with emerging knowledge relevant to social work. Social workers should routinely review the professional literature and participate in continuing education relevant to social work practice and social work ethics.

(c) Social workers should base practice on recognized knowledge, including empirically based knowledge, relevant to social work and social work ethics.

4.02 Discrimination

Social workers should not practice, condone, facilitate, or collaborate with any form of discrimination on the basis of race, ethnicity, national origin, color, sex, sexual orientation, age, marital status, political belief, religion, or mental or physical disability.

4.03 Private Conduct

Social workers should not permit their private conduct to interfere with their ability to fulfill their professional responsibilities.

4.04 Dishonesty, Fraud, and Deception

Social workers should not participate in, condone, or be associated with dishonesty, fraud, or deception.

4.05 Impairment

(a) Social workers should not allow their own personal problems, psychosocial dis-

tress, legal problems, substance abuse, or mental health difficulties to interfere with their professional judgment and performance or to jeopardize the best interests of people for whom they have a professional responsibility.

(b) Social workers whose personal problems, psychosocial distress, legal problems, substance abuse, or mental health difficulties interfere with their professional judgment and performance should immediately seek consultation and take appropriate remedial action by seeking professional help, making adjustments in workload, terminating practice, or taking any other steps necessary to protect clients and others.

4.06 Misrepresentation

(a) Social workers should make clear distinctions between statements made and actions engaged in as a private individual and as a representative of the social work profession, a professional social work organization, or the social worker's employing agency.

(b) Social workers who speak on behalf of professional social work organizations should accurately represent the official and authorized positions of the organizations.

(c) Social workers should ensure that their representations to clients, agencies, and the public of professional qualifications, credentials, education, competence, affiliations, services provided, or results to be achieved are accurate. Social workers should claim only those relevant professional credentials they actually possess and take steps to correct any inaccuracies or misrepresentations of their credentials by others.

4.07 Solicitations

(a) Social workers should not engage in uninvited solicitation of potential clients who, because of their circumstances, are vulnerable to undue influence, manipulation, or coercion.

(b) Social workers should not engage in solicitation of testimonial endorsements (including solicitation of consent to use a client's prior statement as a testimonial endorsement) from current clients or from other people who, because of their particular circumstances, are vulnerable to undue influence.

4.08 Acknowledging Credit

(a) Social workers should take responsibility and credit, including authorship credit, only for work they have actually performed and to which they have contributed.

(b) Social workers should honestly acknowledge the work of and the contributions made by others.

5. Social Workers' Ethical Responsibilities to the Social Work Profession

5.01 Integrity of the Profession

(a) Social workers should work toward the maintenance and promotion of high standards of practice.

(b) Social workers should uphold and advance the values, ethics, knowledge, and mission of the profession. Social workers should protect, enhance, and improve the integrity of the profession through appropriate study and research, active discussion, and responsible criticism of the profession.

(c) Social workers should contribute time and professional expertise to activities that promote respect for the value, integrity, and competence of the social work profession. These activities may include teaching, research, consultation, service, legislative testimony, presentations in the community, and participation in their professional organizations.

(d) Social workers should contribute to the knowledge base of social work and share with colleagues their knowledge related to practice, research, and ethics. Social workers should seek to con-tribute to the profession's literature and to share their knowledge at professional meetings and conferences.

(e) Social workers should act to prevent the unauthorized and unqualified practice of social work.

5.02 Evaluation and Research

(a) Social workers should monitor and evaluate policies, the implementation of programs, and practice interventions.

(b) Social workers should promote and facilitate evaluation and research to contribute to the development of knowledge.

(c) Social workers should critically examine and keep current with emerging knowledge relevant to social work and fully use evaluation and research evidence in their professional practice.

(d) Social workers engaged in evaluation or research should carefully consider possible consequences and should follow guidelines developed for the protection of evaluation and research participants. Appropriate institutional review boards should be consulted.

(e) Social workers engaged in evaluation or research should obtain voluntary and written informed consent from participants, when appropriate, without any implied or actual deprivation or penalty for refusal to participate; without undue inducement to participate; and with due regard for participants' well-being, privacy, and dignity. Informed consent should include information about the nature, extent, and duration of the participation requested and disclosure of the risks and benefits of participation in the research.

(f) When evaluation or research participants are incapable of giving informed consent, social workers should provide an appropriate explanation to the participants, obtain the participants' assent to the extent they are able, and obtain written consent from an appropriate proxy.

(g) Social workers should never design or conduct evaluation or research that does not use consent procedures, such as certain forms of naturalistic observation and archival research, unless rigorous and responsible review of the research has found it to be justified because of its prospective scientific, educational, or applied value and unless equally effective alternative procedures that do not involve waiver of consent are not feasible.

(h) Social workers should inform participants of their right to withdraw from evaluation and research at any time without penalty.

(i) Social workers should take appropriate steps to ensure that participants in evaluation and research have access to appropriate supportive services.

(j) Social workers engaged in evaluation or research should protect participants from unwarranted physical or mental distress, harm, danger, or deprivation.

(k) Social workers engaged in the evaluation of services should discuss collected information only for professional purposes and only with people professionally concerned with this information.

(l) Social workers engaged in evaluation or research should ensure the anonymity or confidentiality of participants and of the data obtained from them. Social workers should inform participants of any limits of confidentiality, the measures that will be taken to ensure confidentiality, and when any records containing research data will be destroyed.

(m) Social workers who report evaluation and research results should protect participants' confidentiality by omitting identifying information unless proper consent has been obtained authorizing disclosure.

(n) Social workers should report evaluation and research findings accurately. They should not fabricate or falsify results and should take steps to correct any errors later found in published data using standard publication methods.

(o) Social workers engaged in evaluation or research should be alert to and avoid conflicts of interest and dual relationships with participants, should inform participants when a real or potential conflict of interest arises, and should take steps to resolve the issue in a manner that makes participants' interests primary.

(p) Social workers should educate themselves, their students, and their colleagues about responsible research practices.

6. Social Workers' Ethical Responsibilities to the Broader Society

6.01 Social Welfare

Social workers should promote the general welfare of society, from local to global levels, and the development of people, their communities, and their environments. Social workers should advocate for living conditions conducive to the fulfillment of basic human needs and should promote social, economic, political, and cultural values and institutions that are compatible with the realization of social justice.

6.02 Public Participation

Social workers should facilitate informed participation by the public in shaping social policies and institutions.

6.03 Public Emergencies

Social workers should provide appropriate professional services in public emergencies to the greatest extent possible.

6.04 Social and Political Action

(a) Social workers should engage in social and political action that seeks to ensure that all people have equal access to the resources, employment, services, and opportunities they require to meet their basic human needs and to develop fully. Social workers should be aware of the impact of the political arena on practice and should advocate for changes in policy and legislation to improve social conditions in order to meet basic human needs and promote social justice.

(b) Social workers should act to expand choice and opportunity for all people, with special regard for vulnerable, disadvantaged, oppressed, and exploited people and groups.

(c) Social workers should promote conditions that encourage respect for cultural and social diversity within the United States and globally. Social workers should promote policies and practices that demonstrate respect for difference, support the expansion of cultural knowledge and resources, advocate for programs and institutions that demonstrate cultural competence, and promote policies that safeguard the rights of and confirm equity and social justice for all people.

(d) Social workers should act to prevent and eliminate domination of, exploitation of, and discrimination against any person, group, or class on the basis of race, ethnicity, national origin, color, sex, sexual orientation, age, marital status, political belief, religion, or mental or physical disability.

Appendix B

International Federation of Social Workers, The Ethics of Social Work: Principles and Standards

1 Background

Ethical awareness is a necessary part of the professional practice of any social worker. His or her ability to act ethically is an essential aspect of the quality of the service offered to clients.

The purpose of IFSW's work on ethics is to promote ethical debate and reflection in the member associations and among the providers of social work in member countries.

The basis for the further development of IFSW's work on ethics is to be found in *Ethics of Social Work: Principles and Standards* which consists of two documents, *International Declaration of Ethical Principles of Social Work* and *International Ethical Standards for Social Workers*. These documents present the basic ethical principles of the social work profession, recommend procedures when the work presents ethical dilemmas, and deal with the profession's and the individual social worker's relation to clients, colleagues, and others in the field. The documents are components in a continuing process of use, review and revision.

2 International Declaration of Ethical Principles of Social Work

2.1 Introduction

The IFSW recognises the need for a declaration of ethical principles for guidance in dealing with ethical problems in social work.

The purposes of the *International Declaration of Ethical Principles* are:

1. to formulate a set of basic principles for social work, which can be adapted to cultural and social settings,
2. to identify ethical problem areas in the practice of social work (below referred to as "problem areas"), and
3. to provide guidance as to the choice of methods for dealing with ethical issues/problems (below referred to as "methods for addressing ethical issues/problems").

Compliance

The *International Declaration of Ethical Principles* assumes that both member associations of the IFSW and their constituent members adhere to the principles formulated therein. The IFSW expects each

Published by International Federation of Social Workers, P.O. Box 4649, Sofienberg, N-0506 Oslo, Norway; October 1994. Adopted by the IFSW General Meeting, Colombo, Sri Lanka, July 6–8, 1994.

member association to assist its members in identifying and dealing with ethical issues/problems in the practice of their profession.

Member associations of the IFSW and individual members of these can report any member association to the Executive Committee of the IFSW should it neglect to adhere to these principles. National associations who experience difficulties adopting these principles should notify the Executive Committee of IFSW. The Executive Committee may impose the stipulations and intentions of the *Declaration of Ethical Principles* on an association which neglects to comply. Should this not be sufficient the Executive Committee can, as a following measure, suggest suspension or exclusion of the association.

The *International Declaration of Ethical Principles* should be made publicly known. This would enable clients, employers, professionals from other disciplines, and the general public to have expectations in accordance with the ethical foundations of social work.

We acknowledge that a detailed set of ethical standards for the member associations would be unrealistic due to legal, cultural and governmental differences among the member countries.

2.2   The Principles

Social workers serve the development of human beings through adherence to the following basic principles:

2.2.1.   Every human being has a unique value, which justifies moral consideration for that person.

2.2.2.   Each individual has the right to self-fulfilment to the extent that it does not encroach upon the same right of others, and has an obligation to contribute to the well-being of society.

2.2.3.   Each society, regardless of its form, should function to provide the maximum benefits for all of its members.

2.2.4.   Social workers have a commitment to principles of social justice.

2.2.5.   Social workers have the responsibility to devote objective and disciplined knowledge and skill to aid individuals, groups, communities, and societies in their development and resolution of personal-societal conflicts and their consequences.

2.2.6.   Social workers are expected to provide the best possible assistance to anybody seeking their help and advice, without unfair discrimination on the basis of gender, age, disability, colour, social class, race, religion, language, political beliefs, or sexual orientation.

2.2.7.   Social workers respect the basic human rights of individuals and groups as expressed in the *United Nations Universal Declaration of Human Rights* and other international conventions derived from that Declaration.

2.2.8.   Social workers pay regard to the principles of privacy, confidentiality, and responsible use of information in their professional work. Social workers respect justified confidentiality even when their country's legislation is in conflict with this demand.

2.2.9.   Social workers are expected to work in full collaboration with their clients, working for the best interests of the clients but paying due regard to the interests of others involved. Clients are encouraged to participate as much as possible, and should be informed of the risks and likely benefits of proposed courses of action.

2.2.10.   Social workers generally expect clients to take responsibility, in collaboration with them, for determining courses of action affecting their lives. Compulsion which might be necessary to solve one party's problems at the expense of the interests of others involved should only take place after careful explicit evaluation of the claims of the conflicting parties. Social workers should minimise the use of legal compulsion.

2.2.11. Social work is inconsistent with direct or indirect support of individuals, groups, political forces or power structures suppressing their fellow human beings by employing terrorism, torture or similar brutal means.

2.2.12. Social workers make ethically justified decisions, and stand by them, paying due regard to the *IFSW International Declaration of Ethical Principles* and to the *International Ethical Standards for Social Workers* adopted by their national professional association.

2.3 Problem Areas

2.3.1. The problem areas raising ethical issues directly are not necessarily universal due to cultural and governmental differences. Each national association is encouraged to promote discussion and clarification of important issues and problems particularly relevant to its country. The following problem areas are, however, widely recognized:

1. *When the loyalty of the social worker is in the middle of conflicting interests*
   - between those of the social workers own and the clients
   - between conflicting interests of individual clients and other individuals
   - between the conflicting interests of groups of clients
   - between groups of clients and the rest of the population
   - between systems/institution and groups of clients
   - between system/institution/employer and social workers
   - between different groups of professionals
2. *The fact that the social worker functions both as a helper and controller*
   The relation between these two opposite aspects of social work demands a clarification based on an explicit choice of values

in order to avoid a mixing-up of motives or the lack of clarity in motives, actions and consequences of actions. When social workers are expected to play a role in the state control of citizens they are obliged to clarify the ethical implications of this role and to what extent this role is acceptable in relation to the basic ethical principles of social work.

3. *The duty of the social worker to protect the interests of the client will easily come into conflict with demands for efficiency and utility*
   This problem is becoming important with the introduction and use of information technology within the fields of social work.

2.3.2. The principles declared in section 2.2 should always be at the base of any consideration given or choice made by social workers in dealing with issues/problems within these areas.

2.4 Methods For The Solution of Issues/ Problems

2.4.1. The various national associations of social workers are obliged to treat matters in such a way that ethical issues/problems may be considered and tried to be solved in collective forums within the organization. Such forums should enable the individual social worker to discuss, analyse and consider ethical issues/problems in collaboration with colleagues, other expert groups and/parties affected by the matter under discussion. In addition such forums should give the social worker opportunity to receive advice from colleagues and others. Ethical analysis and discussion should always seek to create possibilities and options.

2.4.2. The member associations are required to produce and/or adapt ethical standards for the different fields of work, especially for those fields where there are complicated ethical issues/problems as well as areas where the ethical principles of social work may come into conflict with the respective country's legal system or the policy of the authorities.

2.4.3. When ethical foundations are laid down as guidelines for actions within the practice of social work, it is the duty of the associations to aid the individual social worker in analysing and considering ethical issues/problems on the basis of:

1. The basic *principles* of the Declaration (section 2.2)
2. The ethical/moral and political *context* of the actions, i.e. an analysis of the values and forces constituting the framing conditions of the action
3. The *motives* of the action, i.e. to advocate a higher level of consciousness of the aims and intentions the individual social worker might have regarding a course of action
4. The *nature* of the action, i.e. help in providing an analysis of the moral content of the action, e.g. the use of compulsion as opposed to voluntary co-operation, guardianship vs participation, etc.
5. The *consequences* the action might have for different groups, i.e. an analysis of the consequences of different ways of action for all involved parties in both the short and long term.

2.4.4. The member associations are responsible for promoting debate, education and research regarding ethical questions.

3 International Ethical Standards for Social Workers

(This section is based on the *International Code of Ethics for the Professional Social Worker* adopted by the IFSW in 1976, but does not include ethical principles since these are now contained in the new separate International Declaration of Ethical Principles of Social Work in section 2.2 of the present document.)

3.1 Preamble

Social work originates variously from humanitarian, religious and democratic ideals and philosophies and has universal application to meet human needs arising from personal-societal interactions and to develop human potential. Professional social workers are dedicated to service for the welfare and self-fulfilment of human beings; to the development and disciplined use of validated knowledge regarding human and societal behaviour; to the development of resources to meet individual, group, national and international needs and aspirations; and to the achievement of social justice. On the basis of the *International Declaration of Ethical Principles of Social Work,* the social worker is obliged to recognise these standards of ethical conduct.

3.2 General Standards of Ethical Conduct

3.2.1. Seek to understand each individual client and the client system, and the elements which affect behaviour and the service required.

3.2.2. Uphold and advance the values, knowledge and methodology of the profession, refraining from any behaviour which damages the functioning of the profession.

3.2.3. Recognise professional and personal limitations.

3.2.4. Encourage the utilisation of all relevant knowledge and skills.

3.2.5. Apply relevant methods in the development and validation of knowledge.

3.2.6. Contribute professional expertise to the development of policies and programs which improve the quality of life in society.

3.2.7. Identify and interpret social needs.

3.2.8. Identify and interpret the basis and nature of individual, group, community, national, and international social problems.

3.2.9. Identify and interpret the work of the social work profession.

3.2.10. Clarify whether public statements are made or actions performed on an individual basis or as representative of a professional association, agency or organisation, or other group.

3.3 Social Work Standards Relative to Clients

3.3.1. Accept primary responsibility to identified clients, but within limitations set by the ethical claims of others.

3.3.2. Maintain the client's right to a relationship of trust, to privacy and confidentiality, and to responsible use of information. The collection and sharing of information or data is related to the professional service function with the client informed as to its necessity and use. No information is released without prior knowledge and informed consent of the client, except where the client cannot be responsible or others may be seriously jeopardized. A client has access to social work records concerning them.

3.3.3. Recognise and respect the individual goals, responsibilities, and differences of clients. Within the scope of the agency and the client's social milieu, the professional service shall assist clients to take responsibility for personal actions and help all clients with equal willingness. Where the professional service cannot be provided under such conditions the clients shall be so informed in such a way as to leave the clients free to act.

3.3.4. Help the client—individual, group, community, or society—to achieve self-fulfilment and maximum potential within the limits of the respective rights of others. The service shall be based upon helping the client to understand and use the professional relationship, in furtherance of the clients legitimate desires and interests.

3.4 Social Work Standards Relative to Agencies and Organizations

3.4.1. Work and/or cooperate with those agencies and organizations whose policies, procedures, and operations are directed toward adequate service delivery and encouragement of professional practice consistent with the ethical principles of the IFSW.

3.4.2. Responsibly execute the stated aims and functions of the agency or organizations, contributing to the development of sound policies, procedures, and practice in order to obtain the best possible standards or practice.

3.4.3. Sustain ultimate responsibility to the client, initiating desirable alterations of policies, procedures, and practice, through appropriate agency and organization channels. If necessary remedies are not achieved after channels have been exhausted, initiate appropriate appeals to higher authorities or the wider community of interest.

3.4.4. Ensure professional accountability to client and community for efficiency and effectiveness through periodic review of the process of service provision.

3.4.5. Use all possible ethical means to bring unethical practice to an end when policies, procedures and practices are in direct conflict with the ethical principles of social work.

3.5 Social Work Standards Relative to Colleagues

3.5.1. Acknowledge the education, training and performance of social work colleagues and professionals from other disciplines, extending all necessary cooperation that will enhance effective services.

3.5.2. Recognise differences of opinion and practice of social work colleagues and other professionals, expressing criticism through channels in a responsible manner.

3.5.3. Promote and share opportunities for knowledge, experience, and ideas with all social work colleagues, professionals from other disciplines and volunteers for the purpose of mutual improvement.

3.5.4. Bring any violations of professional ethics and standards to the attention of the appropriate bodies inside and outside the profession, and ensure that relevant clients are properly involved.

3.5.5. Defend colleagues against unjust actions.

3.6 Standards Relative to the Profession

3.6.1. Maintain the values, ethical principles, knowledge and methodology of the profession and contribute to their clarification and improvement.

3.6.2. Uphold the professional standards of practice and work for their advancement.

3.6.3. Defend the profession against unjust criticism and work to increase confidence in the necessity for professional practice.

3.6.4. Present constructive criticism of the profession, its theories, methods and practices

3.6.5. Encourage new approaches and methodologies needed to meet new and existing needs.

IFSW Homepage General Directory Activities Publications Partnerships information
    Contact IFSW: secr.gen@ifsw.org
    Last updated 13 September 2000
    Designed and produced by X Kommunikation

Appendix C

Council on Social Work Education Curriculum Policy Statement for Baccalaureate Degree Programs in Social Work Education

B1.0 Scope and Intent of the Curriculum Policy Statement

B1.1 This document sets forth the official curriculum policy for the accreditation of baccalaureate (BSW) programs of social work education by the Council on Social Work Education. It supersedes all prior statements of curriculum policy for the baccalaureate program level.

B1.2 The Curriculum Policy Statement establishes mandates for minimum requirements for the curricula of baccalaureate programs to be accredited by the Council. The policy statement specifies certain content areas and requires that they be logically related to each other, to the purposes and values of social work set forth in this document, and to the purposes, mission, resources, and educational context of each professional program. The statement does not prescribe any particular curriculum design.

B1.3 Each program is responsible for making every faculty member, student, field instructor, and administrator associated with the program aware of the content of the Curriculum Policy Statement.

B2.0 Relationship to Accreditation Standards

B2.1 The Commission on Accreditation of the Council develops standards by which social work education programs are evaluated for accreditation. These standards pertain to the organization, administration, and curriculum implementation of programs of social work education. Curriculum standards are derived from and must conform with this Curriculum Policy Statement.

B3.0 Premises Underlying Social Work Education

B3.1 The purpose of social work education is to prepare competent, effective social work professionals who are committed to practice that includes services to the poor and oppressed, and who work to alleviate poverty, oppression, and discrimination.

B3.2 Social work education is based upon a specific body of knowledge, values, and professional skills. It is grounded in the profession's history and philosophy. Education for the profession promotes the development and advancement of knowledge, practice skills, and services that further the well-being of people and promote social and economic justice. Social work education is responsible for the production and application of research and scholarship aimed at advancing social work practice.

B3.3 Programs of social work education are offered at the baccalaureate, master's, and doctoral levels. Doctoral programs are not accredited by the Council.

B3.4 Programs of social work education maintain close, reciprocal, and ongoing relationships with social work practitioners and with groups and organizations that promote, provide, or seek to influence social policies and social work services. Responsibility for initiating these relationships rests with social work education programs. Effective programs develop and maintain systematic communication with these individuals and groups.

B3.5 The effectiveness of any profession depends on the active engagement of its members in continuous learning. Programs of social work education strive to promote continuing professional development of students and faculty. Programs seek to teach students how to become lifelong learners who are motivated to continue developing new knowledge and skills throughout their careers.

B3.6 Effective social work education programs recognize the interdependence of nations and the need for worldwide professional cooperation.

B3.7 Social work education programs assume a leadership role within the profession by offering curricula that are at the forefront of the new and changing knowledge base of social work and its supporting disciplines.

B4.0 Purpose of Social Work

B4.1 The profession of social work is committed to the enhancement of human well-being and to the alleviation of poverty and oppression. The social work profession receives its sanction from public and private auspices and is the primary profession in the provision of social services. Within its general scope of concern, professional social work is practiced in a wide variety of settings. It has four related purposes:

B4.1.1 The promotion, restoration, maintenance, and enhancement of the functioning of individuals, families, groups, organizations, and communities by helping them to accomplish tasks, prevent and alleviate distress, and use resources.

B4.1.2 The planning, formulation, and implementation of social policies, services, resources, and programs needed to meet basic human needs and support the development of human capacities.

B4.1.3 The pursuit of policies, services, resources, and programs through organizational or administrative advocacy and social or political action, to empower groups at risk and to promote social and economic justice.

B4.1.4 The development and testing of professional knowledge and skills related to these purposes.

B5.0 Purpose and Structure of Baccalaureate Social Work Education

B5.1 The purpose of professional social work education is to enable students to integrate the knowledge, values, and skills of the social work profession into competent practice. The achievement of this purpose requires clarity about learning objectives and expected student outcomes, flexibility in programming and teaching to accommodate a diverse student population, and commitment of sufficient time and resources to their education.

B5.2 Two levels of social work education are accredited by the Council on Social Work Education: the baccalaureate and the master's. The baccalaureate level prepares students for generalist social work practice, and the master's level prepares students for advanced social work practice in an area of concentration. These levels of education differ from each other in the depth, breadth, and specificity of knowledge and skill that students are expected to synthesize and apply in practice.

Both levels of social work education must provide a professional foundation curriculum that contains the common body of the profession's knowledge, values, and skills. This common base is transferable among settings, population groups, and problem areas. The baccalaureate level of social work education must include a liberal arts perspective and the professional foundation content, which prepares students for direct services with client systems of various sizes and types.

B5.3 Professional social work education at the baccalaureate level takes place in accredited baccalaureate degree-granting colleges and universities.

B5.4 All baccalaureate social work programs must:

B5.4.1 Provide content about social work practice with client systems of various sizes and types.

B5.4.2 Prepare graduates to practice with diverse populations.

B5.4.3 Provide content about the social contexts of social work practice, the changing nature of those contexts, the behavior of organizations, and the dynamics of change.

B5.4.4 Infuse throughout the curriculum the values and ethics that guide professional social workers in their practice.

B5.4.5 Prepare graduates who are aware of their responsibility to continue their professional growth and development.

B5.5 The baccalaureate curriculum must be based upon a liberal arts perspective and must include the professional foundation.

B5.6 The baccalaureate curriculum must be developed and organized as a coherent and integrated whole.

B5.7 Graduates of a baccalaureate social work program will be able to:

B5.7.1 Apply critical thinking skills within the context of professional social work practice.

B5.7.2 Practice within the values and ethics of the social work profession and with an understanding of and respect for the positive value of diversity.

B5.7.3 Demonstrate the professional use of self.

B5.7.4 Understand the forms and mechanisms of oppression and discrimination and the strategies of change that advance social and economic justice.

B5.7.5 Understand the history of the social work profession and its current structures and issues.

B5.7.6 Apply the knowledge and skills of generalist social work to practice with systems of all sizes.

B5.7.7 Apply knowledge of bio-psychosocial variables that affect individual development and, behavior, and use theoretical frameworks to understand the interactions among individuals and between individuals and social systems (i.e., families, groups, organizations, and communities).

B5.7.8 Analyze the impact of social policies on client systems, workers, and agencies.

B5.7.9 Evaluate research studies and apply findings to practice, and, under supervision, to evaluate their own practice interventions and those of other relevant systems.

B5.7.10 Use communication skills differentially with a variety of client populations, colleagues, and members of the community.

B5.7.11 Use supervision appropriate to generalist practice.

B5.7.12 Function within the structure of organizations and service delivery systems, and under supervision, seek necessary organizational change.

Liberal Arts Perspective

B5.8 A liberal arts perspective enriches understanding of the person-environment context of professional social work practice and is integrally related to the mastery of social work content. The baccalaureate professional program in social work is built upon a liberal arts perspective.

B5.9 A liberal arts perspective provides an understanding of one's cultural heritage in the context of other cultures; the methods and limitations of various systems of inquiry; and the knowledge, attitudes, ways of thinking, and means of communication that are characteristic of a broadly educated person. Students must be capable of thinking critically about society, about people and their problems, and about such expressions of culture as art, literature, science, history, and philosophy. Students must have direct knowledge of social, psychological, and biological determinants of human behavior and of diverse cultures, social conditions, and social problems.

B5.10 Determination of whether students have acquired a liberal arts perspective is left to the judgment of each social work program's faculty. Each program must clearly explicate the requirements for training in a liberal arts perspective and the rationale for those requirements.

B6.0 Baccalaureate Curriculum Content

B6.1 The baccalaureate curriculum must include a liberal arts perspective and the professional foundation. The professional foundation includes content on social work values and ethics, diversity, social and economic justice, populations-at-risk, human behavior and the social environment, social welfare policy and services, social work practice, research, and field practicum. Baccalaureate programs must achieve integration among these professional content areas. Curriculum areas do not need to be taught in discrete courses, but mastery of the professional curriculum must occur through classroom experiences and field practice. The baccalaureate social work curriculum must cover, but is not necessarily limited to, the professional foundation.

B6.2 The curriculum design of each program must identify a coherent approach for the selection of research and theories offered. Every part of the baccalaureate curriculum must strengthen the student's understanding and appreciation of a scientific, analytic approach to building knowledge for the delivery and evaluation of practice. Content provided in each curricular area must be relevant to the objectives, philosophy, and mission of the individual program and must facilitate the student's understanding of how the knowledge relates to social work practice.

Social Work Values and Ethics

B6.3 Programs of social work education must provide specific knowledge about social work values and their ethical implications and must provide opportunities for students to demonstrate their application in professional practice. Students must be assisted to develop an awareness of their personal values and to clarify conflicting values and ethical dilemmas. Among the values and principles that must be infused throughout every social work curriculum are the following:

B6.3.1 social workers' professional relationships are built on regard for individual worth and dignity, and advance by mutual participation, acceptance, confidentiality, honesty, and responsible handling of conflict.

B6.3.2 social workers respect individuals' right to make independent decisions and to participate actively in the helping process.

B6.3.3 Social workers are committed to assisting client systems to obtain needed resources.

B6.3.4 Social workers strive to make social institutions more humane and responsive to human needs.

B6.3.5 Social workers demonstrate respect for and acceptance of the unique characteristics of diverse populations.

B6.3.6 Social workers are responsible for their own ethical conduct, the quality of their practice, and for seeking continuous growth in the knowledge and skills of their profession.

Diversity

B6.4 Professional social work education is committed to preparing students to understand and appreciate human diversity. Programs must provide curriculum content about differences and similarities in the experiences, needs, and beliefs of people. The curriculum must include content about differential assessment and intervention skills that will enable practitioners to serve diverse populations.

Each program is required to include content about population groups that are particularly relevant to the program's mission. These include, but are not limited to, groups distinguished by race, ethnicity, culture, class, gender, sexual orientation, religion, physical or mental disability, age, and national origin.

Promotion of Social and Economic Justice

B6.5 Programs of social work education must provide an understanding of the dynamics and consequences of social and economic injustice, including all forms of human oppression and discrimination. They must provide students with the skills to promote social change and to implement a wide range of interventions that advance the achievement of individual and collective social and economic justice. Theoretical and practice content must be provided about strategies of intervention for achieving social and economic justice and for combating the causes and effects of institutionalized forms of oppression.

Populations-at-Risk

B6.6 Programs of social work education must present theoretical and practice content about patterns, dynamics, and conse-

quences of discrimination, economic deprivation, and oppression. The curriculum must provide content about people of color, women, and gay and lesbian persons. Such content must emphasize the impact of discrimination, economic deprivation, and oppression upon these groups.

Each program must include content about populations-at-risk that are particularly relevant to its mission. In addition to those mandated above, such groups include, but are not limited to, those distinguished by age, ethnicity, culture, class, religion, and physical or mental disability.

Human Behavior and the Social Environment

B6.7 Programs of social work education must provide content about theories and knowledge of human bio-psycho-social development, including theories and knowledge about the range of social systems in which individuals live (families, groups, organizations, institutions, and communities). The human behavior and the social environment curriculum must provide an understanding of the interactions between and among human biological, social, psychological, and cultural systems as they affect and are affected by human behavior. The impact of social and economic forces on individuals and social systems must be presented. Content must be provided about the ways in which systems promote or deter people in maintaining or achieving optimal health and well-being. Content about values and ethical issues related to bio-psycho-social theories must be included. Students must be taught to evaluate theory and apply theory to client situations.

Social Welfare Policy and Services

B6.8 Social welfare policy and services content must include the history, mission, and philosophy of the social work profession. Content must be presented about the history and current patterns of provision of social welfare services, the role of social policy in helping or deterring people in maintaining or achieving optimal health and well-being, and the effect of policy on social work practice. Students must be taught to analyze current social policy within the context of historical and contemporary factors that shape policy. Content must be presented about the political and organizational processes used to influence policy, the process of policy formulation, and the frameworks for analyzing social policies in light of the principles of social and economic justice.

Social Work Practice

B6.9 At the baccalaureate level, professional social work education prepares students for generalist practice with systems of all sizes. Practice content emphasizes professional relationships that are characterized by mutuality, collaboration, and respect for the client. Content on practice assessment focuses on the examination of client strengths and problems in the interactions among individuals and between people and their environments.

Social work practice content must include knowledge, values, and skills to enhance the well-being of people and to help ameliorate the environmental conditions that affect people adversely. Practice content must include the following skills: defining issues; collecting and assessing data; planning and contracting; identifying alternative interventions; selecting and implementing appropriate courses of action; using appropriate research to monitor and evaluate outcomes; applying appropriate research-based knowledge and technological advances; and termination. Practice content also includes approaches to and skills for practice with clients from differing social, cultural, racial, religious, spiritual, and class backgrounds, and with systems of all sizes.

B6.10 Each program must explicate the ways in which students are prepared for generalist practice.

Research

B6.11 The research curriculum must provide an understanding and appreciation of a scientific, analytic approach to building knowledge for practice and to evaluating service delivery in all areas of practice. Ethical standards of scientific inquiry must be included in the research content.

The research content must include quantitative and qualitative research methodologies; analysis of data, including statistical procedures; systematic evaluation of practice; analysis and evaluation of theoretical bases, research questions, methodologies, statistical procedures, and conclusions of research reports; and relevant technological advances.

B6.12 Each program must identify how the research curriculum contributes to the student's use of scientific knowledge for practice.

Field Practicum

B6.13 The field practicum is an integral component of the curriculum in social work education. It engages the student in supervised social work practice and provides opportunities to apply classroom learning in the field setting.

B6.14 Field education at the baccalaureate level requires a minimum of 400 hours in field practicum.

B6.15 Each educational program must establish standards for field practicum settings that define their social work services and practices, field instructor assignments and activities, and student learning expectations and responsibilities. Individual programs may organize their practice in different ways but must ensure educationally directed, coordinated, and monitored practicum experiences for all students. All programs must provide:

a. A placement that is based upon the objectives of the educational program and the learning needs of each student.

b. Structured learning opportunities that enable students to compare their practice experiences, integrate knowledge acquired in the classroom, and expand knowledge beyond the scope of the practicum setting.

c. Support for field practicum instructors by:

1. Sharing pertinent information about practicum students.

2. Providing information about the organization and content of the educational curriculum, emphasizing the interrelationships among human behavior, social policy, research, and practice content.

3. Providing information about the sequencing of course content.

4. Articulating clear practice and evaluation goals for the field practicum and for each student.

5. Offering orientation and training programs.

B6.16 The baccalaureate practicum must provide the student with opportunities for:

a. The development of an awareness of self in the process of intervention.

b. Supervised practice experience in the application of knowledge, values and ethics, and practice skills to enhance the well-being of people and to work toward the amelioration of environmental conditions that affect people adversely.

c. Use of oral and written professional communications that are consistent with the language of the practicum setting and of the profession.

d. Use of professional supervision to enhance learning.

e. Critical assessment, implementation, and evaluation of agency policy within ethical guidelines.

B7.0 Avenues of Renewal

B7.1 Programs of social work education must remain vital and progressive by actively pursuing ongoing exchanges with the practice community and other essential groups, and by developing and assessing new knowledge and technology.

B7.1.1 Programs must establish and maintain close, reciprocal, and ongoing relationships with social work practitioners, and use those relationships continuously to evaluate the total curriculum.

B7.1.2 Programs must establish and maintain relationships with groups that develop, implement, and benefit from social policies and services.

B7.1.3 Programs must establish and maintain involvement with professional associations and with academic disciplines and departments.

B7.1.4 Programs must assume responsibility for systematic, high-quality scholarship that assesses social work practice and develops new knowledge.

Adopted 6/24/94

Appendix D

Council on Social Work Education Curriculum Policy Statement for Master's Degree Programs in Social Work Education

M1.0 Scope and Intent of the Curriculum Policy Statement

M1.1 This document sets forth the official curriculum policy for the accreditation of master's (MSW) programs of social work education by the Council on Social Work Education. It supersedes all prior statements of curriculum policy for the master's program level.

M1.2 The Curriculum Policy Statement establishes mandates for minimum requirements for the curricula of master's programs to be accredited by the Council. The policy statement specifies certain content areas and requires that they relate logically to each other, to the purposes and values of social work as set forth in this document, and to the purposes, mission, resources, and educational context of each professional program. The statement does not prescribe any particular curriculum design.

M1.3 Each program is responsible for making every faculty member, student, field instructor, and administrator associated with the program aware of the content of the Curriculum Policy Statement.

M2.0 Relationship to Accreditation Standards

M2.1 The Commission on Accreditation of the Council develops standards by which social work education programs are evaluated for accreditation. These standards pertain to the organization, administration, and curriculum implementation of programs of social work education. Curriculum standards are derived from and must conform to this Curriculum Policy Statement.

M3.0 Premises Underlying Social Work Education

M3.1 The purpose of social work education is to prepare competent and effective social work professionals who are committed to practice that includes services to the poor and oppressed, and who work to alleviate poverty, oppression, and discrimination.

M3.2 Social work education is based upon a specific body of knowledge, values, and professional skills. It is grounded in the profession's history and philosophy. Education for the profession promotes the development and advancement of knowledge, practice skills, and services that further the well-being of people and promote social and economic justice. Social work education is responsible for the production and application of research and scholarship aimed at advancing social work practice.

M3.3 Programs of social work education are offered at the baccalaureate, master's, and doctoral levels. Doctoral programs are not accredited by the Council.

M3.4 Programs of social work education maintain close, reciprocal, and ongoing relationships with social work practitioners and with groups and organizations that promote, provide, or seek to influence social policies and social work services. Responsibility for initiating these relationships rests with social work education programs. Effective programs develop and maintain a systematic process of communication with these individuals and groups.

M3.5 The effectiveness of any profession depends on the active engagement of its members in continuous learning. Programs of social work education strive to promote continuing professional development of students and faculty. Programs seek to teach students how to become lifelong learners who are motivated to continue the development of knowledge and skills throughout their careers.

M3.6 Effective social work education programs recognize the interdependence of nations and the need for worldwide professional cooperator.

M3.7 Social work education programs must assume a leadership role within the profession by offering curricula that are at the forefront of the new and changing knowledge base of social work and its supporting disciplines.

M4.0 Purpose of Social Work

M4.1 The profession of social work is committed to the enhancement of human well-being and to the alleviation of poverty and oppression. The social work profession receives its sanction from public and private auspices and is the primary profession in the provision of social services. Within its general scope of concern, professional social work is practiced in a wide variety of settings and has four related purposes:

M4.1.1 The promotion, restoration, maintenance, and enhancement of the social functioning of individuals, families, groups, organizations, and communities by helping them to accomplish tasks, prevent and alleviate distress, and use resources.

M4.1.2 The planning, formulation, and implementation of social policies, services, resources, and programs needed to meet basic human needs and support the development of human capacities.

M4.1.3 The pursuit of policies, services, resources, and programs through organizational or administrative advocacy and social or political action, to empower groups at risk and to promote social and economic justice.

M4.1.4 The development and testing of professional knowledge and skill is related to these purposes.

M5.0 Purpose and Structure of Master's Social Work Education

M5.1 The purpose of professional social work education is to enable students to integrate the knowledge, values, and skills of the social work profession into competent practice. The achievement of this purpose requires clarity about learning objectives and expected student outcomes, flexibility in programming and teaching to accommodate a diverse student population, and commitment of sufficient time and resources to the educational process.

M5.2 Two levels of social work education are accredited by the Council on Social Work Education: the baccalaureate and the master's. The baccalaureate level prepares students for generalist social work practice, and the master's level prepares students for advanced social work practice in an area of concentration. These levels of education differ from each other in the depth, breadth, and specificity of knowledge and skill that students are expected to synthesize and apply in practice.

Both levels of social work education must provide the professional foundation curriculum that contains the common body of knowledge, values, and skills of the profession. This common base is transferable among settings, population groups, and problem areas. The master's level of social work education must include the professional foundation content and concentration content for advanced practice in an identifiable area.

M5.3 Professional social work education at the master's level takes place in accredited colleges and universities. It requires the equivalent of two academic years of full-time study and leads to a professional degree at the master's level. Entry into the MSW program does not require completion of the BSW degree.

M5.4 All master's social work programs must:

M5.4.1 Provide content about social work practice with client systems of various sizes and types.

M5.4.2 Prepare graduates to practice with diverse populations.

M5.4.3 Provide content about the social contexts of social work practice, the changing nature of those contexts, the behavior of organizations, and the dynamics of change.

M5.4.4 Infuse throughout the curriculum the values and ethics that guide professional social workers in their practice.

M5.4.5 Prepare graduates who are aware of their responsibility to continue their professional growth and development.

M5.5 The master's curriculum must be based upon a liberal arts perspective and must include the professional foundation and one or more concentrations.

M5.6 The master's curriculum must be developed and organized as a coherent and integrated whole.

M5.7 Graduates of a master's social work program are advanced practitioners who can analyze, intervene, and evaluate in ways that are highly differentiated, discriminating, and self-critical. They must synthesize and

apply a broad range of knowledge as well as practice with a high degree of autonomy and skill. They must be able to refine and advance the quality of their practice as well as that of the larger social work profession. These advanced competencies must be appropriately integrated and reflected in all aspects of their social work practice, including their ability to:

M5.7.1 Apply critical thinking skills within professional contexts, including synthesizing and applying appropriate theories and knowledge to practice interventions.

M5.7.2 Practice within the values and ethics of the social work profession and with an understanding of, and respect for, the positive value of diversity.

M5.7.3 Demonstrate the professional use of self.

M5.7.4 Understand the forms and mechanisms of oppression and discrimination and the strategies and skills of change that advance social and economic justice,

M5.7.5 Understand and interpret the history of the social work profession and its current structures and issues.

M5.7.6 Apply the knowledge and skills of a generalist social work perspective to practice with systems of all sizes.

M5.7.7 Apply the knowledge and skills of advanced social work practice in an area of concentration.

M5.7.8 Critically analyze and apply knowledge of bio-psycho-social variables that affect individual development and behavior, and use theoretical frameworks to understand the interactions among individuals and between individuals and social systems (i.e., families, groups, organizations, and communities).

M5.7.9 Analyze the impact of social policies on client systems, workers, and agencies and demonstrate skills for influencing policy formulation and change.

M5.7.10 Evaluate relevant research studies and apply findings to practice, and demonstrate skills in quantitative and qualitative research design, data analysis, and knowledge dissemination.

M5.7.11 Conduct empirical evaluations of their own practice interventions and those of other relevant systems.

M5.7.12 Use communication skills differentially with a variety of client populations, colleagues, and members of the community.

M5.7.13 Use supervision and consultation appropriate to advanced practice in an area of concentration.

M5.7.14 Function within the structure of organizations and service delivery systems and seek necessary organizational change.

M5.8 Duplication and redundancy of content mastered at the baccalaureate level must be avoided in master's programs. Specifically, BSW graduates who enter MSW programs should not repeat professional foundation content in the master's program that has been mastered in the BSW program. In order to verify mastery and to prevent unproductive repetition, master's programs must develop explicit policies and procedures relevant to admission, course waivers, substitutions, exemptions, or advanced placement. Credit for advanced placement can be granted only for content in the professional foundation. Advanced placement signifies mastery of required content but does not necessarily signify exemption from credit hours. The program must clearly explain specific policies and procedures for advanced placement.

Liberal Arts Perspective

M5.9 A liberal arts perspective enriches understanding of the person-environment context of professional social work practice and is integrally related to the mastery of social work content. This perspective is prerequisite to the master's professional program in social work.

M5.10 A liberal arts perspective provides an understanding of one's cultural heritage in the context of other cultures; the methods and limitations of various systems of inquiry; and the knowledge, attitudes, ways of thinking, and means of communication that are characteristic of a broadly educated person. Students entering the professional curriculum must be capable of thinking critically about society, about people and their problems, and about expressions of culture such as art, literature, science, history, and philosophy. Students must have knowledge about social, psychological, and biological determinants of human behavior and of diverse cultures, social conditions, and social problems.

M5.11 Determination of whether students have acquired a liberal arts perspective is left to the judgment of the faculty of each social work program. Each program must clearly explicate the requirements for attaining a liberal arts perspective and the rationale for those requirements.

M6.0 Master's Curriculum Content

M6.1 The curriculum at the master's level must include both foundation and concentration content. The professional foundation includes content on social work values and ethics, diversity, social and economic justice, populations-at-risk, human behavior and the social environment, social welfare policy and services, social work practice, research, and field practicum. Concentration content includes knowledge, values, and skills for advanced practice in an identifiable area. Master's programs must achieve integration among these content areas. Curriculum areas do not need to be taught in discrete courses, but mastery of the curriculum must occur through classroom experiences and field practice. The master's social work curriculum must cover, but is not necessarily limited to, the professional foundation and the concentration content.

M6.2 The curriculum design of each program must identify a coherent approach to selecting the research and theories offered. Every part of the master's curriculum must strengthen the student's understanding and appreciation of a scientific, analytic approach to building knowledge for the delivery and evaluation of practice. Content provided in each curricular area must be relevant to the objectives, philosophy, and mission of the individual program and must facilitate the student's understanding of how the knowledge relates to social work practice.

M6.3   The Professional Foundation

M6.4   New advances in practice knowledge, as well as the accumulated knowledge of social work education and the social work profession, determine the specific content required for the professional foundation. The professional foundation curriculum must include content on social work values and ethics, diversity, social and economic justice, populations-at-risk, human behavior and the social environment, social welfare policy and services, social work practice, research, and field practicum.

Social Work Values and Ethics

M6.5   Programs of social work education must provide specific knowledge about social work values and their ethical implications, as well as opportunities for students to demonstrate their application in professional practice. Students must be assisted to develop an awareness of their personal values and to clarify conflicting values and ethical dilemmas. Among the values and principles that must be infused throughout every social work curriculum are the following:

M6.5.1   Social workers' professional relationships are built on regard for individual worth and dignity, and are advanced by mutual participation, acceptance, confidentiality, honesty, and responsible handling of conflict.

M6.5.2   Social workers respect the individual's right to make independent decisions and to participate actively in the helping process.

M6.5.3   Social workers are committed to assisting client systems to obtain needed resources.

M6.5.4   Social workers strive to make social institutions more humane and responsive to human needs.

M6.5.5   Social workers demonstrate respect for and acceptance of the unique characteristics of diverse populations.

M6.5.6   Social workers are responsible for their own ethical conduct, the quality of their practice, and seeking continuous growth in the knowledge and skills of their profession.

Diversity

M6.6   Professional social work education is committed to preparing students to understand and appreciate human diversity. Programs must provide curriculum content about differences and similarities in the experiences, needs, and beliefs of people. The curriculum must include content about differential assessment and intervention skills that will enable practitioners to serve diverse populations.

Each program is required to include content about population groups that are particularly relevant to the program's mission. These include, but are not limited to, groups distinguished by race, ethnicity, culture, class, gender, sexual orientation, religion, physical or mental disability, age, and national origin.

Promotion of Social and Economic Justice

M6.7   Programs of social work education must provide an understanding of the dynamics and consequences of social and economic injustice, including all forms of human oppression and discrimination. They must provide students with the skills to promote social change and to implement a wide range of interventions that further the achievement of individual and collective social and economic justice. Theoretical and practice content must be provided about strategies of intervention for achieving social and economic justice and for combating the causes and effects of institutionalized forms of oppression.

Populations-at-Risk

M6.8 Programs of social work education must present theoretical and practice content about patterns, dynamics, and consequences of discrimination, economic deprivation, and oppression. The curriculum must provide content about people of color, women, and gay and lesbian persons. Such content must emphasize the impact of discrimination, economic deprivation, and oppression upon these groups.

Each program must include content about populations-at-risk that are particularly relevant to its mission. In addition to those mandated above, such groups include, but are not limited to, those distinguished by age, ethnicity, culture, class, religion, and physical or mental disability.

Human Behavior and the Social Environment

M6.9 The professional foundation must provide content about theories and knowledge of the human bio-psycho-social development, including theories and knowledge about the range of social systems in which individuals live (families, groups, organizations, institutions, and communities). The human behavior and social environment curriculum must provide an understanding of the interactions among human biological, social, psychological, and cultural systems as they affect and are affected by human behavior. The impact of social and economic forces on individuals and social systems must be presented. Content must be provided about the ways in which systems promote or deter people in the maintaining or achieving optimal health and well-being. Content about values and ethical issues

related to bio-psycho-social theories must be included. Students must be taught to evaluate theory and apply theory to client situations.

Social Welfare Policy and Services

M6.10 The foundation social welfare policy and services content must include the history, mission, and philosophy of the social work profession. Content must be presented about the history and current patterns of provision of social welfare services, the role of social policy in helping or deterring people in the maintenance or attainment of optimal health and well-being, and the effect of policy on social work practice. Students must be taught to analyze current social policy within the context of historical and contemporary factors that shape policy. Content must be presented about the political and organizational processes used to influence policy, the process of policy formulation, and the frameworks for analyzing social policies in light of principles of social and economic justice.

Social Work Practice

M6.11 The professional foundation prepares students to apply a generalist perspective to social work practice with systems of all sizes. Foundation practice content emphasizes professional relationships that are characterized by mutuality, collaboration, and respect for the client system. Content on practice assessment focuses on the examination of client strengths and problems in the interactions among individuals and between people and their environments.

Foundation practice content must include knowledge, values, and skills to enhance the well-being of people and to help ameliorate the environmental conditions that affect people adversely. Practice content must include the following skills: defining issues; collecting and assessing data; planning and contracting; identifying alternative interventions; selecting and implementing appropriate courses of action; using appropriate research to monitor and evaluate outcomes; applying appropriate research-based knowledge and technological advances; and termination. Practice content also includes approaches and skills for practice with clients from differing social, cultural, racial, religious, spiritual, and class backgrounds, and with systems of all sizes.

Research

M6.12   The foundation research curriculum must provide an understanding and appreciation of a scientific, analytic approach to building knowledge for practice and for evaluating service delivery in all areas of practice. Ethical standards of scientific inquiry must be included in the research content.

The research content must include qualitative and quantitative research methodologies; analysis of data, including statistical procedures; systematic evaluation of practice; analysis and evaluation of theoretical bases, research questions, methodologies, statistical procedures, and conclusions of research reports; and relevant technological advances.

M6.13   Each program must identify how the research curriculum contributes to the student's use of scientific knowledge for practice.

Field Practicum

M6.14   The field practicum is an integral component of the curriculum in social work education. It engages the student in supervised social work practice and provides opportunities to apply classroom learning in the field setting.

M6.15   Field education at the master's level requires a minimum of 900 hours in field practicum.

M6.16   Each educational program must establish standards for field practicum set-

tings that define their social work services and practices, field instructor assignments and activities, and student learning expectations and responsibilities. Individual programs may organize their practice in different ways but must ensure educationally directed, coordinated, and monitored practicum experiences for all students. All programs must provide:

a. Placements based upon the objectives of the educational program and the learning needs of each student.

b. Structured learning opportunities that enable students to compare their practice experiences, integrate knowledge acquired in the classroom, and expand knowledge beyond the scope of the practicum setting.

c. Support for field practicum instructors by:
   1. Sharing pertinent information about practicum students.
   2. Providing information about the organization and content of the educational curriculum, emphasizing the interrelationships among human behavior, social policy, research, and practice content.
   3. Providing information about the sequencing of course content.
   4. Articulating clear practice and evaluation goals for the field practicum and for each individual student.
   5. Offering orientation and training programs.

Foundation Practicum

M6.17   The purpose of the foundation practicum is for the student to apply foundation knowledge, skills, values, and ethics to practice.

M6.18   The foundation practicum must provide the student with opportunities for:

a. The development of an awareness of self in the process of intervention.

b. Supervised practice experience in the application of knowledge, values and ethics, and practice skills to enhance the well-being of people and to work toward the amelioration of environmental conditions that affect people adversely.

c. Use of oral and written professional communications that are consistent with the language of the practicum setting and the profession.

d. Use of professional supervision to enhance learning.

e. Critical assessment, implementation, and evaluation of agency policy within ethical guidelines.

M6.19   Concentration Curriculum

M6.20   The central purpose of the master's curriculum is to prepare students for advanced social work practice in an identifiable concentration area. Each program must clearly explicate for each concentration the (1) conceptualization and design, (2) expected educational outcomes, and (3) content.

Conceptualization and Design

M6.21   A concentration provides a context within which advanced practice skills and knowledge are acquired. A conceptual framework, built upon relevant theories, shapes the breadth and depth of knowledge and practice skills to be acquired.

Programs have the freedom to establish concentrations within an organizing framework that is consistent with the purpose of social work and its traditional values. The organizing framework for concentrations must have curricular coherence and logic, and must be anchored in the liberal arts and the professional foundation. The program must have sufficient resources to support the concentrations offered. Frameworks and perspectives for concentrations that are frequently offered by programs include fields of practice, problem areas, populations-at-risk, intervention methods or roles, and practice contexts and perspectives. Combinations of concentrations are permitted.

Concentration Outcomes

M6.22   Each master's program must apply foundation content to the central issues relevant to the areas of concentration. Programs must determine educational outcomes for each concentration offered.

Concentration Content

M6.23   Concentration content must be designed to prepare students for advanced practice. The emphasis of content areas must be relevant to the concentration and may vary across concentrations.

Concentration Practicum

M6.24   The concentration practicum for master's social work education must clearly support the student's area(s) of concentration.

M7.0   Avenues of Renewal

M7.1   Programs of social work education must remain vital and progressive by actively pursuing ongoing exchanges with the practice community and other essential groups, and by developing and assessing new knowledge and technology.

M7.1.1   Programs must establish and maintain close, reciprocal and ongoing relationships with social work practitioners, and use those relationships to continuously evaluate the total curriculum.

M7.1.2   Programs must establish and maintain relationships with groups that develop, implement, and benefit from social policies and services.

M7.1.3   Programs must establish and maintain involvement with the professional associations and with disciplines and departments in the academic community.

M7.1.4   Programs must assume responsibility for systematic and high-quality scholarship that assesses social work practice and develops new knowledge.

Adopted 6/24/94

Appendix E

MSW Programs in the United States

MSW Programs

Alabama

University of Alabama, School of Social Work, Box 870314, Tuscaloosa, AL, 35487-0314

Arizona

Arizona State University, School of Social Work, Box 871802, Tempe, AZ 85287-1802

Arkansas

University of Arkansas, Little Rock, School of Social Work, 2801 South University, Little Rock, AR 72204

California

California State University, Fresno, Department of Social Work Education, 5310 Campus Dr., Fresno, CA 93740-0102

California State University, Long Beach, Department of Social Work, 1250 Bellflower Blvd., Long Beach, CA 90840-0902

California State University, Sacramento, Division of Social Work, 6000 J St., Sacramento, CA 95819-6090

California State University, San Bernardino, Department of Social Work, 5500 University Parkway, San Bernardino, CA 94207

Loma Linda University, Master of Social Work Program, Department of Social Work, Loma Linda, CA 92350

San Diego State University, School of Social Work, 5500 Campanile Dr., San Diego, CA 92182-4119

San Francisco State University, School of Social Work, 1600 Holloway Ave., San Francisco, CA 94132

San Jose State University, College of Social Work, One Washington Square, Suite #215, San Jose, CA 95192-0124

University of California at Berkeley, School of Social Welfare, 120 Haviland Hall, Berkeley, CA 94720-7400

University of California at Los Angeles, Department of Social Welfare, 3250 Public Policy Building, Box 951656, Los Angeles, CA 90095-1656

University of Southern California, School of Social Work, 699 W. 34th St., MRF Bldg., Rm. 214, Los Angeles, CA 90089-0411

Colorado

Colorado State University, Department of Social Work, 127 Education Building, Fort Collins, CO 80523-1586

University of Denver, Graduate School of Social Work, 2148 S High St, Denver, CO 80208-2886

Connecticut

Southern Connecticut State University, Graduate Social Work Program, P R Lang Social Work Center, 101 Farnham Ave, New Haven, CT 06515

University of Connecticut, School of Social Work, 1798 Asylum Ave, W Hartford, CT 06117

Delaware
Delaware State College, Department of Social Work, 1200 N Dupont Hwy, Dover, DE 19901-2277

District of Columbia
The Catholic University of America, Natl Catholic School of Social Service, Washington DC 20064

Gallaudet University, Department of Social Work, 800 Florida Ave NE,Washington, DC 20002-3695

Howard University, School of Social Work, 601 Howard Pl NW, Washincton, DC 20059

Florida
Barry University, Ellen Whiteside McDonnell School of Social Work, 11300 NE Second Ave., Miami, FL 33161

Florida International University, School of Social Work, 3000 NE145th St, Ac-1 Bldg., Suite 234, N Miami, FL 33181

Florida State University, School of Social Work, C2412 University Center, Tallahassee, FL 32306-2024

University of Central Florida, School of Social Work, P.O. Box 163358, Orlando, FL 32828

University of South Florida, School of Social Work, Soc 107, 4202 E Fowler Ave, Tampa, FL 33620-8100

Georgia
Clark Atlanta University, School of Social Work, JP Brawley Dr. at Fair St SW, Atlanta GA 30314-4391

University of Georgia, School of Social Work, 105 Tucker Hall, Athens, GA 30602

Hawaii
University of Hawaii at Manoa, School of Social Work, 2500 Campus Rd., Honolulu, HI 96822

Idaho
Boise State University, School of Social Work, 1910 University Dr, Boise, ID 8372

Illinois
Aurora University, School of Social Work, 347 S Gladstone Ave, Aurora, IL 60506-4892

Loyola University of Chicago, School of Social Work, 820 N Michigan Ave, Chicago, IL 60611

Southern Illinois University at Carondale, School of Social Work, Quigley Hall, Carbondale, IL 62901-4329

University of Chicago, School of Social Service Administration, 969 E. 60th St., Chicago, IL 60637

University of Illinois Chicago, Jane Addams Coll of Social Work,mc 309, 1040 W Harrison St, Chicago, IL 60607-7134

University of Illinois at Urbana-Champaign, School of Social Work, 1207 W. Oregon St., Urbana, IL 61801

Indiana
Indiana University, School of Social Work, Education/Social Work Bldg, 902 W New York St, Indianapolis, IN 46202-5156

Iowa
University of Iowa, School of Social Work, 308 North Hall, Iowa City, IA 52242-1223

Kansas
University of Kansas, School of Social Welfare, Twenty Hall, Lawrence, KS 66045-2510

Kentucky
University of Kentucky, College of Social Work, 619 Patterson Office Tower S. Limestone, Lexington, KY 40506-0027

University of Louisville, Raymond A. Kent School of Social Work, Oppenheimer Hall, Louisville, KY 40292

Louisana

Louisana State University, School of Social Work, Huey P. Long Field House, Baton Rouge, LA 70803

Southern University at New Orleans, School of Social Work, 6400 Press Dr., New Orleans, LA 70126

Tulane University, School of Social Work, 6823 St. Charles Ave., New Orleans, LA 70118-5672

Maine

University of Maine, School of Social Work, 5770 Annex C, Orono, ME 04469

University of New England, School of Social Work, Hills Beach Rd., Biddeford, ME 04005

Maryland

University of Maryland,Baltimore, School of Social Work, Louis L Kaplan Hall, 525 W Redwood St, Baltimore, MD 21201-1777

Massachusetts

Boston College, Graduate School of Social Work, Mcguinn Hall 140 Common Wealth Ave., Chestnut Hill, MA 02167-3807

Boston University, School of Social Work, 264 Bay State Rd., Boston, MA 02215

Salem State College, School of Social Work, 352 Lafayette St, Salem, MA 01970

Simmons College, Graduate School of Social Work, 51 Commonwealth Ave, Boston, MA 02116-2307

Smith College, School of Social Work, Lily Hall, North Hampton, MA 01063

Springfield College, School of Social Work, 263 Alden St., Springfield, MA 01109-3797

Michigan

Eastern Michigan University, Department of Social Work, King Hall, Rm #411, Ypsilanti, MI 14197

Grand Valley State University, School of Social Work, 25 Commerce St. SW, Grand Rapids, MI 49503

Michigan State University, School of Social Work, 254 Baker Hall, E Lansing, MI 48824

University of Michigan, School of Social Work, 1080 S. University, Ann Arbor, MI 48109-1260

Wayne State University, School of Social Work, 201 Thompson Home, 4756 Cass Ave., Detroit, MI 48202

Western Michigan University, School of Social Work, Kalamazoo, MI 49008-5034

Minnesota

Augsburg College, Social Work Department, 2211 Riversdale Ave., Minneaplois, MN 55454-1351

Coll of St Catherine/ University of St Thomas, Department of Social Work, Mail # Lor 405, 2115 Summit Ave, St Paul, MN 55105

University of Minnesota-Duluth, Department of Social Work, 220 Bohannon Hall, Duluth, MN 55812

University of Minnesota-Twin Cities, School of Social Work, 400 Ford Hall, 224 Church St. SE, Minneapolis, MN 55455

Mississippi

University of Southern Mississippi, School of Social Work, Box 5114, Hattiesburg, MS 39406-5114

Missouri

Saint Louis University, School of Social Service, 3550 Lindell Blvd., St. Louis, MO 63103

University of Missouri Columbia, School of Social Work, 701 Clark Hall, Columbia, MO 65211

Washington University, The George Warren Brown School of Social Work, Campus Box 1196, One Brookings Dr., St. Louis, MO 63130-4899

Nebraska
University of Nebraska Omaha, School of Social Work, Annex 40, 60th & Dodge st, Omaha, NE 68182-0293

Nevada
University of Nevada Las Vegas, School of Social Work, 4505 Maryland Pk, Las Vegas, NV 89154-5032

University of Nevada-Reno, School of Social Work, Buisness Building Rm 523, mail stop 090, Reno, NV 89557-0068

New Jersey
Rutgers- The State University of New Jersey, School of Social Work, 536 George St., New Brunswick, NJ 08903

Rutgers-The State University of New Jersey, School of Social Work, Camden Campus, 327 Cooper St., Camden, NJ 08102

Rutgers-The State University of New Jersey, School of Social Work, 707 Hill Hall, Newark, NJ 07102

New Mexico
New Mexico Highlands University, School of Social Work, Singer Hall, Rm 205, Las Vagas, NM 87701

New Mexico State University, Department of Social Work, Po Box 30001 Dept 3sw, Las Cruces, NM 88003-8001

New York
Adelphi University, Masters in Social Work Program, South Ave., Garden City, NY 11530

Columbia University, School of Social Work 622 W 113th St, New York, NY 10025-7982

Fordham University, Grad School of Social Service, 113 W 60th St, New York, NY 10023-7479

Hunter College of the City University of New York, School of Social Work, 129 E. 79th St., New York, NY 10021

New York University, Shirley M. Ehrenkranz School of Social Work, 1 Washington Square North, New York, NY 10003

Roberts Wesleyan College, M.S.W. Program, 2301 Westside Dr, Rochester, NY 14624-1997

State University of New York, University at Albany, School of Social Work, 135 Western Ave., Albany, NY 12222

State University of New York at Buffalo, School of Social Work, 359 Baldy Hall, Buffalo, NY 14260-1050

State University of New York at Stony Brook, School of Social Work, School of Social Welfare, Health Sciences Center Level 2, Rm 093, Stony Brook, NY 11794

Syracuse University, School of Social Work, Sims Hall, 123 College Pl, Syracuse, NY 13244-1230

Yeshiva University, Wurzweiler School of Social Work, Belfer Hall, 500 W. 185th St., New York, NY 10033

North Carolina
East Carolina University, School of Social Work, Ragsdale Bldg Rm 208a,Greenville, NC 27858-4353

University of North Carolina at Chapel Hill, School of Social Work, Tate-Turner-Kuralt Building CB #3550, 301 Pittsboro St., Chapel Hill, NC 27599-3550

North Dakota
University of North Dakota, Department of Social Work, Box 7135, Grand Forks, ND 58202-7135

Ohio

Case Western Reserve University Mandel School of Applied,10900 Euclid Ave, Cleveland, OH 44106-7164

Ohio State University, College of Social Work, 1947 College Rd., Columbus, OH 43210-1162

Ohio University-, Department of Social Work, 531 Morton Hall, Athens, OH 45701-2979

University of Cincinnati, School of Social Work, P.O. Box 210108, Cincinnati, OH 45220

Oklahoma

University of Oklahoma, , School of Social Work, Rhyne Hall, 1005 Jenkins, Norma, OK 73019-0475

Oregon

Portland State University, Graduate School of Social Work, Po Box 751, Portland, OR 97207-0751

Pennsylvania

Bryn Mawr College, Graduate School of Social Work, 300 Airdale Rd, Bryn Mawr, PA, 19010-1697

Marywood University, School of Social Work, 2300 Adams Ave., Scranton, PA 18509

Temple University, School of Social Administration, Ritter Hall Annex, 13th St and Cecil B Moore Ave, Philadelphia, PA 19122

University of Pennsylvania, School of Social Work, 3701 Locust Walk, Philiadelphia, PA 19104-6214

University of Pittsburgh, School of Social Work, 2117 Cathedral of Learning, Pittsburghgh, PA 15260

Widener University, Center for Social Work Education, One University Place, Chester, PA 19013

Puerto Rico

Interamericana, Universidad, Trabajo Social, Arecibo PR 00614-4050

University of Puerto Rico, Beatriz Lassalle Graduate School of Social Work, P.O. Box 23345, San Juan, PR 00931-3345

Rhode Island

Rhode Island College, School of Social Work, 600 Mount Pleasant Dr, Providence, RI 02908

South Carolina

University of South Carolina, College of Social Work, Columbia, SC 29208

Tennessee

University of Tennessee, College of Social Work, 109 Henson Hall, Knoxville, TN 37996-3333

University of Tennessee, College of Social Work, 822 Beale St., Rm. 220, Memphis, TN 38163

University of Tennessee, College of Social Work, 1720 W. End Ave., Rm. 230, Nashville, TN 37203

Texas

Our Lady of the Lake University, Worden School of Social Service, 411 SW 24th St, San Antonio, TX 78207-4689

University of Houston,Graduate School of Social Work, Houston, TX 77204-4492

University of Texas Arlington, School of Social Work, Box 19129, Arlington, TX 76019

University of Texas at Austin, School of Social Work, 1925 San Jacinto Blvd., Mail Code: D3500, Austin, TX 78712

Utah

Brigham Young University, School of Social Work, 221 Knight Mangum Bldg, Po Box 24472, Provo, UT 84602-4472

University of Utah, Graduate School of Social Work, Social Work Bldg, Salt Lake City, UT 84112

Vermont
University of Vermont, Department of Social Work, 228 Waterman Bldg, Burlington, VT 05405

Virginia
Norfolk State University, E R Strong Sch of Social Work, 2401 Corprew Ave, Norfolr, VA 23504

Radford University, School of Social Work, Box 6958, Radford, VA 24142

Virginia Commonwealth University, School of Social Work, 1001 W. Franklin St., P.O. Box 842027, Richmond, VA 23284-2027

Washington
Eastern Washington University, Inland Empire School of Social Work and Human Services, Ms 19 , 526 5th St, -Cheney, WA 99004-2431

University of Washington, School of Social Work, 4101 15th Ave., NE, Seattle, WA 98105-6299

Walla Walla College, Graduate School of Social Work, 204 S College Avenue, College Place, WA 99324-1198,

West Virginia
West Virginia University, School of Social Work, Po Box 6830, Allen Hall, Morgantown, WV 26506-6830

Wisconsin
University of Wisconsin-Madison, School of Social Work, 1350 University Ave., Madison, WI 53706-1510

University of Wisconsin-Milwaukee, School of Social Work, P.O. Box 786, Milwaukee, WI 53201

Master's Programs in Candidacy

Alabama
Alabama A & M University, Graduate Social Work Program, P.O. Box 1417, Normal, AL 35762

Alaska
University of Alaska at Anchorage, Department of Social Work, 3211 Providence Dr., Anchorage, AK 99508-8230

California
California State University-Stanislaus, Master of Social Work Department, 801 W. Monte Vista Ave., Turlock, CA 95382

Georgia
Savannah State College, M.S.W. Programs, Po Box 20553, Savannah, GA 31404

Valdosta State University, Division of Social Work, 1500 Patterson St., Valdosta, GA 31698

Indiana
University of Southern Indiana, Social Work Department, 8600 University Blvd, Evansville, IN 47712

Kansas
Washburn University, Department of Social Work, 1700 College, Topeka, KS 66621

Louisiana
Grambling State University, School of Social Work, Po Box 907, Grambling, LA 71245

Michigan
Andrews University, Social Work Department, Nethery Hall, Berrien Springs, MI 49102

Mississippi
Jackson State University, Graduate School of Social Work,3825 Ridgwood Rd, Jackson, MS 39211

Missouri
Southwest Missouri State University, School of Social Work, 901 South National Ave., Professional Building, Suite 200, Springfield, MO 65804

New Hampshire
University of New Hampshire, Department of Social Work, 15 Library Way, Murkland Hall, Durham, NH 03824-3596

New Jersey
Kearn College, Master of Social Work Program, Hutchinson Hall Rm. 305, Morris Ave., Union, NJ 07083

North Carolina
North Carolina A&T State University/University of North Carolina at Greensboro, Joint Master of Social Work, 1601 E. Market St., Greensboro, NC 27411-0002

Ohio
Cleveland State University/University of Akron, Joint Master's of Social Work, 2227 Prospect Ave., Cleveland, OH 44115

Puerto Rico
Universidad Interamericana de PR, Graduate Social Work Program, Recinto Metropolitano, Po Box 191293, San Juan PR 00919-1293

Texas
Southwest Texas State University, Department of Social Work/Walter Richter Institute, 601 University Dr., San Marcos, TX 78666-4616

A p p e n d i x F

Permanent Missions to the United Nations

Afghanistan afgun@undp.org
Albania albun@undp.org
Algeria dzaun@undp.org
Andorra andun@undp.org
Angola agoun@undp.org
Antigua and Barbuda atgun@undp.org
Argentina argun@undp.org
Armenia armun@undp.org
Australia ausun@undp.org
Austria autun@undp.org
Azerbaijan azeun@undp.org
the Bahamas bhsun@undp.org
Bahrain bhrun@undp.org
Bangladesh bgdun@undp.org
Barbados brbun@undp.org
Belarus blrun@undp.org
Belgium belun@undp.org
Belize blzun@undp.org
Benin benun@undp.org
Bhutan btnun@undp.org
Bolivia bolun@undp.org
Bosnia and Herzegovina bihun@undp.org
Botswana bwaun@undp.org
Brazil braun@undp.org
Brunei Darussalam brnun@undp.org
Bulgaria bgrun@undp.org
Burkina Faso bfaun@undp.org
Burundi bdiun@undp.org
Cambodia khmun@undp.org
Cameroon cmrun@undp.org
Canada canun@undp.org
Cape Verde cpvun@undp.org
Central African Republic cafun@undp.org
Chad tcdun@undp.org
Chile chiun@undp.org
China chnun@undp.org
Colombia colun@undp.org

Comoros comun@undp.org
Congo cogun@undp.org
Costa Rica cosun@undp.org
Cote d'Ivoire civun@undp.org
Croatia hrvun@undp.org
Cuba cubun@undp.org
Cyprus cypun@undp.org
Czech Republic czeun@undp.org
Denmark dnkun@undp.org
Djibouti djiun@undp.org
Dominica dmaun@undp.org
Dominican Republic domun@undp.org
Ecuador ecuun@undp.org
Egypt egyun@undp.org
El Salvador salun@undp.org
Equatorial Guinea gnqun@undp.org
Eritrea eriun@undp.org
Estonia estun@undp.org
Ethiopia ethun@undp.org
Fiji fjiun@undp.org
Finland sanomat.yke@formin.fi
France fraun@undp.org
Gabon gabun@undp.org
Gambia gmbun@undp.org
Georgia geoun@undp.org
Germany germany@un.int
Ghana ghaun@undp.org
Great Britain gbrun@undp.org
Greece grcun@undp.org
Grenada grdun@undp.org
Guatemala gtmun@undp.org
Guinea ginun@undp.org
Guinea-Bissau gnbun@undp.org
Guyana guyun@undp.org
Haiti htiun@undp.org
Honduras hndun@undp.org
Hungary hunun@undp.org

Iceland islun@undp.org
India indun@undp.org
Indonesia idnun@undp.org
Iran irnun@undp.org
Iraq irqun@undp.org
Ireland irlun@undp.org
Israel isrun@undp.org
Italy itaun@undp.org
Jamaica jamun@undp.org
Japan jpnun@undp.org
Jordan jorun@undp.org
Kazakstan kazun@undp.org
Kenya kenun@undp.org
Democratic People's Republic of Korea
   prkun@undp.org
Republic of Korea korun@undp.org
Kuwait kwtun@undp.org
Kyrgyzstan kgzun@undp.org
Lao People's Democratic Republic
   laoun@undp.org
Latvia lvaun@undp.org
Lebanon lbnun@undp.org
Lesotho lsoun@undp.org
Liberia lbrun@undp.org
Libya lbyun@undp.org
Liechtenstein lieun@undp.org
Lithuania ltuun@undp.org
Luxembourg luxun@undp.org
Former Yugoslav Republic of Macedonia
   mkdun@undp.org
Madagascar mdgun@undp.org
Malawi mwiun@undp.org
Malaysia mysun@undp.org
Maldives mdvun@undp.org
Mali mliun@undp.org
Malta mltun@undp.org
Marshall Islands mhlun@undp.org
Mauritania mrtun@undp.org
Mauritius musun@undp.org
Mexico mexun@undp.org
Federated States of Micronesia
   fsmun@undp.org
Moldova mdaun@undp.org
Monaco mcoun@undp.org
Mongolia mngun@undp.org
Morocco marun@undp.org
Mozambique mozun@undp.org
Myanmar mmrun@undp.org

Namibia namun@undp.org
Nepal nplun@undp.org
Netherlands nldun@undp.org
New Zealand nzlun@undp.org
Nicaragua nicun@undp.org
Niger nerun@undp.org
Nigeria ngaun@undp.org
Norway norun@undp.org
Oman omnun@undp.org
Pakistan pakun@undp.org
Palau plwun@undp.org
Panama panun@undp.org
Papua New Guinea pngun@undp.org
Paraguay pryun@undp.org
Peru perun@undp.org
Philippines phlun@undp.org
Poland polun@undp.org
Portugal prtun@undp.org
Qatar qatun@undp.org
Romania romun@undp.org
Rwanda rwaun@undp.org
Russian Federation rusun@undp.org
Samoa wsmun@undp.org
San Marino smrun@undp.org
São Tomé and Principe stpun@undp.org
Saudi Arabia sauun@undp.org
Senegal senun@undp.org
Seychelles sycun@undp.org
Sierra Leone sleun@undp.org
Singapore sgpun@undp.org
Slovakia svkun@undp.org
Slovenia svnun@undp.org
Solomon Islands slbun@undp.org
Somalia somun@undp.org
South Africa zafun@undp.org
Spain espun@undp.org
Sri Lanka lkaun@undp.org
St. Kitts and Nevis knaun@undp.org
St. Lucia lcaun@undp.org
St. Vincent and the Grenadines
   vctun@undp.org
Sudan sdnun@undp.org
Suriname surun@undp.org
Swaziland swzun@undp.org
Sweden sweun@undp.org
Syrian Arab Republic syrun@undp.org
Tajikistan tjkun@undp.org
Thailand thaun@undp.org

Togo tgoun@undp.org
Trinidad and Tobago ttoun@undp.org
Tunisia tunun@undp.org
Turkey turun@undp.org
Turkmenistan tkmun@undp.org
Uganda ugaun@undp.org
Ukraine ukrun@undp.org
United Arab Emirates areun@undp.org
United Republic of Tanzania
   tzaun@undp.org
United States of America usaun@undp.org
Uruguay uruun@undp.org
Uzbekistan uzbun@undp.org
Vanuatu vutun@undp.org

Venezuela venun@undp.org
Viet Nam vnmun@undp.org
Yemen yemun@undp.org
Yugoslavia yugun@undp.org
Zaire zarun@undp.org
Zambia zmbun@undp.org
Zimbabwe zweun@undp.org

Permanent Observer Missions

Holy See vatun@undp.org
Switzerland cheun@undp.org
Palestinian National Authority
   palun@undp.org

Appendix G

International Federation of Social Workers Member Associations

Federacion Argentina de Asociaciones de Profesionales del Servicio Social
Padre Buodo 516 C.P. 6300 Santa Rosa,
La Pampa, Argentina
Phone: (54) 2954 425538; Fax: (54) 2954
433443
E-mail: faapss@infovia.com.ar

Australian Association of Social Workers Ltd.
P.O. Box 4956, Kingston, ACT 2604,
Australia
Phone: (61) 2 6273 0199; Fax: (61) 2
6273 5020
E-mail: aaswnat@aasw.asn.au
Homepage: www.aasw.asn.au

Österreichischer Berufsverband Diplomierter SozialarbeiterInnen
Mariahilferstrasse 81/1/3/14, A-1060
Vienna, Austria
Phone: (43) 1 587 4656; Fax: (43) 1 587
46 56 10
E-mail: oebds@ins.at
Homepage: www.sozialarbeit.at

Bahrain Society of Sociologists
P.O. Box 26488, Manama, Bahrain
Phone and Fax: (973) 727 485

Belorussian Association of Social Workers
Ms. Marina Naranovich, V Khoruzhya
Str. 16-161, Box 179, Minsk 220123,
Belarus
Phone: (375) 17 260 2686; Fax: (375) 17
2346 435
E-mail: basw@nsys.by
Homepage: www.basw,unibel.by

Union Professionnelle des Associations Francophones d'Assistants Sociaux (UFAS)
42, rue Brognez, B-1060 Bruxelles,
Belgique
Phone: (32) 2 522 9104; Fax: (32) 2 726
21 25

Syndicat National des Techniciens Sociaux du Benin
07 BP 99 Sainte Rita, Cotonou,
Republique du Benin
Phone: (229) 331 603; no fax information available

Colegio Nacional de Trabajadores Sociales de Bolivia
Casilla Postal 13592, La Paz, Bolivia
Phone: (591) 315 740; Fax: (591) 2 366
104

Conselho Federal de Serviço Social (CFESS)
Setor Comercial Sur, Quadra 02, Bloco
C, Sala 312/17 Ed. Serra Dourada,
CEP 70300-902, Brasilia D.F., Brazil
Phone: (55) 61 233 1652; Fax: (55) 61
223 2420
E-mail: cfess@persocom.com.br
Homepage: www.cfess,org.br

Bulgarian Coordinating Body for IFSW-Membership (correspondence to both):

Bulgarian Association of Social Workers
"Trayanovi vrata" str. 107/A, 32, Sofia
1408, Bulgaria
Phone: (359) 2 517 374; Fax: (359) 2 598
113

Organisation of Social Workers in Bulgaria
21, Hristo Belchev str, Sofia 1000, Bulgaria
Phone: (359) 2 244 865; Fax: (359) 2 211
032

Canadian Association of Social Workers
383, Parkdale Avenue, Suite 402, Ottawa,
ON K1Y 4R4, Canada
Phone: (1) 613 729 6668; Fax: (1) 613
729 9608
E-mail: casw@casw-acts.ca
Homepage: www.casw-acts.ca

Colegio Asistentes Sociales de Chile
Calle Dieciocho 45, Piso 4, Depto. 401,
Casilla 2324, Santiago, Chile
Phone: (56) 2 671 7382; Fax: (56) 2 696
2199
E-mail: vivigo@netline.cl
Homepage: www.cmet.net/profesional

China Association of Social Workers
Ma Xue-Li, President, No 9 Huang Cheng
Gen Nan Jie Xicheng District, Beijing
100032, People's Republic of China
Phone and Fax: (86) 10 66 08 4345

**Federación Colombiana de Trabajadores
Sociales (FECTS)**
Sra . Libia Christina Santos, President,
Calle 19, No. 32-19, Barrio San Alonso,
Bucaramanga, Santander, Colombia
Phone: (57) 76 455 266; Fax: (57) 76 346
144
E-mail: federacioncts@yahoo.com

**Sociedad Cubana de Trabajadores Sociales
de la Salud**
Calle L No 406 e/23 y 25 Vedado, CP
10400, Ciudad Habana, Cuba
Phone and Fax: (53) 7 29 1671
E-mail: socutras@infomed.sld.cu

Cyprus Association of Social Workers
M. Malamo Neophytou, President, Nikou
Theofanous S., Pallouriotisa, Nicosia,
Cyprus
Phone: (357) 2 437 443; Fax: (357) 2 439
130
E-mail: syms@iname.com

**Association of Social Workers in Czech
Republic**
Mirovická 19, Kobylisy, 182 00 Prague 8,
Czech Republic
Phone: (42) 2 900 54568; no fax informa-
tion available

**Danish Co-ordinating Body for IFSW-Mem-
bership (correspondence to all three):**

Danish Association of Social Workers
P.O. Box 69, DK-1003 Copenhagen K,
Denmark
Phone: (45) 33 91 30 33; Fax: (45) 33 91
30 69
E-mail: aam@socialrdg.dk
Homepage: www.socialrdg.dk

**HK/Kommunal—Danish Union of Commer-
cial and Office Employees/Local Govern-
ment**
H. C. Andersens Boulevard 50, DK–1780
Copenhagen V, Denmark
Phone: (45) 33 30 43 59; Fax: (45) 33 30
44 49
E-mail: 44est@hk.dk
Homepage: www.hk-kommunal.dk

National Federation of Social Educators (SL)
Brolæggerstræde 9, DK–1211 Copen-
hagen K, Denmark
Phone: (45) 33 96 28 00; Fax: (45) 33 96
29 96
E-mail: sl@sl-dk.dk
Homepage: www.sl-dk.dk

**Asociacion Dominicana de Trabajadores
Sociales Profesionales Inc. (ADOTRASOP)**
Aparado Postal 4936, Santo Domingo,
Dominican Republic
Phone: (1) 809 583 9393; Fax: (1) 809
5871 8177
E-mail: giselda.blanco@codetel,net.do

Union of Social Professions of Egypt
32 Gaber Ibn Haian Street, Dokky, Giza,
Egypt
Phone: (20) 2 349 7980; Fax: (20) 2 765
214

Faeroe Islands Association of Social Workers
Postrúm 1191, FR -110 Tórshavn, Faeroe
Islands
Phone: (298) 3 15480; Fax: (298) 3 18850
E-mail: alma@post.olivant.fo

Union of Professional Social Workers
Rautatieläisenkatu 6, SF-00520 Helsinki,
Finland
Phone: (358) 9 877 0270; Fax: (358) 9
149 6440
E-mail: upsw@sostl.fi
Homepage: www.sostl.fi

Association Nationale des Assistants de Service Social (ANAS)
15, rue de Bruxelles, F-75009 Paris,
France
Phone: (33) 1 45 26 33 79; Fax: (33) 1 42
80 07 03
E-mail: anas@travail-social.com
Homepage: www.altern.org/anas/index.
htm

Deutscher Berufsverband für Sozialarbeit, Sozialpädagogik und Heilpädagogik e.V.
Friedrich-Ebert Strasse 30, D-45127
Essen, Germany
Phone: (49) 201 820 780; Fax: (49) 201
8207 840
E-mail: geschaeftsstelle@dbsh.de
Homepage: www.dbsh.de

Ghana Association of Social Workers (GASOW)
Mrs Ernestina Adams-Lomotey, President, P.O. Box OS 924, Osu-Accra,
Ghana
Phone: (233) 21 242 022 or (233) 21
665298; Fax: (233) 21 662683

Hellenic Association of Social Workers
19, Tositsa Street, 106 83 Athens, Greece
Phone: (30) 1 883 4818; Fax: (30) 1 882
7071

Hong Kong Social Workers Association
Duke of Windsor Social Service Building,
Room 703, 15 Hennessy Road, Wan-
chai, Hong Kong
Phone: (852) 2528 1802; Fax: (852) 2528
0068
E-mail: hkswa@hkswa.org.hk
Homepage: www.hkswa.org.hk

Szociális Munkások Magyarországi Egyesülete
1094 Budapest, Liliom u. 8, Hungary
Phone: (36) 1 216 2866; Fax: (36) 1 216
2867
E-mail: 352@cspc.hu

Iceland Association of Social Workers
Lagmuli 7, P.O. Box 5150, 125 Reykjavik,
Iceland
Phone: (354) 581 4322; Fax: (354) 588
9239
E-mail: soc-work@itn.is

National Co-ordinating Committee of Professional Social Workers (NCCPSW)
c/o Mr. M. V. Sriganesh, Convener, 69/03,
Shankaramutt Road, Bangalore-
560004, India
Phone: (91) 80 600 600; Fax: (91) 80 334
0357

Irish Association of Social Workers
114–116, Pearse Street, Dublin 2,
Ireland
Phone: (353) 1 677 4838; Fax: (353)1 671
5734
E-mail: iasw@iol.ie

Israel Association of Social Workers
93, Arlosorov Street, Histadrut Building,
Tel Aviv, Israel
Phone: (972) 3 692 1180; Fax: (972) 3
692 1148
E-mail: info@isassw.org.il
Homepage: www.isassw.org.il

Associazione Nazionale Assistenti Sociali
Largo F.Anzani19 Androne C Scala A
int.6, I-00153 Roma, Italy
Phone: (39) 06 58 33 33 23; Fax: (39) 06
58 17 99 40
E-mail: cesdiss@iperbole.bologna.it

Japanese Co-ordinating Body for IFSW-Membership (correspondence toall three):

Japanese Association of Certified Social Workers
Floor 3, Sakurai Building, 4-5 Koujimati,
Chiiyoda-ku, Tokyo 102-8482,Japan
Phone: (81) 3 5275 3580; Fax: (81) 3
5275 0139
E-mail: info@jacsw.or.jp
Homepage: jacsw.or.jp

Japan Association for Medical Social Work
Win Yotsuya 1110, 2-18 Sumiyoshi-chou,
Shinjuku-ku, Tokyo 162-0065, Japan
Phone: (81) 3 5366 1057; Fax: (81) 3
5366 1058
E-mail: jaswhc@d3.dion.ne.jp

Japanese Association of Social Workers
No. 8 Kojimachi Bldg., Rm. B-557, 4-5,
Kojimachi, Chiyoda-Ku, Tokyo 102,
Japan
Phone: (81) 3 3221 1877; Fax: (81) 3
3221 6523
E-mail: jasw@netlaputa.ne.jp

Kenya National Association of Social Workers
P.O. Box 74223, Nairobi, Kenya
Phone and Fax: (254) 2 740 039
E-mail: assk@cepac.africaonline.com

Korean Association of Social Workers
Mr. Kim Yoong II, President, 9th Floor,
No. 24-2 World Vision Bldg., Yoido-
dong, Young Deung Po-Ku, Seoul 156-
010, Korea
Phone: (82) 2 786 0190; Fax: (82) 2 786
0191
E-mail: kasw@welfare.net
Homepage: www.kasw.or.kr

Kuwait Association of Social Workers
P.O. Box 34100, Adeiliya, 73251 Kuwait
Phone: (965) 252 3472; Fax: (965) 256
3492

Latvian Co-ordinating Body for IFSW-Membership (correspondence to both):

Latvian Association of Professional Social and Care Workers
Ed. Smilga Street 46-204, LV-1002 Riga,
Latvia
Phone: (371) 701 2260; Fax: (371) 701
2341
E-mail: soc@transdata.lv

Union of Municipal Social Workers in Latvia
c/o The Union of Municial Workers in
Latvia
M. Pils icla 1, LV-1002 Riga, Latvia
Phone: (371) 701 2153; no fax or e-mail
information available

Lebanese Co-ordinating Body for IFSW-Membership (correspondence to both):

Association des Assistants Sociales du Liban
Université Saint Joseph, c/o Ecole
Libanaise de Formation Sociale,
P.O. Box 115076, Beirut. Lebanon
Phone: (961) 1 614947; Fax: (961) 1
614048
E-mail: hirani@dm.net.lb

Social Worker's Syndicate in Lebanon
c/o National Council of Social Services,
Badaro Str., Building No. 97, 2nd
Floor, P O Box 116/5410, Beirut,
Lebanon
Phone: (961) 1 380675; Fax: (961) 384202
E-mail: enaam@cyberia.net.lb

Lesotho Social Workers' Association
c/o Box 7406, Maseru, Lesotho
Phone: (266) 313194; Fax: (266) 310429

Lithuanian Social Workers' Association
Lakstingalu 7, Vilnius, Lithuania
Phone: (370) 44 36 82; Fax: (370) 2
611672

Association Nationale des Assistantes d'Hygiène Sociale, Assistantes Sociales et Infirmières Graduées du Luxembourg
10, avenue Guillaume, L-1650 Luxembourg
Phone: (352) 44 36 82; Fax: (352) 44 30 29
E-mail: marc.meyers@fm.etat.lu

Former Yugoslavian Republic of Macedonia
Headquarters Humanitarian Organisation "Dare Gambaz" 91000 Skopje, Macedonia
Phone and Fax: (389) 91 228 106

Malaysian Association of Social Workers
D/A 5-2-1 Taman Seri Endah, Jalan 3/149B, Seri Petaling, 57000 Kuala Lumpor, Malaysia
Phone: (60) 3 294 8221

Maltese Association of Social Workers
11 a, Piazza Filippo Scriberres, Florina, VLT 15, Malta
Phone: (356) 246 846; Fax: (356) 446 677
E-mail: masw@orbitet.mt

Mauritius Association of Professional Social Workers (MAPSOW)
Mr. Kishore Ramgoolam, Secretary General, Royal Road, Isidore Rose, Quatre Cocos, Mauritius
Phone: (230) 413 4244; Fax: (230) 413 2990
E-mail: kcramgoolam@hotmail.com

Mongolian Association of Social Workers
Department of Social Work, Pedagogical University, Post Office-49, Box 29, Ulaanbaatar, Mongolia
Phone: (972) 1 328 261; no fax information available
E-mail: swdep@magicnet.mn

Nederlandse Vereniging van Maatschappelijk Workers (NVMW)
P.O. Box 6057, 3503 PB Utrecht, Netherlands
Phone: (31) 30 2948603; Fax: (31) 30 2939225
E-mail: maatswk@nvmw.org
Homepage: www.nvmw.org

Organisashon di Trahadornan Sosial Unf (OTSU)
P.O. Box 4719, Willemsad, Curacao, Netherlands Antilles
Phone: (599) 9 7377047 or (599) 9 7364374; Fax: (599) 9 7364376

Aotearoa New Zealand Association of Social Workers
P.O. Box 1072, Dunedin, New Zealand
Phone: (64) 3 477 5793; Fax: (64) 3 479 0571
E-mail: natoffice@nzasw.org.nz

Asociacion Nicaraguense de Trabajadores Sociales "Mildred Abaunza"
Campo Herois y Martires, Apartado Postal 3257, Managua, Nicaragua
Phone: (505) 2 23765; no fax information available

Association Nigerienne es Travailleurs Sociaux (ANTS)
B.P. 11386, Niamey, Niger
Phone: (227) 73 30 37; Fax: (227) 73 24 61

Nigeria Association of Social Workers
Mr. Alhaji Gbindin-Idowu, President, Block 4, Flat 3, Housing Estate, Caulcrick Close, P.O. Box 8629, Ikeja, Lagos State, Nigeria
Phone: (234) 1 497 9030, ext 4086 or (234) 1 901 5000, ext 4086; Fax: (234) 73 460 097 (c/o Global 2000, Jos)
E-mail: ifeomaumolu@yahoo.com

Norwegian Union of Social Educators and Social Workers (FO)
Postboks 4693, Sofienberg, N-0506 Oslo, Norway
Phone: (47) 23 06 11 70; Fax: (47) 23 06 11 14
E-mail: kontor@fobsv.no
Homepage: www.fb.no/fo/index.htm

Colegio de Asistentes Sociales del Peru
Centro Comercial San Felipe No 63, Lima 11, Peru
Phone and Fax: (51) 1 463 0523

Philippine Association of Social Workers, Inc. (PASWI)
Room 210, Philippine Social Science Center, Commonwealth Ave., UP Diliman, P.O. Box 205, Quezon City, Philippines
Phone: (63) 2 922 9621, local 308; Fax: (63) 2 924 4178
E-mail: paswi@pworld.net.ph

Polish Association of Social Workers
Mr. Arkadiusz Glimasinski, President
Ul. Akacjowa 4/4, PL-41-902, Bytom, Poland
Phone: (48) 32 281 3023; Fax: (48) 32 281 8093
E-mail: bops@pro.onet.pl

Association of Trained Social Workers (APSS)
Av. Casal Ribeiro 37 - 1, 1000 Lisboa, Portugal
Phone: (351) 21 315 2810; Fax: (351) 21 354 3313
E-mail: apss@mail.pt

Romanian Coordinating Body for IFSW-Membership (correspondence to both):

Romanian Association for the Promotion of Social Work (ARPAS)
Prof. Dr. Elena Zamfir, 9, Schitul Magureanu, Sector 5, Postcode 70761, Bucharest, Romania
Phone: (40) 1 614 0010 or (40) 1 312 1791; Fax: (40) 1 638 2376 or (40) 1 312 1791
E-mail: ezamfir@swork.swork.uniluc.ro

Romanian Social Workers Association
Ms. Adriana Median, Strada Costache Conachi Nr. 14, Bloc 7, Scara A, Ap. 32, Sector II Bucharest, Romania
Phone: (40) 1 781 1071 or (40) 1 653 6114

Union of Social Pedagogues and Social Workers
7 a, Pavel Korchagin Str., 129278 Moscow, Russia
Phone and Fax: (7) 095 283 8492; Fax: (7) 095 283 8314
E-mail: LTchainikova@racu.ru

Singapore Association of Social Workers
Family Resource and Training Centre, Blk. 324 Clementi Ave 5, No. 01-209, Singapore 120324
Phone: (65) 775 4776; Fax: (65) 778 0609
E-mail: president@sasw.org.sg
Homepage: www.sasw.org.sg

Association of Social Workers in Slovak Republic (ASPS)
Dr. Vladimir Labath, President, Znievska 26, Bratislava 5, 85105, Slovak Republic
Phone: (421) 7 638 14132; Fax: (421) 7 638 14132
E-mail: asps@netex.sk
Homepage: www.asps.sk

Interim Committee: Social Workers' Associations (ICSWA)
B O Box 2800, Kempton Park 1620, South Africa
Phone: (27) 11 975 7106; Fax: (27) 11 975 7108
E-mail: famsa@global.co.za

Consejo General de Colegios Oficiales de Diplomados en Trabajo Social y Asistentes Sociales
Campomanes, 10-1, 28013 Madrid, Spain
Phone: (34) 91 541 5776/7; Fax: (34) 91 559 02 77
E-mail: consejo@cgtrabajosocial.es
Homepage: www.cgtrabajosocial.es

Sri Lanka Association of Professional Social Workers

191, Dharmapala Mawatha, Colombo 07, Sri Lanka

Phone: (94) 1 68 92 02 / 68 92 03 or (94) 1 68 91 59; Fax: (94) 1 68 91 59

Swedish Coordinating Body for IFSW-Membership (correspondence to all three):

Titti Fränkel, Akademikerförbundet SSR

Box 12800, S-112 96 Stockholm, Sweden

Phone: (46) 8 617 44 33; Fax: (46) 8 617 44 11

E-mail: t.frankel@akademssr.se

Homepage: www.akademssr.se

Yvonne Ahlström, SKTF (Swedish Union of Local Government Officers)

P.O. Box 7825, S-103 97 Stockholm, Sweden

Phone: (46) 8 789 64 01; Fax: (46) 8 789 64 83

E-mail: y.ahlstrom@sktf.se

Homepage: www.sktf.se

Sveriges Socionomförbund

Peter Lamming, Illerstigen 16, S-170 71 Solna, Sweden

Phone: (46) 8 85 20 42; Fax: (46) 8 405 43 80

E-post: peter.lamming@social.ministry.se

Schweizerischer Berufsverband Soziale Arbeit (SBS)

Postfach, Schwarztorstrasse 22, CH-3001 Bern, Switzerland

Phone: (41) 31 382 28 22; Fax: (41) 31 382 11 25

E-mail: sbs@datacomm.ch

Homepage: www.sozialinfo.ch/sbs

Tanzania Association of Social Workers

P.O. Box 7732, Dar-Es-Salaam, Tanzania

Phone: (255) 51 150335; no fax information available

Social Workers' Association of Thailand

Mr. Elawat Chandraprasert, President, Building 5, Floor 4, Department of Public Welfare, Krung Kasem Road, Promprup, Bangkok 10100, Thailand

Phone: (66) 2 281 7053 or (66) 2 281 3800 or (66) 2 281 3199, ext. 7602; Fax: 66) 2 281 7053

E-mail: prachuab@loxifo.co.th

National Association of Social Workers of Uganda (NASWU)

Mr. Max Alfred Anyury, General Secretary, P.O. Box 1131, Kampala, Uganda

Phone: (256) 41 532693; Fax: (256) 41 347545

E-mail: Manyuru@avumuk.ac.ug

Ukrainian Association of Social Pedagogues and Specialists in Social Work

Irina Zvereva, St. Vorovskogo 2, 252053 Kiev, Ukraine

Phone: (7) 044 212 1423; Fax: (7) 044 220 4003 or 220 0412

British Association of Social Workers

16, Kent Street, Birmingham B5 6RD, United Kingdom

Phone: (44) 121 622 3911; Fax: (44) 121 622 4860

E-mail: i.johnston@basw.co.uk

Homepage: www.basw.co.uk

Asociation de Asistentes Sociales del Uruguay (ADASU)

Ejido 1435, Apto 103, Montevideo, Uruguay

No information about phone and fax number available for the moment

Email: adasu@chasque.apc.org

National Association of Social Workers

750 First Street NE, Suite 700, Washington, DC 20002-4241, United States

Phone: (1) 202 408 8600; Fax: (1) 202 336 8313

E-mail: LDiaz@naswdc.org

Homepage: www.socialworkers.org

National Association of Social Workers

P.O. Box 5369, Harare, Zimbabwe

Phone: (263) 4 726 997; Fax: (263) 4 771 802

E-mail: nasw-z@icon.co.zw

Index

Note: Page numbers in boldface refer to glossary terms.